"INVASION ON!"

"INVASION ON!"

D-DAY, THE PRESS, AND THE MAKING OF AN AMERICAN NARRATIVE

STEPHEN M. RUSIECKI

Naval Institute Press
Annapolis, Maryland

Naval Institute Press
291 Wood Road
Annapolis, MD 21402

Library of Congress Cataloging-in-Publication Data
Names: Rusiecki, Stephen M, author.
Title: "Invasion on!" : D-Day, the press, and the making of an American narrative / Stephen M. Rusiecki.
Other titles: D-Day, the press, and the making of an American narrative
Description: Annapolis, Maryland : Naval Institute Press, [2023] | Includes bibliographical references and index.
Identifiers: LCCN 2023003984 (print) | LCCN 2023003985 (ebook) | ISBN 9781557509209 (hardcover) | ISBN 9781557502827 (ebook)
Subjects: LCSH: World War, 1939-1945–Campaigns–France–Normandy–Press coverage–United States. | World War, 1939-1945–Campaigns–France–Normandy–Public opinion. | World War, 1939-1945–Radio and the war. | World War, 1939-1945–United States–Public opinion. | Mass media and public opinion–United States–History–20th century. | Press and propaganda–United States–History–20th century. | Propaganda, American–History–20th century. | Public opinion–United States.
Classification: LCC D756.5.N6 R86 2023 (print) | LCC D756.5.N6 (ebook) | DDC 940.54/21421–dc23/eng/20230214
LC record available at https://lccn.loc.gov/2023003984
LC ebook record available at https://lccn.loc.gov/2023003985

♾Print editions meet the requirements of ANSI/NISO z39.48-1992 (Permanence of Paper).
Printed in the United States of America.

31 30 29 28 27 26 25 24 23 9 8 7 6 5 4 3 2 1
First printing

I dedicate this book to my beautiful and loving wife, Angie, and to my son, Jonathan, who has grown into a singularly exceptional person. I am forever grateful for their love and continuing support.

CONTENTS

FOREWORD

As the sun rose across the United States on Tuesday, June 6, 1944, American workingmen and women from Maine to California prepared for another day on the job in a nation immersed in a war effort of unprecedented proportions. Students and teachers readied for a new day of school; housewives planned their daily homemaking chores. By now, nearly a thousand days into America's involvement in World War II—it had been 912 days since Pearl Harbor, to be exact—Americans on the home front had settled into a routine in a society dominated by rationing, the draft, and an unceasing flow of war news from overseas theaters in which U.S. military forces were actively engaged. According to the American media, news from the front was mostly positive, but U.S. citizens fully grasped that the end was not yet in sight.

Early risers that Tuesday followed their normal morning routine and switched on their living room radios—and all at once everything changed. The event all Americans had anticipated for months—"D-Day," the Allied invasion of western Europe—had finally begun. Local switchboards buzzed. Citizens gathered on street corners, in town squares, churches, and classrooms to converse, to pray, to meditate. It was undeniably the biggest news day since Pearl Harbor. The war, everyone knew, had just entered a new and decisive phase, and perhaps for the first time the glimmer of the proverbial light at the end of the tunnel had shown itself.

The old saying goes that history is one-sided because it is written only by the winners. Stephen Rusiecki's *"Invasion On!"* contributes significantly to the historiography of World War II by delving into this adage in an innovative and resourceful way. In the case of the Normandy invasion, he notes in a convincing manner that not only has the history of D-Day for the most part been written by the winners in the eight decades since the invasion, but the groundwork for this historical analysis was carefully laid even *before* the invasion took place. It is a fresh and enlightening view into one of the most scrutinized events of World War II.

The western Allies undertook dozens of distinct "D-Day" invasions throughout World War II, both before and after June 6, 1944, but as Rusiecki points out, U.S. print and radio media had clearly established ahead of time to the American public that there would be only one D-Day of foremost significance to the Allied war effort—the invasion of German-occupied western Europe. When Americans listened that Tuesday morning to the edgy voices of radio broadcasters announcing that "D-Day had begun," they knew exactly what that meant and grasped straight away that the main military effort of the western Allies in World War II had commenced. Rusiecki fittingly quotes an October 1942 American trade journal editorial in which the writer declared, "The more thoroughly the people of the United States understand this war, the harder they will work to win it." On Tuesday, June 6, 1944, Rusiecki points out that civilians on the home front undeniably appreciated the magnitude of the events unfolding in Normandy, practically on a real-time basis—an unprecedented event in wartime.

Our understanding of a momentous historical event such as D-Day of course changes over time as new details emerge, veterans' memories loosen, and young historians—not yet born at the time of the occurrence—introduce fresh perspectives. But as Rusiecki so meticulously reveals, in 1944 a powerful media hammered home a unified theme to its readers and listeners, one that has endured for nearly eighty years. That theme emphasized that in the gamut of Allied military efforts in World War II, D-Day was something remarkably special and would in the war's aftermath be remembered by the American public as the most decisive event of the conflict.

For six decades, I have watched how D-Day historiography has evolved, from my attendance at age eight, with my father, at one of the first showings of the film *The Longest Day* at the Warner Theater in Times Square—a still-vivid memory despite my youth—to my involvement at the seventy-fifth anniversary commemoration of the invasion in

Normandy in June 2019. I have contributed to that historiography over that span by writing three books on American involvement in the invasion. But as I read Stephen Rusiecki's *"Invasion On!"* I fully appreciated his perspective that in order to grasp how we examine the invasion in the twenty-first century, it is vital to understand how the media initially shaped our images of that great event.

It is a highly valuable contribution to our perception of D-Day, and for that reason I urge all students of World War II history—even those already familiar with the Normandy invasion—to read and learn from it.

Joseph Balkoski
May 2022

ACKNOWLEDGMENTS

Any comprehensive historical study requires the assistance and encouragement of fellow scholars and supporters. That said, this book would not have been possible without the mentorship and tireless support of my dissertation advisor at George Mason University, Dr. Christopher H. Hamner. Christopher helped me to approach the topic with a level of enthusiasm and depth of understanding that made my research and writing into a true labor of love. I am forever in his debt.

Many thanks are due to my other committee members, Dr. Alison Landsberg and Dr. Sam Lebovic, for their superlative feedback and efforts to help me reshape my thinking about the project, which ultimately made my work so much better. I am also grateful for the support of my many professors at George Mason University, whose faith in my abilities provided an added boost to my spirit. Without the moral and intellectual support of Dr. Jane Turner Censer, Dr. Jack Censer, Dr. Meredith Lair, and Dr. Cynthia Kierner, this study would be a lesser piece of work. I am equally indebted to my close friend, preeminent D-Day historian Joseph Balkoski, who gave me unfettered access to the archives of the 29th Infantry Division at the Fifth Regiment Armory in Baltimore, Maryland. I am also grateful to the late Andrew "Andy" Rooney of *60 Minutes* television fame, who took the time to answer my questions about the attitudes and perspectives of U.S. war correspondents in the European theater of operations, of which he had been one. I must also thank Tricia Gesner of the Associated Press, who helped me track down and obtain permissions for several of the AP wire photos reproduced in this book. Lastly, I owe a debt of gratitude to Aden Nichols for his adept copyediting abilities and for making this book a polished product. Thank you one and all.

The views expressed in this publication are mine and do not necessarily reflect the official policy or position of the Department of Defense or the U.S. government. I alone am responsible for any errors in interpretation or fact that appear in this book.

INTRODUCTION

The Birth of an American Narrative

The men of Normandy had faith that what they were doing was right, faith that they fought for all humanity, faith that a just God would grant them mercy on this beachhead or on the next. It was the deep knowledge . . . that there is a profound, moral difference between the use of force for liberation and the use of force for conquest. You were here to liberate, not to conquer.

—Ronald Reagan, 6 June 1984[1]

Standing at a podium on 6 June 1984 under gray Norman skies in front of a stone monument shaped like a dagger, his hair slightly tussled by a gentle breeze and with the English Channel's choppy waters roiling behind him, President Ronald Reagan delivered what many now label as his famous "Boys of Pointe du Hoc" speech to a rapt audience of American and European D-Day veterans. This spot, Reagan reminded his audience, had been a battlefield forty years earlier, a place where young troops of the 2nd Ranger Battalion, "champions who helped free a continent," scaled the cliffs of Pointe du Hoc under heavy German fire in order to seize and destroy German artillery pieces threatening the Invasion fleet.[2] Americans, sleepy-eyed and yawning due to the time difference, watched at home on early morning news shows. Reagan celebrated not only the gallantry of American fighting men that day; he also brought together all the key themes associated with America's standing narrative of D-Day in this single speech, themes developed four decades earlier on the very day the Invasion took place.

Although the purpose of his speech was decidedly political and targeted toward America's Cold War Communist adversary, the Soviet Union, Reagan succeeded in synthesizing into this single oration four key themes that encompassed the narrative behind how all Americans came to imagine D-Day, a uniquely American account developed the moment the Invasion happened. First, he celebrated the grand scale of the Invasion, hyperbolically casting it as "a giant undertaking unparalleled in human history," even though he acknowledged the Soviet Union's major contribution in defeating the Wehrmacht. Second, he cast all American soldiers as moralistic liberators, young "boys" who took up arms to "liberate, not to conquer." These young GIs, claimed Reagan, fought for freedom and democracy, driven by a love for liberty and a hatred of "tyranny." Third, the virtuous motives of these young American men sanctified their endeavor, thus giving "Providence" a "great hand in the events that would unfold" on the beaches and cliffs of Normandy. "God," insisted the president, "was an ally in this great cause," and the prayers of those fellow Americans at home "filling the churches" that Tuesday morning further buttressed the overarching devotion that undergirded the troops' collective valor. Lastly, highly moral, divinely inspired senior leaders—such as the sole American general mentioned by Reagan, Maj. Gen. Matthew Ridgway, commander of the 82nd Airborne Division—were the right officers to lead these men in battle. Under their exceptional leadership, the troops would neither "fail" nor "forsake" God and the folks at home. In short, according to Reagan's rendition, D-Day was the seminal, liberating battle of World War II, a divinely sanctioned enterprise fought by intrepid, liberty-loving soldiers led by the best leaders of any army or navy in the world. Period.[3]

In the forty years leading up to President Reagan's Pointe du Hoc speech and in the decades that followed, Americans routinely built upon, and in many ways reconstructed and reimagined, this thematically fashioned and highly anodyne narrative of D-Day. In those intervening years, historians and media outlets provided a plethora of details about what precisely occurred on the Invasion beaches, details that have filled out much of America's understanding of what happened that day on the landing shores, in the air, and on the water. Despite this profusion of additional details, the four themes Reagan communicated on the cliffs of Pointe du Hoc have remained constant and ever-present aspects of the

American D-Day story, especially in the American public's consciousness. These interrelated themes have become the very bedrock of how the nation continues to perceive and chronicle the Invasion, an event elevated through hyperbole to myth-like prominence. These themes, and the overarching story line they shape, have become a touchstone in America's collective understanding of the nation's contribution to winning the war, as well as its own sense of exceptionalism.

In the years immediately following the Invasion, and years before Reagan's 1984 speech, the themes comprising America's D-Day narrative found ready reinforcement through an avalanche of books, magazines, and films. When Gen. Dwight D. Eisenhower published *Crusade in Europe* (his memoir of World War II) in 1948, he revived the principal theme of the Invasion as a mighty endeavor—the seminal undertaking of the war in Europe—prosecuted by "the mightiest fighting force the two Western Allies [the United States and Great Britain] could muster."[4] The religiously charged connotation of his book's title evoked another key theme: Eisenhower's own belief in the Invasion as a sacred undertaking, a "crusade" for liberty and peace. And Eisenhower's plainspoken, first-person presence in the book conjured up another core theme in the D-Day narrative: that only America's finest senior officers—men like Eisenhower—had led the Allied troops, especially American GIs, to a just and noble victory.

These core themes found further purchase in the works of historians and journalists alike. When historian Gordon A. Harrison published the official U.S. Army "Green Book" history of D-Day, *Cross-Channel Attack* (1951), he further characterized the operation as "the supreme effort of the Western Allies in Europe—the consummation of the grand design to defeat Germany."[5] Several years later, Cornelius Ryan published *The Longest Day* (1959), in which he emphasized the ground-level activities of the average fighting man, especially the American GI. In doing so, Ryan revived the thematic trope of American citizen-soldiers as reluctant, youthful warriors who fought gallantly under the leadership of America's finest officers. When Hollywood transformed Ryan's tome into a major film production in 1962 featuring the era's biggest movie stars, the American public once again bore witness to the precise themes that had framed their collective narrative of D-Day as it materialized on the very day the Invasion began.[6] These four significant and uniquely American D-Day themes reappeared most tellingly during a 1964 CBS television broadcast on the twentieth anniversary of D-Day in which former-president Eisenhower revisited the Invasion beaches with Walter Cronkite. As both men sat under an overcast June sky among the uniformly arrayed headstones in the American military cemetery overlooking Omaha Beach, a serious and subdued Eisenhower reflected on the scale of the Invasion; on the noble, sacred purpose behind the operation ("to preserve freedom"); and on the fact that many thousands of good, young men, American and Allied alike, "died for ideals such as these." The solemnity of Eisenhower's demeanor on camera reinforced the scale and gravity of the operation. Leaders like him represented the very best America had to offer at that moment in time—men with the right stuff to succeed in such a massive enterprise.[7]

President Reagan's speech in 1984 reenergized American interest in D-Day and how all Americans continued to perceive the Invasion, sometimes at the expense of their Allied partners' contributions and in some cases at the expense of a more critical examination of America's and its soldiers' participation in the war. For instance, like Reagan's oration, Stephen E. Ambrose's *D-Day June 6, 1944: The Climactic Battle of World War II,* published a decade later in 1994, once again channeled the thematically framed American narrative of the operation. Ambrose's title reflected his interpretation of the Invasion as the pivotal event of the war, something truly "staggering in its scope."[8] Although Ambrose included the British and Canadian involvement in D-Day, he concentrated primarily on the American contribution. He also focused on the average American soldier's grit, valor, and virtue, as well as the uniquely gifted and qualified American commanders who led these troops. Fellow Americans at home, wrote Ambrose, further sanctified their troops' endeavor by flocking to churches in order to satisfy an overwhelming "impulse to pray."[9]

A few years later Tom Brokaw credited his National Broadcasting Company (NBC) documentary chronicling the fortieth anniversary of D-Day as awakening him to his own youthful memories of the war, in turn compelling him to add another thematic (and uncritically nostalgic) layer to the D-Day trope of America's troops as gallant and virtuous citizen-soldiers, particularly those men who participated in the Invasion. Brokaw's *The Greatest Generation* (1998), a culturally influential paean to the World War II generation, recast the men who fought the war as universally exceptional in every sense of the word—a characterization later contested by many historians and veterans alike.[10] That same year, the American public bore witness to a stunning visual representation of America's soldiers landing under direct enemy fire on Omaha Beach. The opening sequence of Steven Spielberg's *Saving Private Ryan* (1998) laid bare the stark reality and abject horror faced by America's courageous young men as they charged headlong into withering enemy fire on the beaches of Normandy. The shocking and gory images of this remarkably realistic representation of ground combat reinforced with immense power the enormity of the operation and the remarkable sacrifice of the young GIs who stormed the beaches.[11] This thematic frame, along with the other three, has endured well into the twentieth century through a plethora of popular history books, magazines, and television documentaries. In fact, in crafting the nation's most widely used undergraduate history textbook, *Give Me Liberty! An American History* (2017), Eric Foner described the Invasion as "the most massive sea-land operation in history."[12]

Throughout the seventy-nine years following the Allied Invasion of Normandy on 6 June 1944, four significant themes, previously unidentified in any other scholarship, have consistently attended America's enduring narrative of D-Day:

- The singular importance of this specific Invasion, through its scope, scale, and stated goals, in ultimately ending the war in Europe.
- The sacralization of the enterprise as a "Great Crusade."
- The remarkable competence and skill of senior American and Allied commanders.

- The exceptional valor and abilities of the American soldier, sailor, and airman.

These thematic frames have found solid purchase among Americans and have shaped their perceptions of D-Day and what the operation should mean to them. Most significantly, these themes have resisted efforts over time to recast their overstated, gauzy qualities in favor of a more realistic, and more sobering, D-Day narrative.

But how did this thematically constructed—and enduring—American narrative of D-Day originate? Did this narrative develop haphazardly over time through an amalgamation of widely disparate sources and means? Not in the least. America's D-Day narrative has its roots in the moment the Invasion took place, communicated to the American public by the only institutions available in 1944 with the authority, power, and reach to do so—the radio networks and daily newspapers.

America's radio networks and newspapers, each a powerful conveyor of information to a well-connected American populace, developed the standard D-Day narrative through a combination of official- and correspondent-generated source materials and a professional ethos that recognized the Invasion for what it was—the biggest story of the war up to that point in time. The themes they developed to shape the narrative are themselves unsurprising. What is surprising is the degree to which the radio and newspaper media seized upon, and then vigorously advanced, the four common themes shaping the D-Day narrative on a single day—6 June 1944.

America's press corps and radio networks had spent nearly six months preparing for what most members of the news media at home and abroad knew instinctively was an event of great historical import. D-Day's success would force the Germans to fight on three separate fronts—in France, in the Soviet Union, and in Italy—compelling Adolf Hitler, now under pressure from three sides, to split his forces and thus bring the war in Europe to a speedier conclusion. With these factors in mind, these news professionals in both the print and broadcast worlds knew they had a role to play in the Invasion, and that role included keeping the American people informed and supportive of the war effort.

Ultimately, this central belief in D-Day's importance served as the foundational principle guiding all D-Day reporting and had the greatest effect in shaping the thematic frames that defined how the American public came to understand the D-Day storyline on the very day it happened—and beyond. In fact, that first thematically framed version of the landings proved so powerful that it has become the template for the way generations of Americans have continued to imagine the landings.

Neither government dicta nor policies issued prior to the Invasion drove the way America's news editors and war correspondents reported the D-Day Invasion. Instead, Operation Overlord's status as the war's most critical event, and the other thematic frames that arose around that core theme, came about instinctively and organically from within the press and radio industries. The men with the greatest agency in these two news industries—white, educated, middle-aged men (and a few women)—agreed to treat the Invasion as director of the Office of War Information (OWI) Elmer Davis saw it: an event of "'tremendous' consequence."[13] These professional newsmen knew a big story when they saw one—and D-Day fit the bill.

But D-Day was not an event manufactured by the press for self-serving purposes; it was not what historian Daniel J. Boorstin has termed a "pseudo-event," a news story fabricated to make something reportable in order to satisfy the public's need for a dramatic, newsworthy event and, perhaps, to pull in more advertising dollars. The press knew it had the power "to make a reportable event [and] thus the power to make experience," but it did not manufacture D-Day as a major news event.[14] D-Day was always going to be a highly newsworthy affair in the greater context of the war up to that point in time. Instead, America's newspapers and radio networks supercharged the significance of D-Day primarily by developing, and then adhering to, a common narrative of D-Day on the very day the Invasion occurred.

The press advanced this common narrative of D-Day most effectively through each of the two medium's trade journals—*Editor & Publisher (E&P)* and *Broadcasting and Broadcast Advertising (BBA)*. The running discourse between these two journals encouraged editors and war correspondents alike to view the Invasion the same way—as a seminal, sacred undertaking led by America's best senior leaders and fought by the very best of America's young, courageous men.

This study argues that radio and newspapers gave birth to a precisely framed narrative of D-Day on the very day the Invasion occurred, a narrative that formed the very foundation of how Americans have come to understand and commemorate the Invasion over the past seventy-nine years, despite efforts to ground that narrative in greater reality. America's radio and print media combined on that Tuesday, 6 June 1944, to deliver to the American people a deliberately constructed narrative of what would become for them the seminal event of World War II—D-Day. The narrative crafted by these two news platforms helped to amplify in the minds of all Americans the historical significance of D-Day from the moment it occurred. Their initial reporting hammered these themes consistently throughout the coverage, essentially drowning out other potential narratives that might have complicated portrayals of the action on the blood-soaked Invasion beaches. These themes ultimately laid the groundwork for a more entrenched, and distinctly American, collective memory of the Invasion in the decades that followed. While not the focus of this study, memory clearly informs this overall analysis. Whereas memory studies generally emphasize and analyze the *receivers* of a given narrative, this study focuses exclusively on the *developers* and *transmitters* of that narrative. Despite these differing methodologies, both narrative-making and memory-making often work in tandem with each other.

Within this overarching framework, this study will seek to explain how America's collective understanding of D-Day—essentially the American D-Day story—was born. In order to answer this query, this project will explore in detail the mechanics of precisely how radio broadcasts and newspapers gathered and communicated facts, images, impressions, attitudes, and meaning in the twenty-four-hour period of 6 June 1944 and reveal how that reportage formed a common narrative that would remain fixed in the American consciousness for decades to come.[15] By addressing the process of news reporting during D-Day, this study also explores precisely what information was available to the press;

how the press assigned meaning to, or perceived, that information; and what information remained unavailable to the press on 6 June 1944 due to censorship or procedural reporting breakdowns caused by the friction of war. In sum, this study is about the process by which the print and broadcast media developed a thematically structured narrative of D-Day in the moment, a narrative that elevated D-Day to a status enjoyed by those few events in American military history that essentially defined the conflicts of which they were a part, such as Bunker Hill and Gettysburg.[16] This process was complicated and included many players—war correspondents, military officials, newspaper editors, radio commentators, military analysts, and the American public—and all shared a certain degree of historical agency in shaping the final outcome of the common D-Day narrative. These players managed to work cooperatively in many ways, even while separated geographically and chronologically, to contribute to the production of common themes that shaped the narrative. This collaboration yielded a communal and largely sanitized American story line of D-Day. The purpose of this study is not to evaluate the accuracy of the D-Day reporting but to emphasize the key thematic frames involved.

◆ ◆ ◆

This media-facilitated narrative of D-Day, with its four attendant themes, was thrust upon a country that was remarkably heterogeneous in ethnic and racial composition, religious affiliation, and political beliefs. Furthermore, America's political leaders were alarmed by how "public complacency" in the form of strikes, absentee workers, and low recruiting numbers "was damaging the war effort."[17] Despite these disparate factors, the print and broadcast media managed to coax all Americans to see D-Day through a single nationalistic prism. Even though D-Day was an Allied operation, the U.S. news media presented the Invasion almost exclusively as an American-only enterprise that nearly eclipsed the contributions of British, Canadian, French, and other Allied participants. Most tellingly, the overarching importance the media lent to the Invasion supplanted the greater, more significant combat achievements of the Soviet Union's Red Army, which ultimately broke the back of German land power on the eastern front and suffered heavily in the process. For instance, the Red Army's offensive against the Wehrmacht's Army Group Center beginning on 23 June 1944, Operation Bagration, cost the Soviets 178,000 lives over twenty-six days—approximately 6,846 killed in action per day. D-Day cost the Allies 4,414 lives, of which 2,499 were American. Thus, in a single day, the Red Army lost more than double the men the Americans lost on D-Day. In Russian eyes, Allied losses on D-Day were negligible by comparison; D-Day was not the main thrust destined to end the war but merely a supporting effort.[18] The American-centric media campaign ignored such a perspective. Instead, American radio broadcasts and newspapers mythologized D-Day as the decisive World War II event, an endeavor that marked the beginning of the end for Nazi Germany. They depicted U.S. combat power as a direct extension of the American values of freedom, democracy, and the rights of all people to live in peace and prosperity.[19] America's journalists became D-Day's primary mythmakers.

The development of a uniquely American narrative about D-Day arose as a largely organic, but intentional, effort orchestrated by numerous actors inside and outside of the media. As mutually reinforcing institutions, the broadcast and print media demonstrated a unique brand of historical agency by leveraging the power of their respective platforms and professional ethos to communicate a shared perspective of D-Day and its meaning. These two mediums, each generally served by the same news wire sources, wove a thematic tapestry of meaning around the operation using information already filtered by military censors and again by the wire services. Through these filters, General Eisenhower's Supreme Headquarters Allied Expeditionary Force (SHAEF) and other government agencies succeeded in controlling some of the thematic messaging about D-Day—all while adhering in principle to what the OWI called America's "strategy of truth." In the case of D-Day, that strategy generally prevailed but proved somewhat fungible.[20]

One of the principal drivers behind the nature of this thematic messaging was the standing fear that the Invasion might not succeed. In many ways the Western Allies viewed D-Day—the spearhead of Operation Overlord—as a highly consequential, all-or-nothing venture.

A cross-Channel assault was the only way they could strike at the heart of Hitler's armies and conclude the war. In fact, the specter of failure haunted General Eisenhower so much that on the eve of the Invasion, he scrawled a draft communiqué accepting sole responsibility if Overlord should fail. In an inspiring moment of genuine leadership, Eisenhower insisted, "If any blame or fault attaches to the attempt[,] it is mine alone."[21] This underlying fear of failure colored the themes emanating from SHAEF's official press releases and from the typewriters and pens of the hundreds of U.S. war correspondents covering the Invasion. What SHAEF and these reporters needed to communicate to the Allied home fronts (and the American home front in particular) was a measured sense of optimism, hope, and confidence that the Invasion would succeed. Most of all, they needed to sustain public support in America not only for this D-Day but for subsequent "D-days" should this first attempt fail.

The Invasion of Normandy was not the American armed forces' first invasion during the war, but D-Day was different, especially in how the broadcast and print media portrayed it. They cast Operation Overlord as something unique and in a class of its own. The reporting on these other invasions prior to D-Day lacked the same power, uniqueness, and exclusivity that came to typify much of the D-Day reportage, reflecting America's pent-up trepidation over the highly anticipated cross-Channel assault and the Allied leadership's nagging doubts about success. When the United States engaged in its first true invasion prior to D-Day, the landings on the Solomon Islands in the Pacific on 7 August 1942, American newspapers did not even report the operation until two days later, on 9 August 1942 (a consequence of military censorship), and only then as a front-page story competing with dozens of other front-page news items. Those newspapers that did make the landings a headline event even eschewed the word "invasion" in favor of "offensive."[22]

Other American invasions leading up to D-Day, such as the landings in North Africa (Operation Torch) on 8 November 1942 and in Sicily (Operation Husky) on 10 July 1943, received greater emphasis and timelier, same-day reporting from the broadcast and print media. In fact, the word "invasion" appeared more often in the headlines. However, these major stories still competed significantly with other front-page accounts of political and domestic matters. For example, the headlines splashed across the 8 November 1942 edition of the *Detroit Free Press* declared, "U.S. Invading French Bases in West and North Africa." Competing for privileged news space on that same front page, however, were articles labeled "Rural Lawmakers to Control Michigan" and "War-Plant Strike Ended by Toolmen."[23] The same approach typified other newspapers' handling of the North Africa landings.[24]

The newspaper reporting of the Sicily landings on 10 July 1943 reflected the same general approach evident in the newspaper coverage of North Africa. The events still competed with other stories for front-page space, but certain characteristics of the reporting—the inclusion of front-page maps and the more frequent use of the word "invasion"—demonstrated an evolution in coverage that portended the kind of unique reporting that would epitomize how newspapers treated D-Day on 6 June 1944. A sense of scale and scope also became apparent in the reporting on Sicily through the headlines used by some newspapers. The *New Castle News* of Pennsylvania, for example, proclaimed, "Allied Forces Open Huge Invasion Move in Sicily," while the *Indianapolis Star* reported, "Sicily Invaded; Eisenhower Troops Leap Mediterranean From Africa."[25] The *Akron Beacon Journal* and *Dunkirk Evening Observer* (New York) came closest to approximating the headlines that would dominate mastheads on D-Day by belching forth banner headings that read, respectively, *"Invasion!"* and *"Invasion Is On!"*[26] Despite this evolution of "invasion" reporting in America's newspapers, the print media's treatment of D-Day—with oversized, dramatic headlines; home-front calls to prayer; and exclusive "extra" editions—still set the Invasion of 6 June 1944 apart from all others preceding it.

Broadcast coverage of these earlier invasions also underscored the extreme shift in how radio would relate news of D-Day to the American people. On that day (and for the first time ever) the networks allowed a breaking news story to eclipse the entire day's commercial schedule solely in favor of Invasion news. Such a decision was remarkable in 1944 since these networks were, according to author John McDonough, a struggling "medium dominated by entertainment and paid for by advertisers."[27] Advertising dollars equated to survival. In contrast to D-Day reporting, radio reports of the Solomon Islands and North Africa landings lacked the sense of immediacy and consequence that characterized the Invasion's coverage. In each case, for instance, the Columbia Broadcasting System's (CBS) *World News Early Morning Report* included only brief overviews of both landings synthesized within the early morning war news summaries. The broadcast on 8 November 1942 treated the North Africa landings with more importance and some greater detail, mainly mentioning the number of invasion forces (140,000) and the names of key American commanders in the operation, such as Eisenhower and Lt. Gen. George S. Patton Jr. But like the reportage on the Solomon Islands landings three months earlier, CBS still rolled up news of the invasion into its larger morning report, even though Operation Torch was America's initial ground-combat foray against the vaunted German war machine.[28]

The American reporting of D-Day far surpassed the kind of war reportage the American public had come to expect when they purchased a newspaper at the local newsstand or tuned in to the radio. The print and broadcast media worked in unison on D-Day to communicate a basic, thematic narrative to a fully connected American public. Thus, when the American public awoke the day after the Invasion, Wednesday, 7 June 1944, the themes communicated through the previous day's reportage had already formed the foundation for a fixed, thematically based impression of D-Day as the most important military operation of the war, a sacred undertaking led primarily by the United States and its gifted military leaders and executed on the ground and in the air by dedicated, valorous, pure-hearted American fighting men who fought to advance America's image as a nation of righteous, liberating "crusaders" in a world of godless barbarians.

These thematic frames and the narrative they conveyed, however, fell flat in the eyes of America's Black citizens. In fact, the emerging D-Day narrative was in direct tension with the attitudes and reporting found in the newspapers published by and for the Black community. Although the Black newspapers clearly supported the Invasion, in their own ways they rebuffed the American D-Day narrative advanced by the mainstream newspapers and radio networks, instead calling into question how these themes could find purchase in a segregated, Jim Crow America that excluded 10 percent of its citizens from the privilege of engaging in direct combat with the enemy. These consistent efforts by the Black press to resist discrimination, even in the face of government accusations of seditious rabble-rousing, revealed the incomplete and exaggerated nature of the D-Day narrative's thematic frames.[29] In excluding the Black population from sharing in the Invasion effort, America's largely White mainstream news media risked its much-heralded sense of objectivity and inclusiveness. In the end, the emerging D-Day narrative remained impervious to any efforts by the Black press to reshape it and be more inclusive.

In many ways, reporting America's participation in D-Day through a thematically flattering, racially exclusionary, anodyne, and even jingoistic lens was as much a gamble for the press as Overlord was for the Allies. What if D-Day failed? The press had gone all-in on framing D-Day as an operation undertaken by the best leaders and soldiers, so how might the public feel about those same leaders and troops if, say, Overlord failed and another invasion had to take place in 1945 elsewhere in France? Their collective credibility was at stake—and the D-Day narrative that would have emerged on 6 June 1944 would have appeared far less triumphant and optimistic. But they did not have to approach the Invasion reportage that way; they had other options. For instance, when reporting on major battlefield events during World War I, America's newspapers maintained a more subdued tone, such as the straightforward reportage on the fighting at Belleau Wood in June 1918. Papers like Wyoming's *Sheridan Enterprise* on 12 June 1918 still highlighted in bold letters that "U.S. Guns Check Advances" by the Germans; but in general, their war-related reporting followed a more thematically neutral framework and appeared alongside front-page stories that had nothing to do with the fighting in France—despite President Woodrow Wilson's government-run propaganda effort to whip up support for the war. Other American newspapers in 1918, such as Philadelphia's *Evening Public Ledger*, held to the same approach.[30]

But in the United States, the press' total and unequivocal commitment to the Invasion's success evidently mirrored a larger American desire to end the war as directly and as quickly as possible—and D-Day was the new starting point. Without doubt, American reporters were cheerleaders for the home team. In fact, the nature of their reportage assumed the trappings of 1940s-era sports reporting, in which journalists rooted for their teams by using overblown, snappy language and by accentuating the "greatness" of their sports heroes, despite the obvious human frailties and limitations of these personalities. In the end, what made D-Day unique was that the people who reported it, while still committed to high journalistic standards, were willing members of "Team America," a phenomenon unique to World War II and one that would fade completely by Vietnam, when the press not only quit the team but completely left the proverbial stadium. As the much-touted operation aimed directly at the heart of the Wehrmacht, D-Day had become a thing unto itself.

But as distinctive as D-Day had become in the eyes of the American radio networks and daily newspapers, the media-constructed narrative of the Invasion resulted from deliberate choices that had the potential to backfire. For instance, the networks and newspapers could have chosen to evoke less optimistic themes in favor of producing a more sobering, more blood-stained, and in some ways more accurate D-Day storyline than the more anodyne and comforting one that materialized on the day of the Invasion. First, the news media may have collectively chosen to downplay the overall significance of the Invasion to the greater war effort to hedge their bets against the potential failure of such an ambitious and massive enterprise. Second, they could have easily eschewed the "Great Crusade" rhetoric and any overtures to sacralize the Invasion based upon their past experiences with a notoriously similar government propaganda effort during World War I that whipped up a war fervor among the public, eventually leaving Americans feeling deceived and suspicious of news and government messaging. Third, the news media could have tempered its portrayals of the Invasion's senior leaders to emphasize not only their strengths and successes but also their past battlefield foibles in order to suggest that the success of such a massive, as-yet-untried amphibious operation rested on men whose ability to lead such an operation remained an open question. And last, if the war correspondents had not suffered from a structural breakdown that prevented their eyewitness dispatches of the bloody, vicious fighting on places like Omaha Beach from reaching their editors, then these horrific accounts might have very well imbued the D-Day narrative with a more somber and frightening tone that could have enervated the fighting spirit of the American home front. In the end, the themes that finally emerged to shape the D-Day narrative represented a combination of editorial choices and structural shortfalls, but the news media's gamble paid off. The Invasion succeeded, validating the more anodyne D-Day reportage that emerged over the airwaves and in the newspapers and allowing the four themes shaping that narrative to linger over time and contribute directly to how Americans came to mythologize the Invasion.

As soon as World War II ended, this almost mythic, media-enabled impression of the Invasion would become a standard trope among Americans in subsequent decades as, in the words of historian Michael Dolski, a "morality tale of America's selfless sacrifice to restore order in the world."[31] This impression echoed the very same themes communicated to the American people by the radio networks and newspapers on D-Day at the moment the Invasion happened, essentially validating the staying power of the American Invasion narrative as constructed by the national media. The greatest validation eventually came in the form of presidential-level commemorations of the Invasion, which leaned heavily upon the American D-Day narrative for inspiration and direction.

◆ ◆ ◆

This study will describe in detail how the press—through the radio and the newspapers—crafted the narrative and communicated the themes that became the foundation for how America has continued to perceive the story of D-Day, 6 June 1944. Chapter 1 establishes the media landscape and other factors that directly affected the creation and fundamental shape of the Invasion story line. Chapter 2 discusses the primary theme—the Invasion's significance to the global war effort as a whole—as reporters developed it through the first immersive radio broadcasts in the early morning hours of 6 June 1944. Chapter 3 expands that story by exploring how the newspapers stepped in hours later to solidify that same theme using visual devices such as evocative headlines, detailed maps, and actual photographs of Invasion activities. Chapter 4 continues with the newspapers' efforts to give greater shape to the emerging D-Day narrative with wire-service summaries splashed on the front pages. Chapter 5 shifts to a different theme, the sacralization of the Invasion. It shows how the radio and newspapers developed and then advanced the idea of the landings in near-religious terms rather than as a straightforward military operation. Chapter 6 explores how radio and the press collectively gave rise to the final two themes—the best leaders leading the very best soldiers—through newspaper features and eyewitness broadcasts. Chapter 7 brings the final D-Day narrative into sharp relief by exploring how the four themes and the D-Day story line drafted around these themes have endured in America's consciousness for more than three-quarters of a century, principally through the speeches of American presidents at national D-Day commemorations. Although the context and political purposes behind their speeches at these major commemorations changed over the years, the D-Day narrative and its four themes remained largely unaltered.

CHAPTER 1

Anticipating the "Explosion"

America's News Landscape on the Eve of D-Day

The stress of public feeling among the peoples of the United Nations has been so great during the past months of expectancy that the release of pent-up emotion on D Day will have the character of an explosion.

—Gen. Dwight D. Eisenhower, "D Day Guidance for the Press," 31 May 1944[1]

The enduring, thematically structured D-Day narrative developed by America's news media on the day of the Invasion and conveyed to the American people as the foundational story line of the operation was the product of a unique wartime news environment that at once enabled, complicated, and sometimes contradicted that very scenario. This D-Day narrative was born under extraordinary conditions that saw an otherwise highly competitive news industry set aside self-interest and even profits in the service of what American journalists considered to be the critical, war-winning enterprise in the European theater of operations. Remarkably, newspapers and radio managed to agree upon this standard narrative almost organically, as a natural, journalistic response to this all-important venture. Therefore, exploring how Americans consumed news in 1944 is essential to understanding how such a homogenous narrative came to be.

I will break down my analysis of news consumption into five specific areas:

1. the newspaper establishment and the news wire services that supplied that industry with information

2. the radio industry and its sometimes strained but symbiotic relationship with America's newspapers
3. the notorious legacy from World War I of any news reporting that smelled like blatant propaganda and how that legacy influenced the way the news media reported D-Day
4. the impact of governmental and military censorship on the media's developing D-Day narrative
5. the remarkable pre-Invasion discourse between the press and radio industries through their trade journals, which not only established a loose working relationship between both news industries but also laid the groundwork for the Invasion narrative that would follow.

Another factor affecting how Americans responded to, and seized upon, the D-Day story line was, quite simply, angst. Gen. Dwight D. Eisenhower, the supreme Allied commander, gave voice to this concern in his "D Day Guidance for the Press" issued to all overseas war correspondents on 31 May 1944. In this document Eisenhower revealed his trepidation about the tension of a war-weary populace. He wanted the war correspondents attached to his SHAEF headquarters to consider the impact the initial news of the Invasion would have on the public and to channel this "release of pent-up emotion" into war-winning activities on the home front. Much of that emotion had built up within America in the six months leading up to the Invasion.[2]

Until that violent Sunday morning of 7 December 1941, when Japanese naval forces attacked Pearl Harbor, the people of the United States had only watched from afar as the Germans in Europe and the Japanese in the Pacific engulfed the world in a global conflagration that would eventually consume millions of lives.[3] After the sneak attack on the U.S. homeland, the war had touched all Americans in different ways, evoking reactions ranging from confidence to fear about what lay ahead. As the war dragged on, British and American planners in England meticulously crafted a blueprint for what the Allies hoped would be the beginning of the end of the war in Europe: the much-anticipated cross-Channel Invasion. For American planners in particular, the ambitious operation—a source of great debate, disagreement, and rancor between the British and American allies—ultimately became what historian David M. Kennedy described as "the supreme and jealously guarded foundation stone of anti-German strategy."[4] Eisenhower relinquished command of the Mediterranean theater upon his appointment as the supreme Allied commander on 24 December 1943, and the Invasion was tentatively set for the following year.

Eisenhower's new posting fired the imagination of all Americans with the hope that perhaps this revelation signaled the beginning of the end of the war in Europe. For the Americans who had been suffering the brunt of years of hard fighting in North Africa and the Mediterranean, the real test was yet to come. The Allies were about to get a taste of what their Soviet counterparts had been facing since 1941 half a world away on the eastern front—the full might of the Wehrmacht. Up to that point, the British and American forces had only engaged a handful of German divisions at any given time in the Mediterranean. Nearly fifty German divisions would be waiting for them on the other side of the English Channel.[5]

Historian Michael C. C. Adams described World War II as "a brutalizing experience," with "anonymous mass destruction [as] the dominant characteristic."[6] America's radio networks and newspapers had made most Americans aware of that painful fact. For that reason, Americans just wanted to get the job done; when the Invasion finally arrived, the American people greeted it with both anticipation and trepidation. The mechanisms for communicating that event were already well in place and primed to create an enduring, media-generated narrative of the operation that Americans would come to know as Operation Overlord, the Allied Invasion of Europe—D-Day.

◆ ◆ ◆

During World War II, Americans received their news of the war through four main sources: newspapers, radio, occasional newsreels shown in theaters, and letters from the men and women serving in uniform.[7] However, for news of D-Day at the moment the Invasion was happening, the nation relied principally on two of these communication mediums—newspapers and radio. Both media forms ultimately worked hand in hand, and sometimes from within a comingled structure, to communicate the news of the events on the beaches of Normandy and to explain what it should mean to the nation at large.

Newspapers did the most to convey a more detailed, visually stimulating version of the thematically framed D-Day narrative. Newspapers enjoyed a long history in America as a cultural artifact that did not merely distribute news but also built a "psychologically potent entity"[8] in the form of an "imagined community" of the kind described by sociologist Benedict Anderson.[9] Through Anderson's notion of the common ceremony of readership, newspapers connected all Americans to the greater world around them, a world well beyond the local limits of their own towns, cities, and states.[10] In addition to the power to publicly include, to legitimize, to invest with meaning, and to amplify the significance of any reported event, the newspaper had the unique ability to take such an event and transform it into another cultural artifact known as "news." The newspaper would then develop from that "news" a thematically framed story line, one that would eventually serve as the foundation for a commonly accepted narrative of that event.[11] In this sense, the American newspaper exemplified "the most representative carrier and construer and creator of modern public consciousness."[12]

On the eve of D-Day, America had more than enough newspapers to connect this American "public consciousness" to a common narrative about the Invasion. The number of newspapers serving the American public on 5 June 1944 numbered 11,974. This number included newspapers produced on a rather varied schedule—daily, triweekly, semiweekly, weekly, fortnightly, semimonthly, monthly, and bimonthly. Since many weekly, specialty, and other less frequently produced newspapers (such as Black newspapers) published their editions on Fridays and since the Invasion began on a Tuesday, the daily newspapers became the primary source of Invasion news for all Americans. Excluding Sunday and foreign editions produced by the daily newspapers, the number of dailies reporting D-Day to the nation on Tuesday, 6 June 1944, stood at 1,859, which included morning (387), all-day (3), and evening (1,469) editions. When D-Day finally came, some daily newspapers produced multiple editions (sometimes three or four) in the form of "extras" throughout the day and into the night on 6 June 1944.[13]

News of the world came to these newspapers through the wire services. In 1944 the three main wire services were the Associated Press (AP), the United Press (UP), and the International News Service (INS).[14] According to David Lloyd Jones, the "press wire services best exemplif[ied] press concentration," suggesting that these services dominated the messaging about the world's events and the way Americans saw those events—with D-Day as a case in point.[15]

Another news wire service that received almost no attention from the White-dominated press—the Associated Negro Press (ANP)—was struggling for a national voice. The ANP provided opinion and other news material to Black newspapers that served as a stark counterpoint to the Whites-only narratives filling the daily newspapers and radio airwaves. The opinion pieces supplied by the ANP were packed with demands for racial justice and appeals to allow Black men to fight alongside White troops. But the ANP's offerings never found their way into White newspapers or the D-Day narrative, principally because Black calls for civil rights complicated America's wartime claim to be fighting for liberty and democracy for all.[16]

The AP was the largest and most successful of the three main wire services; it was also the first true cooperative news-gathering organization in America.[17] Each subscribing newspaper contributed its own news, which in turn entitled that paper to the news gathered by all other member newspapers in the system. By contrast, the UP and INS wire services conducted their own news gathering at home and overseas and then sold their news bulletins directly to client newspapers.[18] At any given time during the war, seven hundred reporters worked overseas to gather, write, and transmit war news to America's newspapers. Many of these reporters worked for the three main wire services while others worked directly for individual or syndicated newspapers or magazines such as *Life*, *Collier's*, or *Newsweek*. On D-Day, a veritable battalion of reporters—estimated at around five hundred—covered the Invasion, many of whom hailed from the U.S. wire services.[19]

In practical terms, when a wire service reporter on assignment overseas as a war correspondent crafted a news story for transmission to the stateside newspapers, the report came in the form of a bulletin, often a verbatim statement provided by an official source, or a properly written news piece ready for publication complete with the reporter's byline. The reporter, after receiving censorship approval at the source (a specific military headquarters, for example), would then communicate the news item to the wire service's main clearinghouse for further censorship as necessary. That clearinghouse, such as the AP's London Bureau, transmitted the copy by wire to another stateside node (such as the AP's New York Bureau), which would then transmit it to all members in the AP cooperative or, in the case of the UP and INS, to all direct-purchase clients.

Subscribing newspaper offices throughout the United States maintained Teletypewriter Exchange (TELEX) machines. The receiving TELEX machines printed the news bulletin or story sent by the wire service in all capital letters, capturing not only the news item but the date and time the wire service sent it.[20] Newsroom editors, who made the key decisions about the content and framing of the news, could either choose to publish verbatim what the wire service sent them or turn it over to a rewrite man to revise the style, reorganize it, reframe it, or abridge it. In the newspaper world, rewrite men stood at the top of the "reportorial hierarchy." The more experienced rewrite men had developed the ability over time to take stale facts and information and, drawing upon rich backgrounds and well-honed writing skills, make the story interesting or attention grabbing.[21] Some rewrite men often went too far in "spicing up" the copy, though. Wartime cartoonist Sgt. Bill Mauldin, best known for his Willie and Joe characters, thought stateside newspaper editors should clamp down on their overly "enthusiastic" rewrite men, who loved to describe "'smashing armored columns,' the 'ground forces sweeping ahead,' and 'victorious, cheering armies.'" Frontline reporters like Mauldin worried that such hyperbolic language might adversely affect the morale of the GIs by separating the news from their harsh reality. In Mauldin's view, the GIs were no fools.[22]

Of the three main wire services, the AP stood out as the gold standard. The AP was founded in May 1848 as a cooperative news-gathering enterprise among six New York City newspapers. It existed solely for the benefit of its members.[23] The electromagnetic telegraph had exploded on the scene only five years earlier and transformed the nation overnight, providing citizens across the westward-expanding nation with a wealth of commercial information and, later, hard news. The new AP intended to embrace fully the opportunities the telegraph presented or risk obsolescence. By the summer of 1848, the AP began selling news to outside clients in cities such as Philadelphia and Baltimore. Its client list expanded rapidly in the years that followed.[24]

The AP's burgeoning reputation as a news agency that Americans could trust hinged on its journalistic philosophy of objectivity. Since the AP gathered news that appeared in scores of newspapers across the United States with diverse political leanings, the copy it produced had to remain free of editorializing in order to satisfy all customers. The focus on objectivity was essentially a belief in facts, a distrust of societal values and biases, and a firm commitment to their separation. Because of this devotion to objectivity, many commentators over the years promoted the AP as "the ideal of journalism," even when objectivity was far from the norm in journalism. Instead, telling stories and editorializing remained the mainstays of journalism well into the early twentieth century.[25] During World War I, when Woodrow Wilson's Committee on Public Information (CPI) co-opted so many journalists into the government's propaganda activities, Americans began to see the news as tainted and skewed. Subjectivity in reporting became a topic of debate among citizens and reporters alike. Remarkably, World War I reaffirmed the AP's ability to gather accurate, reliable, objective facts, especially since the agency often corrected the erroneous reporting of other news services.[26]

Despite its commitment to objectivity, the AP recognized the damage the CPI had done to any notion of reportorial objectivity in journalism. It acknowledged that separating reporters from the news they produced was unrealistic; value systems and personal beliefs almost always crept into any news item. In 1925, the AP responded by signing news stories with the reporter's byline, thus paving the way for "interpretive reporting," which allowed journalists to assign meaning to the events they reported.[27] This interpretive approach dominated much of the AP's reporting on D-Day. The AP also transformed wire service journalism in 1935 with the development of the AP Wirephoto, adding a visual component to the news by simultaneously transmitting over the same wires crisp, clear photographs to accompany the written copy. On 6 June 1944, many of the photographs of the Invasion boasted "AP Wirephoto" as their source.[28]

◆ ◆ ◆

Although the AP and the other major wire services became the principal drivers behind the information that appeared as news in America's newspapers, one other wire service, the ANP, and the newspapers it supplied remained on the margins of what the Black community saw as the "White man's" newspapers. When D-Day finally arrived, the thematically framed narrative these White newspapers conveyed did not go unchallenged. In fact, the emerging D-Day narrative in the mainstream press was in direct tension with the newspapers published by and for America's Black community, some 13 million strong.[29] The Black press, boasting 210 weekly newspapers with a circulation of more than 1,808,060 by the end of the war, consistently poked holes in the American social values and sense of exceptionalism that permeated the daily White newspapers.[30] The Black press over the years had unfailingly served as a medium through which "white America's ideals and institutions [had] been upheld and its deviations from these denounced."[31] Thus, the Black press, while signaling support for the Invasion, did not fully accept the emerging American D-Day narrative, but instead called into question how the themes framing that narrative could prevail in a segregated, Jim Crow America that excluded 10 percent of its citizens from the privilege of engaging in direct combat with the enemy.

Since America's Black newspapers were all weeklies (with but one exception), Black Americans used them to supplement the news they got from radio and daily newspapers, which tended to omit stories highlighting the wartime participation and achievements of Black service members.[32] By the time the first weeklies hit the stands on the Friday or Saturday following the Invasion, the D-Day storyline and its attendant themes had already permeated the American consciousness. Thus, while still supporting the Invasion and vigorously advocating the purchase of war bonds, the Black press could only add the contributions of Black troops to the Invasion narrative after the fact.[33] Black editors essentially forced the inclusion of Black soldiers into the D-Day story as full members of General Eisenhower's "crusaders." For instance, Kansas City's *The Plaindealer* of 16 June 1944 boasted front-page headlines proclaiming, "Well Trained [Black] Units Follow Orders Given By Eisenhower," and "Negroes In Heat Of Invasions [*sic*] Die With Whites."[34] These headings cut straight to the point of the Double V campaign, which the *Pittsburgh Courier*, the Black weekly with the nation's highest circulation, had initiated on 7 February 1942 as a direct assault on racial discrimination in America.[35] The Double V stood for victory at home (against discrimination) and victory abroad (against the Axis enemy).[36] But the primary aim of the campaign was to encourage all Blacks to "fight for the right to fight" because, as far as many Black leaders and editors were concerned, spilling Black blood would earn them precious leverage to push for equal status with Whites after the war.[37] The consistent efforts of the Black press to resist discrimination, even in the face of government accusations of seditious rabble-rousing, revealed the incomplete and exaggerated nature of the D-Day narrative's thematic frames.[38] Ultimately, the mainstream White press in many ways risked its professional credentials by pushing such an incomplete, thematically shaped narrative that in the end excluded certain groups of Americans from the storyline.

◆ ◆ ◆

The second of the two main communications mediums supplying the American public with news of the war—radio—lacked the long history and cultural entrenchment enjoyed by newspapers, but the broadcast industry still played a prominent role in shaping the initial draft of the D-Day narrative. In fact, World War II marked the very first involvement of commercial broadcasting in a major American conflict, placing its role and subsequent performance as a legitimate conveyer of D-Day news under the microscope.[39] Commercial radio had only come of age in America in the early 1920s and offered Americans a new way of imagining the world through sound. Perhaps most significantly, radio transformed and extended the public sphere by circulating information and ideas with greater immediacy and synchrony.[40] In this sense, the ritual of radio listenership adhered strictly to clock time, since people across the country, regardless of which of the four time zones they occupied, could tune in to the very same broadcast at the very same moment throughout the nation, even though clock time in each of the zones differed. Although people read newspapers each day around the same time, radio's unique capacity to broadcast in real time allowed people to listen to the same news or other programs at *exactly* the same moment, further strengthening the ability of both radio and newspapers to communicate common themes and narratives about major news events such as D-Day nearly simultaneously.[41]

The ability to provide information quickly and concurrently across the nation made radio the American people's first source of information about wartime events. Radio proved highly attractive because the medium allowed "imaginative listeners" to "feel a world at war Out There in a way that newspapers could only faintly provoke."[42] During the war, Americans listened to approximately four-and-a-half hours of radio programming per day, the bulk of which occurred between 7 p.m. and 10:30 p.m. each night.[43] A poll taken shortly after D-Day on 20 June 1944 revealed that 63 percent of the Americans surveyed preferred to get their national and foreign news from the radio. But when asked if they usually tried to get more details later from newspapers, they responded "yes" by an overwhelming 77 percent. Even though they appreciated the greater details offered by newspaper reporting, many Americans preferred the personal touch of a radio commentator's human voice, which had the power to command respect and trust.[44]

Despite their stated preference for radio, Americans remained a nation of newspaper readers even as they purchased home radio sets in vast numbers (425 sets for every 1,000 persons by 1942).[45] In fact, Americans had begun reading even more newspapers, with daily newspaper circulation nearly doubling in the thirty-five years following 1920. During the interwar period, radio supplemented the newspapers, but print remained the bedrock of America's news.[46] Even so, newspapers and radio worked in tandem throughout the war to provide Americans with immediate, in-depth war news, primarily because many radio stations owned newspapers. Conversely, several forward-looking newspapers in the early 1920s purchased their own radio stations as a means of leveraging the unique characteristics of both media forms to enhance information circulation nationwide and to generate greater profits.[47] This nascent concept of the media corporation afforded the roughly 7 percent of newspapers owning radio stations between 1923 to 1929 far greater power and influence beyond their small numbers. The number of newspaper-owned stations continued to grow into the 1930s until newspapers owned 30.6 percent of the AM stations and 18.2 percent of the newer FM band stations by 1944.[48] The cumulative effect of the D-Day news transmitted by these newspaper-radio corporations was a more consistent and coordinated presentation of Invasion information and thematically framed messaging to the American public.[49]

Not all newspapers responded eagerly to the emergence and growth of radio as a news platform. Many newspapers and the American citizens they served viewed radio as a means of providing entertainment and local programming—and nothing more. Americans in the interwar period witnessed this cohort of newspapers engaging in a decade-long, unified offensive against radio beginning in 1924 colloquially known as the Press-Radio War. This "war" began when newspapers began to believe that the radio networks' efforts at news presentation posed a threat to the long-standing relationship between the wire services and the newspapers. Moreover, newspapers saw themselves as America's primary cultural mechanism in the "social communication process," and radio could bypass them in real time and speak directly to the American public. Control over the means of communication meant "power over the domain of meaning-making"; power over political discourse, especially since FDR often used radio to bypass newspapers; and power "to shape the cultural agenda, public opinion, and the nature of discourse." This power determined how all Americans defined and experienced reality. Newspapers fought mightily to avoid losing this power but eventually lost to radio in the mid-1930s when, following a brief boycott on wire-service memberships to radio stations, the major wire services decided to sell news directly to radio stations. Thus, the Press-Radio War ended with a whimper.[50]

One line of argument that newspaper reporters employed against radio commentators during the Press-Radio War was that on-air broadcasters lacked the professional legitimacy and objectivity to report the news properly and accurately. Print journalists themselves had struggled in the 1920s with questions about journalistic standards, ethics, training, and professional identity, particularly following charges of extreme subjectivity and bias during World War I.[51] Newspaper reporters viewed radio newscasters as complicating any efforts to create a new postwar professional identity for journalists. In their view, radio newscasters communicated the news using sensationalistic, show-business styles of delivery designed to evoke strong emotional responses. They also claimed that radio news was simply too short and lacked the depth and intellectual engagement that only printed news could provide. Newspapers allowed readers to absorb information at their own pace—to page back and forth through the different features and stories. By contrast, print journalists argued, if a listener missed something said by a radio announcer, the listener could not ask to hear it again, thus causing truth to get lost in the telling. These accusations generally proved baseless, since radio broadcasters did in fact apply the same news-gathering techniques as print reporters and conformed to the same code of objectivity. In fact, many radio staff members had shifted from print to air, the most famous of whom were Lowell Thomas, formerly of the *Chicago Journal*, and H. V. Kaltenborn, formerly of the *Brooklyn Eagle*.[52]

Since commercial radio's inception, the United States had remained alone among the world's major nations in entrusting the growing broadcasting system to major private corporations rather than to the state.[53] Prior to and during World War II, totalitarian nations such as Germany, Italy, and the Soviet Union retained strict government control over radio and used it to shape public opinion.[54] The United States did not use radio in this manner, despite America's standing as the most "radio-conscious" nation in the world, boasting 37 percent of the world's radio stations. During the war, Axis nations only had 62 radio sets per 1,000 persons compared to 425 per 1,000 persons for the United States.[55]

In 1944 NBC, CBS, the Mutual Broadcasting System (MBS), and the Blue Network represented the four major broadcast networks in the United States, and they all functioned as private enterprises that affiliated with radio stations throughout the country.[56] Congress declared the airwaves public property through the Radio Act of 1927. This legislation empowered the government to license commercial radio to private users, such as the networks, for fixed, renewable terms. Newspapers, on the other hand, faced no such licensing strictures. Licensing also prevented small groups of owners from dominating the limited number of frequencies and gaining too much political and economic power.[57]

Despite regulating the airwaves, the United States generally shied away from any semblance of direct control over radio broadcasting or the content of that broadcasting, except in emergency situations. For instance, the Communications Act of 1934 allowed the government to shut down or take control of radio stations in the national interest after a presidential proclamation of war, an authority the government exercised often during World War II for special announcements or war-related programming, such as the type that attended the D-Day Invasion.[58] Even though the radio networks fell under the Federal Communications Commission's (FCC's) direct oversight, the National Association of Broadcasters recognized radio's potency in wartime and imposed its own code on radio in December 1941 (well ahead of the forthcoming Office of Censorship's guidelines) by banning programming that might trigger public hysteria through the use of news flashes or other dramatic techniques.[59]

Despite radio's unique contributions to the transmission of news and entertainment throughout America before and during World War II, commercial radio was first and foremost a business. One of the major reasons newspapers purchased radio stations was to increase profits. Radio became big business and a commercial success specifically because the combined newspaper-radio corporations, in possession of nearly one-third of the nation's stations, fought to make that success a reality.[60]

Radio needed revenue to survive, and that revenue came in boatloads from a multitude of advertisers who routinely sponsored radio programming on all networks. For example, the *CBS Program Book* for spring 1944 listed 104 paying sponsors. One of those sponsors, American Oil Company, bankrolled the *CBS World News* with Edward R. Murrow each Thursday on fifty-five CBS stations. Likewise, the Bayer Company subsidized the *American Melody Hour* on Tuesdays while General Mills, Inc. underwrote the Kitty Foyle serial drama from Monday through Friday each week.[61] Concerned radio watchdogs at the time such as Sherman H. Dryer, director of Radio Productions at the University of Chicago, worried that such reliance on advertising dollars would compromise radio's ability to broadcast harsh truths that might alienate audiences and advertisers alike.[62] Notwithstanding such concerns, radio forged ahead to become so successful that major networks could devote between 20 and 30 percent of their programming to war news by 1944.[63]

In September 1938 radio took a significant step forward toward earning its news spurs when broadcasters combined with print journalists to provide riveting, complementary coverage of the Munich Crisis. The two major radio networks, NBC and CBS, dispatched correspondents to Europe to cover the growing emergency as Adolf Hitler, whose Nazi government had already annexed Austria on 12 March 1938, threatened to occupy Czechoslovakia's Sudetenland. From 12 to 29 September 1938, well-known American radio broadcasters such as Edward R. Murrow, William Shirer, and H. V. Kaltenborn delivered constant, up-to-the-minute coverage of the unfolding crisis to rapt audiences in the United States. The listening public heard the actual voices of the key political players—Hitler, Neville Chamberlain, Edvard Beneš, Édouard Daladier, and Benito Mussolini—for the first time during an unfolding, real-world drama as the European leaders abandoned the Sudetenland to Germany in a futile effort to thwart another world war. Most American listeners were hooked. They quickly developed a new habit of seeking their news on radio first only to follow up with newspapers for added details, maps, and other visual extras that radio could not provide. Newspaper circulation spiked as radio news continued to employ the Munich model well into the war. CBS sent its most seasoned and trusted broadcaster, Edward R. Murrow, to London in 1940 to broadcast live from British rooftops, chronicling the dramatic effects of German bombers pummeling London. By June 1944 radio was more than ready to take on D-Day.[64]

◆ ◆ ◆

As the radio networks and newspapers throughout the United States prepared to communicate news of D-Day to a restless American public, the specter of propaganda hung heavy in the air. Suspicion of government efforts to propagandize the public had the potential to become the greatest barrier between the media and the American people in conveying news of any wartime event, especially news of D-Day. American distrust in propaganda-style messaging—essentially any overt attempt to whip up ideological fervor for the war or cast the Axis enemies as bloodthirsty monsters—had its roots in the CPI, which Woodrow Wilson established during World War I to convert a pacifist American public into, according to Noam Chomsky, "a hysterical, war-mongering population which wanted to destroy everything German . . . [and] go to war and save the world."[65] In a moment of genuine understatement, in 1942 Sherman H. Dryer claimed that Americans were "suffering a mild neurosis on the subject of propaganda" as a result of the tricks perpetrated upon them by the CPI.[66] Postwar attitudes to the CPI's efforts were far from "mild." And since Wilson's CPI co-opted the efforts of many journalists in his nationwide propaganda effort, the broadcast and newspaper media during World War II had to tread lightly and avoid any behavior Americans might recognize as tools from the CPI's old kit bag.

In its most basic sense, propaganda connotes a process designed to shape perceptions systematically and deliberately, to manipulate cognition, and to direct behavior to achieve an outcome desired by the propagandist. Its core purpose is to convey an ideology as part of an intended outcome, and propagandists often employ many means and methods—including truths, half-truths, and limited truths—to achieve their planned goals.[67] This definition of propaganda describes precisely how the CPI functioned during World War I. In turn, the lingering effects of the CPI's actions on Americans during World War II demands a clear understanding of just how the CPI influenced public attitudes and ideology a generation earlier, some messaging of which the media—and even senior military leaders such as General Eisenhower—dared to resurrect on 6 June 1944.

The Committee on Public Information represented the first modern government propaganda operation.[68] The Great War, as it was commonly called prior to World War II, began on 28 July 1914, but an isolationist America, led by the religiously devout and progressive Woodrow Wilson, stood on the sidelines. Wilson's efforts to mediate a "peace without victory" failed as American grievances against Germany mounted with the growing German submarine threat and the discovery of the notorious Zimmerman telegram inviting Mexico to side with Germany against the United States. On 2 April 1917, Wilson asked Congress to declare war and Congress acceded.[69] Less than two weeks later, on 14 April 1917, Wilson signed Executive Order 2594 creating the CPI, a committee comprised of the secretaries of State, War, and Navy and a civilian chairman, George Creel.[70]

Wilson, who believed God had ordained his presidency and that the nation would redeem civilization, charged Creel with promoting the war to an isolationist America and whipping up anti-German sentiment. Creel, an experienced journalist, zealous reformer, and Wilson acolyte, embraced his new charter with amazing fervor. He employed every method available to recalibrate American thinking to reflect Wilson's war aims by uniting public opinion in support of the war and to persuade Americans to sacrifice so that democracy might survive.[71] Blinded by his own zealotry, Creel insisted that behind the front lines was another equally intensive struggle—"the fight for the minds of men, for the 'conquest of their convictions,' and the battle-line ran through every home in every country."[72]

Creel's CPI staff quickly set about generating thousands of images and ideas communicated through various mediums. According to Creel, the "printed word, the spoken word, the motion picture, the telegraph, the cable, the wireless, the poster, the sign-board—all these were used in our campaign to make our own people and all other peoples understand the causes that compelled America to take arms." The divine sanction of the mission, the horror of German atrocities perpetrated on civilians, and the German threat to the United States coalesced as key themes of the CPI's intensive wartime propaganda.[73] This concentrated, exaggerated, and misleading messaging campaign ultimately succeeded, creating a "war psychosis" among the populace that proved crucial to providing moral and material support to the armed forces.[74]

In addition to the CPI's propaganda efforts, Creel attempted to establish the very first program of voluntary censorship in the press. With Wilson's backing, Creel furnished unenthusiastic editors with guidelines, asking them to avoid reporting on troop and ship movements, the size of the expeditionary forces, the location of American bases, new war material, and so on on—all matters of military security. Although the censorship guidelines generally kept this type of information from the public, some newspapers made inadvertent or intentional slips.[75] The program ultimately failed because, as Creel himself admitted after the war, the "scale and diversity" of the American press defied his ability to manage them.[76] This combination of propaganda and censorship only succeeded in giving Americans at home a distorted picture of what their troops were facing in the trenches of France.[77]

When the war ended and America walked away empty-handed, Americans felt deceived. Congress refused to ratify the Treaty of Versailles, and Woodrow Wilson failed to make the United States a member of his own brainchild for collective world security—the League of Nations.[78] The result was that Americans were left with dead sons and unfulfilled promises. A disillusioned populace quickly scapegoated Creel and his propaganda efforts.[79] Investigations in the 1920s exposed much of the German atrocity propaganda as pure fabrication. Although Creel had argued that the Germans were the ones who sullied the term "propaganda," the CPI was in fact guilty of making the term in America a synonym for lies.[80] By the time World War II exploded upon the global stage, the carnage of the previous war and its hollow calls for American idealism and patriotism remained all too fresh in the minds of most Americans, particularly the parents of the young men that America was calling to arms.

Overt propaganda of the type generated by Creel's minions a generation earlier did not emerge during World War II. The government completely avoided any such attempts at employing fictive accounts of atrocities or other apocryphal stories to whip up pro-war sentiment. The Japanese attack on Pearl Harbor had already served that purpose. Most importantly for the news-minded American public, the broadcast and print media generally avoided any such propaganda techniques, instead allowing government-sponsored messages about practical operational security measures and self-affirming American ideals to fill newspapers and airtime. For this reason, the press retained credibility with Americans, although the populace remained guarded about the type of messaging it received from all sources.

One major reason CPI-style propaganda failed to emerge was the absence of a similar propaganda agency within FDR's government. Like his fellow Americans, FDR had despised the CPI's behavior and swore off any efforts to manipulate public sentiment.[81] He resisted calls within his own administration to create such an organization. FDR preferred to let the federal government's agencies handle their own messaging. However, in October 1941, just weeks before Pearl Harbor, FDR heeded his advisors and created the Office of Facts and Figures (OFF) under the leadership of poet and writer Archibald MacLeish, a fellow detractor of the CPI.[82] MacLeish's primary task involved providing government war facts and data to the press, which MacLeish did but within the boundaries of his own ideological framework—a strategy of truth. This policy meant that in a liberal democracy, the government had to provide the honest facts to the people and trust them to make up their own minds. Liberal democracies could engage in total war without undermining democracy. For MacLeish, this framework responded directly to "the existential struggle with fascism" and public fears that FDR's government would taint the press with Creel-style propaganda.[83] This high-minded ideal governed the OFF's interactions with the media, but friction developed as the press interpreted the agency's data in its own unique ways, often subverting the intended messaging. By early 1942 military censorship restrictions significantly jeopardized the OFF's information-distribution activities and its credibility.[84] Most tellingly, America's involvement in the war after Pearl Harbor demanded a much stronger messaging effort than the one employed by the OFF. Bickering with other competing information agencies such as the Office of the Coordinator of Information (OCOI) and its Foreign Information Service further darkened the information and public relations landscape.[85]

In response to the confusion and bickering, a reluctant FDR, still apprehensive about creating anything resembling a CPI-like agency, agree to combine all foreign and domestic information efforts into one organization—the Office of War Information (OWI).[86] On 13 June 1942 FDR signed Executive Order (EO) 9182 establishing the OWI, which subsumed into its structure the various information agencies, such as the OFF, the Office of Government Reports, the OCOI and its satellites, and the Division of Information of the Office for Emergency Management.[87] FDR signed the EO on the sole condition that Elmer Davis, a Rhodes scholar and one of America's most well-known and trusted journalists, agree to head the agency.[88] The press was pleased, particularly since Davis adopted MacLeish's guiding framework—the strategy of truth. Davis fully intended to erase America's bitter memories of the CPI.

The OWI's core functions as outlined in EO 9182 reflected a fundamentally different charter than the one issued to Creel twenty-five years earlier. The OWI would not create its own messaging content from whole cloth but instead, "through the use of press, radio, motion picture, and other facilities . . . *facilitate* the development of an informed and intelligent understanding, at home and abroad, of the status and progress of the war effort" and any accompanying government policies. The OWI, according to the executive order, would "coordinate the war informational activities of all Federal departments and agencies for the purpose of assuring an accurate and consistent flow of war information to the public and the world at large."[89]

In actual practice, the OWI engaged in a variety of messaging activities. For example, Davis's staff took proposed messages from government agencies on topics such as war bonds or the need for workers with special skills, crafted them into one-minute radio transcriptions, and issued them to stations to "plug" as part of their programming.[90] Other efforts included disseminating posters with pragmatic messages reflecting FDR's, and the nation's, practical goal of winning the war quickly.[91]

Overall, the OWI's war messaging tended to comport with the ambiguous war aims offered up by FDR's "Four Freedoms"—freedom of speech, freedom of worship, freedom from want, and freedom from fear—and the American people's preconceived notions of their own exceptionalism. By the time D-Day took place, such thematically framed messaging had become the cultural backdrop to much of the war reporting ingested by the average American. The messaging had, according to Susan A. Brewer, "blended facts with inspiring and reassuring cultural beliefs," blurring the boundary between what was true and what Americans wanted to believe.[92] Clearly, the strategy of truth as a guiding principle had become "truth" only as the American citizenry and official government sources defined it, ultimately laying the groundwork for the post–World War II "good war" myth.

Aside from reinforcing the practical aspects of winning the war for somewhat imprecise war aims, the OWI's propaganda efforts—a "propaganda of truth"—did little to influence directly how the press reported D-Day. The War Department and the Navy Department generally did not cooperate well with Davis, and some members of Congress even accused the OWI in 1943 of serving as a "New Deal publicity center" aimed at supporting FDR's bid for a fourth term. Consequently, on 18 June 1943 Congress voted to pull funding from the OWI for much of its domestic propaganda activities, leaving Davis with a more robust foreign propaganda operation based in London that engaged almost solely in traditional wartime propaganda activities and psychological warfare directed at the enemy.[93] The government organization that would have the greatest impact on what the press reported on D-Day was one that prevented, rather than facilitating, certain information from reaching the American public—the Office of Censorship (OC).

◆ ◆ ◆

No other government program impacted news of D-Day more than the censorship program, which served as the principal filtration and gatekeeping apparatus for information about D-Day as well as a shaping mechanism for the dispatches issued by newspaper and broadcast journalists about the Invasion. Although sensitive to censorship, most Americans realized that no modern nation, even a liberal democracy, could prosecute a war successfully without controlling or suppressing some information.[94] FDR acknowledged the public's inherent aversion to censorship, but he also recognized that "the experience of this and of all other Nations has demonstrated that some degree of censorship is essential in wartime, and we are at war."[95]

On 19 December 1941, less than two weeks after the Japanese attack at Pearl Harbor, FDR formalized in an executive order what had been an earlier, less structured program of voluntary censorship in the United States.[96] Executive Order 8985 not only established the OC but also appointed its director, a trusted, lifelong newspaperman named Byron Price who, like FDR and most Americans, abhorred censorship.[97] As a senior member of the AP—America's premier wire service—Price enjoyed extraordinary credibility among the press corps and the public in general, especially for his calm and judicious nature.[98] In Executive Order 8985, FDR charged Price and the OC with censoring information of potential value to the enemy transmitted "through the medium of the mails, radio, or cable . . . or by any other means." Most significantly, the order read, "The Director of Censorship is authorized to take all such measures as may be necessary or expedient to administer the powers hereby conferred."[99]

Price immediately set to work building a comprehensive structure to enact the censorship program. By 15 February 1942, the OC's six divisions—Postal, Cable, Press, Broadcasting, Reports, and Administrative—were in full operation. A month later, the OC formally accepted the transfer of all Army and Navy personnel engaged in censorship. Despite the addition of 15,000 military personnel, Price's assistant director, Theodore F. Koop, explained that "censorship *by* the military *of* the military and of persons and places under military jurisdiction" was beyond the OC's purview. In other words, the Army and the Navy retained much of their own authority for censorship of their personnel, including the censorship of dispatches issued by accredited newspaper and radio war correspondents in the theaters of operation.[100]

Even before his new staff members had settled into their duties, Director Price implemented a key aspect of the executive order—voluntary censorship. By 15 January 1942 Price issued the first *Code of Wartime Practices* outlining what types of sensitive military information newspapers and broadcasters should avoid disseminating in the interest of national security.[101] George Creel and his CPI had attempted a similar program of voluntary censorship during World War I, but the program failed because of the sprawling nature of the media at the time. Also, Creel had blended censorship with his aggressive propaganda activities, and the press misunderstood how to implement his guidelines.[102] Price's efforts, by contrast, succeeded in grand fashion. Recognizing Creel's mistakes, Price avoided an early effort at mixing propaganda with censorship by resisting calls to combine the OC with the OWI.[103] Price used a light touch with America's print and broadcast journalists, offering them assistance with the code and helping to clarify issues on a twenty-four-hour basis. Price placed great faith in his fellow reporters to do the right thing.

Between 15 January 1942 and 15 May 1945, the OC issued five editions of the press and broadcasting codes.[104] The codes came in the form of small five- to eight-page pamphlets, one version of which applied to the newspapers and the other to radio. The first code asked that newspapers withhold information related to troops, ships, planes, fortifications, production, weather, photographs, maps, and general topics (such as naming the units to which casualties were assigned).[105] The news section of the broadcasters' code was nearly identical except for the weather, reports of which, if given in real time, could allow German U-boats in the Atlantic to triangulate weather patterns in their area for the next few days.[106] The broadcasters' code also differed by addressing radio-unique programming; the code requested that stations avoid music-request programs, quiz programs, and forums so that enemy agents could not use the radio to send coded messages to their handlers.[107]

One important aspect of Price's approach was his desire to avoid censoring government information. The information emanating from public relations officers normally combined, in his view, publicity and enemy-directed propaganda, which defied any attempts at disentanglement. To avoid Creel's mistake of blending censorship with propaganda, Price developed the principle of "appropriate authority," in which any qualified government source could violate the OC's codes. For Price, the OC was not the appropriate agency to suppress official government information.[108] Moreover, Price had already sensed confusion between the role of the OC and the OWI. On 15 November 1942 he signed an agreement with Elmer Davis specifying that the OC would censor outgoing OWI broadcasts for security purposes only and not for policy reasons. The line of demarcation between both agencies was clear: the OC kept information from the enemy that would endanger the Allies, while the OWI disseminated, at home and overseas, information and propaganda messaging designed to bolster the Allied cause.[109] The system was a "patchwork" that frustrated the more security-minded officials concerned with leaks from "appropriate authorities" within the government. According to Sam Lebovic, the OWI and the agencies tried to keep information secure at the source while the OC served as the "safety net" by catching material before it hit the newspapers or airwaves.[110]

Despite the government's imperfect efforts at safeguarding all state secrets, the OC's program of voluntary censorship proved remarkably successful, particularly in the lead-up to D-Day.[111] In the months before the Invasion, Price refocused the OC's efforts strictly on operational security matters instead of issues related to economics and morale. Price also cautioned editors on all fronts against speculation about where the Invasion would take place. Everyone, especially the Germans, knew the Invasion would originate from Britain. The open questions were where, when, and how?[112] In the end, the OC succeeded in keeping the enemy in the dark thanks to voluntary censorship. At the same time, the OC kept the American public guessing as well.[113]

◆ ◆ ◆

By 5 June 1944—the eve of the Invasion—the media architecture in the United States stood ready to help mold the thematic frames that ultimately gave shape to an enduring D-Day narrative on the day the operation unfolded. America's press corps and radio networks had spent the better part of six months preparing for what the OWI's Elmer Davis predicted would be days of "'tremendous' consequence to the U.S. Press."[114] In other words, the press had a role to play in the Invasion by keeping the American people informed and supportive of the war effort. For their part, the government agencies that played important roles in constructing that narrative—Davis's OWI and Price's OC—participated in these preparations to varying degrees. In the end, Americans' central belief that the Invasion was the war's most significant event up to that time served as the foundational precept guiding the collective planning for reporting D-Day. It had the greatest effect in shaping how the American public would come to see the D-Day story and beyond.

How did that perception of the Invasion's overall significance come to dominate the thinking and outlook of America's press and radio editors, and even their correspondents in the field? Did government dicta or policies issued on the eve of the Invasion steer America's reporters toward casting their Invasion reporting in a specific light? Not at all. The Invasion's status as the war's most critical event, and the other thematic frames that arose around that core theme, came about instinctively and organically from within the press and radio industries. The men with the greatest agency in these two news industries—White, educated, middle-aged men (and a few women) who were largely beholden to a Whites-only perspective—agreed collectively in the run-up to D-Day that they would report the Invasion as Elmer Davis and others had already described it: as an event of "'tremendous' consequence."[115] These press and radio men were professionals, and they knew a big story when they saw one—and D-Day was such a story.

Perhaps the most effective way they communicated this common perspective of D-Day across industry lines was by establishing and maintaining a running discourse between each medium's trusted and oft-read trade journals—*Editor & Publisher* (*E&P*) and *Broadcasting and Broadcast Advertising* (*BBA*). These weekly trade journals not only addressed the business mechanics of each news industry, they also chronicled the nature of each industry's pre-Invasion preparations, often in precise detail. This effort clearly spoke to the Invasion's importance in the eyes of journalists serving both the print and broadcast mediums. And since many newspapers owned radio stations, these two trade journals were undoubtedly common reading in both industries.[116] In effect, the newspaper and radio worlds engaged in a common discourse through each other's trade journals, essentially creating through these journals a kind of intellectual framework, a sort of mental ecosystem, that compelled editors and war correspondents alike to see the Invasion as the war's seminal event. In turn, they developed a loose working relationship that enabled them to act upon the narrative from within this common framework.

In the context of D-Day, the conversation between the trade journals began soon after FDR announced in December 1943 that Gen. Dwight D. Eisenhower would command the cross-Channel Invasion. The 29 January 1944 issue of *E&P* featured a story about Eisenhower's visit back home to the United States that same month, sparking a flurry of pre-Invasion interest and reporting among the trade journals.[117] For the next six months following the Eisenhower report, *E&P* featured stories that underscored the extensive D-Day preparations made by the AP and the UP as well as technical and other details of the overseas planning efforts between the SHAEF and each news industry's war correspondents. At the same time, *BBA* expressed in great detail the nature of the various radio networks' stateside and overseas preparations as well as the preparatory "War Clinics" conducted by networks such as NBC to evaluate and improve their wartime reportage.[118] In all, the collective messaging taking place between the newspapers and radio worlds through these two trade journals advanced one common, essentially unchallenged, theme through their pre-Invasion reporting, a theme that cast D-Day as the most significant operation of the entire war. And since the world had nearly six months of foreknowledge about D-Day's inevitable occurrence sometime in the spring of 1944, the newspapers and radio networks enjoyed an unprecedented opportunity to build up D-Day as they saw it—the biggest story of World War II. Thus, the dominant theme comprising the media-constructed D-Day narrative—the Invasion's extraordinary significance to the greater war effort—became the foundational premise from which all the other themes shaping the D-Day narrative would arise. This theme stemmed directly from the print and broadcast media's dual convictions that D-Day was the biggest story of the war and that the American people had a right to know as many facts about the Invasion as possible and as quickly as possible.

In addition to the stories about technical preparations for the coming Invasion filling the pages of *E&P* and *BBA*, readers were regaled with discussions of government policies or guidelines about how to report the war. Surprisingly, no single government-issued policy directed America's newspapers and radio networks to tilt or shade their reporting of the Invasion in a certain manner. In fact, the OWI did not issue any specific guidelines to the news media about how to shape their collective reporting. The only official policy proffered by the OWI in the run-up to the Invasion emerged in April 1944, when the agency distributed a war news policy focused not only on the upcoming Invasion but on the reporting of all military operations; the policy guidance offered no D-Day-specific guidance whatsoever. Instead, it dealt with the practical mechanics related to the release of information and under what circumstances information should be released. According to a description of the policy in the 17 April 1944 issue of *BBA*, "Military security will strictly govern the release of forthcoming news on military operations" and whenever a theater commander withholds information, that commander must submit that information to Washington, DC, for review. The policy further specified that the "OWI and the War and Navy Departments are in agreement that news of military and naval operations should be made public as soon and as fully as military security permits."[119] Thus, the larger concern about the D-Day reportage did not involve ways in which the narrative might develop in the news media but only how the information that would build that narrative flowed from war correspondents to their editors in the United States for subsequent processing and dissemination to an American public eager to know details of the Invasion as it happened.

The closest the OWI came to issuing any type of Invasion-reporting guidance appeared in the form of a statement made by Elmer Davis, reported in the 29 May 1944 issue of *BBA*, in which the OWI chief called upon all media "to retain as much operating normalcy as is possible" on D-Day and to avoid exploiting the Invasion to justify home-front measures. "The news of the invasion," declared Davis, "will speak for itself."[120] Remarkably, and perhaps to Davis's chagrin, the radio networks heeded only part of his call. The subsequent reporting on radio, and for that matter in the newspapers, would not exploit the Invasion for personal or proprietary gains, but the notion that the radio and the press would retain any semblance of operating "normalcy" was already out the window.[121] Despite not issuing any official guidance regarding the D-Day reportage, the OWI instead actively supported the news wire services, syndicated newspapers, and radio networks with extra overseas cables and additional frequencies in order to help the war correspondents get their stories back to London and then on to the United States as quickly as possible.

The policy guidance that came closest to approximating a particular way to report the Invasion did not appear in the trade journals but instead came from General Eisenhower in his "D Day Guidance for the Press" issued in London on 31 May 1944 that was directed only at war correspondents. Eisenhower warned the correspondents that the "release of pent-up emotion on D Day will have the character of an explosion" and that all reporting should attempt to channel this "uncontrolled detonation" to "do the most good for the Allied War Effort." Since the supreme commander offered this rather ambiguous charter solely to the reporters in the field, newsrooms back in America had no idea what this secret document had advised their reporters to do.[122]

In the end, America's newspapers and radio networks enjoyed a generally unconstrained, loosely cooperative environment within which to shape a common, thematically framed narrative that would tell all Americans what they needed to know about the Invasion without alienating them from the war effort. As a professional caste of journalists, they knew that public support would prove essential to victory, so the themes they advanced to shape the common, enduring D-Day narrative had to resonate with their audiences and not alienate them.

◆ ◆ ◆

The cooperative spirit and shared perspective of D-Day that developed between the press and broadcast industries through their trade journals was most evident in how both industries quickly came together to dampen the effects of a massive reporting gaffe that took place only seventy-two hours before the Allies launched the operation. On Saturday, 3 June 1944, at precisely 4:39 p.m. eastern war time (EWT), a teletype operator in the AP's London office accidentally transmitted a false report that the Invasion had begun, a report that went out over America's airwaves before the AP could kill the transmission. The radio networks immediately retracted the bulletin. The newspaper world picked up the story the next day to explain to the American people—in a genuine act of transparency—what had happened. These quick reactions to the false newsflash suggested both news industries clearly understood that their credibility was at stake on the very eve of what each one considered, and what their trade journals insisted, was the greatest operation of the war.

The most revealing aspect of the AP's false Invasion flash was the range of immediate reactions among Americans—from cheers of jubilation to quiet prayers to stunned silence, all of which justified General Eisenhower's suspicion that Americans harbored a "pent-up emotion" that was ready to explode.[123] Clergymen throughout the nation rang church bells and summoned congregations to special prayer services. Radio station WOL in Washington, DC, observed a full minute of on-air silence. In Manhattan, a baseball game between the New York Giants and the Pittsburgh Pirates stopped when the announcer broke in to proclaim that the Allies had invaded France. The fans met the news with cheers of approval, which quickly subsided when the announcer asked in a solemn tone that everyone rise for a minute of silent prayer.[124] But mere minutes after the AP's flash message clicked out over the TELEX, another message followed that rescinded the first message: "BUST THAT FLASH. BUST EISENHOWER."[125] The message had been a mistake. D-Day remained set for some unknown future date—and that date was not 3 June 1944. The news industry's most trusted wire service, the AP, had been the source of the blunder. But what had happened?

The continuing demand for speed and accuracy in wire-service reporting had led to the false Invasion flash that electrified America on Saturday, 3 June 1944.[126] A young teletype operator in the London AP office, Joan Ellis, wanted to practice crafting the very message she might find herself sending to the world in a matter of days or even hours—news of the Allied Invasion of Normandy. Obsessed with speed and accuracy, Joan found time during her hectic Saturday evening shift to practice her teletypewriter speed. When an operator typed a message for broadcast, the letters perforated a paper tape with a series of holes that when connected to a reader converted each letter into an electronic impulse. A reader connected to the network transmitted these electronic impulses over the circuits as a coherent message. As Joan began typing her practice message—"URGENT PRESS ASSOCIATED NYK FLASH—EISENHOWER'S HQ ANNOUNCES ALLIED LANDINGS IN FRANCE"—a shift supervisor handed her an actual report on Soviet activities on the eastern front for immediate transmission. When Joan tore off her practice tape, she failed to get all of it before typing and then transmitting the Soviet war report. As a result, both the practice Invasion message and the actual Soviet report went out over the wire.[127]

Despite the AP's later admission that "the error slipped through the most elaborate system of safeguards and censorship ever established both by the Associated Press and Allied authorities," the false Invasion flash threatened to harm the news media's reputation on the eve of the war's biggest operation. Even though the accidental transmission further demonstrated how the broadcast media could connect all Americans almost instantaneously in a common narrative about a single event transpiring at the moment it happened, the immediate challenge for the radio and newspaper industries was to restore any lost confidence among the American public about the media's combined ability to report the news of D-Day reliably and accurately once the Invasion actually began.[128] Thus, the pre-Invasion discourse in professional journals and the loosely cooperative relationship between the respective news platforms paid dividends when Joan Ellis's slip-up hit the airwaves. Both the radio and newspaper worlds had already recognized and implicitly agreed on, the significance of the Invasion in the greater war effort and to their roles as journalists in helping D-Day succeed.

In a seemingly coordinated, complementary response to Joan Ellis's mistake, the radio networks immediately retracted the report after the AP killed it and admitted to the false nature of the transmission. In corresponding fashion, the newspapers did their part the following day by explaining to the American public exactly what had happened and who was at the source of the mistake. *The Battle Creek Enquirer and News* in Michigan reported on its front page that "AP Blames Operator's Error For False Flash on Invasion." Denver's *Rocky Mountain News* of 4 June 1944 printed the AP's own in-depth explanation of the mistake with a headline that read, "London Girl Sends False Invasion Flash," which cast the error as an unfortunate human failing in the midst of a tense and extraordinary time in world history. Ultimately, Joan Ellis became a figure worthy of public empathy, and the detailed mea culpa stories appearing in the newspapers quelled the scandal.[129] As a further testament to the cooperative nature of the pre-Invasion press-radio relationship, the radio networks, the newspapers, and the wire services gave no evidence of exploiting the error for their own purposes.

◆ ◆ ◆

Despite the wide range of reactions by many Americans in the face of the false Invasion flash, waning public support for the war was no secret to the

American press corps, and this knowledge almost certainly had an impact on how the newspapers and broadcast networks shaped their portrayal of the D-Day story. But working from a common, agreed-upon theme—that of the Invasion's grand significance—the newspapers and radio used what their war correspondents overseas cabled to them and what the official sources distributed to craft a narrative that would share common themes across the nation's newspapers and airwaves. The nation's war-weariness was painfully evident through increased worker absenteeism, strikes, and a decrease in voluntary enlistments. The OWI had conducted its own analysis of the nation's attitude in relation to the war effort. They unveiled a spike in selfishness and a reluctance to do their part in a manner on par with the soldiers' sacrifices on overseas battlefields. America's senior military leaders, most notably Gen. George C. Marshall, became concerned.[130] The American public believed the war was now a downhill venture, so further sacrifices were unnecessary. Thus, local and national newspapers, major wire services, and the major radio networks all converged reflexively on a common set of themes to produce an optimistic realism that would encourage the average American to see the Invasion in the best light. In other words, the newspapers and networks, as an instinctively natural occurrence, gravitated toward the four major themes that would frame the D-Day narrative—the Invasion as a significant, sacred event carried out by America's well-trained and gallant soldiers under the leadership of the very best senior leaders the nation could muster. This resulting D-Day narrative was not objective reality, but it was not a blatant, propagandistic falsehood either. The media simply gave the public an Invasion narrative they needed at the moment to boost their spirits and offer hope. Ultimately, the ground truth was not as noble as the received version, and most Americans with a discerning eye knew the difference. But they also needed the morale boost that came with such reporting.

The American people needed to know that D-Day was a significant step forward in seeing the war through to a speedy, victorious conclusion and that public support for the war still mattered.

One additional factor that further influenced the themes that arose around the D-Day news narrative stemmed from the American war correspondents' firmly held belief that their reporting would contribute directly to the Invasion's success and eventual victory. The pages of the trade journals expressed this conviction as early as October 1942, when *E&P* amplified Elmer Davis's call early in the war that "the more thoroughly the people of the United States understand this war . . . the harder they will work to win it."[131] This charter served to imbue the overseas war correspondents with a powerful sense of responsibility for D-Day's success. In this context, reporters saw themselves not as neutral observers but as members of the Allied fighting team using direct, factually based news as ammunition to counter German propaganda as only a liberal democracy could. The war correspondents came to see themselves as active participants in the Invasion, essentially foot soldiers wielding words and images rather than rifles and bullets.

Perhaps the most powerful voice appearing in the trade journals' pages that empowered the war correspondents came directly from the supreme commander himself—General Eisenhower. *E&P* printed Eisenhower's initial guidance to the war correspondents in February 1944, in which the supreme commander "stated that by their combined efforts they could help defeat the Axis."[132] Another journal report described how Eisenhower, upon assuming command of the Invasion forces, directed that all press and radio representatives in his command receive full support in order "to report the invasion of Western Europe quickly, accurately, fully."[133] With this kind of support from the very top of the command hierarchy, the correspondents could only believe that their contributions would be what *E&P* described as a "Vital War Weapon."[134] According to the journal, a twenty-four-page booklet issued by SHAEF to all field commanders explained that each commander's support to the war correspondents was essential, because only a "speedy and complete flow of news to the United States" would allow the newspapers and radio networks to use "our own truthful information to counteract that from the enemy."[135] Such a powerful responsibility handed to these journalists likely helped lure well-known broadcasters, such as CBS's foreign correspondent Charles Collingwood, out of the United States and overseas to cover the Invasion.[136]

And so, from within the pages of their own trade journals, America's war correspondents came to see themselves as performing a different, more influential role in the Invasion than simply serving as an objective observer and recorder. The trade journals told them that they were part of the greater war-winning effort, and they embraced that role enthusiastically. They produced the kinds of news reports and Invasion narrative that helped instill much-needed optimism while sustaining public support for the war effort. These American reporters were members of the "home team," and they were clearly rooting for the American troops. Andy Rooney, former *Stars and Stripes* reporter in the European theater of operations, made no apologies for his and his fellow war correspondents' attitudes about their roles in the war. "We were all on our side in [World War] II," Rooney declared after the war. "We were agreed on who the enemy was." Moreover, he explained, the "American public wanted to see its soldiers portrayed as the good guys[,] and journalists gave them that."[137]

◆ ◆ ◆

Speculation and anticipation of the Invasion intensified in the American media and among the "jittery" populace beginning in May 1944.[138] Most Americans understood that fairer weather and calmer seas meant that D-Day was imminent. News of the massive pre-Invasion aerial bombardments on occupied France further suggested that D-Day would occur at any moment. *Time* magazine reported in its 1 May 1944 issue that British and American bombers had flown 25,000 sorties in only seven days in order to soften up the Wehrmacht's coastal defenses and inland targets. The magazine proclaimed that the "air assault on Europe had reached its fiercest pitch yet." *Time* also reported that diplomatic communication channels had closed, and the radio airwaves had gone silent, isolating the Germans from any information that might tip the Allies' hand.[139]

Although Byron Price had cautioned the press about speculating where the Invasion might take place, newspapers, radio, and even news magazines engaged in deliberate conjecture about where the Allies would land. The Pas de Calais was the narrowest cross-Channel route between Britain and the Continent, compelling both the German armed forces and the Allied citizenry to keep a close eye on that potential landing spot. *Time*'s editions of 1 May 1944 and 15 May 1944 each included maps of the French coastline, one of which the editors labeled "Invasionland." This particular map identified the locations of cliffs, high rocky coast lines, beaches, and other key terrain features along the French coast, all in an effort to divine where the great enterprise might take place.[140]

The print and broadcast media had no idea that a massive Allied deception operation code-named Fortitude blanketed the Invasion plan and prevented them and the Germans from pinpointing the landing location. The press even reported as fact certain details of the disinformation campaign, making them unwittingly complicit in propagating untruths both to the Germans and to the American public. The core theme of the Allied ruse was that Lt. Gen. George S. Patton Jr., in command of the fictional First U.S. Army Group (FUSAG), would lead the main Invasion force and strike near the Pas de Calais. Any other landings, such as those in Normandy, could only be diversions or feints. Patton had spent months in the doghouse for slapping two GIs in Sicily, but neither the Germans nor the American public could believe that Eisenhower would sideline America's best field general. That belief alone made Fortitude plausible and a success.[141]

Throughout the month of May, as the print and broadcast media prepared for and rehearsed how they would report D-Day, tension among home-front Americans reached a near fever pitch. When the AP's Joan Ellis sent her false Invasion flash on 3 June 1944, the American public's reaction confirmed that pre-Invasion anxiety. The subsequent letdown and confusion following the false flash served only to spur anticipation for D-Day. Thus, when broadcast and print media finally reported that the Invasion had occurred, journalists of all types had a highly receptive American public with fertile minds awaiting every tidbit of information they could absorb. The thematically framed American D-Day narrative had begun to take shape.

CHAPTER 2

"Invasion by Airwave"
Radio Spearheads the D-Day Narrative

Men and women of the United States, this is a momentous hour in world history. This is the invasion of Hitler's Europe—the zero hour.

—Robert St. John, *NBC News* commentator,
3:33:37 a.m. EWT, 6 June 1944[1]

In CBS's New York newsroom the clock ticked past midnight EWT, signaling the beginning of a new day—Tuesday, 6 June 1944. Jesse Zousmer, CBS's night news editor, and his nighttime news crew welcomed what seemed like another uneventful graveyard shift. Zousmer and his team had known for days that news of the Allied Invasion of occupied France—D-Day—could erupt across the wire service machines at any moment or belch forth from CBS's shortwave overseas monitoring station. However, on this night the thirteen teletype machines chattered with their normal monotonous rhythms. The tickers for the AP, UP, INS, OWI, and Reuters (the British wire service) all churned out routine wartime news reports. Against this backdrop of clattering teletype machines and the *clackety-clack* of reporters typing out copy, radio station KNX in Los Angeles piped in the sounds of Lennie Conn's orchestra over the entire 143-station network. All seemed well.

Everything changed at thirty-seven minutes past midnight. In the newsroom, the bell on the AP's ticker rang not once, not twice, but five times. Zousmer and his crew rushed to the teletype machine and watched in stunned silence as the ticker spelled out a news bulletin: "LONDON TUESDAY JUNE (AP)—THE GERMAN NEWS AGENCY TRANSOCEAN SAID TODAY IN A BROADCAST THAT THE ALLIED INVASION HAD BEGUN." Zousmer immediately telephoned and awakened the head of CBS news, Paul White. Zousmer told the groggy White, who struggled to shake off the effects of a sleeping pill, that the news team could not verify the report. The specter of the Joan Ellis mishap two days earlier compelled both Zousmer and White to hesitate. Across town, the INS's night editor hesitated for the same reason. No one wanted to initiate another false news flash of the Invasion. After a few minutes, the INS news editor decided to push the message across the wire to his subscribing newspapers. Zousmer immediately informed White that the same German report had just come over the INS ticker. White blurted out, "Get it on the air!" At forty-eight minutes past midnight, Ned Calmer broke into Lennie Conn's musical broadcast: "We are interrupting this program to bring you a special bulletin. A bulletin has just been received from the London office of the Associated Press which quotes the German Transocean News Agency as asserting that the invasion of Western Europe has begun."[2]

Seven minutes earlier, across town in NBC's New York newsroom, the network's announcer broke into the musical program to proclaim that the NBC shortwave monitoring station had just picked up from London the same report issued by the German Transocean News Agency. Excessive caution prompted by the Joan Ellis incident had prevented CBS from scooping NBC by mere minutes. The NBC announcer warned the listening audience that the report still lacked confirmation by Allied sources. In both the CBS and NBC newsrooms, the OWI ticker remained ominously silent, offering no official Allied confirmation of the German report. However, for those members of the American public listening to these bulletins broadcast over two of the four major networks, something big was afoot.[3] Night shift workers and night owls alike in all time zones knew that even without complete confirmation of the German reports, the Invasion had surely begun—and radio had spearheaded the reporting. In doing so, radio laid the foundation for a narrative of the Invasion that would unfold in the print and broadcast media over the next twenty-four hours, a thematically framed storyline that would endure in America's collective consciousness for decades to come.[4]

◆ ◆ ◆

Radio's unique capacity to report breaking news events with immediacy and dramatic impact signaled to all Americans on the morning of 6 June 1944 that an event of historic, seminal importance was upon them. The most significant aspect of the emerging American narrative rested in D-Day's immense significance, scope, and scale as communicated to the American public during radio's build-up to the Invasion and, most significantly, in the way news of the Invasion unfolded over the airwaves in real time. Although it substantially influenced other themes framing the narrative, radio did the most to cement firmly in the minds of all Americans on 6 June 1944 that the Invasion—Operation Overlord—was the most significant, crucial event of the entire war.

Radio's most direct contribution to this primary theme occurred in three ways. First, the radio networks engaged in a highly publicized level of pre-Invasion preparation that the American public had never experienced with earlier wartime operations, such as the landings in North Africa and Sicily. This publicity of the advanced preparation also provided a separate, underlying narrative: relating the technical details and procedural guidelines demonstrated how radio, in trying to prove its mettle as a new and legitimate medium for news reporting, brought to bear state-of-the-art technology to craft a powerful, immersive, and enduring chronicle of the Invasion for the American public.

Radio's second direct contribution to marking D-Day as the war's seminal event occurred when the medium spearheaded breaking news of the Invasion. As the nation's first source of Invasion news, radio held the listening audience captive in what John McDonough described as "a state of synchronous national tension" by drawing them into unfolding, real-time news coverage.[5] Normally passive listeners became fully engaged participants as the news narrative of D-Day unfolded, involving them directly in the narrative-making process at the moment of the event's occurrence.

Finally, radio brought listeners directly into the chaotic immediacy of D-Day and combat in general by airing a plethora of on-the-spot, eyewitness news reports from radio correspondents embedded with the troops. Some of these reports, recorded on site and broadcast as soon as available, transfixed audiences by capturing as closely as technical limitations would allow the chaos of combat through actual battlefield sounds.

All told, the networks' publicity campaigns concerning their pre-Invasion broadcasting preparations; the listening audience's direct immersion in the construction of the D-Day narrative as news of the Invasion broke; and the enhanced ability of radio correspondents to use new wire recorders to capture the intimacy of battle through sound produced a powerful story line of the Invasion. Though this aural reportage was incomplete and lacking in crucial but as-yet unknown details, radio managed to invest it with an enduring quality. Interestingly, the radio coverage of D-Day proved to be much less American-centric than the newspaper stories published later in the day. The broadcast networks relied on British and Allied sources, which not only afforded listeners a more inclusive, accurate, and comprehensive perspective of the Invasion but also forced them to confront a developing narrative that did not focus solely on the American contribution. Radio's paradigm-breaking involvement in the American public's understanding of D-Day proved central in elevating the Invasion to the status it maintained for subsequent decades as the single most important military operation of World War II—at the very moment the Invasion occurred.

◆ ◆ ◆

The American public received its earliest indication that D-Day would be something completely different, something far more important than any other Allied operation up to that point, when the radio networks publicly advertised on the airwaves and in their trade journal, *BBA*, the exceptional steps they were taking to bring breaking news of the Invasion into America's living rooms. In the six months before the German Transocean News Agency signaled to a stunned American public that D-Day had begun, the four broadcast networks (along with various independent stations) had engaged in an unprecedented level of preparation to ensure that when news of the Invasion finally broke, they would be ready. Network executives knew that America and the world would tune in and experience what David M. Kennedy described as "powerful voices flow[ing] out over airwaves and wash[ing] over listeners by the millions."[6] Such preparations following on the heels of the 24 December 1943 announcement that General Eisenhower would command the Invasion, and publicized on the air and in the trade journal *BBA*, ultimately helped to shape the overarching message that D-Day did in fact represent the war's seminal military operation—the beginning of the end for the Axis powers. Each network wanted to report breaking news of D-Day quickly but accurately and with an expediency and professionalism that would help radio prove its mettle as a viable news source.

Aside from the tremendous stakes associated with the Invasion's success, the broadcasting industry itself had an immense stake in ensuring that radio rose to the occasion when news of the Invasion broke. As late in the war as June 1944, the radio networks still felt they had something to prove. Contemporary commentators and observers of American radio during World War II saw great promise in radio's capacity as an alternative source of original news for the American public. These pundits knew radio could bring the war and D-Day directly into America's living rooms, creating for the average listener a powerful psychological bond with the dramatic events unfolding in another part of the world.[7] This psychological advantage, and its attendant contribution to the D-Day narrative, was due primarily to the power and dramatic appeal of the human voice, which commanded respect and trust; to the immediacy of radio communication; and to the fact that listening to a radio broadcast required less effort than reading a newspaper.[8] Above all, radio enjoyed confidence and public respect among the American populace as "a great uniting force" in much the same way that the notion of common newspaper readership united all Americans into a single, imagined community.[9] Although radio could point to some pre-war and wartime successes, such as NBC's first broadcast from war-torn Manchuria in 1932 and the combined CBS and NBC coverage of the Munich Crisis in September 1938, critics still believed radio had room for improvement.[10]

The University of Chicago's director of Radio Productions, Sherman H. Dryer, argued in 1942 that "radio [was] on trial before the American public," primarily because the networks tended to punctuate their daily programming with constant, seemingly uncoordinated wartime news flashes announced by overly excited commentators. In these cases, radio served not to inform but to alarm. Other criticisms included bad taste in juxtaposing war-related news flashes with product-placement advertisements.[11] Still other critics continued to charge radio news with an absence of depth and variety.[12] Many of these same criticisms had surfaced during the Press-Radio War of the 1920s and 1930s and continued to vex radio's efforts to earn an equal place alongside newspapers, even though by June 1944 a large number of newspapers owned radio stations.[13] These criticisms clearly informed the networks' preparations for reporting D-Day and helped to ensure accurate, consistent, and common thematic messaging across the board on 6 June 1944.[14]

D-Day had all the makings of a major media event, and the networks had no intention of squandering the opportunity.[15] With all the various criticisms and compliments attending radio's image during World War II, the network news chiefs left nothing to chance. In a pamphlet chronicling the network's D-Day performance, NBC declared, "Chance figured prominently" in "planning for this comprehensive coverage of the biggest news in world history." In other words, thorough planning had to prevent dumb luck from robbing the network of its opportunity to seize the reporting initiative when news of D-Day finally burst across the wires. William F. Brooks, veteran director of NBC's News and Special Events, insisted on "coverage that would assure American listeners the most accurate, most comprehensive account, literally step-by-step, of every phase of the attack."[16] On 30 April 1944, Brooks took to the air and explained to NBC's listeners that D-Day would be "an operation in which there is no margin for error." He promised that NBC programs would avoid "'scare' news or invasion rumors."[17] NBC intended to avoid anything that smacked of Creel-style boosterism and bluster, which would only alienate audiences.

Paul White, the head of CBS news, generally agreed with NBC's preparatory approach, but in a memorandum issued in late February 1944, he offered more specific guidelines. White channeled criticisms leveled by the newspapers during the Press-Radio War and from contemporary pundits; he chided his network's announcers and directed them to maintain "an informative, unexcited demeanor at the microphone"; to provide sources; to avoid risking accuracy; and to use "care in [their] choice of words." Moreover, White cautioned, "Respect the listener's trust. Remember that winning the war is a hell of a lot more important than reporting it."[18] *BBA* reported that John Whitmore, manager of Mutual Broadcasting System's (MBS's) news division, focused on intensifying alertness among the MBS news staff so the newsroom would be ready when D-Day finally arrived.[19]

Stateside radio preparations for D-Day—now viewed as the world's best-kept "non-secret"—focused principally on the various network headquarters located in New York. All networks implemented specific provisions designed to assume instantaneous control in order to get Invasion news on the air immediately.[20] All 143 of CBS's affiliated stations, for instance, began testing, reassigning personnel, and rehearsing for breaking Invasion news coverage at the network's direction.[21] Selecting the right announcers with the proper mood and manner quickly became a high priority. Since networks lacked visually identifiable mastheads like their newspaper cousins, announcers would have to rely on the signature uniqueness of their voices, on using catchphrases, and on consistently repeating their networks' call letters in order verify the source of the broadcast to the listening public.[22] *BBA* explained that each network maintained a talented stable of commentators and military analysts, all of whom were ready to go on the air immediately when the time came.[23] While newspapers tended to rely heavily on a single news editor shaping the news each paper printed, radio announcers and on-air military analysts had equal or greater agency in shaping the emerging narrative as information spewed rapidly from the wires. As such, network newsrooms depended heavily on keeping their news-teletype machines in excellent working order. These machines, like the thirteen chattering away in CBS's New York newsroom, provided vital links to the wire services transmitting from London, the planned focal point of all Invasion news.[24]

The networks made little effort to keep their various pre-Invasion preparatory activities to themselves. They wanted the public and members of their own industry to know that radio would be ready when D-Day arrived. Therefore, each network engaged in some manner of pre-Invasion publicity, partly as news and partly as self-promotion, to demonstrate that even before D-Day took place, Americans should view it as the seminal event of the war.[25] The hyperbolic language used to describe these preparations only furthered the notion that D-Day was, according to *BBA*, "the greatest military incursion in history" and that radio would be performing "the most intensive news coverage task in history" with "a degree of military-radio collaboration never before achieved."[26] As the most vocal publicity organ for radio, *BBA* left no doubt that D-Day would be radio's greatest test, and the editorial board wanted to raise the stakes so that when radio rose to the occasion, the industry could enjoy bragging rights.

Another example of the importance the networks placed on keeping the public informed of their preparations occurred on 14 May 1944 when CBS's Paul White broadcast a detailed plan for how the network would respond to the first Invasion flash. This broadcast formed the basis for a memorandum White issued the next day to all 143 CBS affiliates. In that memorandum, like his earlier February message, White explained that the first reports of D-Day might come from German sources, so transmission of such a report would depend upon the news judgment of the editor in charge. In this situation, cautioned White, the network commentator would provide the source of the flash message to the American public in case it proved to be part of a German deception plan. In effect, CBS would not become an unwitting propaganda conduit for Nazi misinformation.

Some networks also informed the public that they would be adjusting their broadcasting hours. Many of the network news chiefs worried that owing to the six-hour time difference between London and the East Coast, the first news flash of D-Day would occur when the network airwaves were dormant. On average, the four major networks broadcast for eighteen hours a day.[27] Most networks had sign-off periods between the hours of 2 a.m. and 5 a.m.[28] In an effort to avoid missing that first breaking flash, CBS teletyped its affiliates on 2 June 1944 that until further notice, the full network would operate until 3:05 a.m. EWT.[29] The networks feared that if they were asleep at the switch when D-Day broke, radio as a serious news medium might suffer irreparable harm in the public's eye.

◆ ◆ ◆

The government had a great stake in ensuring that the radio networks provided accurate news of the Invasion, principally to avoid arousing the specter of misinformation or audience manipulation resulting from erroneous reporting. According to *BBA*, the OWI, the OC, and the War Department extended a helping hand to the four broadcast networks. The OWI and the public relations offices of both the Army and the Navy offered to furnish network and other correspondents in London and, ultimately, France with geographical, chronological, and biographical data on a twenty-four-hour basis to supplement the news originating from overseas. The OWI offered similar twenty-four-hour assistance from Washington for all stateside broadcast operations and even published telephone contact numbers in the 29 May 1944 edition of *BBA*.[30]

In breaking old paradigms to report D-Day, the networks created new ones. Throughout the month of May 1944, *BBA* highlighted many of these specific preparations. MBS's John Whitmore developed his own unique telephone "fan-out system" so the network could rapidly notify selected MBS executives throughout the country, who in turn would relay the same notifications to other MBS affiliates.[31] CBS developed a unique device called "World on a Panel" for news chief Paul White in which the executive could push a colored button on a multibutton panel on his own desk and open the airwaves to a waiting correspondent somewhere in the world who was ready to broadcast on a clear channel. The staffers called this system "Paul White's piano."[32] CBS also installed a pine cupboard for its announcers holding a microphone on a 60-foot cable connected to a switch that bypassed all systems, allowing the correspondent to wander into the noisy newsroom and broadcast directly to listeners in 27 million American homes breaking news the moment it ticked off the teletype machines. Such well-publicized preparations only served to elevate D-Day's importance to all Americans.[33]

Broadcast preparations in London, the designated focal point for all radio and press coverage, were as meticulous and well-publicized as those arrangements made by the stateside network headquarters.[34] Once the Invasion began, news came over the air from three sources: announcers in New York (the men farthest from the action), who broadcasted wire-service reports; pool correspondents in London, who could actually see what they were reporting on; and from the handful of broadcast reporters who managed "to reach directly into the ambiance of battle" by recording on-the-spot news stories using cumbersome wire recorders provided by the armed forces and then sending the taped reports by shortwave to the United States.[35] As an example of the importance placed on getting news of the Invasion to American listeners as quickly as possible, SHAEF assigned David Sarnoff, president of the Radio Corporation of America (RCA) and NBC's chairman of the board, to oversee all radio traffic arrangements from SHAEF headquarters in London. Now holding a direct commission as an Army Signal Corps colonel, Sarnoff, working closely with Col. E. M. Kirby, chief of the Radio Branch of the War Department's Bureau of Public Relations, used his vast wireless and telegrapher expertise to ensure that radio traffic would flow smoothly from the European theater of operations to the American public.[36]

The specific pre-Invasion broadcasting arrangements made in London and outlined in detail to the public in *BBA* appeared daunting. Sarnoff and Kirby had to ensure that enough transatlantic circuits remained in operation for at least eighteen hours a day to facilitate steady radio news traffic to the United States; that consolidated studios were up and running so the Army and all four major networks could work closely together; that the on-site broadcast censors would expedite their processes; that the networks would agree to waive their restrictions on using recordings in place of live reports; and that radio reporters representing individual stations or regional networks would receive the same accreditation from SHAEF.[37] Additionally, a four-person committee of American correspondents—headed by Robert Bunnelle, the AP's London bureau chief, and including Edward R. Murrow, CBS's European staff chief—represented the interests of the combined American press and broadcast media during the pre-Invasion preparations in London. A separate committee representing just the four networks and chaired by NBC's London bureau chief, Stanley P. Richardson, worked out the details of joint broadcasting operations. These committee members held numerous meetings with officers from SHAEF's Public Relations Division, headed by U.S. Army brigadier general T. J. Davis, to address such weighty matters as censorship, the number of available radio channels, and the use of portable transmitters. They worked night and day to cover all bases in the run-up to D-Day. Everyone knew that once the Invasion began, the flurry of news emanating from the field would develop a powerful momentum unto itself.[38]

Perhaps the most challenging aspect of the pre-Invasion preparations involved an innovative approach to providing comprehensive D-Day coverage to all networks equally: the Invasion pool. The pool required all networks to share their reporting uniformly with each other to ensure that no single network scooped another. This collective approach tempered the competitive streak that characterized all networks, which traditionally used such news scoops to attract more advertising dollars. Most significantly for narrative-building, the pool remained committed to ensuring that the home-front listening community received a common thematic message on 6 June 1944.[39] *Newsweek* reported that on 30 April 1944, the OWI established a new, powerful radio station in England, the American Broadcasting Station in Europe (ABSIE). Its mission was to bombard German-occupied territories with pre- and post-Invasion American propaganda. Once the Invasion began, the ABSIE assumed the added mission of supplying the pool with a dedicated transatlantic shortwave frequency that allowed all four networks to broadcast their stories simultaneously when necessary.[40] Since the pool gave the networks equal access to all incoming reports (including reports from the British Broadcasting Company and the Canadian Broadcasting Corporation), well-known veteran broadcasters such as Edward R. Murrow could not identify their reports as originating from a specific network. Inside the British Ministry of Information building, the network representatives would type their copy and use broadcast booths to announce their news stories to the United States—but only after the pool's censors made their chop. The broadcast pool became one of the great success stories of D-Day.[41]

While the pool worked out the nitty-gritty details for ensuring that Invasion news reached the networks' bureaus in New York and elsewhere quickly and efficiently, the networks and *BBA* revealed to the American public a preparation detail that further reinforced D-Day's significance. The home front learned that the correspondents who would provide Invasion news to American listeners were undergoing months of rigorous training with their assigned infantry, airborne, and other units. These men—and some women—were putting their lives on the line to embed themselves with the troops going into actual combat in order to bring the story to all Americans. Naturally, if these correspondents, all hailing from America's broadcast networks, wire services, newspapers, and newsmagazines, hoped to keep up with the troops, they had to be in shape and well-integrated with the men they would follow into battle. The troops generally trusted the reporters, all of whom had to undergo accreditation and earn the imprimatur of SHAEF in order to be present in the field.[42] In fact, on 11 May 1944, General Eisenhower sent a letter to all commanders requiring them to provide "accredited war correspondents all reasonable assistance" so that these reporters could "transmit to the public the conditions under which men from their countries are waging war against the enemy."[43] When D-Day finally arrived, nearly fifty radio correspondents from the four major networks and independent stations carried credentials.[44]

The most daunting news filter facing all these embedded correspondents proved to be the field commander, whose decisions about what information to release and when proved absolutely central in shaping the story line that ultimately led to the formulation of the American D-Day narrative. But these commanders, as well as the armed forces and the federal government, knew the importance of getting Invasion news to an anxious home front. In April 1944, the OWI outlined the war news policy the networks and the print media would follow when reporting on military operations. First and foremost, the Army and Navy agreed with OWI that news of all military operations should be made public as soon as military security conditions permitted. The authority behind all releases, however, rested directly with the field commanders. If operational security and other conditions allowed for the release of information related to Army, Air Corps, and Navy operations, then commanders on the ground could release it for immediate publication as soon as the censors cleared it.[45] *BBA* explained that a commander's decision to withhold the release of information would depend on local conditions and security implications, and these factors may not always be obvious or explainable to war correspondents or the public. In other words, the information received by correspondents and subsequently their listening audiences was contingent upon each commander's judgment, which in turn gave that commander remarkable power over how the narrative of D-Day would unfold through the media.[46] Moreover, the receiving stateside networks had to apply another self-censorship filter to the already censored information coming from overseas based upon the *Code of Wartime Practices for American Broadcasters* issued by the OC.[47]

As spring 1944 approached, everyone in the United States knew that fairer weather in Europe would mean that D-Day was imminent. No one knew when or where, and that uncertainty contributed to an ever-increasing tension as May turned into June.[48] In turn, local radio stations made their own innovative plans for reporting D-Day to the masses. Station KTFI in Twin Falls, Idaho, for instance, took the unusual step of issuing studio tickets to selected listeners, giving them ringside seats to the Invasion broadcasts.[49] Many local radio stations would get extra help from their government and religious leaders in letting the public know the moment D-Day began. For instance, like many other towns throughout the United States, Elmira, New York, intended to herald news of the Invasion by tolling all church bells.[50] Many of these preparations on the home front received an unexpected test run on 3 June 1944 with the AP's false Invasion flash. Two days later, on the evening of 5 June 1944 at 9:30 p.m., FDR addressed 34 million American listeners on all four networks, proclaiming that Rome had fallen to the Allies.[51] Meanwhile in London, several hours before FDR's Rome broadcast, the OWI's Brewster Morgan (an alumnus of CBS) assembled the radio station chiefs and executives and ushered them into a large map-filled room. A spokesman said, "You are here for the night, perhaps longer. You will not be allowed to leave this room or to telephone until we give you permits." The real D-Day was here.[52]

◆ ◆ ◆

Although radio's well-publicized preparations on both sides of the Atlantic conveyed the impression that an event of great significance to the war and to history loomed on the horizon, nothing compared to the impact of the American public's full immersion in the unfolding D-Day drama in real time. As soon as the networks aired the first German report that the Invasion had likely begun, radio "held the nation hostage to a terrible incertitude." For the first time, the average American listener became part of the story, experiencing the drama unfolding in the moment with all its uneven rhythms, gaffs, and uncertainties. While newspapers traditionally provided some order to the news and a wider "curriculum of meaning," radio on D-Day did just the opposite.[53] According to John McDonough, "Radio blurted out everything" on D-Day.[54] *Time* magazine later proclaimed that listeners that night "had an experience they will remember to their graves." "Into their living rooms," *Time* continued, "came the voices of history."[55] During the initial hours of their Invasion coverage, the networks did the most to elevate in America's collective psyche the grand significance of D-Day as the leading theme attending America's collective narrative of the Invasion. They seized the average American in an unrelenting and powerful grip—a "continuous and mesmerizing suspense" that would not let go.[56] By the time the sun rose on the East Coast, the first newspaper editions would trade places with the networks and further reinforce to the American public that D-Day was indeed the seminal operation of the war—and radio had led the way.

The first crucial feat achieved by the networks and the one that allowed listeners to find themselves immersed in the growing narrative at the outset was the speed with which they resurrected their newsroom operations in the dead of night. As soon as the German Transocean News Agency report hit the wires and the networks' shortwave monitoring stations, the networks put their pre-Invasion preparations to the test. Their first challenge was to assemble their respective news staffs, analysts, and commentators—the people who would convey the narrative of D-Day to an anxious, deeply engrossed listening public. The four networks and many independent stations initiated telephone notification plans, such as MBS's elaborate telephone "fan-out system," to muster their newsroom staffs, engineers, writers, and even musicians.[57] Thanks to these advanced preparations, the networks had their ace news teams in place in little over an hour and well before SHAEF confirmed that D-Day had begun.

Much of radio's unique influence over the listening population rested in the power of the human voice and the respect it commanded. Therefore, the networks relied almost entirely on their most well-known, well-respected announcers to broadcast the Invasion news to an eager listening audience. These commentators, whose familiar voices would carry the Invasion news to the American public, went right to work. NBC's star announcer—the pipe-smoking, bearded Robert St. John—was one of the first of the prominent commentators to take to the airwaves from New York. He broadcasted skillfully for more than ten hours aided only by a bottle of cough syrup.[58] Sydney Moseley was the first of MBS's announcers to reach a microphone as the rest of his five-man news team arrived and took turns in the broadcasting chair.[59] Likewise, G. W. Johnstone, Blue's director of news, arrived quickly in the network's New York studios, mustered his team of commentators, and put them on the airwaves.

Perhaps the most familiar and respected announcer to broadcast news of D-Day's developing drama was CBS's Bob Trout, whose nearly twenty-four-hour, nonstop broadcasting feat prompted *BBA* to brand him as the "Iron Man of D-Day commentators."[60] As soon as news of the German report broke, Paul White awakened Trout by phone and told him, "This could be it. Better get here." After dressing hastily, Trout arrived by cab at the CBS studios and promptly took to the microphone.[61]

Unlike the other networks, CBS stood out by concentrating its D-Day coverage almost solely on Trout's familiar voice, offering listeners a trusted and credible source for the developing Invasion narrative. Trout immediately established "a tone of cool elegance and restraint" in keeping with Paul White's earlier guidance that all CBS commentators maintain an "unexcited demeanor" when reporting the Invasion.[62] John McDonough summed up Trout's performance on 6 June 1944 as "an unmitigated masterpiece of broadcasting."[63]

The networks' star announcers did not face the listening public without some interpretative assistance from specially selected and well-known analysts, who lent coherence, meaning, and context to the kaleidoscope of Invasion details washing over American listeners. These analysts, like the commentators they backstopped, had their own ideas about what a discerning American public should know and understand about D-Day, affording them a great deal of agency in shaping the emerging D-Day narrative. Their personal resumés gave their voices even greater authority. According to Sherman H. Dryer, "Americans have always looked up to 'experts' and to people of prominence . . . to respect the man with the 'know-how.'"[64] Several of the networks enlisted the assistance of such individuals—highly regarded men with experience and pedigrees that lent them instant credibility. Bob Trout received exceptional support at the microphone from a man known throughout the United States as the "dean of military analysts"—Major George Fielding Eliot. The American public knew of the fifty-year-old Eliot from his many published works and from his often bluntly stated assessments about America's military potential. His credibility as a soldier came from his remarkable military resumé, which included service in World War I at places like Gallipoli and Passchendaele. Like Trout, Eliot remained cool and composed behind the microphone. The CBS account of the network's D-Day coverage later explained that the "virtue of a military analyst is that he can keep his shirt on when people around him tend to lose theirs in the rising gale." For CBS, Eliot clearly fit the bill.[65]

NBC's Robert St. John enjoyed the privilege of having the "dean of news analysts" at his side—H. V. Kaltenborn.[66] Kaltenborn started his radio career with CBS in 1928 before moving over to NBC in 1940. While at CBS he had gained both fame and respect as one of many commentators (Edward R. Murrow among them) who brought the Munich Crisis of 1938 into America's living rooms and hooked the public on the power of radio news. Although Kaltenborn lacked the extensive military experience of CBS's Eliot (Kaltenborn served during the Spanish-American War), he had an extensive background in foreign affairs and international politics. Most Americans knew him for his ability to speak extemporaneously for long periods and for his ability to analyze any situation with remarkable clarity.[67] Analysts like Kaltenborn and Eliot helped America's listening public sift through the often disjointed and chaotic news reports streaming in from London throughout 6 June 1944 and to interpret what the steadily developing narrative should mean to them. Ultimately, the implications of a military analyst and a political analyst at competing networks seemed benign in the context of the broader D-Day narrative that was unfolding. Both analysts seemed to have struck an effective balance for their respective listeners without tilting the narrative in one direction or another.

How the American listening public processed the breaking news in the moment remained less clear than the networks' efforts to broadcast it. Yet the record reveals that even considering the late hour, the American people had tuned in on their own initiative or had received word from others to switch on the radio. Just as the networks' key players arrived in their studios, the first bulletins recounting the German news reports had in fact caused the nation to stir. Night-shift workers and night owls throughout America quickly tuned in when they received word that D-Day may have finally arrived. By 2:30 a.m., CBS's Network Operations Center reported that all 143 affiliated stations from Portland, Maine, to Los Angeles and from Grand Forks, North Dakota, to Miami were on the air and ready for what may come.[68] In the East and Midwest, utility companies noted abrupt surges in kilowatt outputs as the public switched on lights and radios. Night-shift operators scrambled with busy switchboards as callers telephoned neighbors and urged them to tune in. Members of station KGBH in Harlingen, Texas, phoned listeners who had sent in postcards asking the station to awaken them when the Invasion began.[69] In Manhattan, CBS awoke a very sleepy Mayor Fiorello LaGuardia at the mayor's request.[70] Within ninety minutes of the first bulletin at thirty-seven minutes after midnight EWT, a "highly keyed up" America was awake, tuned in, and experiencing firsthand the drama of D-Day as it unfolded.[71]

The networks scrapped their programming schedules and launched into a twenty-four-hour news cycle.[72] Media outlets—networks and independent stations alike—cancelled almost all sponsorship advertising, an unprecedented and highly significant act. News of D-Day now drove all programming schedules. The Blue Network issued a mimeographed statement from Executive Vice-President Edgar Kobak that Invasion news now had precedence over all other programming.[73] Mutual warned that D-Day bulletins would interrupt or displace any commercial programming that the network might still decide to air. CBS's Ned Calmer announced at 1:30 a.m. as part of his newscast that CBS will "be on duty all night and let you know if the [German] report is true."[74] NBC's president Niles Trammell took perhaps the strictest approach by cancelling all commercial and sustaining programs as long as Invasion coverage warranted such an approach.[75] In fact, exactly one minute before the scheduled sign-off time at 3 a.m., NBC announced that the network would remain on the air and broadcasting Invasion news throughout the night.[76] The networks had cleared the way for D-Day news—and only D-Day news—to command their airwaves.

Network cancellations of most commercial advertising was no small thing to the American listening public in 1944. The networks survived solely on a steady diet of sponsorship dollars, so average American listeners—even during the war years—became accustomed to hearing sponsorship tag lines attached to their favorite radio programs. Unlike newspapers, in which readers could skip advertisements, advertising on radio was what contemporary radio pundit Gunnar Horn described as "inescapable."[77] Listeners simply had to endure advertising as part of the listening experience. Never before had a breaking news story, not even the attack on Pearl Harbor, preempted an entire day's commercial listening schedule.[78] CBS had even warned their advertisers as early as 17 May 1944 that D-Day might result in dropped advertising.

With the networks now free of commercials, the three-hour period following the initial German report and leading up to Allied confirmation of the Invasion at 3:32 a.m. EWT proved to be the most frustrating, the most engrossing, and the most compelling for America's radio listeners. Rapt audiences listened with an increasing intensity as speculation about the Invasion ran rampant throughout the networks' bulletins. While radio had often received scorn from critics for its use of dramatization to convey news, the networks and independent stations had no control over the storyline being thrust upon them; other actors outside the networks drove the emerging, and chaotic, narrative. The very fact that Allied confirmation from SHAEF, the OWI, or the War Department had not validated the German reports added to the dramatic tension. The networks could not control the flow of information they received—they could only manage it.

The operations at CBS during the turbulent three-hour period following Ned Calmer's interruption of Lennie Conn's orchestra at forty-eight minutes after midnight EWT are illustrative of the radio networks' efforts to wrestle with and make sense of the developing narrative for America's listeners. Calmer provided listeners with the first of many warnings that night that Allied confirmation had yet to surface and that the German broadcast might be nothing more "than a German propaganda move or a fishing expedition for information." Calmer further reminded his audience that British prime minister Winston Churchill had in fact warned everyone that "feints and diversions" would precede the attacks, suggesting that any misinformation coming over the airwaves was part of the Invasion plan and not any calculated, Creel-style propaganda ploy aimed at American audiences.[79] Calmer ended the initial broadcast suggesting that the Invasion may have actually begun with an airborne drop near the Seine estuary as Allied bombers pummeled Calais and Dunkirk. With nothing left to report, Calmer resumed the suspended musical programming, leaving listeners on tenterhooks. The American public was now experiencing something atypical, something unscripted, with radio.

The lack of Allied confirmation undoubtedly heightened the drama of the radio coverage. Even at CBS, skepticism still pervaded the newsroom: was the Invasion really happening or was it a German ruse? Suffering from a paucity of information, Erwin Darlington aired his regular newscast at 1 a.m. and rebroadcast the German rumor. Paul White's failed attempts to contact Edward R. Murrow in London only reinforced the news crew's suspicion that the German report was false. At 1:30 a.m., as Ned Calmer returned to the air to repeat his earlier broadcast, CBS's shortwave monitoring station picked up the BBC broadcasting directly to the Continent. The BBC, closely monitored by resistance forces in occupied Europe, warned coastal residents of Holland, Belgium, and France that this message was "an urgent instruction from the Supreme Commander." The announcer stated in stark terms, "The lives of many of you depend upon the speed and thoroughness with which you obey," especially for "all who live within 15 kilometers [twenty-two miles] of any part of the coast." The transmission further explained that a "new phase in the air attack has begun" and that warnings would only come within an hour preceded by leaflets. The broadcast went on to offer step-by-step instructions about how and where people in affected areas should evacuate.[80] This announcement involved the broadcast and print media in the Allied deception plan. Operation Overlord included no attacks along the Belgian or Dutch coastlines; the plan was to keep the Germans guessing and to dupe them into holding their forces in place in anticipation of landings that would never come.[81]

At 2 a.m. Bob Trout took to the microphone in Studio 9 and in his steady, reserved tone, provided a comprehensive, eight-minute recap of everything CBS had received from overseas, including the BBC message to occupied Europe. Although Trout cautioned once more against German chicanery, doubt about the German reports' veracity began to fade quickly. Trout quoted the German news sources as stating, "The long-expected Anglo-American invasion appears to have begun." Trout further explained that the "German-controlled Calais radio came on the air today with this announcement in the English language: 'This is D-Day! We shall now bring music for the Allied invasion forces.'" In fact, much of the early Invasion news reported by Transocean and later by the Third Reich's state press agency, Deutsches Nachrichtenbüro GmbH (or DNB), proved generally accurate, prompting the OWI's Elmer Davis to declare to the press in Washington, DC, later that morning that Transocean and the DNB "are trying to build up a reputation for accuracy so that they can put one over on the Allies later."[82] Davis's concern reflected a larger political apprehension for the U. S. government and the Allies in general that the German news organs might try to exploit the Invasion to earn legitimacy for future propaganda efforts. Trout's news broadcast also included a summary of the BBC transmission and additional reports from Transocean and DNB about bombings at Le Havre (earlier reports about bombings at Calais and Dunkirk proved false), airborne drops in Normandy, and the fact that "German naval forces have engaged enemy landing craft off the coast." These details caused Trout's intensifying newscast to radiate a kind of "heat lightning." The random collage of emerging details began adding up to the real thing.[83] Still, Trout cautioned, the "Germans are quite capable of faking this entire series of reports."[84] American listeners were hooked.

For the first time, the listening public heard from a highly regarded expert who, like them, was struggling to make sense of a developing news story in the moment. After his report, Trout yielded the microphone to Major Eliot, who began offering his own cautious interpretation of the information obtained from all sources thus far. In his nasally voice, Eliot warned, "We must begin by assuming . . . or understanding . . . that these German reports might be an outright lie." Eliot explained that any Allied actions could be feints designed "to draw German forces to other places," suggesting to American listeners that the available information might be sprinkled liberally with misinformation as part of Operation Fortitude. After reviewing some of the same details provided by Trout a few minutes earlier, Eliot explained to the audience that just like the average listener, CBS (and the other networks) were picking apart inconsistencies in the German reports in real time, such as the obvious error made by the Germans when reporting landings near the Somme estuary instead of the Seine estuary. Eliot opined that if the German reports proved accurate, many of the details they were reporting would make sense. In closing, Eliot insisted that "any military analysis must remain fragmentary and uncertain as long as it is based only on German reports which have so frequently proved to be unreliable in the past."[85]

The information coming off the tickers quickly became too random and scattershot for Bob Trout to compile into coherent newscasts, so he added to a day of radio "firsts" by figuratively pulling his listeners into the studio and sharing with them how news of what in fact might be D-Day was unfolding at the source.[86] He fished inside his pocket for what the CBS staff had christened as "That Key," unlocked the new pine cupboard, and removed the microphone connected to a sixty-foot cable. With the flip of a switch, Trout now spoke to the entire network within the United States. In what likely came across to transfixed listeners as an act of dramatic flair, Trout swung open the door to Studio 9 and entered, immediately filling the airwaves with the chatter of thirty journalists and the loud, ceaseless rattle of thirteen teletype machines churning out reports from the various wire services.[87]

With the long cable trailing behind him, Trout took the audience on a remarkable auditory tour of the newsroom, stopping at each ticker to read precisely what was coming over the teletype machines, identifying each news service by name as he went. Americans virtually "walked" with Trout for the next eighteen minutes as he brought them directly into the unfolding drama of D-Day. As Trout trooped the teletype line, he explained that the wire services were "now hammering out every scrap of information they can get" and that the long pauses the audience heard indicated a paucity of fresh reportage. Trout stopped first at the Reuters teletype machine, which was ticking out a report on SHAEF's warning to residents along the French coastline. He then moved on to the INS ticker as it clacked out another German report announcing the Invasion. Suddenly, Trout heard five bells chime on the AP's machine, prompting him to rush over and read a tantalizing piece of breaking news: London radio, not German radio, was broadcasting a message in Dutch telling underground members to report to their leaders and to avoid military installations. After matter-of-factly offering up this new information,

Trout continued his tour by stopping at the UP and other teletype machines, following his direct quotations from their printed copy with "crisp and unruffled sequences of his own objective interpretation."[88] Then, after pausing at the silent OWI ticker and commenting again on the absence of official confirmation of the German reports, he encountered Major Eliot, who explained on the air that the recent report about the London radio message to the Dutch resistance might in fact point toward the real Invasion.[89]

Eliot's fresh analysis and Trout's unique tour into the seemingly chaotic belly of broadcast news-making likely exacerbated tensions among the American populace as they struggled with CBS and the other networks to confirm or deny the scattered influx of information and bulletins.[90] By involving the audience in the developing narrative, the haphazard first hours of Invasion reportage did in fact hold "America in a state of synchronous national tension." That suspense would soon reach a crescendo.[91]

The dramatic denouement of the Invasion narrative burst over the airwaves for a spellbound audience with the kinetic immediacy of radio: the official Allied announcement broadcast directly from London that Operation Overlord had begun. While Trout read a fresh AP bulletin over the air, one of six telephones on Paul White's desk "piano" rang with a message from the War Department in Washington, DC, alerting CBS to "Stand by for an important message over FAX Army Signal Corps Channel at 3:32: zero."[92] At NBC, the same alert from London prompted Robert St. John to declare, "Ladies and gentlemen, we may be nearing a fateful hour."[93] Back at CBS, White quickly signaled to Trout, who responded, "Go ahead, London." Crackling static over the London-based circuit added to the growing expectation that something big was about to come over the airwaves.[94]

After a brief pause, at precisely 3:32:05 a.m. EWT, the "arid, clear, unmodulated" voice of Col. R. Ernest Dupuy, SHAEF's public relations officer, broke through the static. As a former commentator on NBC's *Army Hour* program, the fifty-seven-year-old Dupuy had a voice that was familiar to listening audiences. The distinguished looking, neatly mustachioed Dupuy was also a noted military historian who had coauthored with his friend and colleague, CBS's George Fielding Eliot, a popular book in 1937 titled *If War Comes*.[95] From a studio within London's Ministry of Information, Dupuy spoke in a deliberate, emotionless monotone in keeping with the gravity of his pronouncement: "This is Supreme Headquarters, Allied Expeditionary Force. The text of Communiqué Number 1 will be released to the press and radio in 10 seconds. Repeat, 10 seconds from now." This dramatic pause undeniably kept both newsmakers and listeners on the edge of their seats. After drawing a deep breath, Dupuy read from his transcript: "Under the command of General Eisenhower, Allied naval forces, supported by strong air forces, began landing Allied armies this morning on the northern coast of France." He repeated the communiqué and then abruptly stated that his transmission was now over.[96] SHAEF had intentionally kept the text of the communiqué brief and free of specific details, such as the nationality of the troops involved, until "there [was] an assurance that the Germans [had] reasonably accurate information of [the Allied troops'] composition."[97] This absence of detail not only worked against the Germans but also against a fact-hungry American public and the emerging D-Day narrative.

The dramatic on-air confirmation of D-Day sent shock waves through listeners, lending credence to the assertion that the press is in fact a culturally powerful transmitter and amplifier of information in the public sphere. Radio's effectiveness as a powerful news medium became most evident when back inside the CBS studios, Bob Trout proclaimed in a clear, deliberate voice, with pauses between each word for maximum effect, "This . . . means . . . invasion." At NBC, Robert St. John built upon the emerging D-Day narrative's dominant theme by asserting, "The world's greatest military undertaking is underway." But he quickly tempered any relief or excitement his audience may have felt by reminding his listeners of war's terrible cost. He warned that in this great undertaking and beyond, "Casualties may reach a dreadful toll."[98] At CBS, Trout verified the text of the communiqué now emanating from OWI's formerly silent ticker and then offered up a sober assessment to his listeners of the breaking story: "The character of the whole broadcast has changed."[99] With Allied confirmation that D-Day had begun, Trout and St. John had become the journalists with the greatest influence over what Americans should know about D-Day and what it should mean to them. In effect, they functioned as their respective networks' editorial boards—all concentrated in the guise of one person.

In a manner that newspapers could never replicate, radio suddenly deluged the American public with an avalanche of information and commentary that underscored the significance of D-Day to the Allied war effort. The absence of information originating from SHAEF shifted into a sudden whirlwind of official announcements, many read by the leaders overseas who were directly involved in making history. At CBS, as Bob Trout was still commenting on Communiqué Number 1, a voice in the background blurted out, "Go to London! Go to London!" Likewise, an unknown voice on NBC suddenly jumped in and exclaimed, "And now, ladies and gentlemen, for a special broadcast, we take you to London, England." A technician's voice broke in through the static, allowing the listening audience to experience fully the unevenness and sheer immediacy of the unfolding story. The voice then counted down to the breaking London broadcast with an unintentional but tension-building melodramatic flair: "Ten seconds, stand by. Eight seconds. Five seconds. Stand by. Three. Two." Suddenly, at 3:37:40 a.m. EWT, the well-known voice of Edward R. Murrow broke through the static of OWI's London transmitter reading General Eisenhower's Order of the Day. The message was transmitted across all networks simultaneously; SHAEF had distributed it in hard copy hours earlier to all participants of the Invasion.[100]

Each network broadcast Murrow's forceful, even-toned, opening flourish of Eisenhower's communication to his Invasion troops: "Soldiers, Sailors and Airmen of the Allied Expeditionary Force! You are about to embark upon the Great Crusade, toward which we have striven these many months." In language replete with highly religious and moralistic overtones, Eisenhower reminded his troops of the ultimate purpose of their great venture—"the destruction of the German war machine" and "the elimination of Nazi tyranny"—while pointing out the extreme difficulty of the task they faced. The Germans, he reminded them, were "well trained, well equipped and battle-hardened"; they would "fight savagely." But Eisenhower injected a fierce sense of optimism into the second half of the message, invoking the numerous defeats the "United Nations have inflicted upon the Germans" leading up to 1944. With home-front support and the contributions of Allies on other fronts, Eisenhower wrote, the "tide has turned." Together with these Allies, the "free men of the world are marching together to Victory!" Eisenhower ended the message by expressing his "full confidence" in the "courage, devotion to duty and skill in battle" of the Allied troops in his charge, invoking the "blessing of Almighty God" in achieving "nothing less than full Victory!"[101] In this short missive, Eisenhower had encapsulated nearly all of the key themes underlying the developing narrative of D-Day—its grand scope and scale; its high-minded, sacred purpose; and its faith in the fighting skill of the average soldier, sailor, and airman. In effect, Eisenhower's message to his troops mirrored the way the American people saw themselves reflected in D-Day—as defenders of democracy, as liberators, and as reluctant combatants—even though the message's intended audience was the entire Allied Expeditionary Force. The inherent contradictions of that reflection for people of color in the United States, particularly those people living under the Jim Crow laws, did not seem to matter at this moment. The power of D-Day as a news event overwhelmed all such contradictions.

Within the span of seven minutes or less, American listeners had absorbed the essential narrative and thematic framework that would shape the American D-Day narrative. The networks' experts, primed for the task, quickly took the lead in guiding American listeners through the complexities of the developing storyline. At NBC, H. V. Kaltenborn took to the microphone at 3:39 a.m. and in his clear patrician accent summed up the content and meaning of Communiqué Number 1 and the Order of the Day. In keeping with the grandiosity afforded the Invasion by the coverage up to that point, Kaltenborn proclaimed, "The great adventure has begun. The final chapter in the history of the Second World War is being written." With a clumsy suddenness that marked the Invasion transmissions up to that point, a voice cut Kaltenborn off midsentence and exclaimed, "Five seconds. Standby by for a pool broadcast." An unknown announcer speaking from London introduced and then read a report written several hours earlier by correspondent Herbert M. Clark from one of the Invasion fleet's flagships. Clark's report described the massive invasion fleet—nearly twenty-three miles of boats—from the deck of his flagship anchored in an unknown British port, a sweeping description of the armada that helped Americans visualize the grand scope and scale of D-Day. Before the networks and the listening public could absorb the whirlwind of information coming in thus far, another call came in at 3:46 a.m. for the networks to cut to London. Eisenhower was coming on the air.

At 3:47 a.m., America heard for the first time on D-Day the voice of the man leading the Invasion, Gen. Dwight D. Eisenhower. His was the first of such voices from key Allied leaders they would hear that day. In a prerecorded message, Eisenhower directly addressed the very people in Western Europe whom the Allies had come to liberate. Americans listening from home sat front and center as the Supreme Allied commander spelled out his instructions to the resistance forces on the continent. "People of Western Europe," intoned Eisenhower calmly in his familiar midwestern accent, a "landing was made this morning on the coast of France by troops of the Allied Expeditionary Force." Eisenhower then explained that together with assistance from the Russians, "the hour of your liberation is approaching." He warned the resistance forces, particularly those forces in France where the landings had taken place, not to react prematurely and risk their lives needlessly. Eisenhower explained that when he needed them to act, he would call on them. He offered his regret for the damage and losses inflicted by the operation and explained that the landings were "but the opening phases of the campaign in Western Europe." Great battles lay ahead, and "together we shall achieve victory."[102]

The multinational scale of D-Day became apparent to American listeners when immediately following Eisenhower's broadcast, the exiled leaders of Norway, the Netherlands, and Belgium spoke from London directly to their own people in their native languages (followed immediately by English translations). These voices confirmed for the American public that the Invasion, and the war more broadly, had a higher purpose and objective beyond any parochial concerns Americans might have harbored about their daily existence. Each leader echoed Eisenhower's instructions to avoid premature uprisings, to bide their time, and to stay close to their radios for the supreme commander's orders to act.[103] Radio had allowed Americans to pierce the veil that normally obscured military operations in real time and, in doing so, firmly linked home-front listeners not simply with their soldiers fighting overseas, but with the very people those soldiers were trying to liberate.[104]

Immediately after the last exiled leader spoke, the first of multiple reports came over the airwaves in a method that only radio could provide: an eyewitness account broadcast from London to spellbound audiences in America. Wright Bryan, from NBC affiliate WSB in Atlanta, was the first radio correspondent to return to England with an eyewitness report of the Invasion. As we shall see, Bryan's account was only the first of many such eyewitness broadcasts from correspondents throughout D-Day, aired live or by recording, that helped lure American listeners into experiencing the Invasion vicariously.[105]

After being subjected to nearly four hours of continuous, rapid-fire broadcast coverage, listeners' reactions in all U.S. time zones clearly indicated that America had been paying attention to the Invasion news.[106] For listeners on the West Coast, the first German bulletin had sounded while they were at the tail end of their prime listening hours. Most people were still awake. Now, well into the coverage, listeners across the country had crossed the midnight hour but were still glued to their radios. Many nighttime activities had ceased; for instance, the casinos in Reno, Nevada, shut down when news of D-Day broke.[107] Back on the East Coast, the regular editions of the newspapers had gone to press, and the hastily assembled "5 a.m. extras" began rolling out. The networks had shouldered the first Invasion news admirably; but even as the newspapers began contributing to the evolving Invasion narrative from a visual perspective, the networks and independent stations continued to fill the airwaves with breaking news and summaries. For its part, CBS calculated that by 4:43 a.m. EWT the network had broadcast 29,000 words on the Invasion.[108]

The networks continued to broadcast fresh pool reports from London, such as the summary provided at 4:40 a.m. by NBC's John Vandercook, who salted his report liberally with evocative and descriptive phrases. He further underscored the Invasion's scope and importance proclaiming, "Millions of people will say today, 'This is really it!'" Vandercook continued, "The great [British general Bernard] Montgomery of Egypt and North Africa" is leading the landing forces and that "General Eisenhower calls this mighty mission 'The Great Crusade.'"[109] Immediately following Vandercook's report, an NBC reporter in Washington read a statement from retired Gen. John J. Pershing in which the former American Expeditionary Force commander linked the legacy of his doughboys who fought for liberty in World War I to the current war of European liberation fought by the sons of those very same men. Pershing declared: "I have every confidence that they, together with their gallant brothers-in-arms, will win through to victory."[110]

More correspondent eyewitness reports continued to pour in from London as the very first photographs approved by the censors for wirephoto and telephoto transmission began clogging up numerous circuits for more than an hour at a time, slowing down the incoming news reports from overseas.[111] In scattershot fashion, analysts at the various networks chimed in with interpretative summaries of the military situation.[112] CBS's Bob Trout and NBC's Robert St. John continued their marathon broadcasting sessions.[113]

By 5:45 a.m. fresh news from overseas had slowed dramatically and fell into a "repetitive rut," causing all networks in turn to lapse into "a circular frenzy of recapitulation and interpretation," which had the effect of reinforcing the details of the emerging D-Day narrative for American listeners.[114] So far the Invasion story had what CBS characterized as "only one solid bone to this story"—Communiqué Number 1—"and the newsmen abroad and at home [had] gnawed it white."[115] For more than five hours, the emerging narrative of D-Day hung on a single, terse official dispatch around which censor-approved eyewitness reports and summations, many of which the networks had begun to rebroadcast repeatedly, attempted to add meat to the "solid bone."[116] As a result, the networks began filling the gaps between redundant broadcasts of Communiqué Number 1 and Eisenhower's Order of the Day with martial music or piano interludes or whatever news became available.[117] Most networks followed this pattern throughout the rest of the day, allowing audiences to absorb more fully all aspects of the D-Day narrative.

By 10 a.m. Bob Trout was making his twenty-fifth broadcast; his military analyst, Major Eliot, was on his tenth.[118] At NBC, Robert St. John was about to launch into his twenty-third broadcast.[119] But the scarcity of fresh news from overseas prompted CBS to return to some regularly scheduled programming at 10 a.m., beginning with a soap opera called *Valiant Lady* followed by *Light of the World* and other shows.[120] Before cutting to *Valiant Lady,* Trout explained that CBS would interrupt the programming with any breaking news. Trout, the "Iron Man of D-Day commentators" who had broadcast nearly nonstop up to that point, finally went home and fell asleep.[121] As promised, Douglas Edwards broke in after *Valiant Lady* long enough to announce a tidbit of news: FDR had just asked the nation to join him around the radio in prayer that night at 10 p.m. EWT.[122] For its part, NBC remained program-free for the twenty-four-hour period of D-Day coverage on the order of network president Niles Trammell. At 9:29 a.m. EWT, Robert St. John, whose multiple turns at the microphone throughout D-Day nearly matched Trout's performance, reminded listeners that NBC would only air news punctuated by brief musical interludes.[123]

The question for all networks soon became: were Americans still listening? As soon as *Valiant Lady* went on the air, CBS tasked an expert crew of telephone interviewers to conduct a CBS-Hooper survey and call thousands of listeners in order to glean a sense of what people felt about the news they were hearing. Were they hearing too much or too little news? Did they prefer a return to their usual programs? The researchers called thousands of homes in metropolitan areas across the country over a nearly three-hour period. The results were impressive. Between 8 a.m. and noon EWT, 218 percent of the number of radios normally tuned in at this time of year were "going wide open."[124] Listeners responded to the polling by insisting on more news. Americans were indeed listening. From their homes, offices, factory floors, truck cabs, and schools, Americans were inextricably connected to each other and to a common D-Day narrative by the shared ritual of radio listenership. CBS got the message loud and clear and at 12:41 p.m., it cancelled all succeeding commercial programs.[125]

Throughout the day and leading up to FDR's nationwide prayer at 10 p.m., the American public continued to hear statements or the actual voices of numerous key Allied leaders, which contributed to the sense of the enormity and importance of the Invasion. At 6:50 a.m., Bob Trout and Ned Calmer reported on Winston Churchill's statement to the House of Commons, in which the prime minister described the Invasion fleet as an "immense allied armada," reassuringly noting that D-Day was proceeding according to plan.[126] Churchill offered up fresh data that spoke to the magnitude of the Invasion: 11,000 Allied aircraft were providing cover for 4,000 ships and smaller craft as they crossed the English Channel to France.[127] At 11:30 a.m. CBS carried General Charles de Gaulle's statement to the French people, the only network to deliver the Free French leader's remarks live and with a running translation. By this point the networks, although still relying on pool reports, began to diverge into their own programming decisions. The fact that de Gaulle's remarks were broadcast live solely on one network reflected this growing shift.[128] At 1:39 p.m., NBC rebroadcast a reading of General Montgomery's message to the troops, in which the 21st Army Group commander expressed confidence in the Allied forces under his command and reminded them that they have been "given the honor of striking a blow for freedom which will live in history."[129]

One of the most significant voices heard by Americans on D-Day echoed through radio sets nationwide in the midafternoon hours on the East Coast—the voice of England's King George VI. Over a clear channel, the king recited in a halting, deliberate manner words of encouragement to his subjects for the "supreme test" they now faced and a solemn call to prayer. "This time the challenge is not to fight to survive," he exhorted, "but to fight to win the final victory for the good cause."[130] President Roosevelt later matched the monarch's call to prayer in England with his own call to prayer in the United States set for later that night—and "radio was the pulpit."[131]

The networks further enhanced D-Day's import by seeking out and broadcasting the comments or actions of political leaders throughout the United States, particularly members of Congress. Oddly enough, early morning broadcasts from Washington, DC, suggested an eerie silence in the nation's capital that belied the furiously evolving narrative then unfolding across the airwaves. The White House offered no reaction, and the State Department building remained dark.[132] Network representatives from NBC, CBS, and Blue had only begun broadcasting from the Pentagon at 4:43 a.m. with nothing more than color commentary and military interpretations from high-ranking Army officers.[133] Secretary of War Henry Stimson later told the press that "he got the surprise of his life" when he heard the news of D-Day on his bedside radio at 4:20 a.m.[134] The timing of the world's best-kept "non-secret" clearly enjoyed an extraordinary level of operational security even within the highest halls of the American government.

Remarkably, one of the first statements broadcast by a political leader took place outside Washington, DC, and included an extraordinary and dramatic ringing of the Liberty Bell. Speaking with an echo from within Independence Hall in Philadelphia, Mayor Bernard Samuel explained the importance of the bell to American freedom and that "now, through radio, let [the bell] indeed proclaim liberty throughout the land and the return of liberty throughout the world." He then rang the Liberty Bell multiple times as the networks cut back to other news.[135] The Invasion's significance soared.

By 12:30 p.m., the American public began hearing statements directly from senators and representatives.[136] While most of these statements exuded optimism about the Invasion's ultimate success, some senators seeded their overemphasis of D-Day's significance with glaring notes of caution. Like his fellow senators, Maine's Republican minority leader, Wallace H. White Jr., declared D-Day as "one of the most momentous days in the world's history." "It is shadowed with the possibility of disaster," he cautioned, "but it has within [it] the substantial promise of a glorious ending." NBC's Morgan Beatty even reported at a late-afternoon news conference attended by 181 reporters that a confident FDR had also warned about overconfidence, maintaining that such bullishness was dangerous to the war effort.[137]

Throughout the day each network continued to broadcast tidbits of news, using news roundups to synthesize into a common picture what had already happened and what was still unfolding in Normandy. At 5 p.m. London warned the networks that Communiqué Number 2 was forthcoming—only the second report to originate from SHAEF after a fourteen-hour drought of officially sanctioned facts—but a minor glitch prevented American listeners from ever hearing it. Through it all, the networks overcame most technical difficulties to keep the news flowing, but radio failed when it came to Communiqué Number 2. Despite frantic scrambling at CBS, for instance, the London cue channel remained silent as the communiqué's full text suddenly clicked over the Reuters ticker followed promptly by the AP and UP teletypes. Radio stations had missed broadcasting the second communiqué directly from their London circuit before the wire services and the newspapers received the text. The one-page missive summed up the naval operations leading up to the beach landings, how assault forces moved to the beaches under cover of aerial bombardment and naval gunfire, and how airborne and glider-borne forces had landed successfully. In all, according to the message, naval casualties were light, and the Germans offered little fighter or antiaircraft opposition. Ultimately, the newscasters would incorporate the contents of the communiqué into their future broadcasts, but for all its successes on D-Day, radio had stubbed its toe.[138]

Radio's coverage of the first twenty-four hours began to wind down soon after FDR broadcast his prayer for the Invasion's success. For its part, radio had allowed all Americans to peek behind the curtain not only when it came to building a common narrative but to "pierce the veil" of combat by doing something that newspapers could not do—inject listeners directly into the raw experience of what FDR termed "the violence of war" through eyewitness reports given in the correspondents' own voices and idiom.[139]

◆ ◆ ◆

Eyewitness reports from correspondents, some broadcast in the correspondents' own voices or transcribed and then read on the air by announcers, represented radio's most original contribution to the developing narrative of the Invasion. The sense of personal involvement that radio provided in the unfolding drama of D-Day, complete with technical gaffs and miscues, had already drawn listeners to their radio sets in pursuit of every morsel of fresh news. Sprinkled liberally throughout the daylong hodgepodge of news reports, prayers, and official statements were eyewitness reports provided by radio correspondents who accompanied the Allied bomber crews and assault troops. Those on-the-spot reports spoken in the correspondents' own voices and idiom had the greatest impact in expressing not only the magnitude of the Invasion effort but also some of the violence and chaos that attended such a massive endeavor. It was those eyewitness accounts that offered emotionally charged, visceral portrayals of combat that came closest to placing listeners on the battlefield, exposing them to sounds they had never heard before over the radio. Edward R. Murrow had already paved the way with his live broadcasts of German air raids on London in 1940, but his reports, although replete with the sounds of air-raid sirens and antiaircraft fire, lacked the intimacy of close combat.[140] Instead, the eyewitness accounts broadcast on D-Day, whether described from within a studio or recorded directly on the front lines, came closest to revealing to American listeners what John Keegan deemed "the face of battle."[141] The end result was collective storytelling at its most powerful, for never had journalism, according to John McDonough, "ever possessed such [a] direct and transcendent effect."[142]

Remarkably, most of these highly impactful eyewitness broadcasts did not reach American listeners' ears in real time, which is what the networks had hoped to achieve. The danger, uncertainty, and chaos of combat, as well as the censorship considerations, rendered real-time, on-site broadcasts practically and technically unfeasible. Under these circumstances the correspondents first had to get themselves or their recordings back to England before the process could bring the story to the air. Some radio correspondents who returned to London by plane or boat were able to broadcast their own accounts from the pool studio in the basement of the British Ministry of Information building. Even before D-Day began, Col. David Sarnoff and Col. E. M. Kirby, who oversaw SHAEF's pre-Invasion radio preparations, had to secure an agreement from the networks to break a longstanding taboo among radio journalists—the use of recordings for on-the-spot reports.[143] The networks believed recordings sacrificed the immediacy and integrity of live broadcasting and the network-level exclusivity that came with such in-the-moment reporting, but such an approach proved impractical during D-Day.[144] For correspondents flying with aircrews or accompanying landing craft loaded with assault troops, live broadcasts were technically impossible.[145] They were possible, however, from aboard naval craft, but emitting sound signatures while aboard ship might reveal a vessel's location to the enemy. Moreover, censors could not control the content of live broadcasts, and that fact alone became the greatest consideration for requiring the use of recorders.

The Army and Navy became the unlikely underwriters of the press' new on-site recorder technology by agreeing to provide each radio pool correspondent with one recording device and if necessary, an engineer to operate it. These bulky electrical recorders could play back the recording immediately without further processing.[146] The brand of recorder the Navy provided—the Recordgraph, Commando Model—proved remarkably effective for capturing sound with clear fidelity.[147]

The London pool established a reasonably efficient system for processing these on-the-spot eyewitness recordings. For those correspondents who recorded ready-for-broadcast recordings, the correspondent delivered the recording to London either by courier or in person (which involved a daunting trip that could last anywhere from a couple of hours to half a day depending on the mode of transportation—plane or boat). Next a censor reviewed the contents, and a technician made the required edits in the pool's studio. The pool then transmitted the report from

London on shortwave. When the networks in the United States received the transmission, they rerecorded it and broadcast it nationwide through their affiliates. Many correspondents used their recorders for notetaking, which aided them in crafting a detailed, written account of what they had witnessed for direct broadcast in their own voices following a censorship review. Since these reports were part of the larger pooling agreement, every network had full access to every eyewitness report, thus ensuring the widest dissemination to listeners throughout America.[148] Of all the numerous eyewitness accounts broadcast through the network pool on D-Day, the most impactful and memorable came from three American correspondents hailing from three different networks—NBC's Wright Bryan, CBS's Richard Hottelet, and the Blue Network's George Hicks. Of these three men, George Hicks used his recorder with the most stunning effect.

One of the more impactful eyewitness reports transmitted to the networks on D-Day was also the first to reach American listeners. The report hailed from NBC correspondent Wright Bryan, and it hit the airwaves in the United States at 4:17 a.m. EWT—less than an hour after SHAEF issued Communiqué Number 1. Bryan was a thirty-nine-year-old commentator for NBC's affiliate in Atlanta, WSB, and managing editor of the *Atlanta Journal*. He accompanied a "stick" of paratroopers on the flight to their insertion point and returned with the aircraft to England, where he made his way back to the London pool studios. Using verbal notes from his recorder, Bryan dashed off a thirteen-minute, painstakingly detailed account of his Invasion experience written in an "I was there" style. After clearing it through the censors, Bryan broadcast his narrative in his distinctive southern twang to the combined networks in New York.[149]

Bryan opened his broadcast by explaining that he had just returned from riding in a C-47 transport aircraft nicknamed "The Snooty," which had just dropped seventeen paratroopers led by a lieutenant colonel, complete "with their arms, ammunition, and equipment, into German-occupied France." The power of Bryan's narration rested in his steady, matter-of-fact delivery and his attention to detail, even describing enemy tracers arcing upward into the sky and the distant sound of small arms fire on the ground below. Bryan explained that he had spent two days with the paratroopers prior to the jump; for the first time, he personalized the Invasion for listeners by inserting names into the story. He explained how a Major Richardson called all pilots to the briefing room on the eve of the Invasion, questioning them about their readiness for the mission. He further drove home the Invasion's human dimension by naming the 1st Squadron commander, Lt. Col. David Daniel, as well as the officer's hometown of Birmingham, Alabama. He even described how the Ninth Air Force commander, Lt. Gen. Lewis H. Brereton, stood on the runway cheering on his departing aircraft.

Once off the ground, Bryan offered even greater intimate details about the conduct of the flight by "Pilot Pete" and the actions of the paratroopers themselves—details that would allow listeners to identify more closely with their young men in harm's way. He described how Lt. Col. Robert Cole, the senior officer on board, walked among his men, handing out motion sickness pills and telling them to catch a quick nap.[150] Bryan also moved among the dozing paratroopers, asking one soldier if the young man had confidence in his parachute. The soldier, whom Bryan identified as Pvt. Robert C. Hillman of Manchester, Connecticut, replied that his chute was "okay" because his mother had checked it. "You see," explained the soldier, "my Mom works at the Pioneer Parachute Company in our town." No other anecdote could have made more of a connection with or had more of an impact on America's listeners than a young soldier linking his faith in his combat equipment to his faith in his own mother's home-front efforts on behalf of the Invasion.

As the aircraft approached the drop zone, Bryan's narrative switched to the fast-paced actions occurring within the plane, providing listeners with a sense of the tension and tempo that soldiers experienced as they prepared to enter combat. He related how Pilot Pete shouted out a thirty-minute warning to Lieutenant Colonel Cole followed by a description of the Normandy countryside and its orderly hedgerows. He captured the dialogue of the moment as Cole addressed his men: "'Are you all set?' asked the colonel. 'Get this thing hooked for me,' he said as he took his own place closest to the door." Bryan watched the green light begin blinking and, "before I could look up, they began jumping." He admitted "I wanted to know how long it would take the eighteen men to jump." But before Bryan could "count 101, 102, 103 to estimate the number of seconds . . . our passengers had left us." In the jostle to exit the plane, though, one paratrooper fell backward heavily, and his comrades pushed him aside and away from the door. According to Bryant, the man was "inconsolable." He had just missed the jump of a lifetime.

Bryan closed his gripping account with a description of the Normandy coastline from above and a strong sense of optimism. Despite his obvious expectations, he had seen no signs of enemy aircraft or antiaircraft fire. Tracers curved upward into the air but at no fixed target. Bryan's narrative suggested that all had gone according to plan and that the Invasion had caught the Germans flat-footed. He closed his broadcast with a rhetorical flourish by proclaiming, "The battle of Europe had begun, and our squadron had delivered the first Allied foot soldiers to their scene of action." Bryan's first-person account moved listeners at home to crave even more such reports—and more would be forthcoming.[151]

Another gripping eyewitness report, one that described a bird's-eye view of an actual beach assault, reached listeners' ears less than an hour after Bryan's broadcast—at 5:07 a.m. EWT. Richard C. Hottelet had returned to England after riding with the first wave of Ninth Air Force B-26 Marauder twin-engine medium bombers as they delivered their payload at low altitude in direct support of the American beach assaults. Like his colleague Wright Bryan, Hottelet crafted a snappy, vivid, brief word picture of what he had seen from his low-flying bomber just as D-Day began. And like Bryan, he broadcast his own report in a matter-of-fact style that underscored key words by deliberate voice inflection. After a brief description of the events leading up to his take-off from England, Hottelet explained that he had "watched the first landing barges hit the beach exactly on the minute of H-Hour." The bombers' mission was to fly a thousand feet above the coastline, explained Hottelet, and "plaster" German coastal fortifications precisely seven minutes before the first landing craft hit the beaches, which Hottelet claimed they had accomplished "as scheduled." Hottelet described in striking detail the "bright orange" sun as it crested the horizon; how "below us the English Channel was a fine, deep blue"; and how white and yellow parachutes dotted the ground—miniscule facts that thrust listeners' imaginations directly into the unfolding Invasion tableau. He described seeing naval vessels that "looked like cruisers firing broadsides on to the shore" as "dozens and scores of white streaks" stretched behind the landing craft heading to the beaches against a backdrop of sheets of flame and a haze of black smoke. Such details drew listeners at home directly into the immediacy of the story.

Hottelet's most gripping details, replete with sensations and smells, came with his narration of the Marauders' bombing run. As the flight ahead dropped its bombs, he explained, the ships offshore resumed firing. "The bombs and the shells burst together on the target. . . . Four-and-a-half-thousand feet up, our plane was rocked by the concussion." And then came the smell: "We got the stench of the explosives" as the bombs detonated below. And through it all, Hottelet's expectations of German resistance, like those of Wright Bryan, went unfulfilled. Hottelet saw no American planes in distress, no German resistance in the ground or air, and no German antiaircraft fire. For listeners, the absence of a German counteraction provided a needed morale boost. Although hesitant to draw a broad conclusion about the Invasion from his narrow perch, he ended his broadcast by declaring that "our air supremacy over the coastal invasion zone today is not seriously challenged." As far as Americans at home were concerned, Hottelet's description, like Bryan's, spelled success, even though seizing the bloodiest and most contested American beach—Omaha—remained an open question. This inability to obtain clearer details contributed to the more anodyne and optimistic version of the narrative emerging from the networks.[152]

While eyewitness accounts read aloud to audiences from a sterile London studio still had the power to fire listeners' imaginations, nothing compared to hearing a report recorded directly in a battle zone replete with the thundering sounds of combat in the background. George Hicks, the Blue Network's London chief, employed his Recordgraph to masterfully capture on tape a genuine, on-the-spot account of the first assault troops hitting the Invasion beaches while he was on board a naval vessel. Hicks's report was the last of the hard-hitting eyewitness accounts broadcast during the first twenty-four hours of Invasion coverage, and it became one of the most memorable accounts aired on 6 June 1944. Hicks, with engineer Bob Massell manning the Recordgraph, recorded his news report at H-Hour, 6 a.m. local European time; but by the time the recording made its way through the screening process in England, the American listening public did not hear it until 11:31 p.m. EWT—nearly eighteen hours later. However, avid listeners were still tuned in and heard all ten minutes of the stunning report before the clock struck midnight, 7 June 1944, on the East Coast.

Hicks, a sixteen-year veteran of radio, opened his report in the straightforward, unemotional style of an experienced broadcaster: "I am speaking now from a tower above the signal bridge of an American naval flagship [USS *Ancon*], and we're lying some miles off the coast of France where the invasion has begun." Hicks then described, using a rich array of adjectives, how landing craft carrying tanks and troops were "churning along" and "bouncing around in the choppy Channel sea" as they passed by his flagship in "irregular lines." The tension increased in Hicks's voice as the Invasion fleet neared the coast of France and the sounds of naval gunfire and aircraft increased appreciably in the background. "It's now becoming quite clear and daylight as six a.m. approaches on June 6th, 1944," said Hicks. "We can hear the thud of shells or bombs landing on the French coastline." At different points in his narration, the thundering sounds of naval gunfire drowned out his voice as "the steel plates [of the bridge] on which we stand vibrate from the concussion of the heavy guns." From his vantage point on the flagship, Hicks witnessed American "battleships lying just a couple of miles off the French shore and firing broadsides into the land" in reply to German "flashes" appearing along the coast. "Overhead, high," explained Hicks, "planes are roaring. I think they just came in and dropped a salvo of bombs on the hilltop before us." The shriek of aircraft overhead nearly drowned out Hicks's stress-tinged voice, prompting him to end his momentary chronicle of the Invasion by declaring that the time was now around 6:30 a.m. and that the "first Allied forces are reaching the beaches in France."[153]

Few Americans on the home front had ever heard the sounds of battle. The fact that a newsman like Hicks would risk his personal safety to cover this story testified to the significance the media placed on D-Day—and certainly with the help of official sources at home and overseas. The raw power of Hicks's report, a story that only radio had the capacity to relate in all its unforgettable authenticity, could only increase the magnitude of the Invasion's importance to the folks at home.[154]

Despite the impact of his beach-assault recording, Hicks became best known for a subsequent report he recorded nearly eighteen hours later, just as Americans on the home front were hearing his H-Hour report for the very first time. Although the networks did not broadcast this second recorded account in the first twenty-four-hour news cycle on D-Day (they first heard it at 11:15 p.m. EWT on 7 June 1944), that second report more than any other broadcast during the Invasion demonstrated radio's ability to influence how and what listeners might think and feel about the Invasion.[155] In this broadcast, recorded shortly after 11 p.m. local European time on 6 June 1944, Hicks described in striking detail, with deafening explosions and the sound of gunfire engulfing him, a German plane strafing the *Ancon*.[156] No other radio broadcast thrust American listeners more directly in the violence of war than this recorded account.

As Hicks switched on the Record ["Recordgraph"] and recorded his impression of fires burning in the growing darkness on the distant French coast, the sound of a low-flying plane above his flagship prompted him to exclaim, "That baby was plenty low!" He acknowledged that the plane was the "first [German] one [he had] seen so far." As the German plane streaked past, the deafening sound of the ship's warning whistle drowned out Hicks's voice, which surfaced sporadically in the sea of noise: "It's planes you hear overhead now . . . they are the motors of Nazis coming and going." He described tracers arcing skyward as he raised his voice over the shouts of the ship's crew members. As the German plane made another pass, the overwhelming sound of machine-gun and 40mm anti-aircraft fire again engulfed Hicks's voice, which evinced clear signs of tension. As the antiaircraft fire paused, Hicks begged his audience to excuse him briefly: "I'll just take a deep breath for a moment and stop speaking." The German plane returned and Hicks blurted, "Here we go again!" The crew's shouts punctuated the thunderous sound of antiaircraft fire as Hicks cheered on the sailors: "Give it to her, boys . . . another one coming over . . . something burning is falling down through the sky . . . it may be a hit plane." Suddenly, the crew's cheering engulfed the airwaves as Hicks bellowed, "They got one!"[157]

The power of this on-the-spot recording, unlike other eyewitness broadcasts, helped to transform American audiences from passive listeners into de facto participants of the Invasion of occupied Europe. Radio had provided them an auditory window into the grim, stark, tension-filled realities of combat. Through Hicks's report, they heard a life-and-death struggle as it happened—and with the likely death of one or more Germans. Stations replayed Hicks's broadcast constantly for the next seventy-two hours, and the report was issued as a record album available for public purchase.[158] Radio had helped to elevate D-Day to a level of significance that would have been impossible in the medium's absence. *BBA* hailed the Invasion as "radio's greatest triumph" and singled out Hicks's remarkable report—and the networks' new embrace of the wire recorder—as the high points of the Invasion coverage. According to *BBA*, "Precedents toppled like duck-pins."[159]

◆ ◆ ◆

The world of radio broadcasting gave itself high marks for its performance on D-Day, not only for its delivery of breaking news over an extended twenty-four-hour period, but also because it had captured the minds and imaginations of the American public and pulled them directly into the Invasion. Radio had earned its spurs by spearheading news of D-Day. Americans had indeed tuned in, and they took away from the realistic, immersive network reports a firm, if overly optimistic, outline of a growing, thematically framed narrative about D-Day. Taken in conjunction with the extensive newspaper coverage of the Invasion, this coverage contributed to how Americans came to see D-Day as the most important event of the war.[160]

The networks had heeded the warning issued by the head of OWI's Domestic Radio Bureau, George P. Ludlam, in the lead-up to the Invasion, cautioning that initial news of the Invasion would be a time of "grave anxiety" for soldiers' families. "They will—and properly—resent any radio message," he cautioned, "which can be interpreted as exploiting the military situation, no matter how patriotic or worthwhile the subject treated." The networks fell in line without exception and followed Edward R. Murrow's roadmap for broadcasting news of the Invasion: "The only thing that counts," said Murrow, "is an honest, coherent account of events."[161]

As midnight approached on D-Day, the straightforward, reasonably accurate reporting by the networks had allowed listeners to feel that not only had they been a part of history in the making, but also that the Allies had likely put the German war machine on its heels. No one could possibly forget such an experience. D-Day had demonstrated that radio "could be an eloquent participant-observer of contemporary history."[162] But in the end the radio networks' reporting, like that of their newspaper brethren that same day, was only as good as their sources. The information gaps in these sources left some of the worst American losses on D-Day unreported and allowed the Invasion narrative to develop into something more hopeful and less representative of the truth. For the troops engaged in the assault, the Invasion was a far bloodier venture than radio was able to report on 6 June 1944, so radio's "participant-observer" capacity came with clear limitations.

Comedian and entertainer Bob Hope perhaps summed up the day's news coverage best in one of the final broadcasts made by NBC on the night of 6 June 1944. Shortly after FDR's prayer at 10 p.m. EWT, Hope spoke over the entire network from a P-38 fighter base near Van Nuys, California. His remarks were heartfelt and passionate: "What has happened these last few hours not one of us will ever forget. How could you forget? You sat up all night by the radio and heard the bulletins, the flashes, the voices coming across from England, the commentators, the pilots returning from their greatest of all missions . . . newsboys yelling on the street. . . . The sun came up and you sat there looking at that huge black headline, that one great black word with the exclamation point, 'Invasion!'" Hope ended with a simple, solemn invocation: "God bless those kids across the English Channel."[163]

CHAPTER 3

"Invasion On!"
Newspapers Take Center Stage

The Invasion Is On! Allies Punch Inland From French Coast. BEACHHEADS SECURE.

—headline, *Akron Beacon Journal*, 6 June 1944[1]

On the East Coast, the major radio networks had been broadcasting news of the Invasion for several hours by the time the first newspapers rolled off the presses and into the hands of a now wide-awake and news-hungry American public. In New York, the *Herald Tribune*, the *Mirror*, the *World-Telegram*, and the *Journal-American* all hit the newsstands between 8 a.m. and 9 a.m. with Invasion headlines and stories. These New York newspapers, like many others across the country, had to retool and rework the editions they had just put to bed shortly before the wire services and broadcast networks sounded the alarm at thirty-seven minutes after midnight EWT that German news organs were claiming the Invasion had begun. The editions slated for circulation on the morning of 6 June 1944 all carried headlines announcing another major story—the capture of Rome by the American Fifth Army. In fact, President Roosevelt had just spoken over the airwaves that evening to all Americans celebrating this significant triumph while also cautioning against premature optimism that an easy victory in Europe was now in the offing. Much to the chagrin of Lt. Gen. Mark W. Clark, commanding general of the Fifth Army in Italy, and the troops under his command, news editors unceremoniously pushed the story of Rome's liberation off America's front pages in favor of D-Day news.

But not every newspaper took the time to revise the morning edition before launching copies onto the streets and into the public's hands. The New York *Daily News,* with a circulation of more than 2 million—the largest in America in 1944—did not wait for the radio networks to garner all the Invasion attention. In fact, *Daily News*-owned local radio station WNEW picked up the German transmission from its own short-wave listening post at thirty-six minutes after midnight and broadcast it locally four minutes later, scooping the AP and other wire services and broadcast networks. Significantly, the *Daily News* produced perhaps the nation's earliest newspaper edition announcing that D-Day had likely begun. The first copy hit the stands at 2:15 a.m. with a headline announcing that "King Gives Up Italy" above a smaller headline proclaiming, "Nazis Report Invasion Move In Sea Fight Off France." Within twenty-five minutes, at 2:40 a.m., the *Daily News* had pushed out another edition with a new headline: "Nazis Report Invasion On." Incredibly, less than forty-five minutes later, another edition appeared with the same headlines but now with a map of the English Channel. A fourth edition followed at 4:03 a.m. minus the map but with a headline in three-inch letters announcing simply, "Invasion Begins."[2]

The *Daily News*'s fast-changing editions exemplified how aggressively newspapers throughout the country reacted to news of the Invasion and sought to get their familiar, socially constructed news products, each replete with journalism's peculiar conventions, codes, and cultural signifiers, into the hands of American readers.[3] Only then, through the mass ceremony of common readership, could all Americans further connect with and become part of the process of creating a common narrative of D-Day at the moment the event occurred.[4] Most importantly, a firm demarcation between the newspapers and the broadcast networks did not exist. Instead, they complemented each other, with newspapers reinforcing the same basic information and thematic frames the networks had aired throughout the night and into the day on 6 June 1944. However, radio never eclipsed newspaper readership; radio further amplified the news and prompted ever-increasing newspaper circulation numbers. The listening public actively sought out newspaper coverage of the

Invasion for more in-depth news and visual representations of the landings. Newspaper circulation skyrocketed.[5]

Radio served as a bridge to the newspapers popping up on newsstands throughout the nation on 6 June 1944. While the broadcast networks gave the American public the sense that D-Day was unfolding in the moment, the newspapers helped arrest that chaotic momentum, giving the American public a chance to absorb and visualize what the airwaves had shared with them throughout the day. For Americans who could only catch snippets of the networks' radio broadcasts, newspapers offered a self-contained, familiar product complete with a front and back page and an abundance of news in between. Newspapers allowed readers to digest, interpret, and take stock of what was happening half a world away. The American public could read, reread, and absorb more fully what was happening without worrying if they were receiving a less complete picture of events than their neighbors or other fellow Americans who had remained glued to radio sets throughout the day. Follow-on "extra" editions added to the unfolding story well into the evening.

Unfortunately, one of the greatest factors hampering how the newspapers communicated the Invasion to the public stemmed from an ongoing shortage of newsprint. While the broadcast networks enjoyed the benefit of plentiful airwave space, the newspaper industry suffered from a paper shortage that significantly affected the content and layout decisions for each edition. While radio "blurted out everything" on D-Day, the newspapers had to pick and choose what made the cut and what did not, creating minor gaps in the newspapers' larger narrative about D-Day.[6] Like the broadcast networks, many newspapers nationwide had to consider the possibility of cutting advertisements to make space for Invasion coverage.[7] The *Seattle Times* felt "the pinch of newsprint rationing" so severely that the paper's editorial board advertised in the 3 June 1944 issue of *E&P* that the *Times*, due to a 42-percent increase in circulation since 1941, had to ration advertising but would still retain its "editorial supremacy."[8]

◆ ◆ ◆

Despite emerging on the scene several hours after news of the Invasion broke, and operating within the constraints of a nationwide newsprint shortage, America's newspapers contributed significantly to all four media-constructed thematic frames that shaped the American D-Day narrative. The newspapers, like the broadcast networks, most effectively communicated to all Americans the first and most dominant theme—that the Invasion represented the most important military operation of the war and the opening chapter of Nazi Germany's demise. D-Day represented something different, something bigger in the context of the global war, so the newspapers responded by portraying the Invasion news in innovative and unprecedented ways. The newspapers used visual tools to underline specific themes in the Invasion coverage in a way that more ephemeral radio broadcasts could not.

First, the nation's newspapers employed unique, eye-catching, often oversized headlines that leapt off the front pages in order to show the American public that D-Day *was* the seminal event of the war up to that point, essentially taking the newspaper as a principal amplifier in the public sphere to an entirely new level.[9] Although some newspapers had used evocative headlines (albeit sparingly) to announce previous operations in the Pacific and Mediterranean, Operation Overlord's headlines stood out as something radically different.[10] These headlines, through their intense and graphic portrayal, had the power to convey the press' shared belief in the importance of the Invasion.

Second, America's newspapers leveraged the use of photographs and maps, two means of graphic representation that only a visual medium like the newspaper could feature, as a further means of communicating the Invasion's unique scope and scale to the American public. The development of the AP Wirephoto gave newspapers across the nation a way to combine the printed word with a visual representation of the news story, thus giving journalists the ability to convey a clearer picture of the news for the reading public.[11]

Finally, nearly every newspaper reporting D-Day employed maps of all sizes to assist Americans in shifting the war's focus and geography away from the Mediterranean and Pacific theaters to a completely new area of operations: the Normandy coastline. Newspapers hastily added sometimes crude arrows to previously prepared maps of the English Channel to point out the numerous reported landing sites along the Normandy coastline, in turn increasing Americans' sense of the operation's broad scope and geographic focus. As both an orientation tool and a measuring stick, these maps further suggested to American readers that the war's global reach had now greatly expanded and the Allies were engaging in a historical undertaking of mammoth proportions.

Although the headlines, photographs, and maps appearing in the mainstream newspapers vigorously promoted the thematic frame casting D-Day as the war's most significant endeavor, the response to the Invasion by America's Black newspapers remained the one factor that destabilized that theme and the news media's greater Invasion narrative. Most Black newspapers, responding to the exclusion of Blacks and other people of color from the D-Day story, simply ignored the Invasion. Someone reading the *Negro Star* in Wichita, Kansas; the *Arkansas State Press*; or the *Echo* in Mississippi on Friday, 9 June 1944, would never know that an event like D-Day, a massive operation elevated in importance by the mainstream press (which was exclusively White), had even happened.[12] The Black newspapers pushed back against the Invasion's underlying message of liberating the oppressed peoples of Nazi-occupied Europe by maintaining their steady drumbeat for greater social justice, instead using their immediate post–D-Day weeklies to push news items with titles such as "Clemency is Requested for Five [Black] Army Men Jailed for Mutiny: Resented Unfairness in Army Life."[13] The Invasion's overarching purpose of liberation fell flat in the eyes of America's Black community, and the Black newspapers treated it as such—a nonevent. The basic question posed by these Black newspapers was clear: when would America's Black community experience "liberation" from the oppression of Jim Crow and racial discrimination?

Surprisingly, a few Black newspapers broke ranks with the greater Black newspaper industry on the subject of D-Day, notably the most influential Black paper with the greatest circulation and reach—the *Pittsburgh Courier*. The *Courier* had created the so-called Double V campaign in February 1942 and had steadily maintained a militant, anti-discriminatory tone that rankled many officials in the U.S. government, even leading to allegations of sedition. However, Blacks had made steady gains by the time D-Day arrived. Black men had received commissions in the Army Air Corps, the Marine Corps, and the Coast Guard. Black women now joined the Women's Army Corps, and the defense plants were hiring Black men in larger numbers. Even the 9 June 1944 edition of the *Echo*, which remained silent about D-Day, published a large advertisement explaining how the U.S. Navy had now opened fifty skilled trade-school jobs to "Colored Men 17 to 18 years of Age."[14] Apparently, these gains motivated a highly circulated Black paper like the *Courier* and even Kansas City's the *Plaindealer* to acknowledge D-Day's importance and feature the word "Invasion" in their main headlines and front-page feature stories.[15] Despite this rupture in the Black newspapers' common front, the gains that elicited some Black newspapers' acknowledgment of D-Day's significance did not result in the inclusion of Black troops in the greater D-Day narrative. In their eyes, D-Day remained a White man's operation.

All told—and despite the exclusion from the Invasion narrative of Blacks and other Americans of color—newspapers, like radio, expressed the enormity and significance of D-Day to all Americans while the actual operation was still underway. Newspapers briefly arrested the steady stream of breaking news at different points in time during 6 June 1944 so that Americans had the opportunity to make greater sense of the emerging narrative and its attendant thematic frames. Although the newspapers, like the broadcasting networks, also expressed varying aspects of the other three themes framing the emerging D-Day narrative, the newspapers' visual (as well as textual) representations of the Invasion perhaps did the most to impress upon the public that Operation Overlord stood out as a pivotal event of great consequence to the war effort, even if more discerning readers did not quite see the Invasion in that light.

◆ ◆ ◆

The most deliberate, most overt means by which newspapers told the American public that D-Day was something special in the broader Allied effort to wrest Europe from Hitler's clutches occurred through the use of headlines. In many ways, the unique and varied "Invasion" headlines splashed across front pages nationwide on 6 June 1944 became iconic representations of how America's newspaper editors wanted to communicate the operation's greater meaning to the public. Almost every American newspaper published that day used the word "Invasion" in its headline, despite the negative connotations the word carried. In the strictest sense, an "invasion" signified an imposition upon someone else's land or a group of people with the intent to intrude, to injure, and to conquer.[16] In other words, invaders were "the bad guys."

Despite the word's negative connotation for the party assuming the role of invader, America's newspapers had used the word liberally to describe previous Allied operations in North Africa and Sicily—but they used "invasion" principally in its verb form. For instance, for the North African landings on 8 November 1942, both the *Cincinnati Enquirer* and Alabama's *Anniston Star* proclaimed, "U.S. Invades North Africa," while the *San Bernardino Daily Sun's* headline read, "American Army Invades French African Colonies."[17] For the Sicily landings in July 1943, the noun form of "invasion" appeared more often, but the dominant approach resembled the verb form used for the North Africa headlines. For example, the 10 July 1943 editions of the *Gettysburg Times* and the *Herald and News* of Klamath Falls, Oregon, each carried headlines declaring, "Allies Invade Sicily," while the *Honolulu Advertiser* opted for the noun form and printed, "Sicilian Invasion Described as Opening of Second Front."[18] The aggressive nature of the Allies' actions likely pleased American audiences, since "invade" suggested that the Allied forces now had the upper hand.

In the period between the Sicily landings in July 1943 and the deliberate preparations for the cross-Channel assault starting in January 1944, D-Day had become reified in America's, and the world's, consciousness through the term "invasion." In fact, D-Day had become *the* "Invasion," a proper, capitalized noun that suggested something bigger and well outside the norm. But the word rankled some Americans' sensibilities, resulting in a minor debate in the editorial pages of some newspapers in May 1944. Specifically, Dr. Douglas Southall Freeman, editor of the *Richmond News-Leader*, found the term insufficient to capture D-Day's true meaning and underlying essence. Freeman convinced the *Washington Post*'s editor and publisher, Eugene Meyer, to publish an editorial in the *Post* declaring the word "invasion" a misnomer for D-Day and promoting "liberation" as the proper term. Meyer agreed and published the editorial on 15 May 1944, arguing that the word "invasion" was "a common or garden episode in warfare"—a "means to a military end." Instead, Meyer asserted to his audience, the "word we need is an expression of the hopes astir in countless breasts in a score of lands." Thus, he insisted, the proper term was "liberation"—"a word of the heart that represented the end and not the means . . . the war aim and not the battle operation." Meyer's high-minded but compelling argument caught the eye of Elmer Davis, director of the OWI, who agreed with the inadequacy of the word "invasion" to describe D-Day. He wrote a letter to Meyer on the same day the editorial appeared in the *Post* to offer his support and to proclaim that he had given standing instructions to OWI's writers in the overseas service to use "liberation" in place of "invasion."[19]

Ironically, most newspaper editors across the nation ignored Meyer and Davis and used the term "Invasion" in their headlines to announce the start of D-Day. These editors knew their reading audiences well and believed the word would resonate with a perceptive American public. In many ways, the term fundamentally modified the D-Day narrative by suggesting a more pronounced shift in the war's initiative away from the Axis and over to the Allies. Hitler and his hordes now had their back to the wall. The Nazi "invaders" had become the "invaded." In this sense, the word carried greater weight and substance. Americans knew liberation was the goal, and they recognized the moralistic aspects of this grand charter as evidenced by all the home-front praying taking place on D-Day. But in the case of D-Day, the Allies, facing a powerful German Wehrmacht replete with seasoned warriors, had to "invade" first before they could "liberate."

The almost universally atypical approach followed by America's newspapers on 6 June 1944 to communicate news of the Invasion took place through an unprecedented increase in the size of headline typesets. Throughout the war and up until D-Day, the editors of America's newspapers generally confined themselves to two-inch headline letters, regardless of the event they were reporting. This standard typeset size undoubtedly stemmed from the newsprint shortage and the resulting problems with printing space. However, when news of D-Day broke, America's editors ignored any such practical constraints and introduced the reading public to eye-catching, sensationalistic, and extraordinarily massive headline sizes that impressed upon the reading public the notion that the Invasion was an event unlike any other during the war. As part of their pre-Invasion planning and preparations, many newspapers had pre-cut front-page plates with the usual one- or two-inch headline letter sizes. However, the "release of pent-up emotion" among the American populace, a phenomenon that General Eisenhower had warned would occur when news of D-Day finally broke, seemingly gripped the editorial staffs of many newspapers, prompting them to retool their front-page plates with outsized headlines.[20]

Many newspapers, while still breaking their own editorial paradigms, made comparatively modest increases to their headline typeset size.[21] In these cases, headline dimensions increased to three inches or slightly more. New York's *Daily News,* in its tabloid format, stuck to its traditional three-inch headline letters, which still proved to be eye-catching. Likewise, in Lansing, Michigan, the *State Journal* proclaimed "Invasion" in three-inch letters but, for added effect, extended the paper's width by two inches. The newspaper's physical size now competed with the headline typeset in suggesting the grand scope and scale of the Invasion. The *Los Angeles Evening Herald and Express* kept the term "Invasion" in its subtitles and instead used three-inch letters to declare "Drive Into France." The *Toledo Times* used the paper's three-and-a-quarter-inch headline to report plainly, "Invasion Starts." In using only a modest one-inch increase in headline size, many American newspapers still managed to convey to readers that D-Day was a paradigm breaker.[22]

But the real paradigm-breaking took place with those newspapers that strove for truly stunning results by employing exceptionally oversized headlines. Many newspapers opted for four- and five-inch letters that dominated the top halves of the newspapers themselves. The various editorial staffs readily traded content space for maximum visual impact. Chicago's *Daily Times*, a tabloid-sized paper like New York's *Daily News*, outdid its New York cousin with evocative four-and-a-half-inch letters silently screaming "Invasion." Similarly, the five-inch word "Invasion" splashed across the front page of the *Detroit News* nearly consumed the top half of the paper. Alongside an enlarged photograph of General Eisenhower and a smaller, one-and-a-half-inch sub-headline reading "Gen. Eisenhower Reports: Big Landings in France," the overall layout had powerful visual impact. The *San Francisco Examiner* pushed its four-inch headline "Invasion Opens!" to the uppermost part of the front page and above the masthead, in turn forcing readers' eyes to the very top and then guiding them down to the bottom of the news-filled page.[23]

Of all the newspapers breaking size paradigms for their headlines, only a handful of papers matched the license taken by the editors of the *San Francisco Chronicle*. The *Chronicle* nearly broke all records by using seven-and-one-quarter-inch typeset to blast the word "INVASION!" from its front page.[24] In fact, the headline had such a striking effect among the populace that an AP photographer captured a group of smiling American civilians and a Free French sailor (most likely in the United States for training) assembled at San Francisco's Powell and Market Streets holding up a copy of the *Chronicle* to reveal the oversized Invasion headline. In this case, the gigantic and highly evocative headline managed to bring Americans and Allies together in a public space to celebrate the Invasion's beginning.[25] For their part, the *Los Angeles Times* and the *Los Angeles Examiner* each used headlines that were nearly as large as those used by the *Chronicle*.[26] The editorial staffs of these papers deliberately sought to evoke maximum impact by employing such visually striking banner headlines.

Numerous newspapers throughout the nation opted for another method to show American readers that the Invasion stood apart from all other military operations—the use of red ink in the headlines and elsewhere on the front pages. Although American newspapers had used color in the past, they did so sparingly—most likely because it smacked of excessive sensationalism (not unlike the oversized headlines). Furthermore, the use of red ink slowed press speed.[27] Even so, many newspapers employed headlines colored in red to grab the public's eye and, undoubtedly, to beat competitors in sales at the newsstands. The *Pittsburgh Sun-Telegraph*, for example, employed oversized, nearly four-inch letters in red that fairly shouted "Invasion" from above the masthead. The *Wichita Falls Record News* in Texas did the same except with slightly smaller three-inch letters. The *Erie-Dispatch Herald* saved front-page news space by sticking to one-and-a-half inch letters but coloring them in red ink to spell out "Invasion," which still elicited the same effect as the other newspapers employing color. Several other papers used red ink, but with headlines highlighting various aspects of D-Day while avoiding the now ubiquitous use of the term "Invasion." For example, the *Abilene Reporter-News* of Texas kept the word "Invasion!" in black ink but at the bottom of the front page while reserving red ink for a comparatively sedate headline just below the masthead—"Allies Land on Coast of France." In most cases, red ink enlivened the broader messaging adorning several front pages. The *Pasadena Independent* made good use of its two-inch red letters to proclaim, "This Is It!" while the *Seattle Daily Times* used red letters to report, "Allies 41 Mi. Inland—Nazis." For its part, San Francisco's *Call Bulletin* used nearly three-inch red letters to assuage anxious audiences with only two words: "Invasion Clicking!" Thus, the extraordinary and widespread use of red ink on the nation's front pages only confirmed for Americans the exceptional nature of D-Day in the greater war effort.[28]

Some newspapers employed highly creative headlines that mixed red ink with unusual graphic and layout patterns, further reinforcing the impression that D-Day was an event like no other. The *Seattle Star* arranged the word "D-Day" in two-inch letters on the left side of the front page but vertically and against a red field, thus altering the traditional visual arrangement of the front page in a unique and eye-catching way. Additionally, and for further effect, the *Star* used salmon-pink paper for the front-page foldout, an equally bold editorial statement given that salmon pink was traditionally reserved for financial and monetary newspapers. The *Montana Standard* took headline creativity to a much higher level by combining one-and-a-half and four-inch letters in red ink to spell out, respectively, "Continent Invaded." This headline's most remarkable feature stemmed from the fact that each of the four-inch letters spelling "Invaded" included within them red-shaded photographic representations of American soldiers, paratroopers, aircraft, ships, and artillery in action. Few newspapers on D-Day measured up to this level of creative license.[29]

One approach to headlines that had become a mainstay among many newspapers during the war—and which editors on D-Day embraced with renewed vigor—was the rich and varied use of aggressive-sounding verbs to describe the troops' assault activities. Syndicated cartoonist Sgt. Bill Mauldin registered his displeasure during the war with such headlines, which often described "smashing armored columns" and "ground forces sweeping ahead." For a front-line soldier like Mauldin, such characterizations failed to capture the slow, hard, painful slogging of true combat. Despite Mauldin's plea that America's newspaper editors "clamp down a little harder on their enthusiastic rewrite men," newspapers on D-Day wholeheartedly indulged in this practice, ostensibly casting America's troops and those of her Allies as owning the initiative on 6 June 1944.[30]

Aside from splashing the word "Invasion" across the front pages, many papers described the Allied troops (much to Mauldin's chagrin) as engaging in an abundance of "smashing." The *Boston Traveler* blared, "Allies Smash Way 9 ½ Miles into France," while the *Cincinnati Times-Star* proclaimed that the "Allies Smash Ahead—Opposition Is Light." The *Journal—Every Evening* (Wilmington, Delaware) pitched in with "Allies Smashing Inland." Other papers chose verbs with even harder-hitting connotations. The *Akron Beacon Journal* posted, "Allies Punch Inland From The French Coast," while Omaha's *Evening World-Herald* declared, "Allied Invasion Armies Rip 'Several Miles Inland.'" Other newspapers described the Allied invaders as "speeding," "slashing," and "cracking" their way through Hitler's Atlantic Wall.[31]

Contrary to this approach, some hometown newspapers eschewed the overblown verbs describing the troop landings in France and instead opted for language that conveyed optimism about the operation's prospects and immediate successes. Editors generally knew their audiences, so their headlines reflected their particular reading population's angst about D-Day. Newspapers that allayed any fears of D-Day's failure or the loss of many young American men would likely make the news more attractive to the public and help maintain support for the war. Thus, many headlines included language suggesting that the Allies were making early progress in the form of "gains." The *Chicago Daily News* reported, "Invaders Gain," while the *Daily News* of Los Angeles exclaimed, "Allies Gain In Invasion!" The *Sun* (New York) stated, "Invasion Gains Several Miles." Some headlines even spoke in the language of winning. The *Columbus Citizen*, while proclaiming broadly that "Allies Invade France," included a caveat that claimed, "Beachheads Won Along North Coast," while the *Fresno Bee* heralded, "Allies Win Foothold In France." Some headlines even attempted to assuage fears of high casualty rates, such as Tennessee's *Elizabethton Daily Star*, which stated that "Allied Troops Smash Way Inland On Broad Front," and added, "Losses Slight." The *San Jose News*'s headline perhaps did the most to calm jittery home-front nerves with a simple message: "Invasion Is O. K. So Far."[32]

Although exploiting front-page headlines as an imagistic pronouncement of the Invasion's broader significance, a few editors used them to temper the otherwise American-centric messaging emanating from the overseas reporting. Since much of the Invasion news appearing in U.S. newspapers hailed from mostly American or pooled sources, some editors wanted to ensure that their audiences recognized the Invasion as a multinational team effort. For these editors, the ubiquitous use in the headlines of the term "Allies" to describe the broader Invasion forces insufficiently drove home that larger point. For instance, the *Toledo Times* in Ohio shared its large "Invasion Starts" headlines with a subhead reading, "Yanks and British Land Along Coast of France," which explicitly gave both American and British troops equal billing. Similarly, the *Wichita Falls Record News,* one of several newspapers to use three-inch letters in red ink to proclaim "Invasion," also made room on the front page for a slightly smaller headline claiming, "American, Canadian, British Troops Land On French Coast To Open Historical Invasion." This headline proved more inclusive by crediting the Canadian forces with an equal share of the Invasion burden; in fact, Americans would later learn that Canadian amphibious forces had assaulted one of the five Invasion beaches (code-named Juno) on their own.[33]

The weekly copies of America's Black newspapers published just days after the Invasion largely ignored D-Day as a headline event. Instead, these papers used their headlines to feature stories of strictly Black interest. However, as described earlier, a few Black newspapers featured the Invasion in their headlines, most likely as a gesture to White America in return for recent gains attained by young Black men and women, such as greater opportunity and advancement in the armed forces and in defense work. Even so, the wording of these headlines still managed to cut against the grain of the mainstream newspapers' more bombastic approach by providing a less sanguine version of the Invasion and its purported significance. For instance, the *Plaindealer* used regular two-inch typeset above the masthead of its 16 June 1944 issue to assert that "Combat Units Continue Bloody Invasion Against Nazism" with the caveat that "100,000 Black Troops Now in England." D-Day as a "Bloody Invasion" blatantly countered the more sanitized, more confident headlines appearing on 6 June 1944; but as the rest of the headline suggested, America's Black troops were on the ground and ready to help. The 10 June 1944 issue of the *Pittsburgh Courier* mimicked the mainstream headlines by using three-inch letters to claim, in rather cryptic syntax, "Dixon Covers Invasion: Race Troops Poised for Action." Certainly, the *Courier* wanted to advertise to its readers that their very own Black war correspondent, William Randolph Dixon Jr., was their overseas source of Invasion news, but the second part seemed open to interpretation. Were "Race

Troops" soldiers of color who were ready for action? Or were they just "Troops" who were ready to "Race" into the heart of Nazi-held Europe? In any case, the *Courier* ensured that the notion of race, in some form, found its way into the Black version of the D-Day narrative, regardless of the intended meaning.[34]

The headlines echoed what the political and military leaders wanted to convey to an American public whose attitudes about the war often waxed and waned: the belief that the Invasion was the war's turning point and the beginning of the home stretch to victory in Europe. Thus, the war effort needed the home front's support now more than ever.

Ultimately, these evocative headlines had the imagistic and semiotic power to carry both the emotion and importance of the Invasion with them through the years. These headlines lived on as nostalgically preserved clippings in scrapbooks, as complete newspaper editions hidden for years in cedar chests, or as artifacts in modern museums so that younger generations could discover or rediscover them and experience the power of the breaking news of D-Day as it happened on 6 June 1944. In effect, these headlines retained over the years the visual potency to signal to future generations the importance that America's newspapers had placed on D-Day.

◆ ◆ ◆

Newspapers relied on two other visual aspects of news representation to communicate the scope, scale, and significance of D-Day that radio could not match—the use of photographs and maps. When photographs and maps appeared together in America's newspapers, they worked in concert to portray the stark reality of the Allied war machine as well as the geographic space that such a military force occupied on the ground. When combined, these pictures and maps allowed America's readers on D-Day to rest their imaginations and instead gaze upon genuine images of American troops in action and the geographic space to which the war had now shifted. Journalists could now use pictorial images to augment the stories they communicated through the printed word. The photographs that managed to make their way into America's newspapers on D-Day thanks to AP Wirephoto and other photographic transmission methods had the most impact, even if these handful of images never showed actual combat on D-Day.[35]

These photographs served as the ultimate narrative-building enhancer for D-Day by offering an actual representation of the event as it was occurring. According to Peter Maslowski, "Photography forever altered the human vision of warfare by preserving" direct representations of war "with a vivid immediacy."[36] Photography was so advanced by World War I that it became an official military function; by World War II, photography and the war were "inseparable." In fact, U.S. government officials assumed that larger audiences were more likely to understand and react to visual images than written material, so they cautioned that photographs required greater care and oversight.[37] Ultimately, the Invasion would provide Americans with a substantial photographic chronicle of the war and become "the most intense collective visual experience in the nation's history."[38] But on D-Day itself, photographers only managed to capture an uncharacteristically fuzzy macro view of the operation, which worked to enhance the more optimistic aspects of the Invasion narrative. Grittier images of D-Day would come in the days and weeks that followed, but by that time the press had already firmly established in America's consciousness the less controversial version of the Invasion story—a narrative that resisted fundamental alteration even when the public later learned of the high casualty count on Omaha Beach and how the Invasion almost failed on that same strip of sand and shingle.[39]

As soon as news of D-Day broke, stateside newspaper editors craved eyewitness news reports and, above all, actual photographs showing Operation Overlord in action. Unfortunately, photographs arrived slowly and sporadically on D-Day, forcing editors to turn to their backup plans: stock photographs. The different means of photographic transmission from London to New York—radiophoto, telephoto, and the well-known AP Wirephoto—required dedicated time on the wires, cables, and radio circuits, so they often took low priority compared to the written bulletins.[40] Therefore, stock photographs tended to dominate the early editions, but as actual Invasion images came in, editors used a mix of both to convey visually to readers the immensity of D-Day.

For the most part, stock photographs attempted to portray what readers could not see in the absence of genuine Invasion images. The *Montana Standard* dedicated an entire page to a step-by-step rendering of how the Invasion likely unfolded, beginning with aerial and naval bombardments and reconnaissance activities followed by the first waves of soldiers hitting the shore under smoke screens, paratroopers striking from above, armored units off-loading landing craft, and support units and artillery pieces arriving on the beaches—all illustrated by stock images of training exercises depicting each of these activities. This graphic representation helped readers visualize what was happening half a world away in detailed photographs that spoke to the scope and breadth of the Allied effort. New York's *Daily News* employed a full centerfold spread of stock pictures showing a large paratrooper drop, the British fleet at sea, fully loaded landing craft, beach landings in action, mechanized cavalry vehicles, and a host of Allied fighter planes. Although not actual Invasion photographs, these images gave a powerful sense of the enormous sweep of the Invasion and its many moving parts. The *Akron Beacon Journal*, while splashing the first two actual Invasion images sent by AP Wirephoto across its front page, still used stock pictures of landing craft during a training exercise to portray "How The Allied Troops Landed in France Today" as well as early images of the German fortifications along the French coastline.[41] Although the use of preplanned stock photographs by America's newspapers lacked the power of actual Invasion shots, the use of these generic depictions still conveyed a potent sense of D-Day's vastness.

Unfortunately for America's newspapers, actual photographs of the Invasion taking place proved very scarce on D-Day, particularly images of the beach landings. The very same problems that kept correspondents from getting their copy off the American beaches also kept photographers from getting their film back to London. But this was not the biggest problem, especially on the deadliest of the American landing zones, Omaha Beach. Photographers from the Army's Signal Photographic

Companies who landed on the beach along with the civilian correspondents struggled to photograph any part of the assault because they were too busy taking cover from German machine-gun fire.[42] *Life* photographer Robert Capa and his colleague from Acme Newspictures, Bert Brandt, both landed on Omaha and took no chances. After snapping numerous close-up photographs of the bloody frontal assault, both men decided to hitch a ride back to London through a combination of returning landing craft and ships, with jeeps positioned on standby in England to get their photographs through the censors and onto the wires. Brandt was the first to have his pooled pictures grace the front pages of many American newspapers—a mere four hours after Communiqué Number 1 aired. Yet the only examples of Brandt's pictures that made the papers on D-Day were ones he had snapped of the embarkation while sequestered at a British port.[43] Either the censors held back his beach assault photographs, or the pool did not get them over the wires and circuits in time for publication in the 6 June editions.

Capa took the best, most iconic images of the Omaha Beach assault, and his unexposed film managed to survive the perilous return trip to London. He had snapped 106 graphic, close-in pictures of the landings with his Contax camera, but when a nervous darkroom assistant turned the heat too high on the drying negatives, the emulsion melted. Only eight frames survived, and those images presumably did not make it into any of America's newspapers on 6 June 1944. The American public would have to wait more than a week to see Capa's surviving images featured in the 19 June 1944 issue of *Life* magazine. The accompanying text claimed that despite initial reports on D-Day of light opposition, Capa's photographs portrayed "how violent the battle was and how strong the German defenses."[44] Ironically, the blurred images of men splashing through the surf and taking cover behind German obstacles helped capture a true sense of this violence and the raw terror, chaos, and gallantry inherent in such a deadly frontal assault, aspects of the fighting that clearer shots might not have conveyed.[45] These photographs, taken at great personal risk by Capa, captured some essential features of the operation that had the power to alter the optimistic tone surrounding the Invasion narrative that was beginning to crystallize in Americans' collective consciousness on D-Day.

Although the most dramatic images from the American sector did not cross the circuits on D-Day, the few actual Invasion pictures that spooled off the teletype machines on 6 June 1944 arguably had a powerful effect on readers. This handful of photographs, pushed over the wires before 12 p.m. EWT, fell into two basic categories—embarkation activities at the British ports and the Allied naval armada heading toward the French coast.[46] These subjects still conveyed D-Day's magnitude through images of young, heavily equipped GIs marching by the hundreds through quaint British villages toward the docks, boarding landing craft, and even kneeling in the street for a chaplain's blessing. Other images captured the incredible scale of the vast Allied naval armada heading toward the Normandy coastline. These subjects would have proved mundane in any other circumstance, but in the highly censored atmosphere of D-Day, and given the problem of getting film from the beaches to London, they became the most powerful evidence for Americans at home of the massive undertaking known as Operation Overlord.

While the embarkation images touted by most American newspapers as the "first Invasion Pictures" did not portray troops in actual combat, they helped to illustrate the extent of the raw human investment in the Allied enterprise.[47] Three embarkation images in particular became the most widely published photographs to reach America's newspapers on D-Day—each one almost certainly snapped by Acme's intrepid Bert Brandt, who later received credit among his peers as the first war correspondent to deliver beachhead pictures to the pool.[48] The three photographs, although lacking in crisp detail because of obvious attempts by censors to remove or blur certain details such as unit patches, portrayed scores of equipment-laden GIs packing themselves tightly into landing craft docked in an unknown British port. The photographs had the potential to identify certain men, so the photography censors blurred or retouched some of their facial features to conceal their identities. The unintended effect of rendering each GI's face unrecognizable is that American readers could project onto those anonymous personages the faces of their own loved ones who might be Invasion participants, in turn providing a seemingly personal connection to the photographs because of the images' "everyman" character. One of the three images also showed larger landing craft loading half-tracks onto the flat-bottomed vessels, testifying to the remarkable investment in matériel as well as soldiers. Since these images derived from American news sources and were intended for American newspapers, they did not feature other Allied troops. The clear priority for the American news agencies was to get the domestic story of D-Day into America's newspapers first.[49]

Aside from these three ubiquitous embarkation images, other less widely published photographs of these activities appeared in selected newspapers and further contributed to the trope that D-Day was truly an immeasurable undertaking. One of these other images depicted more than a hundred heavily laden, fully armed American assault troops marching in formation down an English street headed for the port and their assigned landing crafts. The soldiers seemed alert and confident, and their numbers alone testified to the human contribution to the operation and its potential cost in lives lost.[50] Another embarkation image showed GIs receiving rations of candy and cigarettes before loading onto their transports. The men found solace in God for their angst as evidenced by another image taken just prior to embarkation and sent out via International News Soundphoto. In this picture, a chaplain in white vestments, hand raised in benediction, blesses scores of GIs kneeling in an English street just prior to boarding their landing crafts.[51] The poignancy of this image suggests a sense of righteousness in their cause but also conveys an underlying fear among the men that the butcher's bill for this enterprise might be very high.

Remarkably, and clearly an exception to the rule on D-Day, New York's *Binghamton Press* featured a racially inclusive portside image sent out by AP Wirephoto depicting Black naval personnel readying their five-inch guns for the cross-Channel assault, thus demonstrating that all Americans were in this operation together. The message was clear: the Invasion was so big that all Americans, regardless of race or creed, had a role to play.[52]

The second category of photographs to appear widely in America's newspapers on D-Day, and which further advanced the trope of D-Day's enormous sweep and importance, were images of the actual Invasion armada at sea. These images, although lacking the impact that images of the actual beach landings would have conveyed, still testified to Overlord's immensity. The first of these images came from a British news source as part of the press pool and portrayed the Invasion armada as seen from the air. The aircraft's wingtip is visible in the foreground while below, stretching out to the water's horizon, are hundreds of Allied warships and landing craft of every type that, according to the caption on the front page of Omaha's *Evening World-Herald*, were awaiting "the historic signal to get under way for the gigantic land, sea, and air assault on Adolf Hitler's Fortress Europa." The image quality suffered from excessive retouching, creating a surrealistic impression of the Invasion fleet and leaving one's imagination to fill in the blanks.[53]

The second most commonly published photograph of the Invasion armada depicted with greater clarity numerous infantry-laden landing craft surging through the English Channel on their way to the Normandy beaches. One added detail not evident in the British aerial image is the presence of dozens of barrage balloons hovering over the advancing fleet as protection against low-flying German aircraft. This detail suggested that at the moment the photographer snapped the image, the Invasion had truly begun and the men cramped inside those landing crafts were about to put themselves directly in harm's way in order to breach the German coastal defenses of Normandy. Even though both images sped over the wire and into the pages of America's newspapers, they did not identify the naval craft as belonging to any single nation but instead, through their blurry, impressionistic quality, represented the collective Allied effort. The scope of the Invasion, despite nation-centric reporting evident in British, Canadian, and American newspapers, involved much more than the efforts of a single Allied nation. Instead, the magnitude of D-Day resulted from the collective efforts and resources of multiple Allied nations, and these two Invasion pictures perhaps made this point most clearly to the American—and Allied—reading public.[54]

The embarkation and armada photographs blended the human element of the Invasion into the larger D-Day landscape, but some late-breaking images on 6 June 1944 managed to bring the human contribution into sharper relief. For instance, the *Seattle Daily Times*, while still printing the embarkation and armada images, added some other just-released AP Wirephoto submissions to its "War Extra" edition that reminded America's reading public that the Invasion's success depended on the sacrifice and gallantry of American soldiers. First, the *Times* added to its photographic essay the now-famous image of General Eisenhower meeting with young members of the 101st Airborne Division at an airfield somewhere in England on the eve of the Invasion. Thanks to stock images used throughout D-Day, readers had a good idea of the perilous nature of airborne operations into enemy territory. These men were unmistakably about to put their lives on the line: the assembled paratroopers' smudged faces and their unit insignia obscured by censors while only the supreme allied commander is identifiable. Americans at home could again project upon these images the faces of their own loved ones, in turn connecting with the Invasion in a way that certainly had personal impact. Finally, the *Times* reserved for the front page another late-breaking D-Day image showing GIs offloading an injured paratrooper from a transport plane somewhere in England under the headline: "First Casualty Back in England." The accompanying caption identified the soldier as the "first American casualty in the Western European invasion" (a questionable assertion given the Invasion's magnitude) and suffering from a "head wound from enemy small-arms fire."[55] At least some Americans could recognize as part of their collective understanding of the Invasion the genuine human cost of war—and as close to seeing the "face of battle" as they could through the American reportage on 6 June 1944.[56]

Although America's newspapers on D-Day did not publish—or even have available—images of graphic combat or dead American soldiers, the photographs that did manage to accompany the written reporting still served as potent visual components that made "a distant war seem real" to an American populace whose continued support was essential to victory.[57] Like the fast-breaking radio coverage and summarized newspaper narratives, the specific images of the Invasion published on 6 June 1944 reminded all Americans that D-Day was bigger and more momentous than anything else in the war up to that time and that the Invasion needed home-front support.

◆ ◆ ◆

In addition to photographs, newspapers offered another visual representation of the Invasion news that helped readers see precisely where Operation Overlord was taking place geographically—maps. Nearly every newspaper on D-Day employed maps of varying sizes to assist Americans in shifting the war's focus and geography away from the Mediterranean and Pacific theaters to a completely new area of operations: the Normandy coastline. The maps increased Americans' sense of the operation's broad scope and geographic focus. In addition to serving as both orientation tools and measuring sticks, maps reminded readers that the war's global reach had now greatly expanded. Most importantly, the maps centered almost exclusively on the English Channel, allowing the American home front to visualize the ominous water obstacle the Allies had to overcome in order to reach the French coastline, further testifying to Overlord's true extent as the operation unfolded on 6 June 1944.

The most commonly used maps gracing the front pages on D-Day originated from the AP, whose regular AP Wirephoto spot map service constantly pushed updated images to its subscribers of the Invasion's operational area.[58] In general, these maps portrayed the southern coast of England—the launchpad of the Invasion armada—and the French coastline stretching from the Belgian border to the tip of the Cotentin Peninsula. Based on contemporary reports and intercepted German radio transmissions, the AP added black arrows pointing to known or suspected areas where landings or other Invasion activities were occurring. But as more and more bulletins appeared throughout the day, the AP struggled to keep up with the changes, in turn conveying to American readers a sense of the Invasion's rapidly expanding scope and magnitude as multiple editions throughout the day featured the frequently updated maps. One signature feature of the AP Wirephoto maps that set them apart from maps created and published by syndicated or individual newspapers was the use of American, British, and Canadian flags behind the various arrows in order to capture visually the multinational nature of the grand enterprise. An oft-published variation of the AP Wirephoto map credited to AP Features included cross-Channel distances from places like Portsmouth to Le Havre (114 miles) and Dover to Calais (22 miles) with additional labels indicating "Wide Sandy Beaches" in Normandy and a "Rocky Coast" near Cherbourg.[59]

Publishing revised maps or updating their own maps proved to be such a challenge to America's newspapers that some production editors resorted to crude solutions to add or shift directional arrows indicating landings or other operational events. The *Rochester Times-Union*, for instance, simply avoided recutting fresh printing plates by inexpertly hand-drawing white arrowhead symbols pointing to places like Dieppe, Le Havre, and Cherbourg.[60] The *Flint Journal* made no effort to keep up with the changing bulletins and instead added one sloppily drawn, double-headed white arrow pointing across the Channel from Portsmouth, England, to the Normandy coastline as if to say in blunt terms, "Invasion happening here."[61] The *New York Daily Mirror* opted for a more professional appearance in its directional arrows. Faced with the same flurry of incoming location changes, managing editor Hinson Stiles cut a series of curved and straight arrows from zinc plates and then glued them onto existing map plates, thus avoiding the delay in having to cut new plates. The final printed product gave the impression of a freshly cut map plate with sharply defined arrows. All of these rapid adjustments signaled to American readers the quickly evolving nature and complexity of the massive cross-Channel operation.[62]

Other newspapers employed more eye-catching efforts in portraying the Invasion's geographical locus. The *Chicago Daily News* published a highly detailed terrain-relief map of the Seine Estuary as seen from the invaders' perspective. Provided by the British Information Service, the relief map identified by name the small French villages and towns dotting the countryside—each one possibly in harm's way as the Invasion's war machine advanced inland.[63] The *Erie Dispatch-Herald* deployed an attention-grabbing, half-page terrain-relief map printed completely in red ink under the heading "Where Invasion Begins." Three large, red arrows traversed the Channel and pointed directly at Dieppe, Caen, and Cherbourg. Below that Invasion map was another large-size map depicting D-Day's anticipated contribution to defeating Nazi Germany by showing long arrows pointing from Le Havre, the suspected landing sites at the time, all the way to Berlin; similar arrows stretched from Italy and Russia to the heart of Berlin as well. This strategic map and its placement of D-Day in the context of the greater war effort conveyed the Invasion's significance and justified its grand scope and scale.[64]

◆ ◆ ◆

Newspapers throughout the nation on D-Day reinforced with great effect the thematic frame presented by the radio networks when news of the Invasion first broke—that D-Day was the most significant, most massive undertaking of the war and the beginning of the end for Hitler's Germany. By making unprecedented use of oversized headlines and by offering readers visual aids in the form of photographs and maps, America's newspapers—filled collectively with news from the same wire-service sources—built a common, impressionistic narrative of D-Day at the moment it was happening. Through common readership, Americans on 6 June 1944 constructed this thematically framed common narrative of D-Day in a way that cemented in their minds what D-Day should mean to all of them and how the operation stacked up in the context of a global war. But headlines, photographs, and maps were not the only means by which America's newspapers on D-Day created this common narrative. Newspapers also leveraged the principal means by which they communicated both facts *and* meaning to their readers—the written news story. Framed within the headlines and other visual representations of the Invasion were front-page news summaries assembled and reported by top war correspondents while the Invasion was underway. These news stories, written in punchy, no-nonsense prose, added greater depth and texture to the larger, more complex narrative, a story assembled from a flurry of nearly nonstop bulletins emanating from official

Allied and German sources. These written news summaries, synthesizing the myriad details bursting forth from overseas sources, contributed significantly to how Americans came to understand D-Day in the years to come. That first dynamic reportage of the Invasion on 6 June 1944 left a lasting impression on America's greater consciousness.

Edward R. Murrow, London, 1944 CBS/Getty Images

Bob Trout, June 1936 CBS/Getty Images

United States senators pose, in bipartisan fashion, around a radio during a pause in their legislative session to check on the Invasion's progress. Their smiles imply optimism that D-Day is going as planned. From left to right are Robert Taft (R-OH), David I. Walsh (D-MA), Tom Connally (D-TX), Arthur Vandenberg (R-MI), and Alben W. Barkley (D-KY). *AP Wire photo*

Striking workers from Wright Aeronautics use the oversized headlines on a copy of the *Cincinnati Times-Star* to celebrate the announcement of D-Day from a café near the plant. Production at the plant halted over a racial issue, a matter that news of the Invasion and the obvious sacrifice of American troops overseas seemingly could not overcome so that war-related production could resume. *Cincinnati Post Collection; Cincinnati History Library and Archives, Cincinnati Museum Center*

A Free French sailor displays the enormous headlines used by the *San Francisco Chronicle* on 6 June 1944 to announce the Invasion. Surrounding the sailor at San Francisco's Powell and Market Streets are U.S. naval personnel and civilians. *AP Wire photo*

The Invasion Is On!

Allies Punch Inland From French Coast

BEACHHEADS SECURE

First Invasion Pictures!

Two of the three most widely published images of the embarkation activities leading up to the cross-Channel assault on 6 June 1944 as they appeared on the front page of the *Akron Beacon Journal*. Censors clearly retouched the image on the right to ensure unit patches or facial features were unrecognizable. The photograph is credited to Associated Press Wirephoto via Signal Corps Radio. Acme Newspicture's Bert Brandt is the likely source of the image. Akron Beacon Journal/IMAGN *Content Services*

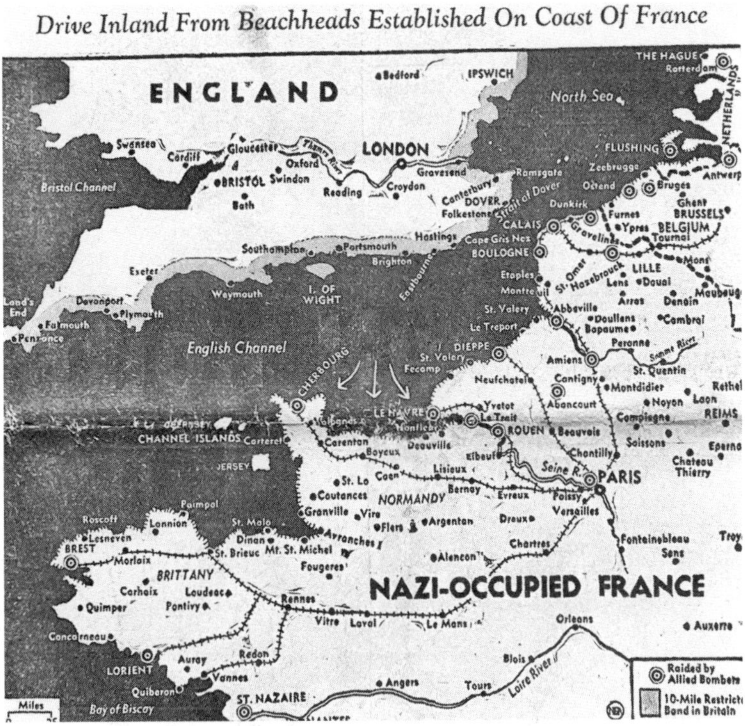

Standard map of the Invasion of the type used by many newspapers on D-Day. This map appeared on the front page of the *Sheboygan Press*. Note the crudely articulated arrows pointing to Le Havre and Cherbourg to identify the known landing sites. Sheboygan Press/IMAGN Content Services

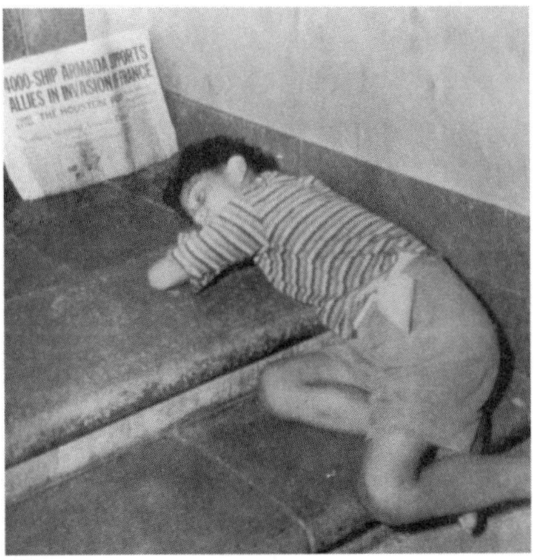

The frenetic pace of the multiple newspaper editions hitting the streets on 6 June 1944 is most evident in this ten-year-old Houston, Texas, newsboy. The original AP caption read: "With only one more invasion extra to sell, he fell fast asleep on the steps of a downtown office building." Note that the copy of the *Houston Post* in the background is already on its third extra of the day. *AP Wire photo/Author's collection*

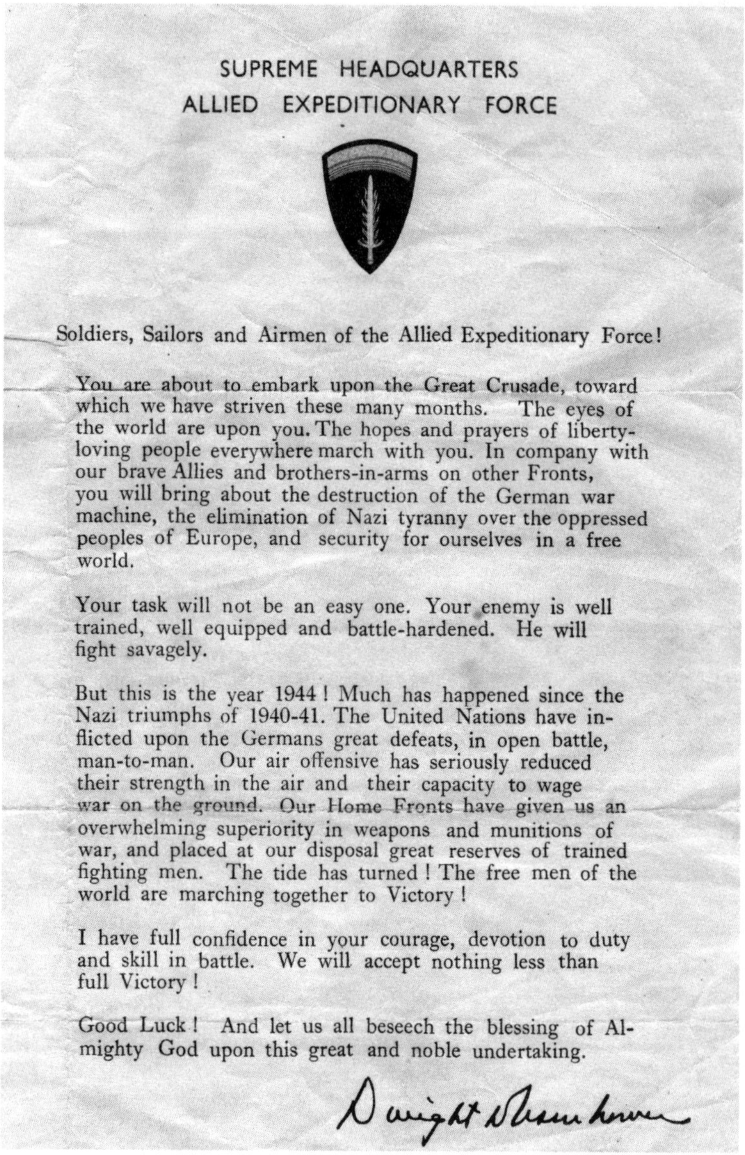

SUPREME HEADQUARTERS
ALLIED EXPEDITIONARY FORCE

Soldiers, Sailors and Airmen of the Allied Expeditionary Force!

You are about to embark upon the Great Crusade, toward which we have striven these many months. The eyes of the world are upon you. The hopes and prayers of liberty-loving people everywhere march with you. In company with our brave Allies and brothers-in-arms on other Fronts, you will bring about the destruction of the German war machine, the elimination of Nazi tyranny over the oppressed peoples of Europe, and security for ourselves in a free world.

Your task will not be an easy one. Your enemy is well trained, well equipped and battle-hardened. He will fight savagely.

But this is the year 1944! Much has happened since the Nazi triumphs of 1940-41. The United Nations have inflicted upon the Germans great defeats, in open battle, man-to-man. Our air offensive has seriously reduced their strength in the air and their capacity to wage war on the ground. Our Home Fronts have given us an overwhelming superiority in weapons and munitions of war, and placed at our disposal great reserves of trained fighting men. The tide has turned! The free men of the world are marching together to Victory!

I have full confidence in your courage, devotion to duty and skill in battle. We will accept nothing less than full Victory!

Good Luck! And let us all beseech the blessing of Almighty God upon this great and noble undertaking.

Dwight D. Eisenhower

Original copy of General Eisenhower's Order of the Day distributed to all participating troops on D-Day *Author's collection*

Whole Nation Kneels In Prayer

The Sheboygan Press

THE PAST IS GONE — WE FACE TO-DAY

VOL. XXXVII, NO. 145 SHEBOYGAN, WIS., TUESDAY, JUNE 6, 1944 PRICE 5 CENTS

INVADE EUROPE!

Allied Troops Land On Coast Of Normandy

Drive Inland From Beachheads Established On Coast Of France

Airborne Units Attack Between Seine And Orne

Wisconsin's *Sheboygan Press* used one-inch letters above the masthead to proclaim on 6 June 1944 that the "Whole Nation Kneels in Prayer." **Sheboygan Press/IMAGN** ***Content Services***

People leaving a synagogue on West 23rd Street in New York City following special D-Day services. The sign indicates that worshippers of all faiths were welcome. *Library of Congress*

Women and men praying at St. Alphonsus Church in Baltimore, Maryland, on 6 June 1944. The *Baltimore Sun*'s editorial staff marked this image for cropping to focus on the four women kneeling in the aisle. This uncropped image illustrates just how women worshippers dominated the churchgoing population on D-Day. Baltimore Sun *Media Group*

President Franklin D. Roosevelt conducting a wartime radio broadcast over the major networks in January 1944. *FDR Presidential Library and Museum*

An AP Wirephoto titled "Invasion Leaders' Wives Broadcast Messages to Their Husbands and Their Troops." From left to right, Mrs. Harold R. Stark, Mrs. Carl A. Spaatz, Mrs. James H. Doolittle, and Mrs. Alan G. Kirk are speaking from NBC's Washington, DC, studio on 6 June 1944. *AP Wire photo*

Unconventional, publicly available media representations of D-Day appeared in the days and weeks following 6 June 1944, allowing members of the American public to purchase these items and reexperience the Invasion in the privacy of their own homes as the press reported it. From left to right, Hagstrom's Invasion Map of Europe, two D-Day commemorative covers postmarked on 6 June 1944, a set of fifteen "Invasion" cards bearing Signal Corps photos of the landings, NBC's four-disc record set of their Invasion-day broadcast, and a 16-mm home version of the D-Day newsreel produced by Castle Films, including the same footage seen in theaters. *Author's collection*

The cathedral-style archway overlooking the entire National D-Day Memorial site in Bedford, Virginia. The archway not only suggests the significance of D-Day in America's collective consciousness, but also gives the rest of the memorial below it an altar-like quality that sanctifies their sacrifice and valor with its realistic statues of GIs emerging from the surf under heavy German fire. *Courtesy Angela Rusiecki*

CHAPTER 4

"Nothing Less Than Full Victory"

Newspapers Seize the Narrative

Supreme Headquarters, Allied Expeditionary Force, June 6—(AP)—American, British and Canadian forces landed by daylight in massive strength on the Normandy coast of France today and sped inland from quickly-established [sic] *beachheads. Gen. Dewight* [sic] *D. Eisenhower told his troops this grand assault was a crusade which must bring "nothing less than full victory."*

—Wes Gallagher, Associated Press
Raw Wire Feed, 6 June 1944[1]

Seasoned war correspondent Wes Gallagher, chief of the AP's Invasion Staff in London, leapt from his chair and tore out of the room and toward the telephone the moment officials at SHAEF released all reporters to submit their first dispatches about the Invasion. It was 9:32 a.m. London time, and SHAEF had just broadcast Communiqué Number 1 to a stunned world. Earlier that morning, SHAEF officials had summoned Gallagher and more than a hundred other war correspondents to report at 6 a.m. to SHAEF headquarters. When the correspondents arrived, the officials locked them inside a conference room and informed them the Invasion was on. However, the journalists could do nothing until the first communiqué announcing D-Day went out over the airwaves. For three-and-a-half hours, Gallagher and his colleagues received official and other reports of the Invasion's progress, enough information for Gallagher to craft a 1,300-word summarized narrative of D-Day that would soon appear as the front-page story on many of America's newspapers.

Gallagher recognized the significance of the story he had just crafted and the importance of beating his competition to the wires. So when the SHAEF officials opened the doors, Gallagher, one of the AP's top reporters, nearly upended his chair. He had already dispatched a hard copy of the story by courier to his boss across town, Robert Bunnelle, the AP's London Bureau chief. But experience had taught Gallagher that a follow-up report via telephone would ensure that the story hit the wire immediately. Thus, the AP's summary of the Invasion became one of the first to appear on the front pages of America's newspapers. It was framed by remarkable headlines, photographs, and maps—all assembled and presented, quite imaginatively, by a variety of editors and their news staffs to convey the D-Day story as it was unfolding to an already anxious reading public.[2]

◆ ◆ ◆

While the visual wonders of newspapers—creative headlines, Wirephoto images, and maps—quickly grabbed the American public's attention about D-Day, the main stories of the Invasion appearing on the front pages of each edition offered newspaper readers a more traditional means of comprehending what was happening half a world away: the news story. These main news stories encapsulated the key, but relatively limited, details that cast D-Day as a major enterprise of breathtaking scale. These stories, like the radio networks' roundups, distilled and then summarized the torrent of bulletins and reports emanating from eyewitness correspondents, official Allied sources, and even German news agencies into a comprehensible but rapidly evolving Invasion narrative, all of which spoke to the enormity of D-Day.

◆ ◆ ◆

The headlines splashed across America's newspapers, while a powerful means of communication in their own right, served a very specific purpose—to draw the reading audience into the main story about the Invasion. These main stories, collected from diverse snippets of information from a multitude of sources, represented the information each newspaper sought to convey to its readers. While radio played upon the dramatic, emotional aspects of news conveyance within a narrative framework, Americans looked to newspapers to arrest the rapid, chaotic transmission of information coming over the airwaves to improve, as postwar studies have shown, the "readers' knowledge of what is going on around them."[3] Radio largely played to the emotions while newspapers principally played to the mind; when combined, both means of news transmission helped convey to the American public the main thematic frame that cast D-Day as the war's most significant undertaking.

The greatest unifying factor enabling the creation of a common Invasion narrative rested on the fact that the newspapers, like their radio cousins, relied primarily on the same three major wire services—the AP, UP, and INS. Of the three, the AP remained the gold standard in unbiased news gathering with the UP and the INS following in that order. Unsurprisingly, the main stories attached to the newspapers' diverse and highly creative headlines came primarily from the AP and the UP. These front-page Invasion summaries, which varied slightly in organization, description, and length, summarized America's understanding of the D-Day narrative and how the American public should view the Invasion, as the AP proclaimed it, as "the greatest overseas military operation in history."[4]

In the same way that radio listeners came to identify with two main commentators on D-Day—CBS's Bob Trout and NBC's Robert St. John—for their larger understanding of the unfolding D-Day narrative, the AP's Wes Gallagher and the UP's Virgil Pinkley, both well-known wire-service correspondents, each commanded the front-page bylines of the main news summaries. The radio networks relied heavily on the same wire-service reports cabled by Gallagher and Pinkley, while the newspapers—privy to the same information—could only bring those details to the American public hours later. Of the two main-story bylines gracing America's front pages on 6 June 1944, Wes Gallagher had the most followed by Virgil Pinkley.[5] Each war correspondent was well-seasoned and well-respected among other journalists in the industry as well as the public. Unfortunately for Gallagher and Pinkley, each man felt he had drawn the short straw by not being able to accompany the assault troops onto the beaches. Gallagher had fractured his spine in a jeep accident in

May 1943 while covering the fighting in North Africa, so this journalist who was considered the pride of the AP—the "bellwether of American correspondents"—instead became chief of the AP's Invasion staff for D-Day. His job was managing and assigning coveted reporting assignments to his colleagues while he remained behind in London to process their incoming reports.[6] Likewise, Virgil Pinkley, as head of the UP service in Europe, considered his role in remaining behind to supervise the UP's London office on D-Day to be one of his "greatest disappointments."[7]

The result of Gallagher and Pinkley remaining in London to process the incoming dispatches was that two of America's most experienced and talented journalists would craft the main front-page stories, essentially the baseline narratives in prose, that documented in a less ephemeral form than radio the developing narrative of D-Day as it occurred. Their assigned roles afforded them perhaps the most direct influence on how America created a very specific, thematically framed storyline of the Invasion. Gallagher's and Pinkley's respective wire services, and the fact that they were part of the larger press pool at SHAEF, ensured that their words and perspectives enjoyed the furthest reach among America's newspapers. Their narratives, like the ones broadcast by their radio colleagues, depended on what tidbits of information could get to London in a timely manner. While many pre-Invasion preparation plans bore fruit for both the radio networks and the newspapers, some fell short—especially for the print journalists and photographers working for the wire services. These shortcomings dictated what information the main newspaper stories could or could not convey as part of the unfolding Invasion narrative. Understanding the nature of the pre-Invasion press planning in the United States and in London is essential to a complete appreciation of how and why the main AP and UP stories featured on America's front pages expressed a very specific, thematically framed storyline.

◆ ◆ ◆

The wire services and newspapers throughout the United States engaged in the same level of pre-Invasion preparation as the broadcast networks to ensure speed and accuracy in reporting when D-Day finally arrived.

They each had call-in plans for their beefed-up news staffs and extended hours for printing-press crews. However, unlike the networks, the newspaper industry confined discussions of its pre-Invasion preparation to industry journals such as *Editor & Publisher* and did not push them overtly onto the public, a consequence of the newsprint shortage. By contrast, the radio networks, with much to prove as a nascent news medium, engaged in a more robust campaign over the more plentiful airwaves and in their trade journal, *Broadcasting and Broadcast Advertising,* to show the American public that radio would be ready when the Invasion kicked off.

The broadcasting networks' greatest concern prior to D-Day rested in their ability to receive uninterrupted voice transmissions live from overseas. On the other hand, the wire services, a longtime staple of the print world, already had sufficient cables in place to receive dispatches through their teletype machines from London or any other overseas node. And for good measure, New York's UP office added a leased wireless circuit as a redundant capability. Thus, getting copy from the wire-service correspondents overseas was not the immediate concern. What concerned the stateside newspapers was their ability to print the tidal wave of dispatches expected to flood all wire-service subscribers when D-Day began and then to distill that large corpus of information, all in accordance with Office of Censorship guidelines, into the few pages available to each newsprint-starved edition. While many newspapers planned extra editions, others did not because the paucity of newsprint precluded such a wartime extravagance. The subject of pulling advertising from the newspapers on D-Day also surfaced, but unlike the radio networks, many newspapers planned to withhold advertising on 6 June 1944, but they never followed through. Newspaper advertising, which was cheaper than airtime, pulled in five times the audience as radio.[8] Since all media survived on the advertising business model, few newspapers saw fit to pull their advertisements.[9]

An equal level of preparation also took place in London for the war correspondents accredited to SHAEF, but the biggest part of that plan—getting written dispatches from the landing beaches back to London and then over the cables to the wire-service offices in New York—fell victim to the friction of war. This shortfall shaped much of the narrative advanced by the newspapers and the media in general. The pre-Invasion press preparations in London focused on two specific areas: accrediting and then assigning the growing number of war correspondents jockeying for a front-row seat to the Invasion and, of course, crafting a plan to get these reporters' hard copy dispatches from the front lines and into the hands of teletype operators in London. In turn, the teletype operators shared the reports worldwide as part of SHAEF's mandate for global pooling during the first days of the operation.[10] Problems in getting dispatches off the beaches ultimately had the most direct influence on the overall content and thematic frames comprising the D-Day narrative.

Accrediting and assigning the vast number of war correspondents proved to be one of the greatest planning challenges for SHAEF's Public Relations Office. In the months leading up to D-Day, correspondents representing 115 news organizations from the United States, Britain, the British Empire, and Canada swarmed into London to bear witness to, and then report on, what SHAEF's head of Public Relations, Brig. Gen. T. J. Davis, deemed as "the biggest news story since the Deluge." Such hyperbolic statements about the Invasion's significance were rife in the halls of the Ministry of Information in London, undoubtedly influencing the attitudes of correspondents who would weave this thematic frame into their reporting.[11] Davis headed a public relations operation responsible for developing and implementing a press plan with a supporting architecture that would ostensibly allow more than five hundred accredited war correspondents to witness the Invasion and then get their stories through the censors and onto front pages and over the airwaves. The plan's success would determine how much or how little information the American public would have access to about D-Day on the very day it occurred.

For the American press, the most talented wire-service and independent newspaper reporters competed and jockeyed for the few spots available on the landing crafts that would ferry assault troops to the beaches. Despite the agreed-upon requirement to pool all news copy, these fiercely competitive reporters still intended to beat their competition by sending the first dispatches from the Invasion beachheads under the name of their wire service, newspaper, or news magazine. Unfortunately for these reporters, only twenty-eight of more than five hundred correspondents from all Allied nations would go in with the first waves, so only a handful of American reporters would accompany the assault troops onto the two American beaches.[12] Those reporters selected for these assignments had to be "fit and experienced in field work," according to the AP's trade magazine *AP Inter-Office*.[13] These selectees, many of whom underwent rigorous training with their assigned assault units, would accompany the troops in uniform wearing only war correspondent insignia and under full equipment, but unarmed.[14] The beaches represented the very epicenters upon which the entire operation's success or failure depended. Any dispatches coming from these locations would unveil to the home front not only the true "face of battle" but also how the American public would perceive the Invasion and its greater meaning. Only the very best, most experienced American war correspondents received these coveted assignments. Ironically, the level of graphic detail these war correspondents sought to convey to the American public was in direct tension with their stateside editors' desire to mediate the D-Day narrative in such a way that it conveyed an optimistic tone that would help allay public angst over the Invasion.

The fourteen war correspondents chosen to land with the first assault waves on the two American beaches, Omaha and Utah, represented the best and most well-known in the business. Of the group, three belonged to the wire services: the AP's Don Whitehead, the UP's Henry T. Gorrell, and the INS's Clark Lee. Whitehead was the most famous of the three; he had earned the nickname "Beachhead Don" for covering more Allied amphibious operations in the European theater than any other reporter.[15] Operation Overlord would be his fifth. Unfortunately for him, Whitehead drew Omaha, the bloodiest of the beaches, while Gorrell and Lee went to Utah. Four other print reporters were part of the mix: John O'Reilly of the *New York Herald Tribune* and John Thompson of the *Chicago Tribune* would accompany Whitehead onto Omaha Beach while Bill Stoneman of the *Chicago Daily News* and Australian Harold Austin of the *Sydney Morning Herald* covered Utah. Two *Life* magazine photographers, Bob Landry and the world-famous Robert Capa, would photograph the landings on Utah and Omaha. Independent photographer Bert Brandt of Acme Newspictures would backstop Capa on Omaha Beach. Four broadcast correspondents, two for each beach, rounded out the group. John MacVane (NBC) and Tommy Grandin (Blue) had Omaha, while Larry LeSueur (CBS) and Bob Dunnett (BBC) claimed Utah.[16] This collective group of correspondents all shared a strong sense of patriotism and adventure, especially the women correspondents who had to watch from afar.[17] However, when SHAEF's Public Relations Office offered the male reporters a chance to jump with the paratroopers to save precious space on the landing craft, nearly all of them demurred. Three female correspondents rushed forward and volunteered, but SHAEF quietly turned them down.[18]

Before a war correspondent could cover D-Day in any capacity, he or she had to be "an employee of a newspaper, magazine, news agency, broadcasting network, photographic agency or newsreel company."[19] Meeting this definition opened the door to accreditation by SHAEF, a process that allowed correspondents access to the battlefields and to military support while limiting through censorship what they could or could not report. In fact, as part of the accreditation process, correspondents agreed in writing to submit all news stories and photographs for censorship before submission.[20] For D-Day, censorship occurred at the source, meaning local commanders had the authority to silence all or some of a correspondent's reportage, ostensibly for security reasons. Some correspondents, like the AP's Edward Kennedy, saw censorship as "heavy-handed."[21] Some young and untrained censors did in fact perform poorly or made quixotic deletions; but for the most part, censorship at the source proved to be fair and generally timely, especially since Brigadier General Davis had implemented an intensive training program for censors prior to D-Day.[22] Agreeing to censorship gave the journalists rare access to senior leaders and to classified planning information about the Invasion, a "peek behind the curtain" of Overlord that further worried a handful of senior SHAEF officers already suffering from security jitters.

The only type of censorship war correspondents refused to countenance was political censorship.[23]

From SHAEF's perspective, accreditation meant "authoritative sanction for a war correspondent to accompany armed forces on military operations, for the purpose of witnessing actual combat" to "impart" what he or she saw "for the information of the public." But in order to fulfill this stated purpose, correspondents had to follow military rules, especially since accreditation made them subject to "military law and regulation." In fact, they had the "assimilated" rank of an Army captain or Navy lieutenant. Not surprisingly, the war correspondents covering D-Day were primarily White males. Women, according to the Public Relations Plan, "were eligible for reaccreditation within assigned quotas." However, their presence in the forward limits of combat zones would be limited to no closer than an Army nurse, roughly three miles.[24]

Black correspondents covering D-Day were also noticeably scarce. During the war, only twenty-seven American correspondents (none of them broadcasters) were Black, including one woman.[25] One of those correspondents, William Randolph Dixon Jr., represented the Black newspaper with the largest circulation in the United States—the *Pittsburgh-Courier.* In his front-page write-up for the *Courier* in the 10 June 1944 issue, Dixon (described by his editor as an "ace war correspondent") proudly proclaimed that he not only represented all of the invading troops, "but millions of colored peoples throughout the world."[26]

Some correspondents bristled at the strictures associated with accreditation and the limits it might place on how they reported the Invasion. The AP's irascible Edward Kennedy believed "credentialing—and the access to communications and transportation support it provided—was a direct way of controlling correspondents."[27] This dependence often brought correspondents into direct tension with the requirements of editors at home and SHAEF's impositions. In the end, "all war correspondents had to operate within two hierarchies"—that of their news organizations and that of the military establishment.[28] But this tug-of-war did not appear to be a significant problem, since most correspondents quickly assimilated into their assigned units and became an integral part of the war effort. Most American war correspondents never wrestled with the postwar charge leveled by Phillip Knightley that their wartime reporting could have been better. Knightley readily admitted that their identification with the cause was "excusable," even considering that some of their reporting bordered on propaganda but never crossed the line like their World War I predecessors. What Knightley found "less excusable" was their "incorporation into the military machine," which had the potential to leave bad news unreported.[29] However, when the Invasion began, no such intentional omissions appeared evident in the reporting of D-Day. The war correspondents, while clearly team players, showed themselves to be genuine professionals dedicated to truth and accuracy, and their Invasion reporting generally reflected these core principles.

One factor that significantly shaped the ability of all accredited war correspondents to bear witness to and report on D-Day was the direct, personal support of the supreme commander himself, Gen. Dwight D. Eisenhower, affectionately known as "Ike." Ike inherently recognized that "public opinion wins wars," so he believed firmly that journalists covering the Invasion required maximum latitude to report what they saw accurately and without bias to the American public—as long as the information was not of value to the enemy.[30] Eisenhower sent a letter to his commanders on 11 May 1944 directing them to provide material support to all war correspondents assigned to their commands as a matter of policy.[31] In recognizing the correspondents' "mission in the war and to assist them in carrying it out," Ike wove them into the Invasion machinery as "quasi staff officers" who were part of the overall operational effort, despite the concerns of some senior leaders that the correspondents might (and likely would) identify too closely with their assigned units.[32]

Ike further sought to shape the thematic overtones of the correspondents' reportage by issuing press guidance on 31 May 1944 advising journalists to avoid conjecture in their reporting or to boast about any reverses suffered by the Germans. The landings would only pierce the "crust," the beach defenses, while even harder fighting lay ahead in subsequent phases. In other words, D-Day might not "cause more than an indentation." But that dent in the fortress, according to Ike's guidance, would be a significant achievement nonetheless. Ike advised the reporters to "sell" the successful landings as "a great feat" and all successes in the phases that followed. Despite the latitude he afforded his correspondents, the supreme commander clearly sought to impose some measure of control on the thematic frames attending their Invasion reporting. Notwithstanding this overt effort to slant the correspondents' reportage, the press guidance still insisted, quite paradoxically, that the war correspondents should "present a correct and sober representation of events as they occur, and to leave the future to unfold itself." The underlying message to the war correspondents was that their "sober representation" of D-Day should praise the operation's great achievement in cracking the German defenses but that they should moderate their reportage to avoid unrealistically boosting the American public's expectations for an early victory.[33]

After accrediting and then assigning the war correspondents who would accompany the first waves, SHAEF's press planners faced a second challenge: cracking the problem of getting news dispatches, film, and wire recordings off the landing beaches and back to London for immediate censorship and rapid transmission to the United States. The war correspondents flying overhead in Allied aircraft had a guaranteed return trip to England, which almost ensured that their high-altitude impressions of the Invasion beaches and the aerial and naval bombing efforts would make the morning airwaves and early newspaper editions in the United States. Unfortunately, the reporters going in with the assault troops, particularly the wire-service and syndicated-newspaper correspondents, had no such guarantees.[34] The American public could only understand what was happening on the Invasion beaches from the print reporters, who could craft more effective, more nuanced, and more contextualized word pictures of D-Day's center of gravity.

Ever since the operations in North Africa, Sicily, and Italy, war correspondents remained collectively aware of the difficulties inherent in getting written stories from the battlefield to their stateside editors.

Syndicated columnist Ernie Pyle, who became a household name during the war for his unabashed portrayals of the average GI in combat, argued that the weakness rested in communications. Pyle told his fellow journalists that he made as many carbon copies as possible of each story but filed only one with the available communications medium. Next, he gave copies to every jeep driver, liaison pilot, or other vehicle driver heading in the direction of a radio terminus or cable node with instructions for personal delivery. Despite Pyle's efforts at redundancy, some stories never reached his syndicate's office in the United States. War correspondents like Pyle came to recognize early in the war that "getting the story was no longer the hardest part of the operation."[35] Getting the story *published* was the real challenge.

Despite these overarching concerns faced by all correspondents, the key planning documents from SHAEF remained notoriously light on detail when addressing how news dispatches would get back to London as part of the early pooling effort. The basic assumption, according to Operation Memorandum Number 24, "Press Policy," was that field commanders would ensure that reporters had the means to file their stories at the outset of D-Day. The document, titled "Public Relations Plan 'OVERLORD,'" offered slightly more detail by tasking the communications officer of Brigadier General Davis's Public Relations Division to prepare a "detailed press communications plan" that "will insure [*sic*] the most rapid, and equalized flow of press, pictorial and broadcast materials through normal channels to the public." In response, Davis's staff organized a publicity and psychological warfare battalion of nearly six hundred personnel to support all correspondents with transportation, communications, billeting, and food for Lt. Gen. Omar N. Bradley's planned 12th U.S. Army Group, which would activate once the troops established the beachheads. However, this organization did not solve the planning conundrum for getting dispatches off the beaches in the Invasion's early stages.[36]

The primary plan to negotiate the "overwater link" across the Channel relied on radio transmitters and teletype circuits provided by the correspondents' assigned units.[37] The backup system was far more complicated. As an interim measure, SHAEF planners organized a shore-to-shore channel around a speedboat-courier system, which would rush the correspondents' early copy, undeveloped film, and wire recordings to southern coastal ports in England, where SHAEF had installed tele-types for wiring news reports and from where motorcyclists could then hurry film and recordings to London news offices. The two groups of correspondents assigned to the American beaches each had two lieuten-ants at their disposal; these officers were equipped with a wire recorder, a generator, a jeep with a radio transmitter, a Morse telegraphic set, and knowledge of the speedboat plan.[38] Despite these preparations, the plan for bridging the overwater link between Normandy and England's south-ern ports seemed tenuous at best.

When the first waves hit the beaches in the American sector at 6:30 a.m. (London time) with their respective war correspondents in tow, things quickly fell apart due to the friction of combat and the basic inad-equacy of the communications plan. Omaha Beach turned into a bloody nightmare, with German machine-gun fire cutting down many of the assault troops as they disembarked. On Utah Beach, the GIs experienced lighter German resistance and suffered far fewer casualties due to a ser-endipitous navigational error that allowed them to avoid the strongest German defenses.[39] When the two pairs of lieutenants supporting the correspondents managed to get onto the beaches, they found that their respective radios could not transmit due to lost antennas or other prob-lems. Moreover, the Navy's courier boats were noticeably absent. Worse still, on Omaha Beach, the reporters' support jeep with the generators and everything else disappeared into a "chuckhole" at the shoreline, forcing the Blue Network's Tommy Grandin and one of the two press-support officers, Lt. George Fuller, to take cover under the cliff facing.[40] Don Whitehead managed to type out a story somewhere on the chaotic beach only to learn that Fuller's jeep and radio were gone; he quickly sought out sailors returning to England as couriers.[41] Whitehead could barely describe what he witnessed on Omaha. He later summed it up for Ernie Pyle with one understated phrase: "It was really awful."[42] In fact, Omaha proved so hot that photographers Capa and Brandt, after snapping numerous pictures on the beach, promptly hitched rides back to England on returning assault crafts. Only Brandt's photographs saw publication on D-Day.[43] NBC's John MacVane reverted to writing brief dispatches on Omaha because the radios he needed for broadcasting were either inoperable or under water. He entrusted his dispatches to an Army public relations officer, who promised to relay them through the Navy back to England. They never arrived. On Utah Beach, Bill Stoneman of the *Chicago Daily News* fumed because the radios he needed to relay his stories back to London were also somewhere under the surf. Like Whitehead and others, Stoneman hunted for couriers headed back to England, praying that his editor would eventually get the copy.[44]

Ultimately, a sketchy communications plan and the vicissitudes of war prevented America's best journalists from giving their readers a true sense of what the most critical part of the Invasion was like for their young men as it was happening on 6 June 1944.[45] This information vacuum on D-Day directly affected the content of the main newspaper narratives crafted by wire service men like the AP's Gallagher and the UP's Pinkley.

In London, both Gallagher and Pinkley had actually begun writing their initial news flashes and narrative summaries not long after the main assault waves hit the American beaches. Both men, along with nearly a hundred other accredited war correspondents, had been sequestered since 6 a.m. in SHAEF's conference room, where someone provided them with the text of Communiqué Number 1 and a general information briefing. SHAEF had outfitted the room with tables and typewriters, so Gallagher, Pinkley, and the other journalists, while waiting for the Invasion's official announcement, could begin typing their initial Invasion narratives for precensorship and immediate release as soon as SHAEF gave the word. During the roughly three-hour period that both men drafted their stories, they only had as their main sources official reports, a handful of eyewitness accounts from high-flying aircraft, and dubious German radio transmissions. No reports had arrived from their two wire service correspondents—the AP's Don Whitehead or the UP's Henry T. Gorrell—who landed on Omaha and Utah Beaches, respectively. In the absence of these critical eyewitness reports, Gallagher still produced a

1,300-word "running story" relying principally on official reports and not on the eyewitness accounts he preferred.[46]

At 9:32 a.m. London time, SHAEF simultaneously released both Communiqué Number 1 and the room full of sequestered correspondents. The reporters scrambled to file their stories and send their news flashes. Wes Gallagher made a beeline to a special telephone line the AP maintained at SHAEF's press quarters. Although he had already sent his news flash and main story by courier to the AP's London office, Gallagher took no risks and phoned his flash directly to his boss, Robert Bunnelle. Thus, thanks to Gallagher, the AP flashed Communiqué Number 1 to the world only one minute after its release, apparently beating the competition. Despite SHAEF's pooling mandate, competition among the wire services and syndicated newspapers proved so fierce that press pooling, which worked so well for the radio networks, functioned only sporadically on D-Day before collapsing within days.[47] Even so, the limited sources available to all wire services and news organizations still drove a common narrative despite individual efforts to upstage the competition. In the meantime, newspapers across the United States that subscribed to the AP and UP services (many subscribed to both) began producing front-page plates with stories under Gallagher's and Pinkley's bylines to accompany the papers' bombastic Invasion headlines. The first drafts of the written Invasion narrative were now coming over the teletype feeds and becoming available for public consumption.

◆ ◆ ◆

The main stories both Wes Gallagher and Virgil Pinkley crafted leading up to the release of Communiqué Number 1 further drove home the common thematic frame that D-Day was in fact the greatest, most significant event of the war. Both men, as well as most journalists on D-Day, liberally seeded their Invasion write-ups with linguistic flourishes proclaiming the Invasion as, in Gallagher's words, "the greatest overseas military operation in history."[48] Accompanying these often grandiose proclamations about the Invasion's significance were numerous details that helped American readers conjure up a sense that the Invasion, for all its scale and complexity, was in fact succeeding. These details, regardless of their sourcing, helped frame the main story coverage in highly optimistic terms, suggesting in some cases that German resistance proved so light that the beach landings, airborne operations, and air-support efforts were occurring almost effortlessly. If SHAEF's press-communications plan for getting reports from the beaches had at least managed some partial success, Gallagher and Pinkley would likely have softened the optimistic tone of their summaries, particularly if they had received dispatches from their reporters on Omaha Beach.[49]

The process by which the news summaries reached the public included a type of silent cooperation between groups of news personnel separated geographically and chronologically. Stateside editors received and processed the information coming over the wires and shaped it for ready consumption by an engaged but discerning American populace. This news production process taking place overseas and in America's newspaper offices affected the content, organization, and framing of both Gallagher's and Pinkley's front-page stories, especially since individual newspaper editors often had their rewrite men thoroughly revise the stories coming off the wires. Generally, the newspapers that printed each man's byline tended to hew closely to the text that ticked off the teletype. However, many newspapers simply rewrote the AP and UP stories so significantly that they did not resemble, in style or tone, the stories submitted by Gallagher and Pinkley. For that reason, many newspapers simply omitted the correspondents' bylines and just identified the wire service by name. Moreover, Gallagher and Pinkley revised their main stories constantly throughout D-Day, adding new information from bulletins, making corrections, and altering their lead-in sentences. Thus, the first 1,300-word main story submitted by Gallagher expanded and changed throughout the day, with differing newspaper editions throughout the country using the latest version spooling off the teletype. Stateside rewrite men sometimes inserted their own interpretative statements to communicate the operation's magnitude or importance, or they swapped out certain words with more colorful synonyms. Despite these continual adjustments by different players in the news-making process, the core themes and details comprising both Gallagher's and Pinkley's narrative summaries proved remarkably similar and consistent, providing to America's readers a common picture of the Invasion that would ultimately shape their collective understanding of D-Day for years to come.

For all their parallels in content and framing, Wes Gallagher and Virgil Pinkley each employed a unique style and tone that came through their respective narratives, regardless of how many rewrite men tinkered with their prose. "Gallagher, for instance, preferred to open each version of his roundups with hard-hitting details colored with superlatives, which helped to transmit at the outset the primary thematic frame of the operation's magnitude. In the version used most often on D-Day, Gallagher opened in the active voice, placing the main participants up front by proclaiming directly that "American, British and Canadian troops landed in northern France this morning." He quickly followed with inflated rhetoric stating that these three Allied nations had just "launch[ed] the greatest overseas military operation in history" under the command of General Eisenhower, who would "accept nothing less than full victory."[50] In the opening flourishes accompanying subsequent revisions, he described these same Allies as "smash[ing] their way inland on a broad front."[51] This language suggested positive action on behalf of the Allied troops, who apparently harnessed such a fierce resolve that they could overcome any resistance. More significantly, identifying by name each of the three main nations participating in Overlord instead of simply lumping them together as "Allies" helped to mitigate some of the nation-centric reporting that characterized much of the American newspapers' coverage on D-Day.

Virgil Pinkley's opening sentences shared a very similar pattern but provided the principal details in a slightly more nuanced, pragmatic tone. For instance, he captured in clear and unbiased language how D-Day had unfolded up to that point: "American, British and Canadian invasion forces landed in northwestern France today, established beachheads in Normandy, and by evening had gotten over the first five or six hurdles." While Gallagher used Eisenhower to evoke optimism and victory,

Pinkley instead referred to practical obstacles overcome by the invaders up to that point. He approached his reporting from within this results-oriented framework and with the expectation that his reading audience felt the same way.[52] Oddly enough, like his colleague, he ended his opening statement with an equally bombastic claim that the invading nations were participating "in the greatest amphibious assault of all time."[53] The similarities in each man's style and tone certainly outweighed any differences, but their subtle stylistic distinctions characterized the unique aspects of how each man approached his reporting.

One other common aspect evident in each of the two reporters' main stories materialized in the firm reliance each man placed on Communiqué Number 1 as the organizing fact around which he framed his front-page narrative. Issued at 9:32 a.m. London time (3:32 a.m. EWT), the communiqué represented what CBS had characterized as the only "solid bone to this story," clearly affirming that the Invasion had truly begun and that it was not an accidental news flash or a German propaganda scheme.[54] The sparsely worded communiqué—"Under the command of General Eisenhower, Allied naval forces, supported by strong air forces, began landing Allied armies this morning on the northern coast of France"—legitimized the overall reporting and confirmed to the American public that D-Day had finally arrived. An early version of Gallagher's narrative positioned the precise text of Communiqué Number 1 immediately after his opening sentence, demonstrating the importance he placed on the official statement. However, in subsequent versions, he wove the missive into the main body of his narrative by stating that "Allied forces had kept silent" until the release, which linked the message's timing directly to SHAEF's operational security strategy.[55] In the UP version, Pinkley blended news of the message into his story's main body by describing it as the "first official word of D-Day," in turn amplifying the statement's legitimacy and the rest of the Invasion narrative.[56] In addition to Communiqué Number 1, each reporter inserted references to Eisenhower's Order of the Day and its "crusading" language into his story, which the radio networks had already broadcast widely throughout America, and the fact that the supreme commander had taken to the airwaves to caution the people of Western Europe to be patient and to avoid "premature uprisings."[57]

The main stories contributed most significantly to conveying the magnitude and scale of the Invasion by quantifying the enormous numbers of aircraft and naval vessels participating in the operation, including the tonnage of bombs dropped and number of naval guns fired. Gallagher's initial story sent over the AP wire included in the first several sentences impressive numbers that undoubtedly drove home the scale of the operation to amazed American readers. In his signature snappy style, Gallagher wrote, "The seaborne troops . . . surged across the channel from England by 4,000 regular ships and additional thousands of smaller craft," and "Eleven thousand planes supported the attack."[58] Pinkley was more overt about the official nature of his sources when he wrote, "Gen. Dwight D. Eisenhower's supreme headquarters revealed that the Allied armies, carried and supported by 4,000 ships and 11,000 planes, encountered considerably less resistance than had been expected."[59]

Seizing upon these numbers and other details, Prime Minister Winston Churchill provided this information to the House of Commons on D-Day, resulting in numerous news stories suggesting that he was the principal source when in fact he served more accurately as an official amplifier of SHAEF's reports. In some cases, Gallagher and Pinkley repeated these numbers in quoting Churchill and described how the British leader used them to communicate the Invasion's magnitude. For example, in the UP narrative appearing on the front page of the *Boston Traveler*, Pinkley stated that "Churchill placed the total number of ships involved at 4000, at least 1000 greater than participated in the invasion of Sicily," which in turn provided a comparison between the two amphibious operations that elevated the scope and scale of Operation Overlord.[60]

Despite the same numbers being reported in both the AP and UP front-page summaries, Virgil Pinkley's UP clearly surpassed the AP in providing even more quantifiable evidence of the Invasion's enormity. Pinkley related that the previous night and into the early morning hours of D-Day, "thousands of Allied planes dropped more than 11,200 tons of bombs on German coastal fortifications," a quantity that testified to the sheer size of the Invasion effort. Pinkley further reported that "200 Allied minesweepers manned by 10,000 officers and men were clearing the approaches to the invasion beaches."[61] In an unusual approach, the rewrite men at the *New York World-Telegram*, subscribers to both the AP and UP, expanded Pinkley's front-page narrative by inserting late-breaking bulletins. The paper, which featured Pinkley's byline for the main story, inserted bulletins from the AP to add further details and numerical quantifications to the main UP story. Pinkley wrote that "warships succeeded in silencing shore batteries and laying smoke screens on schedule." But a modification by a *World-Telegram* rewrite man, who was obviously scanning both the AP and UP press feeds, decided to enhance Pinkley's report by including in brackets an added detail from the AP that "more than 640 naval guns, ranging from four to 16-inch, hurled many tons of shells accurately into the coastal fortifications."[62] Wes Gallagher had included this detail in his initial wire submission. Thus, in order to ensure the most complete picture of the Invasion for their readers, some U.S. newspapers with multiple wire-service subscriptions decided to engage in a localized pooling effort of their own making. Some editors recognized the power of numbers in making a clear point, so the *World-Telegram*, like many newspapers on D-Day, attempted to articulate a common narrative that encompassed as many of the rapidly emerging statistical details as possible.

The geographical enormity of the Invasion became most apparent to American readers through the numerous and hitherto unknown locations along the French coastline strewn throughout Gallagher's and Pinkley's reports. Official missives from SHAEF only confirmed that the landings were taking place along "the Normandy section of northwest France."[63] The Allied headquarters remained silent on all other geographical details. A day earlier, the American public had been following the geography of Italy as the Allies seized Rome, but now the maps appearing on America's front pages suddenly and forcibly redirected their attention to a new part of the world and to completely new place names.

Nearly all the places Gallagher and Pinkley pointed out as landing locations and areas of inland fighting actually originated from intercepted

German radio broadcasts, which cast some doubt on the accuracy of the reports or their potential to serve as propaganda. New place names in France such as Caen, Rouen, Le Havre, Cherbourg, Ouistreham, and Arromanches now appeared scattered throughout the AP and UP main stories because of the German reports. Gallagher and Pinkley each reported that the Germans had repeatedly identified the precise invasion zone as the hundred-mile stretch of coastline between the port city of Le Havre at the mouth of the Seine River and the tip of the Cherbourg Peninsula. For the most part, the German reports proved correct.[64] However, nearly all other German reports identifying landing or fighting locations included inaccuracies, suggesting a desperate attempt by the Wehrmacht and the German media to get a handle on the Invasion and, more significantly, that Overlord's deception plan had kept the Germans guessing.

Despite their inaccuracies, many of the German reports identifying landing and fighting locations and repeated in both AP and UP stories almost certainly created the impression that Overlord was more expansive in scope than it actually was. Gallagher and Pinkley each included a dubious report that Allied paratroopers and German troops were fighting forty-one miles inland near Rouen, which was far away from the actual Allied drop zones.[65] Reports about heavy fighting in Caen were also false; the Allies did not reach the city until after 6 June 1944. Pinkley included in his UP story that the DNB, duped by dummy paratroopers tossed out of Allied aircraft over Le Havre, had to retract their earlier assertion that actual Allied paratroopers had landed near the port city.[66] Perhaps the most apocryphal of the German news reports—which both reporters included in their round-ups—was the false assertion that the Allies had landed on the British Channel Islands of Jersey and Guernsey, which the Germans had occupied since 1940. In fact, both islands would remain in German hands until May 1945.[67] Despite these inaccuracies, those German reports upon which Gallagher and Pinkley relied for their Invasion accounts on 6 June 1944 only served to enhance the thematic frame that Operation Overlord was truly a momentous undertaking.

The AP and UP main stories also evoked a powerful sense of optimism by highlighting official proclamations of D-Day's early successes. In his initial breaking story for the AP, Wes Gallagher included a pronouncement from SHAEF after his opening paragraph that "German opposition was apparently less effective than anticipated." But as a seasoned war correspondent, Gallagher reflexively tempered this optimism by cautioning that the German opposition was also "fierce in many respects."[68] Despite his implicit misgivings about excessive optimism, Gallagher still included a report from SHAEF in a later revised summation that "airborne troops who led the assault before daylight on a history-making scale suffered 'extremely small' losses in the air."[69]

Virgil Pinkley's UP reports picked up on the same optimistic versions from SHAEF about minimal German resistance. Pinkley seized on the minimal resistance allegedly faced by Allied paratroopers and the "light" number of casualties. Pinkley wrote, "Many air-borne [*sic*] missions reported remarkably little anti-aircraft fire," a possible consequence of the massive pre-Invasion bombing effort. An eye-catching detail he inserted after this comment stated, "One large group of troop carriers returned to base without a single flak hole," suggesting to readers that the German defenses had collapsed and that overwhelming success was in the offing.[70] Both Gallagher and Pinkley appeared to become caught up in this wave of optimism, since each reporter liberally seeded his front-page stories with reports highlighting weak German resistance in the skies and at sea. In fact, wrote Gallagher, the "German navy was only represented by a few destroyers and E-Boats."[71] Pinkley reported that the "apparent key to the lightness of the Nazi opposition" rested in the thousands of tons of bombs dropped on German coastal fortifications the night before and on the morning of D-Day.[72] Some readers likely viewed the optimism inherent in these sanguine reports as further enhancing the scope and significance of the Invasion by suggesting that only a massive, all-in enterprise like Overlord could have cracked the German defenses so handily. This excessive optimism essentially ignored General Eisenhower's press guidance, which cautioned the reporters against creating the impression of an early victory.

The extensive bombing and naval gunfire effort in support of the beach landings received much attention in the official reports and subsequently in the front-page stories. Both Gallagher and Pinkley described the pre-Invasion bombing effort in highly expressive terms. Gallagher inserted into his narrative an official report that forty-eight hours before the landings, the Royal Air Force (RAF) and "American bomber fleets dropped a stupendous tonnage of bombs" on the coastal fortifications, turning the German defenses into "a jumping, jagged mass of flames."[73] Gallagher further enhanced the enormity of the bombing campaign by describing how bases in England "resounded to the roar of thousands of airplanes" throughout the night as returning RAF bombers met "big fleets" of American Flying Fortress heavy bombers headed for France.[74] Pinkley's UP report included even more highly descriptive quantifications of the bombing effort, claiming that more than 2,300 American and British heavy bombers had teamed up "in a shattering zero hour bombardment" the night before and on the morning of D-Day to send 7,000 tons of bombs raining down upon the German coastal gun emplacements.[75] Pinkley even broke character once again and indulged in hyperbole by declaring the bombardment to be "the greatest attack launched against a single objective in the history of aerial warfare."[76]

Details of the intense naval gunfire support proffered by SHAEF also enriched the narratives and spoke to the enormity of the cross-Channel effort. Gallagher offered the only hard number describing the scope of the naval-gunfire assault: "640 naval guns, ranging from 4 to 16-inch, hurl[ing] 'tons of shells accurately into the coastal fortifications.'"[77] Pinkley's UP report suggested the close-in nature of the naval gunfire by describing the first Allied assault pushing ashore "under a protective naval barrage of rockets and shells ranging up to 16 inches in diameter."[78] The combined naval and aerial bombardment was, in Pinkley's estimation, "earthshaking."[79]

Strangely enough, Gallagher and Pinkley each became unwitting propaganda organs for SHAEF by relaying official pronouncements about the scale of the Invasion's operational security and the possibility of landings outside Normandy—all part of the greater Allied deception plan. Such measures, both men implied, suggested that an ambitious enterprise such as Operation Overlord relied equally on matching wits *and* combat power with the Germans. For reasons of operational security, wrote Gallagher, SHAEF "kept silent on the [landing] locations, to exploit to the fullest whatever element of tactical surprise the Allies may have gained," in turn suggesting to the beleaguered Wehrmacht that the Normandy landings may have been a feint to draw German combat power away from the real landing zones elsewhere on the Continent. Moreover, Gallagher reported, SHAEF refused to confirm the capture of airfields near Caen or any other German report identifying where the Invasion was taking place.[80] He also added an optimistic note by explaining that in "four previous landings to date[,] the Allies obtained tactical surprise three times—at Anzio, Sicily, and North Africa." Salerno was the outlier. But three of four past successes meant that the Allies had a strong track record when fooling the Germans.[81]

When the topic fell to deliberate deception operations, Gallagher and Pinkley were both inclined to boast about the extensive measures SHAEF had launched against the Germans on D-Day. Pinkley took no issue with relaying a SHAEF spokesman's "hint" or, more accurately, misinformation, that "operations may soon be extended to Holland and possibly to other countries in western Europe."[82] Such pronouncements not only roiled German sensibilities but obviously misled American readers, since the landings were in fact confined solely to Normandy. Both reporters also seized on one detail of deception ingenuity that exemplified the magnitude of the Allied deception effort. Gallagher reported that the Germans (specifically DNB radio) had announced "that in some places, dummy parachutists were dropped to confuse the defense."[83] Pinkley added another facet to this ruse by explaining that the "uniformed dummies" landing north of Le Havre "exploded when touched."[84] These deception features woven into the Invasion narrative only magnified the operation's scope and illustrated the level of effort undertaken by the Allies to dupe the enemy and crack the German coastal defenses.

Much of the information Gallagher and Pinkley wove into their summaries reinforced the same information their own wire services were already providing to the broadcast networks from London and that had been filling the airwaves throughout the day. However, each man included in his respective narrative additional details that expanded upon reports aired by the radio networks, such as information related to the Invasion's troubles with bad weather. In their narrative summaries, both reporters made reference to an official report revealing that SHAEF had, in Gallagher's words, "postponed [D-Day] until today because of bad weather."[85] But Pinkley did not simply mention this point in passing like his colleague or the broadcast networks. Rather, he placed greater emphasis on the weather delay in his UP report by explaining that the "Allied command gave the go-ahead order last night despite strong northwest winds and rain squalls," instead making the decision to invade contingent on the "weather experts [who] forecast improving conditions."[86] From Pinkley's perspective, the weather situation, while "still somewhat unfavorable," could very well have scuttled the entire cross-Channel attack and might still have a significant impact on the ongoing operation. Pinkley's pragmatism and cautiousness, sometimes overridden by hyperbolic statements, still suffused much of his writing.

Other official pronouncements first broadcast over the airwaves and then further amplified by the printed AP and UP stories focused on two British leaders in particular—General Montgomery and Prime Minister Churchill. When SHAEF announced that General Montgomery "led the assault," Gallagher, in a direct attempt to signal Allied unity and promote confidence in the operation's leadership, promptly cast the British general as the "hero of the African desert."[87] Pinkley showed equal enthusiasm for Montgomery and Allied unity by proclaiming the British general as "Monty of El Alamein" and noting specifically that Montgomery led "American, British, and Canadian troops."[88] While much of the American newspaper reporting on 6 June 1944 emphasized American feats of arms, reporting on Allied senior leadership tended to underscore more directly the multinational contributions of talented commanders from both the American and British sides of the Allied venture—another key thematic frame shaping the D-Day narrative.

Prime Minister Churchill became an oft-cited source of official reports, wild optimism, and Allied unity in both radio broadcasts and in the roundups issued by Gallagher and Pinkley throughout the day. According to the reports, Churchill had addressed the British House of Commons twice on D-Day to update the members of Parliament on the Invasion's progress. Since recording devices were forbidden, details of Churchill's pronouncements became available through the larger pooling effort from British news sources.[89] Churchill's statements were rife with hyperbolic declarations (and even a little misinformation) about the Invasion's conduct and progress, further suggesting the operation's extraordinary scale. Gallagher reported in his initial version that an optimistic Churchill had informed Parliament that "the whole operation was 'proceeding according to plan.'"[90] Regarding the Allied airborne operations, Gallagher quoted Churchill as stating that a "record-shattering number of parachute and glider troops were fighting in Caen, nine miles inland," an inaccurate statement from the prime minister given that Allied forces did not reach the city until after 6 June 1944.[91] In his reports, Pinkley gave Churchill a complete platform by quoting the prime minister extensively. He related Churchill's prediction that "the battle will grow constantly in scale and intensity" in the coming weeks and that the Allies had already achieved "tactical surprises." Churchill, wrote Pinkley, deemed the "vast" Overlord plan as "the most complicated and difficult" ever set into motion because it "combined [the] employment of air, land and sea forces in the highest degree of intimacy." And in keeping with his proclamation that "complete unity prevails throughout the Allied armies," Churchill declared that there "is brotherhood in arms between us and our friends, the United States," and that there was complete confidence in the supreme commander and his lieutenants.[92] From a newsgathering perspective, Churchill became one of the best sources available to war correspondents, who were eager for a window into the supreme command's assessment of the Invasion's progress.

Spokesmen at SHAEF ticked off five specific hurdles overcome by the Allies on D-Day, but only the pragmatic Virgil Pinkley opted to list them in order in his UP stories as another way to quantify the mammoth operation's seemingly incredible success on the first day. Gallagher, for his part, simply blended these points throughout his reports. Pinkley parroted the official scorecard by explaining that the first hurdle, the German failure to bomb any English ports and assembly areas, essentially left the Allied forces unmolested as they launched Overlord. The second hurdle, German Luftwaffe attacks on the sea convoys failing to reach "the expected scale," helped the Allies surmount their third hurdle—minesweeping the Channel to the beaches "without much opposition." The fourth hurdle, overcoming the German coastal guns, proved almost effortless in Pinkley's characterization; the ineffectiveness of these German artillery pieces apparently allowed the troops to land on the beaches successfully, but subsequent reports in the days following the Invasion would amend this characterization significantly, particularly for the Americans on Omaha Beach. The fifth, and final, item on the list summed up German opposition as "generally . . . below expectations," especially since the Luftwaffe "had flown only 50 battle area sorties."[93] Each of these points enveloped the Invasion in an aura of overwhelming success that even more cautious and practical correspondents like Virgil Pinkley found difficult to resist. Instead of American readers recoiling at news of a faltering, high-casualty event, they could perceive D-Day as a grand operation that succeeded well beyond expectations, even if certain less palatable details of the Invasion's true difficulties remained absent.

The missing details in Gallagher's and Pinkley's narratives were the result of events unfolding on the landing beaches. On these beaches rested the Invasion's centers of gravity, but the reports crafted by American journalists like Gallagher and Pinkley suffered from information blind spots because the best-laid plans of SHAEF's public relations enterprise had fallen through. Some of America's finest journalists—now accredited war correspondents reporting on the scene—could not get their eyewitness reports from the beaches and into the hands of America's key Invasion chroniclers, the AP's Gallagher and the UP's Pinkley. If the wire services were flying blind in their news-gathering efforts on the beaches, so were the rest of America's newspapers and radio networks. And this news blackout did much to shape the nature of the reporting and the overall narrative produced by both men, keeping the most troubling details about the landings hidden from the American public.

The only eyewitness accounts Gallagher and Pinkley included in their nationally distributed front-page narratives came from observers flying far overhead in Allied bombers or transport aircraft, accounts that proved generally unsatisfying to an American public hungry for details about the beach landings. Unfortunately, the pilots and the war correspondents who flew with them proved to be the only reliable witnesses to the events taking place on the beaches. These accounts only received brief, even lackluster, attention from Gallagher and Pinkley, most likely because each man sought to squeeze as much information into his tightly written stories as possible. Gallagher quoted a returning Canadian fighter pilot as imprecisely describing "a hell of a lot of stuff on the beach" that "looked like tanks" as well as "lots of shooting going on."[94] Pinkley described returning fighter pilots as reporting that "Allied infantrymen were scrambling up the shores . . . apparently without heavy opposition in the early stages."[95] Nothing in these descriptions helped to paint a true picture of the fighting on the beaches, even though Gallagher and Pinkley each had access to at least two detailed aerial accounts from wire service correspondents—the AP's Gladwin Hill and the UP's Collie Small. Hill and Small each managed to publish highly detailed accounts of their aerial adventures as passengers in B-26 Marauder bombers.[96] These stories supplemented the front-page narratives composed by Gallagher and Pinkley, but they did not provide any true sense or clarity about what was taking place down on the beaches. In fact, Gallagher mentioned a nameless AP correspondent (presumably Gladwin Hill) who only reported seeing hundreds of parachutes dotting the landscape as "great naval forces" fired into the German coastal fortifications.[97] While light on specifics within the front-page narratives, these eyewitness testimonies helped to enhance a sense of the Invasion's scope and complexity, simply by leaving certain details, such as the beach landings, to the public's imagination.

Also left to the public's imagination were the roles and contributions of America's Black soldiers and sailors. Gallagher's and Pinkley's summaries did not mention how Black troops had contributed directly to the beach assaults, even though the *Pittsburgh-Courier*'s Black war correspondent on the ground, William Randolph Dixon Jr., had reported that "several all-Negro combat units were being trained to operate in the Invasion, such as field artillery, tank destroyer, and anti-aircraft." Black readers had continued to use their weeklies to supplement the news they received from the mainstream, all-White press, yet the Black weeklies generally omitted news of the Invasion in the days following D-Day. Such silence suggested that the Black press was brooding quietly over the nearly total absence of Black troops in the Invasion coverage.[98]

Instead of sitting quietly on the sidelines, Dixon and his editors at the *Courier* decided to take a page from Gallagher's and Pinkley's playbook by crafting a front-page news summary of the Invasion that mimicked the very stories submitted by these two wire service reporters on D-Day. The *Courier*, with Dixon as their ace reporter, pushed back against the all-White AP and UP narratives in the 10 June 1944 issue with a front-page Invasion news summary that outdid most White newspapers in terms of jingoistic boosterism. Moreover, Dixon's account included at least some commentary on the (presumed) roles of Black troops, allowing him to thumb his nose at the mainstream press for failing to do the same thing. In colorful prose using language that evoked an uncomfortable slavery motif, Dixon exclaimed on the front page, "*This is it!* The skies of *enslaved* [emphasis mine] Europe glowed this morning as the rainbow of liberation . . . cloaked the landing of Allied armies on the northern coast of France." His summary captured many of the key details used by Gallagher and Pinkley, such as General Montgomery's command of the assault troops under "an air umbrella of 11,000 planes," the "ominous roar" of which "vindicated itself as the 'voice of liberation.'" Dixon left no doubt that America's Black community supported the Invasion while still pushing against the glaring hypocrisy of Americans fighting to liberate Europe's "enslaved" peoples—all while ignoring the plight of Blacks living under Jim Crow at home. Dixon commented on the *potential* contribution of Black troops in his Invasion summary, but he admitted that, due to censorship, he was unable "to report whether Negro Americans participated in the initial assault because of the tremendous size of the invasion forces." Dixon recognized that this statement was tentative and weak, causing him to declare, without any evidence, that the "contributions of Negro Americans to date have been magnificent." Ultimately, Dixon's reporting did little in the short term to make the broader American Invasion narrative more inclusive. By 10 June 1944, the all-White American D-Day narrative was already firmly ensconced in the consciousness of most Americans.[99]

On the whole, the primary news summaries of the Invasion appearing on front pages through 6 June 1944 with ever-increasing levels of detail momentarily arrested the chaotic glut of bulletins pouring nonstop over the radio waves. In terms of sheer information volume, radio came out on top; wartime newspapers suffered from space limitations, while the networks "could give a story as much time as it merited."[100] Still, Gallagher's and Pinkley's roundups succeeded in advancing the common thematic frame that D-Day was the most significant operation of the war and an enterprise of staggering magnitude. American readers also took away from these narratives a common picture of a massive military endeavor supported by thousands of aircraft and naval vessels, hundreds of naval guns, and scores of paratroopers and beach-assault troops—all led by American and British commanders who, according to eyewitnesses and official reports, were succeeding beyond expectations. D-Day was measuring up as a triumph.

The front-page news summaries did not vary greatly in style and content from the summaries issued by the wire services to report upon two previous invasions in the European theater of operations—the landings in North Africa on 8 November 1942 (Operation Torch) and the landings in Sicily on 10 July 1943 (Operation Husky). They had a familiar style and delivery that was instantly recognizable to any newspaper reader. Like the summaries crafted by Gallagher and Pinkley, the write-ups for these operations synthesized official reports and whatever morsels of eyewitness testimonies became available in the moment. The principal distinction between the D-Day narrative summaries and the ones crafted for Torch and Husky rested in the fact that two official pronouncements on 6 June 1944—Communiqué Number 1 and Eisenhower's Order of the Day—anchored and infused the D-Day narratives with a power and meaning absent in the North Africa and Sicily accounts.[101] Aside from these two factors, the stylistic and editorial approach to the wire service news summaries stuck to the basic formula for the time.

The true significance of the written summaries of D-Day rested in their culturally familiar pattern of allowing American readers to see the news presented in a particular form, the newspaper. The specific "*codes* and *canons* of culture," as David Paul Nord has branded them, could help enhance narrative-building by presenting American readers with something familiar, the newspaper, while at the same time using that same cultural artifact as a means of communicating new information of national and global significance.[102] This process of nationwide communication had the power to connect people, in turn *collectivizing* the experience of news and generating common conceptions of the same event.[103] Radio remained outwardly communal while textual readings of the Invasion narrative prompted greater individual introspection, allowing for a more intimate personal experience with the reported event. Thus, newspapers could enhance one's individual perception of D-Day in a manner that differed from radio's more communal, and generally more chaotic, flow of information while still merging these personalized experiences with the greater collective narrative through the common ceremony of newspaper readership.

◆ ◆ ◆

Ultimately, newspapers momentarily slowed the pace of the rush of incoming Invasion news, but the newspapers did not unburden readers from having to make sense of this glut of information and its attendant thematic frames.[104] The American reading public had to connect all the information presented into a coherent narrative related to this single event. While the front-page stories written by Wes Gallagher and Virgil Pinkley helped by forming a core summary of the Invasion, readers still had to string together all the various news items, features, and bulletins into a "curriculum of meaning" through a process that Nord has termed "linking." According to Nord, "Readers must find (create, actually) coherence through connection, interpolation, and inference," in turn creating order out of what they had read.[105] In so doing, readers intellectually "experienced" the Invasion, eventually translating that narrative-building experience into a common storyline casting D-Day as the most significant operation of the war. But the printed newspaper had the ability to supplement this textual narrative with visual portrayals of the Invasion through photographs and maps, two means of representation that helped cement the significance of D-Day even further in the minds of American readers.

Although the war correspondents, censors, and editors on the American home front struggled admirably to construct a coherent picture of the Invasion, "one cannot escape the impression," according to Philip Knightley, "that the sheer size of the operation overwhelmed most of them."[106] As historian Steven Casey has averred, for most reporters and their home-front audiences, D-Day "was a distant event, something they could only piece together in vague outlines from the sketchy clues" provided by SHAEF.[107] Many details of the airborne and beach landings never crossed the wires on D-Day, and when these details emerged in the days and weeks that followed, they did little to alter the thematically framed narrative that emerged on 6 June 1944.

◆ ◆ ◆

American newspapers were not alone in conveying the significance and grand scale of D-Day to their respective reading audiences. Newspapers of fellow Allied nations, particularly those 6 June 1944 editions published by the British and Canadian presses, expressed the same basic thematic frame formulated by the American journalists but in subtler ways. For instance, most British and Canadian newspapers did not stun their readers with oversized headlines, but they did employ headline language that voiced a combination of relief, angst, and optimism over the cross-Channel assault. Canada's *Vancouver Sun* came closest to replicating the American approach by printing the headline "Invasion!" in nearly three-inch letters in red ink.[108]

Another difference was that British and Canadian front-page news summaries were not as tightly packaged and more piecemeal than the American versions. However, British and Canadian narrative summaries still carried the same basic news items proffered by the same official sources, including the few eyewitness pilot accounts. The same problems affecting the American efforts to get dispatches and film off the landing beaches and back to London affected correspondents of all nations. The first photographs of British troops on D-Day were lost on their way back to London, so for the first two days after the landings, British editors had to use images of American and Canadian troops hitting the beaches. For the British press in particular, newsprint was also in short supply; like their American colleagues, they limited advertising and the amount of Invasion information they could publish. The British press also did not have the same six-hour head start as their American and Canadian brethren. They received the Invasion bulletins in real time with little opportunity to prepare more comprehensive, more carefully laid out editions before the mid-afternoon deadline. The first British D-Day papers came off the presses as early as 10:30 a.m. London time, but most editions did not reach the stands until the afternoon.[109] Of particular note was the London *Times*' morning edition, which appeared to many observers as "unruffled" by the Invasion news. In a stunning demonstration of editorial panache, the austere *Times* printed news of D-Day where it always printed principal cable news of the day—on page four.[110] For all their similarities and minor differences, American newspapers and radio networks departed significantly from their British and Canadian counterparts on D-Day in one radically different way—they used their respective communications mediums to call Americans to prayer nationwide, transforming D-Day into a sacred event.

CHAPTER 5

The "Great Crusade"

The Press and the Sacralization of D-Day

Soldiers, Sailors and Airmen of the Allied Expeditionary Force! You are about to embark upon the Great Crusade, toward which we have striven these many months. The eyes of the world are upon you. The hopes and prayers of liberty-loving people everywhere march with you.

—Gen. Dwight D. Eisenhower,
Order of the Day, 6 June 1944[1]

An electrified American audience, ears glued to their radios, listened intently at 3:37 a.m. EWT as the voice of CBS's broadcast chief in Europe, Edward R. Murrow, broke through the "fog of static" on Tuesday, 6 June 1944, and in a voice familiar to millions, stoically read General Eisenhower's Order of the Day issued hours earlier to the invading Allied troops.[2] Only five minutes before Murrow's announcement, Col. R. Ernest Dupuy, SHAEF's public relations officer, had read aloud in an "arid, clear, unmodulated voice" the first communiqué from SHAEF announcing the Invasion.[3] Murrow's was the first civilian voice to cross the airwaves from Europe, further confirming that the Invasion had in fact begun. For skeptical listeners, Murrow's proclamation assured the listening public that this D-Day was the real thing and not another false report like the one sent accidentally on 3 June 1944.[4] The rapid broadcast and newspaper reactions to the false flash revealed the incredible tension leading up to the Invasion, a tension near the breaking point for both America's news agencies and the American public at large.[5]

For the previous three hours, the world had relied exclusively on radio reports from German news sources, such as Germany's government-run news agency, Transocean, for information about the long-awaited

Invasion.[6] But now no one in America doubted that D-Day had begun, and Eisenhower's characterization of the Invasion as a "Great Crusade"—a phrase that smacked of George Creel's World War I propaganda and which even for a generally devout 1944 America stood out for its religious overtones and moral righteousness—would receive added emphasis from America's newspapers. The stage was set for a media-enabled "apotheosis" of D-Day, an approach that, according to social historian Mary Louise Roberts, would allow all Americans to imagine D-Day as "a sacred event" in their collective consciousness.[7]

◆ ◆ ◆

Daily newspapers and radio stations throughout the United States, through the shared ceremony of readership and listenership, became the principal enablers of the sacralization of D-Day and its media-constructed narrative in the first twenty-four hours after the Invasion reporting began.[8] With a reasonable wealth of initial news from overseas wire services and from Washington, DC, the newspapers and radio were well postured to invest D-Day with religiously charged rhetoric that would significantly influence the Invasion narrative as it developed in the media on 6 June 1944. These news mediums approached this effort in three ways.

First, the newspapers and radio capitalized on General Eisenhower's characterization of D-Day as a "Great Crusade," casting the Invasion as a religiously charged enterprise carried out by Allied "crusaders" tasked with eliminating "Nazi tyranny over the oppressed peoples of Europe."[9] Second, newspapers and radio instructed the American public on what behavior was acceptable in the face of the Invasion news by framing the nationwide response to D-Day as a universal call to prayer. Although newspapers and radio built upon the religiously tinged language appearing in Eisenhower's Order of the Day, the press independently (and mostly in preplanned fashion) cast the Invasion as a sacred event by becoming active conduits for political and religious leaders at the local and national levels to call all Americans to prayer on D-Day. Third, the newspapers and radio enabled President Franklin D. Roosevelt to end the day's Invasion news cycle on a religious note by widely promoting and then communicating the commander in chief's own spiritual sentiments about D-Day in a special prayer he broadcast personally to the country at 10:00 p.m. EWT. Newspapers and radio widely promoted FDR's scheduled prayer as the capstone event of the day's Invasion reporting by serving as the "pulpits" through which the president could engage in a rare moment of spiritual union with his fellow Americans. Through the power of his personal example, FDR demonstrated to all Americans the importance that prayer would play in leading America along a difficult path to victory while also acknowledging the Invasion as a momentous and sacred event in the war's history.

The sacralization of D-Day represented a longstanding, but very rare, tradition of casting selected military events in American history as sanctified endeavors. Only a handful of historic military events have enjoyed similar treatment in the past two centuries. The tradition began with the American Revolution, in which newspapers and pamphlets imbued the Battle of Bunker Hill on 17 June 1775 with a highly moralistic and sacred meaning. The vessel used for casting Bunker Hill in this light was the personal example of Dr. Joseph Warren, whose bloody death during the battle gave the revolutionary cause its first martyr, thus elevating both Warren and the battle to hallowed status.[10] The tradition continued with a similar sacralization of the Battle of Gettysburg, which took place over the first three days in July 1863 and represented a turning point in the Civil War. With this point in mind, Abraham Lincoln sanctified the battle and the Union dead when he delivered his famed Gettysburg Address. In that brief speech, he lamented the fact that those standing with him lacked the power to "consecrate" and "hallow" this ground. Instead, admitted Lincoln, only the "brave men, living and dead, who struggled here, have hallowed it, far above our poor power to add or detract."[11] Venerated battles such as Bunker Hill and Gettysburg served as antecedents that laid the groundwork for D-Day's elevation to near-transcendental status in America's collective consciousness. Such a characterization clearly set the Invasion apart from any other event during World War II.

◆ ◆ ◆

The sacralization of D-Day began in earnest on 6 June 1944 with Edward R. Murrow's on-air reading of General Eisenhower's Order of the Day and subsequent re-readings (sometimes in various languages) by other broadcasters on different networks. On the East Coast, many of the nation's 60 million radio sets were switched off as Americans slept through much of the early Invasion reporting.[12] On the West Coast, the first reports broke just as many Americans were preparing for bed. The most attentive audiences throughout America proved to be third-shift workers or late-night bar crawlers imbibing one last drink before making their way home. But the audience would grow rapidly as early newspaper editions spread the word that the supreme commander had sent their sons on what many hoped would be one final "crusade" in order to, in FDR's words, "cleanse the world of ancient evils, ancient ills," all of which America had confronted a generation earlier and which now had returned as "Nazi tyranny."[13]

Eisenhower's Order of the Day helped unleash the moralistic and religious sentiment encompassing the news of D-Day, a sentiment that would help the American public conflate the Invasion with the notion of a sacred mission to free the oppressed peoples of Europe from Nazi fascism and barbarism. The paper message given to all Invasion participants on the eve of D-Day represented a statement not just to the addressees—the "Soldiers, Sailors and Airmen of the Allied Expeditionary Force"—but to all Americans as well. Elmer Davis's OWI had set up its London office in July 1942; by D-Day, that office had grown to 1,600 personnel. This team fed SHAEF's press releases to the various wire and syndicated news services through OWI's Washington, DC, office.[14] Thus, Eisenhower's message was certain to reach a wide American audience almost immediately upon public release. With this point in mind, the supreme commander crafted the message carefully with language that would invest the Invasion with starkly moralistic and religious characteristics while essentially "knighting" all members of the Allied Expeditionary Force as "crusaders" destined to fulfill some perceived holy mandate. Essentially, Eisenhower had co-opted the press in lending legitimacy to his Great Crusade.[15]

Eisenhower's brief message was in many ways a straightforward reminder of what the Allies had worked so hard to achieve leading up to the cross-Channel Invasion. He invoked the good-versus-evil trope by singling out "Nazi tyranny" as the true enemy, a rhetorical device that military and civilian leaders alike had deliberately constructed and relied upon in order to cast the war in clear, simple terms.[16] He invoked "liberty" and the Invasion's practical purpose of freeing "the oppressed peoples of Europe," all themes that comported well with American and Allied intentions and self-conceptions. But he cautioned that although the Germans were off balance—thanks to Allied military and home-front efforts—the Allied troops' "task would not be an easy one." The enemy, stated Eisenhower, would "fight savagely," language that channeled both the World War I characterization of the Germans as "Huns" and the American tradition of casting wars as clashes between civilization and barbarism.[17] Yet in spite of singling out these inherent challenges, Eisenhower used the message to communicate his well-known sense of optimism, his faith in his men, and his assurance that they would accept "nothing less than full Victory."

Framing the core content of this message, however, was an even higher-minded, moralistic phrase, one that Eisenhower intentionally rendered in capital letters—Great Crusade. By invoking this phrase in the first line of the message, Eisenhower was imbuing the Invasion with a divine purpose by likening it to the medieval crusades of centuries past, which were military-style enterprises sanctioned by the Latin Church to free the Holy Land from Islamic barbarians. By casting the Invasion in these terms, Eisenhower was sacralizing D-Day in the minds of his troops and of all Americans. They were no longer simply Allied soldiers, sailors, and airmen but holy crusaders on a sacred mission to free the European continent from oppressive, warmongering Nazis. Eisenhower further suggested that the prayers of all Allied nations—those "liberty-loving people everywhere"—fueled the Allied troops' efforts and served as the divine bulwark upon which the troops' moralistic foundation rested. In an unusual juxtaposition between secular and religious language, Eisenhower ended the note with "Good Luck!" and a call to "beseech the blessing of Almighty God upon this great and noble undertaking."

The high-minded, moralistic language running throughout the message was no accident. Eisenhower personally crafted and restructured much of the message's language to communicate clearly what he wanted to say. In the surviving final draft of the message, Eisenhower deliberately circled and then moved two sentences from the bottom of the message to follow immediately after the first sentence announcing the Great Crusade: "The eyes of the world are upon you. The hopes and prayers of liberty-loving people everywhere march with you." In doing so, he shifted to the top nearly all of the message's religiously infused language to ensure that the moralistic framework he was establishing remained clear and precise.[18] He seemingly believed that his moralistic characterization of the Invasion would motivate the troops *and* the American home front to make one last push for victory. By contrast, no such missives ever framed the meaning and moralistic purpose behind battles in the Pacific, possibly because America was fighting a war of vengeance there and not liberation. The idea of Americans as liberators was more in keeping with the American people's conception of themselves and their values. Likewise, Eisenhower's message did not include America's and Britain's ally on the Eastern front—the Soviet Red Army—perhaps for the simple reason that Eisenhower did not have them under his direct command like the Anglo-American Allies or quite possibly because the Soviet Union's brutal application of communism did not reflect Western Allied values and therefore conflicted with Eisenhower's core message. The Russians had simply joined with the Allies out of necessity, and their omission from the Order of the Day, even as a brief reference as fellow Allies fighting a common enemy, proved telling.

Similar messages issued to the troops by FDR and General Montgomery also leveraged religious appeals to God and to prayer but not to the same degree employed by Eisenhower.[19] In his message, FDR reminded the men that they were agents of freedom upon whom America depended, men who were "God-fearing, proud, and courageous people" who, throughout America's history, had "put its freedom under God before all other purposes." Thus, in FDR's mind America rested upon a bedrock of religious values that the people had entrusted its soldiers with protecting. Similarly, General Montgomery, commander in chief of the 21st Army Group and overall commander of amphibious landings, used his "Personal Message from the C-in-C" to inject enthusiasm and confidence into all the Invasion's soldiers on "the eve of this great adventure." He further pointed out the righteousness of the Allied cause, that all should pray that "'The Lord Mighty in Battle'" will go forth with "our armies," and "that His special providence will aid us in the struggle."[20] Compared to these two messages, Eisenhower's message, framed as a crusade, stood out for its far higher-minded invocation of purpose behind the Invasion.

Furthermore, the fact that Eisenhower had crafted a lesser-known second, and completely different, message for his troops on the eve of D-Day confirmed that his characterization of the Invasion as a Great Crusade was a deliberate and, from his perspective, necessary way to infuse new meaning into the Allied Invasion effort. This second message, classified as "Secret," was issued to Invasion leaders at all levels. The instructions were clear: "The following message from the Supreme Commander will be read to troops by an officer after embarkation . . . and only when no postponement of the operation is likely." The verbal transcript represented a significant departure from the crusading rhetoric of the hard-copy message. Eisenhower explained that the troops would soon "be engaged in a great undertaking" to rid Western Europe of "the Nazi tyranny." But the message quickly transformed into a sober, practical warning about each soldier's personal responsibilities as representatives of his respective country. Eisenhower explained that the liberated peoples, who "have suffered great privations," would welcome the Allied troops with open arms but that the soldiers were not to take advantage of this reception and increase these peoples' hardships, particularly by damaging property, infringing upon their rights, or engaging in black-market activities. In short, Eisenhower cautioned, don't behave like the enemy you are fighting and therefore sacrifice your moral high ground.

This remarkable message portrayed the more practical side of the supreme commander, who could invoke religious sentiment while still recognizing the harsh, and even dark, realities of such a massive endeavor as Operation Overlord.[21] The second message suggested the calculated nature and motives behind Eisenhower's Great Crusade language. His biographers have cast him as hailing from "solid Mennonite stock"; but despite being raised in a deeply religious household, he did not wear his faith on his sleeve.[22] He seemed to balance faith and secularism well, invoking luck on one hand and God on the other. Ultimately, the press would not receive copies of this second message to the troops. For those war correspondents within earshot of its reading, the guidelines for self-censorship established by the Office of Censorship and by SHAEF would have prevented transmittal of such classified communications to the U.S. press services. No war correspondent, though, would have wanted to disparage the troops by suggesting that America's young men had the capacity to pillage and plunder the land they were liberating.

Thus, Eisenhower likely sought to use his Great Crusade characterization not simply to boost his troops' morale but to energize American home front efforts in support of the war. Eisenhower understood that most Americans knew the war only from the radio and the press and were "fighting this war on imagination alone."[23] The broadcast and print media became the means by which Eisenhower could enlist American home front support in a way that transcended all Americans' minor privations and invest their collective efforts with greater meaning by recruiting them as "co-crusaders" along with their soldiers, sailors, and airmen fighting overseas.

Yet in characterizing D-Day as the Great Crusade, Eisenhower risked alienating an American public deeply suspicious of high-minded propagandistic claims and crusading rhetoric. They had seen it all before during the previous world war when President Woodrow Wilson's Committee on Public Information, or CPI, headed by muckraking journalist George Creel, aroused a skeptical, isolationist America into supporting American military participation in the war.[24] Creel and his agents sold the war with a religious zeal by stirring up hatred for all things German. He marketed the war through newspapers and other means as "a Crusade not merely to re-win the tomb of Christ, but to bring back to earth the rule of right, the peace, goodwill to men and gentleness he taught."[25] Creel even produced a film in 1918 titled *Pershing's Crusaders,* which opened with Gen. John J. Pershing astride a horse beside a mounted knight in full armor with a cross on his smock—the stereotypical image of a medieval Crusader.[26]

But Creel oversold his message, and Americans felt betrayed by the overt propaganda.[27] For many Americans, the war yielded nothing but dead sons and unfulfilled expectations. The Senate even refused to ratify the Treaty of Versailles.[28] Once World War II began, FDR eschewed any suggestions about creating a similar agency such as Woodrow Wilson's CPI. The Office of War Information (OWI), headed by respected journalist Elmer Davis, operated under a self-proclaimed "strategy of truth" and behaved nothing like Creel's agency.[29] Instead, the OWI coordinated messaging efforts throughout the federal government but did not manufacture information. Despite the CPI's sordid history of what Davis had once characterized as going "grailing" without actually finding the Holy Grail, Eisenhower still wrapped D-Day in the same kind of crusading rhetoric.[30] His Order of the Day allowed the media, particularly newspapers, to frame the Invasion as a highly moralistic and religious endeavor, which comported well with all Americans' belief in freedom and "the special virtue of the American experiment" in democracy.[31]

Despite the troubled history attending any rhetoric casting the war as a crusade, the American broadcast and print media readily accommodated Eisenhower's "Great Crusade" language in the first twenty-four hours of reporting on D-Day. Edward R. Murrow's initial CBS broadcast of the Order of the Day, pooled through other networks such as NBC, imbued the message with a legitimacy and dramatic appeal that newspapers could not replicate. The familiar voice of the trusted Murrow reading Eisenhower's message over the airwaves lent the supreme commander's words an authenticity and immediacy that had the power to impress.[32] But for Murrow's words to have an effect, people had to hear them. Most Americans on both coasts were either asleep or working late shifts when Murrow introduced the nation to Eisenhower's Great

Crusade, limiting the message's initial impact to a reduced listening population. A public opinion survey in June 1944 revealed that 63 percent of Americans preferred radio for their war news, likely because the speed at which radio could dispense news had an allure unto itself.[33] And, since radio stations received their news from the same wire services as newspapers, listeners remained as informed as readers. But Americans had to build radio listening time into their busy schedules, so the more important medium on 6 June 1944 for communicating Eisenhower's Great Crusade message, a medium available for consumption anywhere and anytime, became the newspaper.

Throughout the country, scores of morning newspaper editions followed quickly on the heels of the initial radio broadcasts announcing the Invasion by summarizing or reproducing verbatim Eisenhower's words portraying D-Day as a Great Crusade. Many newspapers carved out space on their front pages for the message's full text or excerpts from it, often juxtaposing the message's language against massive, visually powerful headlines proclaiming the Invasion as "ON!"[34] Several newspapers, such as the *Toledo Times*, reproduced the Order of the Day word for word, either embedded in the main AP and UP stories appearing on the front pages or set apart surrounded by a border.[35] In these cases, the editorial staff offered no comment and instead chose to allow the words to speak for themselves. Ironically, these word-for-word renderings of the message failed to depict the Great Crusade in capital letters, thus robbing the term of the special emphasis the supreme commander intended. Wire feeds from the news services produced text only in capital letters, so the editorial staff of each newspaper had no way of knowing that the original text issued in hard copy to the troops and to overseas war correspondents capitalized the term.[36] Thus, the practical aspect of transmitting news via wire to the United States prevented Eisenhower from communicating fully to the American people his implied assertion that D-Day would not be another failed crusade like World War I, but instead would be *the* Crusade that would finally finish the job.

Some newspapers also highlighted Eisenhower's Great Crusade language as a front-page headline or subheading, lending the term greater marquee status as Eisenhower likely intended. Tennessee's *Johnson City Press-Chronicle* prefaced a complete transcription of the message (still with Great Crusade in lowercase letters) with the larger heading "Eisenhower Starts Men On 'Crusade.'"[37] In a similar approach, the *Knoxville News-Sentinel* capitalized the phrase in a large font subheading proclaiming "'Great Crusade' Is Under Way" as an introduction to the front-page AP story.[38] For its part, the *Miami Herald* used the phrase "Embarking On a Great Crusade" as a larger subheading for one of the segments breaking the dense AP reporting into more digestible chunks.[39]

Despite the limited marquee-style, front-page treatment afforded to Eisenhower's Great Crusade by some newspapers, most editions throughout the country simply included the Great Crusade language in the context of summarizing the Invasion news, mostly on the front page. The most prolific example repeated throughout many of America's newspapers came from the AP's chief of the Invasion staff in London, Wes Gallagher, who, in varying versions of his wire submissions, emphasized the phrase in quotation marks early in the main body of his reporting. One example had Gallagher leading off with the following phrase: "The invasion, which Eisenhower called 'a great crusade,' was announced at 7:32 a.m. Greenwich Mean Time (3:32 a.m., Eastern War Time)." He continued by quoting Communiqué Number 1 and describing how "Eisenhower himself wished Godspeed to the parachutists who were the first to land on the enemy-held soil of France."[40] In follow-up wire submissions for later editions, such as the third Invasion Extra produced by the *Los Angeles Evening Herald and Express*, Gallagher recast his language to read: "Gen. Dwight D. Eisenhower told his troops this grand assault was a crusade which must bring 'nothing less than full victory.'"[41]

Unlike the AP's up-front references to the Great Crusade, UP wire submissions forming the basis for front-page Invasion reporting and authored primarily by the chief of the UP's London office, Virgil Pinkley, did not reveal Eisenhower's words until much later in the main story. The UP-sourced main story in the *Detroit Times* paraphrased the Order of the Day in the fourth paragraph, explaining that the order told "assault groups" that "they were embarking on the 'great crusade toward which we have striven these many months.'"[42] Omaha's *Evening World Herald*, in synthesizing multiple cable dispatches, also reported that Eisenhower had "told his troops this grand assault was a crusade which must bring 'nothing less than full victory.'"[43] Similar summaries crafted by editorial staffs, such as that of the *New York Times*, used diverse wire submissions and still managed to work the lower-case version of the "great crusade" into their main copy.[44]

Some syndicated columnists and newspaper editorial sections even gave Eisenhower's Great Crusade an added boost by reinforcing the greater meaning behind his Order of the Day. Nationally syndicated columnist DeWitt MacKenzie quoted the missive in his column, particularly the "Great Crusade" line, and threw his full weight behind the supreme commander's connotation, arguing that this "is the coup de grace for which we have waited so long—the last great battle to exterminate the Nazi beast."[45] The editorial in the *Journal—Every Evening* from Wilmington, Delaware, channeled Eisenhower's language by proclaiming: "We here in the United States have a vast stake in this crusade. . . . It is a *holy war* against slavery and oppression."[46] The *Toledo Times* perhaps went further than any other newspaper to advance the intended meaning behind the Great Crusade. In hyperbolic language that would have made George Creel proud, the editorial proclaimed: "This is Invasion day! The modern Crusade for the Holy Grail of peace and freedom cannot be accomplished or measured in days or weeks or months." The commentary further invoked the continuing war "of civilization and Christianity against the forces of evil" and how today's "modern Crusaders are hurling themselves against the bastions of evil," an all-out effort requiring America's prayers so that "our boys will go into battle protected by . . . Jesus Christ and the Virgin Mary."[47]

Not all newspaper editorial staffs readily accommodated Eisenhower's Great Crusade language. These few editorial staffs, possibly put off by Eisenhower's resurrection of the propagandistic crusading language of the previous war, pushed any mention of the Great Crusade well to the backs of their Invasion-day editions or, in some cases, avoided the phrase entirely. The *Boston Traveler* inserted into a small space on page 19 the complete text of the Order of the Day without emphasis or comment, but the unobtrusive portrayal of Eisenhower's message, given the impact of the rest of the paper's powerful Invasion reporting, called into question the editorial board's decision.[48] Likewise, the *Daily News* of New York City relegated any mention of the Great Crusade to page 14, literally burying within one column Eisenhower's phrase and the meaning he intended it to evoke.[49]

Despite these isolated instances, most Americans, through the simple ceremony of radio listenership and newspaper readership, knew that their most admired military commander, Gen. Dwight D. Eisenhower, a man entrusted by America and her Allies with leading an extraordinarily complicated seaborne and airborne invasion, had infused that operation with a starkly religious and moralistic meaning, one that cast D-Day in the minds of all Americans as a struggle of good versus evil, or, according to one newspaper's editorial board, a "holy war."[50] Eisenhower's gamble in launching America on another World War I–style crusade appeared to have met with the general approval and support of the nation's press corps, ensuring that Americans nationwide would perceive D-Day as a sacred undertaking reflecting their own sense of exceptionalism and moral superiority.

◆ ◆ ◆

The newspaper and broadcast media built directly upon General Eisenhower's religious overtures by describing most Americans' reactions to the Invasion news as a universal call to prayer, a call reinforced by political and religious leaders who used the news media to establish a social expectation for all people on D-Day—to behave solemnly and to pray. This call to prayer, like the press corps' tacit acceptance and promulgation of Eisenhower's religiously charged rhetoric, enjoyed wide acceptance from an American public that displayed strong evidence of faith in a higher power. The public reactions to D-Day as reported in most newspapers offered the starkest evidence of this widely held faith, but that reporting also helped to shape America's understanding of the Invasion as something transcendent, something sacred that required the active participation and contribution of all citizens in the form of prayer. Such religiously charged reporting never appeared in American newspapers covering earlier invasions in the European theater. The reportage on the invasions of North Africa and Sicily remained strikingly secular in nature when compared to the D-Day reporting. In effect, the call to prayer attending the reporting on D-Day represented anything but a trend. The media was breaking new ground.[51]

Most Americans in 1944 believed in God. In an opinion poll conducted on 15 November 1944, nearly six months after D-Day, 96 percent of all Americans admitted to believing in God—or *a* God, as the survey phrased the question. Only 1 percent claimed no belief in a God while 3 percent remained undecided. Women overall came in ahead of men by 2 percent—97 compared to 95. The proportion of faithful even remained high at 93 percent among younger people from ages twenty to twenty-nine while the highest percentages favored those over thirty.[52] Thus, America at the time of D-Day was a self-admitted nation of believers who likely included prayer in their daily, or at least weekly, wartime regimen.

For many Americans in 1944, the war had placed nearly unbearable stress on Christian belief systems and notions of a benevolent God. Highly popular and widely read books sought to address this crisis in faith following America's first combat actions in early 1942. Archbishop Francis J. Spellman of New York, also the military vicar of the armed forces of the United States, published *The Road to Victory* in 1942 to soothe people's angst, suggesting that America's "fight to save her life" was righteous and that "Peace with Justice after Victory" will only come through "A Second Front of Prayer."[53] In a similar vein, Harry Emerson Fosdick offered a ray of hope in his book *A Great Time to Be Alive: Sermons on Christianity in Wartime* (1944) by suggesting that the war offered Christianity an opportunity to reveal a greater Christian message to a world desperately in need of it. According to Fosdick, who had also broadcasted these sermons over the Blue Network, "This is a great time for great convictions."[54]

Hollywood films of the era covering wartime and home-front subjects also included a combination of overt and subtle references to religion and faith, perhaps to give soldiers and civilians a sense of solace that in the end everything would be all right and that America would prevail. In a *Guy Named Joe* (1943), pilots killed in action never really die; instead, they return as guardian angels for new pilots. In *Since You Went Away* (1943), Lionel Barrymore's local preacher uses as the text of his sermon the last stanza of the "Star-Spangled Banner," converting an American patriotic song into scripture to comfort his home-front flock and to remind them that our cause is just, "and this be our motto—'In God is our Trust.'"[55]

Perhaps the starkest evidence of America's devotion to a higher power appeared in the form of one of the war's most popular poems, Frances Angermayer's "Conversion." In July 1943, Angermayer lay in bed haunted by news from the frontlines and wondered how a soldier facing death would feel "if he did not know God." Twenty minutes later, Angermayer typed out a twenty-six-line poem she titled "Conversion," essentially a prayer for unbelieving soldiers who desired to embrace God from the proverbial foxhole. The poem became an international sensation and was translated into numerous languages. The opening verse revealed a direct appeal to God from a desperate soldier: "Look God, I have never spoken to you—/ But now—I want to say 'How do you do.'" The anonymous soldier admits to finally seeing God in nature's beauty from within the presumed safety of a "shell hole," wondering why he first had to endure such a "hellish place" before "I had the time to see Your face." Upon hearing the signal to attack, the soldier, tears streaming down his face, says, "Well, I have to go now, God—good-by. / Strange—since I met you—I'm not afraid to die." Requests for copies nearly overwhelmed Angermayer and the staff of the tiny publication in which it first appeared, the Catholic weekly *Our Sunday Visitor*.[56] Foxhole conversions among America's fighting men spiked. Most notably, on 6 June 1944, a U.S. Army chaplain ministering to the wounded and dying on a Normandy beach found copies of "Conversion" clutched in the hands of several dying men as "hundreds more" loose copies blew across the sand. The popularity of "Conversion" and its meaning suggested that American soldiers and civilians alike represented a highly receptive audience for any moralistic, religiously charged rhetoric emanating from the radio or newspapers.[57]

Morning editions of most newspapers leveraged their audiences' religious inclinations by immediately characterizing America's response to the Invasion as a nationwide call to prayer, thus establishing a social expectation of prayer for all citizens. These newspapers were essentially instructing all Americans in how to comport themselves on this most important of days. The singular message was that even though the Invasion was happening half a world away, all Americans still had a part to play, even if that part was spiritual in nature.[58] A UP report in the *St. Joseph News-Press* titled "America Reacts to News of Invasion With Prayer" described how several American cities such as New Orleans, Columbus, Tacoma, and Cleveland reacted to the Invasion news by praying.[59] Reporter Malcolm Johnson of New York's the *Sun* described D-Day as "a day of prayer in homes, churches and schools throughout the United States."[60] The *Sheboygan Press* used one-inch letters above the masthead to proclaim "Whole Nation Kneels in Prayer," invoking an image of America as one collective body acting in unison.[61] The *Pasadena Independent* was less subtle in its expectations by directing its readers to "Attend Your Church Today! Pray [to] God for a Righteous Victory and a Lasting Peace."[62] For the most part, newspapers simply characterized the national response in local terms by reporting how their own communities reacted to the news. The *Baltimore News-Post*'s front page declared, "City Turns to Prayer On D-Day," while the *Boston Traveler* claimed, "Thousands Flock to Churches to Pray."[63] The *Binghamton Press* simply summed up America's overall reaction as "a common impulse—an impulse to pray."[64]

In addition to the expectation of prayer, the nation's newspapers advanced another equally important social behavior in keeping with the religious response—calmness and solemnity. Many newspapers explained how news of the Invasion had broken a long-developing tension among all Americans, a tension first made evident in America's pointed reaction to the false Invasion report issued the previous Saturday.[65] Despite a few reports of skeptical Americans questioning the verity of the Invasion reports, most Americans readily accepted the news as fact, calmly and without fanfare.[66] Newspapers throughout the nation reported how local leaders urged people to observe the day "with reverence and solemnity."[67] The closest thing to fanfare, reported the press, was the use of sirens, whistles, and church bells in some towns and cities to announce the Invasion.[68] Tennessee's *Elizabethton Daily Star* explained that when news of D-Day broke, "Church bells rang and whistles shrieked."[69] Factory and fire sirens even served as cues for factory workers and others to pause and pray.[70]

Even though the newspapers served to establish the acceptable social response to D-Day as one of prayer and solemnity, they did so by also providing state and local political leaders a means with which to communicate these expectations to the wider public. Newspaper reports broadly cast these political leaders as the messengers of and agents behind the national response of prayer and solemnity. Although operating independently of the supreme commander, they built upon and enhanced the meaning behind Eisenhower's Great Crusade message. The *Baltimore News-Post* shared Maryland governor Herbert R. O'Conor's and Baltimore mayor Theodore R. McKeldin's proclamations urging solemnity and prayer.[71] The *Boston Traveler* outlined Arthur J. Frawley's, mayor of Lynn, Massachusetts, requirement for all schools to pause for one minute of prayer while also providing Boston's mayor Tobin a forum to announce that "Today is a day for prayer and work." The *Traveler* also reported how the governors of New Hampshire, Maine, and Rhode Island all called for a day of prayer while the *Fresno Bee* published California governor Earl Warren's personal plea for prayer.[72] Likewise, New York's *Daily News* and the *Rochester Times-Union* both announced Mayor Fiorello LaGuardia's appeal for all New Yorkers to pause at 3:30 p.m. that day and "pray for success."[73] Similar requests from other mayors setting specific times for public prayer appeared in numerous newspapers.[74] Ultimately, these political leaders took on the roles of spiritual guides who shaped America's reaction to the Invasion, a reaction that would only enhance the importance of D-Day's sacred meaning for all Americans.

Newspapers also provided local and national religious leaders a medium through which to offer the public specific prayers tailored to the Invasion's success. In providing these devotionals, these religious leaders were symbolically arming all citizens with the necessary tools to meet their social obligation of prayer, further enhancing D-Day's already sacred aura. For example, the *Columbus Citizen* provided prayers crafted by three local religious leaders from three different faiths "to be used in Columbus homes during the invasion," each of which comprised generally similar thematic elements.[75] In an effort to link local communities with America at large, the *Detroit Times* featured locally proffered prayers alongside devotions offered by nationally known religious leaders, such as Archbishop Francis J. Spellman of New York, Bishop Henry St. George Tucker of the Protestant Episcopal Church, and Rabbi Edgar F. Magnin of Los Angeles. The thematic strands running throughout these leaders' devotionals further capitalized upon Eisenhower's rhetoric and the language the press used to describe reactions to D-Day. Spellman's lofty petition singled out America as a source of light in darkness with a special destiny of its own while Tucker's prayer beseeched God to protect the suffering. Magnin and D. Stanley Coors, president of the Michigan Council of Churches, in keeping with Eisenhower's "crusading" rhetoric, each sought victory through prayer and the rise of a new world order.[76] Two other prayers originated from lesser-known congregations—the Church of the Ascension and the Reformed Church of America. Remarkably, the *New York Herald Tribune* included as the fifth prayer a brief missive from England's Archbishop of Canterbury, suggesting an effort to present a theologically united front with America's chief ally in the Invasion.[77] Overall, prayers of this nature appeared in most American newspapers on 6 June 1944, advancing such core themes as protecting the suffering, achieving victory, and cleansing the world of its evil enemies. These prayers clearly smacked of crusaderism and the righteous smiting of a barbaric adversary, all themes that comported well with Eisenhower's own depiction of D-Day as a sacred undertaking.

The newspapers not only provided the practical tools—the prayers—the American public needed to ask for God's grace on behalf of victory, but also where to go within the community to discharge this social expectation. In doing so, America's newspapers on D-Day essentially became bulletin boards for churches and synagogues, which had flung open their doors for citizens eager to express their devotions in a public, communal setting. These newspapers listed specific times for special services while many simply kept their doors open throughout the day for all comers.[78] New York's *Binghamton Press*, for example, proclaimed: "Churches Open Throughout Day."[79] The *Boston Traveler* reported how the aptly named Our Lady of Victory Catholic Church in Boston's South End doubled the usual number of daily masses.[80] The *Cincinnati Times-Star* announced that "Special Church Services Are Held Throughout City and County."[81] Some newspapers even provided schedules of special prayer services conducted in local war plants for nearly all religious denominations.[82] The *Miami Herald*, for example, provided times and locations for services in Presbyterian, Baptist, Methodist, Community, Catholic, and Lutheran churches as well as in Miami's synagogues.[83] Lesser-known denominations, such as Universalists, received equal space in selected papers.[84] The *St. Joseph News-Press* described how all churches in Moberly, Missouri, the hometown of First Army commander Lt. Gen. Omar N. Bradley, had opened their doors within minutes of the first Invasion news flash.[85] Ultimately, America's newspapers, primarily through local reporting, further unified a larger American community of prayer not only by communicating to people the need to pray but where to do it in settings that would allow them to demonstrate publicly that they were doing their part for D-Day's success.

America's newspapers not only publicized the social expectation of prayer as well as when and where people should do it, but many even managed to chronicle specific instances of how Americans at the local and national levels actually responded to this messaging. For the most part, the newspapers demonstrated that people heeded local political and religious leaders' calls to observe D-Day solemnly and with prayer. Many newspapers reported that as soon as church doors opened, people filled the pews.[86] The *Boston Traveler* proclaimed on its front page that "Thousands Flock to Churches to Pray," with the accompanying article describing many men and women in uniform clearly visible among the throngs.[87] The *Evening World-Herald* connected the past to the present by describing how residents of Vincennes, Indiana, rang the old Vincennes cathedral's bell to announce the Invasion. This same bell had announced the British surrender to George Rogers Clark a century and a half earlier, but now it signaled residents to gather immediately in the church to pray before a candle-lit altar.[88] United Press staff correspondent Joseph L. Myler reported how mostly service men and women were among the early worshippers to gather in Washington, DC's, churches.[89] The *Daily News* of Los Angeles painted a dramatic word picture of fathers, mothers, sisters, and wives headed before dawn through "fog shrouded streets to churches to ask divine assistance for their loved ones marching in the armies of liberation."[90]

The most commonly reported collective reaction to D-Day was of people pausing in their workplaces, on the streets, and in schools for a moment of silent prayer. New York's *Binghamton Press* described how thousands of night-shift workers in the Remington Rand Propeller Division plant, upon hearing news of the Invasion over loudspeakers, "stood at attention at machines and benches for one minute of silent prayer." The 17,000 workers at Endicott Johnson, continued the *Press*, broke into small prayer groups throughout the twenty-seven-factory complex.[91] Workers at the Cincinnati Milling Machine Company and at Newman Brothers Brass Works, according to the *Cincinnati Times-Star*, observed two minutes and one minute of silence, respectively.[92] The *Los Angeles Evening Herald and Express* revealed that the Vultee plant's graveyard shift stood silently as an Army chaplain prayed over a loudspeaker for D-Day's success.[93] Similarly, in Hollywood, the house band at the chic, celebrity-filled Clover Club paused as an Army chaplain led the patrons in a prayer, after which "the throngs soberly started homeward."[94] The New York Stock Exchange, according to the *Sun*, suspended trading at 10:58 a.m. for two full minutes.[95] At the request of the mayor of Wilmington, Delaware, "all traffic and work halted—heightening the solemnity of the day."[96] Newspapers publicized the fact that schools in Lynn, Massachusetts, paused for one minute of prayer at the mayor's request while nearly 1,300 teachers and students of Cincinnati's Washington Junior High School pledged allegiance to the flag in unison at 9 a.m.[97] Similar reactions took place throughout America.

For those not engaged in war work or in school on D-Day, the newspapers made clear that America's citizens should not spend 6 June 1944 engaged in pastimes or amusements. Instead, many news bulletins reported that those venues would close for the day so that no one had an excuse not to find a suitable location, in public or in private, to pray. The *Baltimore News-Post* reported on the front page that "many places of amusement, including hundreds of taverns, closed their doors." Additionally, the *News-Post* explained, horse racing at Charles Town and Aqueduct was "called off," the baseball game at "Oriole Park" scheduled for that night was cancelled, and liquor was not sold.[98] Some papers identified many storefronts that had closed in response to the Invasion news.[99] According to New York's the *Sun*, Walter Hoving, the president of Lord and Taylor, closed the store to afford all three thousand employees a chance to pray for victory.[100] Similar closings filled the pages of newspapers throughout the country, driving home to all Americans the media-facilitated expectation that D-Day in America would be a prayer day.

Remarkably, the collective reporting revealed a striking emphasis on women of all ages, using gender-specific language, when describing who was attending, or who *should* attend, prayer vigils. Many newspapers stressed how women of all ages comprised the bulk of worshipers in churches and elsewhere, suggesting a gendered belief that women should set the example for all citizens by diligently and demonstrably fulfilling the social expectation of prayer. The *Binghamton Press* singled out women workers in one of Endicott Johnson's factories as being particularly inclined to leave work to pray in nearby churches.[101] One Boston newspaper described weeping mothers praying with "crumpled V-mail letters held in their hands" and how "some girls and elderly women wept as they lit candles and knelt in prayer."[102] The *Daily News* of Los Angeles specifically identified mothers, sisters, and wives as heading to local churches.[103] The *San Jose News* highlighted fifteen or twenty female workers who stopped packing cherries briefly to go and light candles for the troops at Holy Cross church.[104] The *Seattle Star* described women and children—and "some men"—as flocking to churches.[105] Thus, a standard trope constructed by most newspapers on D-Day was the notion of women as "prayers-in-chief," bearing the greatest share of this social expectation because so many of their men were away from home serving their country.

Several newspapers used photographs to illustrate that fellow citizens were indeed engaging in prayer, particularly women of all ages. The *Erie Dispatch-Herald* provided the most dramatic images by publishing two photographs of kneeling worshipers just above the massive, red-lettered headline "Invasion On!" The left photograph featured the Stout family—Mr. G. W. J. Stout, his wife, and his daughter—praying in St. Peter's Cathedral while the photograph to the right featured three young women, hands clasped in prayer, who, according to the description, were praying for a husband, a brother, and several relatives.[106] The *Baltimore News-Post* splashed a large photograph atop an inside page of eighteen elderly women deeply engaged in prayer. The caption described them as praying in the chapel of the Little Sisters of the Poor Home for the Aged led by Reverend Charles Walker of St. John's Catholic Church. In this case, elderly women set the example for all readers to follow in keeping with the gendered expectations for prayer inherent in most reporting on D-Day.[107] But not all images included only women. Four male International Business Machines employees appeared in a photograph in the *Binghamton Press* pausing beside their assembly lines with heads bowed in silent prayer. Next to it was a snapshot of an elderly gentleman named Andrew Zully in a Polish church praying for his son, a sailor in the Navy; the legend below the picture further linked Mr. Zully's actions with Eisenhower's Order of the Day by quoting from the message that the "'hopes and prayers of all liberty loving peoples' went with the invasion troops today."[108] Mr. Zully had become one of Eisenhower's "crusaders."

A noteworthy photograph appearing in the *Boston Traveler* was one that suggested an effort to overcome racial and ethnic attitudes of the time. A photograph of more than a hundred schoolchildren, taken from an elevated position, depicted them in a "V" formation above a description that read: "32 different racial origins represented here as pupils of the Quincy School, Tyler Street, South End, form a V for Victory in the school yard and say a moment's silent prayer for D-Day."[109] In this case, the obligation to pray for the Invasion's success supposedly transcended racial or other such distinctions, differences that to the all-White mainstream press mattered little at the moment.

Nevertheless, those differences did matter to America's Black community. Almost none of the photographs of Americans praying on D-Day, or for that matter any of the news items discussing prayer, featured the reactions and behaviors of Black Americans, who almost certainly ventured forth into their own churches to pray for the Invasion's success. But since Black newspapers were weeklies and did not hit the stands until three or four days after the Invasion began, they featured nothing about the prayer activities of Blacks or other people of color on 6 June 1944. By that time the rush to prayer was old news and no longer front-page fodder for America's newsprint-constrained Black newspapers. Thus, the portrayal in the mainstream press of Americans praying for D-Day's success appeared, quite unrealistically, as an all-White enterprise—just like the greater Invasion narrative.

According to these photographs and others appearing throughout America's newspapers, the attempt to enshroud D-Day in prayer dominated the press. But perhaps the photograph that offered the most comfort for families with loved ones in harm's way was an actual D-Day embarkation photograph that appeared on the front page of the *New York Journal American*. With a caption headed by the word "Godspeed," the image portrayed an Army chaplain, in white vestments and hand held high, blessing a tightly packed crowd of kneeling soldiers and sailors at a British embarkation port. They are, according to the description, "the first assault troops to be thrown against Hitler's forces on the continent. They are bare-headed, kneeling and solemn."[110] This image perhaps comforted some Americans by suggesting that at least some of their loved ones would be going into battle with God's good graces in hand.

Many newspapers highlighted the individual reactions of certain people as an obvious way to personalize, and further exemplify, what the papers suggested were the proper responses to the message of prayer. Many of these examples focused on individuals whose reactions agreed with the day's social expectations. According to one newspaper, "a young woman [in Washington, DC,] slipped into a seat and prayed silently while tears coursed down her cheeks." In Sheboygan, Wisconsin, reported the same paper, a church janitor's wife received the call announcing the Invasion; but since her husband also worked the night shift at a local defense plant, he was not there to ring the church bell. The wife, Mrs. Sam Katt, ignored any gendered expectations that she might not be able to manage the bells and rung them herself for a solid ten minutes.[111] At 42nd and Eighth Streets in New York, reported the *Sun*, an elderly woman and an eleven-year-old boy dropped to their knees and prayed.[112]

The newspapers also identified some individuals by name whose behavior deserved special mention. The *Boston Traveler* singled out Mrs. Mary Carey, with four sons in service, as the first to arrive at church in Natick, Massachusetts.[113] Twelve-year-old Margie Hamilton received recognition in the *Cincinnati Times-Star* for wearing a pin for her brother, a paratrooper, and for promising to say five prayers for him daily and for other soldiers as well.[114] The *New York Journal American* described how Pfc. Wallace Mathiason, notified of the Invasion by a passerby on East 51st Street, looked toward nearby St. Patrick's Cathedral and said, "I'm not a Catholic, but I can pray here. . . . That's one of the things we're fighting for—freedom of worship."[115] Lt. Leonard Bessman in Washington, reported Chicago's *Daily Times*, a recent escapee from a prisoner-of-war camp in Italy and recipient of the Distinguished Service Cross and Purple Heart, asked "God [to] bless our guys." With a credibility few could match, the *Times* transformed Lt. Bessman into a de facto spokesman for all fighting men overseas by quoting his solemn appeal: "I wish everybody here at home could know what they are going through."[116] Perhaps the most poignant example was the *New York Journal American*'s report that forty-year-old Miss Clara Waxman, upon hearing news of the Invasion, collapsed on a trolley at 42nd Street and Broadway and later died at

Roosevelt Hospital. Miss Waxman in a sense became a casualty of the war through her obviously powerful emotional and empathetic connection with the men fighting in Normandy. The press could offer no greater example of devotion and piety among America's citizens.

Advertisements in numerous newspapers also contributed to the broader call to prayer and to the sacralization of D-Day by using religious language and imagery. Although many newspapers responded to the Invasion by limiting or even omitting advertisements in favor of Invasion-related news, some newspapers instead retained advertisements that furthered the religious messaging already evident in much of the Invasion reportage. The *Boston Traveler* carried numerous advertisements of this nature. For example, a large announcement from Wm. Filene's Sons Company, covering one-third of a page, proclaimed: "On this day when the fate of the world may well hang in the balance, we join our prayers to those of millions of our fellow Americans."[117]

Most of these advertisements, though, used impressive illustrations to drive home their messaging. The *Elizabethton Daily Star* featured a nearly full-page rendering of a soldier in full combat gear bursting through a swastika. Sponsored by the East Tennessee Light and Power Company, the advertisement encouraged readers to attend the special victory services held in their communities and to "Buy more War Bonds—Produce more weapons and food—Pray for Victory!"[118] The *Johnson City Press-Chronicle* included a notice sponsored by Hannah's depicting a large "V" within which appeared illustrations of a soldier, sailor, wife, child, mother, and father, each with hands clasped in prayer under a banner of "Let's Have Faith."[119] The *Boston Traveler* featured a nearly full-page advertisement sponsored by the Jordan Marsh Company with an illustration of George Washington in military uniform kneeling with hands clasped in prayer and surrounded by modern artillery pieces and aircraft. The text above Washington read: "Then conquer we must when our cause it is just and this be our motto 'In God Is Our Trust,'" implicitly comparing Washington to Eisenhower and the supreme commander's moralistic message of a righteous crusade.[120] Franklin Simon of the eponymous New York department store sponsored a drawing in the *Sun* of Albrecht

Dürer's "Hands in the Act of Prayer" with a caption reading "Grant us Thy help in this our need."[121] The *Seattle Star* contained a full-page illustration sponsored by Rhodes Home-Owned depicting Uncle Sam rolling up his sleeves while above him in large letters appeared the message: "Invasion Is On! Let's all Pray—and keep on Working for Victory!"[122]

Even a few political cartoons (among others) appearing in newspapers on 6 June 1944 advanced prayer as the acceptable response to D-Day. As part of his series of "Willie and Joe" cartoons, Bill Mauldin happened by chance or by design on D-Day to produce a cartoon with prayer as the theme. In this case, Mauldin's drawing, seen in multiple newspapers throughout the country, depicted a helmeted Army chaplain holding a prayer service with five GIs (Willie and Joe among them) huddled in a sand-bagged antiaircraft position on the Anzio beachhead in Italy. The chaplain held a prayer book in one hand while cupping the other to his ear, listening for incoming artillery. The caption read, ". . . forever, Amen. Hit the dirt." Although intended both to satirize and to sympathize with soldier life on the front lines, the cartoon clearly suggested to America's public that if soldiers under fire could take the time to pray, Americans on the home front had no excuse not to follow their lead.[123]

While the most obvious and direct messaging about the importance of prayer on D-Day came from the daily newspapers, radio also reinforced this theme by broadcasting numerous "programs of a religious character" throughout the day.[124] The call to prayer quickly became an important feature of the major networks' Invasion news programming. One of the earliest broadcasts came at 7 a.m. EWT over the Blue Network from New York's Catholic archbishop, Francis J. Spellman; Dr. Israel Goldstein; and the Right Reverend William T. Manning. Each of these three religious leaders had prerecorded prayers in advance for the Invasion. Spellman later repeated the same special prayer he read to his worshipers at the noon mass in St. Patrick's Cathedral live over NBC at 2:30 and 5 p.m., allowing a national audience to absorb the power of his firm, resolute, and steady voice as he recited his petition to God.[125] With equal impact, NBC's 140 network affiliate stations—heard by millions throughout America and Canada—all pealed forth at 7:15 a.m. with the sound of Philadelphia mayor Bernard Samuel tapping the Liberty Bell from inside Independence Hall thirteen times to signify the original thirteen states in the Union. In an emotional voice, Samuel said, "Our voices are raised in fervent prayer for the men engaged in this mission for freedom."[126] In Cincinnati, local station WCKY broadcast Archbishop John T. McNicolas's prayer service held in St. Peter and Paul Catholic Church live.[127] Likewise, local pastors in Sheboygan, Wisconsin, led prayers over radio station WHBL at 7 a.m.[128] By mid-morning, Mutual featured Invasion prayers recited by Brig. Gen. William R. Arnold, chief of Army chaplains, and Capt. Stanton W. Salisbury, acting chief of Navy chaplains. Even the armed forces, as the program suggested, were appealing directly to all Americans for the prayers needed to prevail over the Nazi hordes. Mutual also featured an "Hour of Prayer" program at 4:30 p.m. with spiritual messages from the ubiquitous Archbishop Spellman, Rabbi Louis Finkelstein, and the Right Reverend Henry St. George Tucker.[129]

Throughout the day and into the evening, several music and film stars lent their on-air voices along with the power of their celebrity to the call to prayer. Comedian Red Skelton, who was awaiting induction into the U.S. Army the next day, 7 June 1944, read aloud "A Child's Prayer on D-Day" over the NBC network.[130] Popular singer Kate Smith, host of CBS's "The Kate Smith Hour," took to the air at 12 p.m. EWT with a powerful commentary about the Invasion's significance and the need for all Americans to stop and pray. She charged her listeners with concentrating all of their "thoughts on victory" and turning their "earnest, united thought into devout, unceasing prayer to God." She challenged her public to join their prayers with hers at that very moment and, in reinforcing General Eisenhower's Order-of-the-Day rhetoric, to "Pray that our crusaders may be strong" and "speedily accomplish their mission [and] bring their adversaries to unconditional surrender."[131]

Possibly the most gripping, religiously charged radio transmission came at 7:30 p.m. EWT from Hollywood. Popular British actor Ronald Colman read a poem live over NBC; "Poem and Prayer for an Invading Army" was written specially for D-Day by Pulitzer-Prize-winning poet Edna St. Vincent Millay. The Writers' War Board had secretly commissioned Millay to write the prayer in April 1944 for exclusive broadcast by NBC on D-Day.[132]

For nearly ten minutes, Colman's familiar English accent carefully and thoughtfully conveyed Millay's extensive, two-stanza, multithemed poem over America's crackling radio sets. It lamented the sacrifices young men made in war while also serving as a clarion call for all Americans to step up their home-front support. In sophisticated but accessible metaphorical prose, Millay directed her opening lines at home-front America by demanding that the nation's sons "must not go alone / into that burning building!—which today / is all of Europe!" Heroism existed on American soil as well as foreign soil, she claimed, since the very same "blood which warms the veins / of heroes at the front . . . / runs also in our own!" Millay directed her appeals to "Thou Prince of Peace," beseeching God to put an end to this "antique and violent thing / called War" and to "let our boys come home!" A brief moment of silence followed Colman's flawless recitation, contributing further to the impact of Millay's powerful poetic prayer.[133] D-Day had in fact developed a divine aura unto itself.

Although many of the newspapers published on 6 June 1944 characterized the "impulse to prayer" as a spontaneous reaction to D-Day, several of them revealed in their reportage that advance preparations had actually attended many of the special prayer services and radio broadcasts conducted throughout the day. Thus, much like General Eisenhower's religiously charged Order of the Day, the consistent message put forth by the press and broadcast media on D-Day represented a deliberate effort to frame the Invasion as a sacred event, one that mandated through editorials, imagery, language, and printed pronouncements by political leaders the social expectation of prayer. In short, D-Day was to be the most important event of the war, so all Americans had to rally in supporting the final push in both spirit and action.

The advanced preparations to observe D-Day through prayer should not have surprised many Americans, since the false Invasion flash erroneously sent on 3 June 1944 set many of these plans into motion. For example, in its 4 June 1944 edition, Denver's *Rocky Mountain News* reported that the accidental flash message prompted area military installations to initiate preplanned prayer observances, which leaders quickly canceled once the error became known.[134] Many newspapers published on 6 June revealed their own advanced preparations for observing the day through prayer. The *Baltimore News-Post* had prepublished several prayers by religious leaders in an earlier edition for use when D-Day actually arrived.[135] In several cases, clergymen called in to the newspapers early on D-Day to submit preplanned special service schedules so the public would know where and when to pray.[136] Newspapers had almost certainly prepared many of the elaborate, religiously charged advertisements that appeared in D-Day editions in advance. Likewise, local and national religious leaders had also prewritten the Invasion prayers published by newspapers on their behalf on 6 June 1944, particularly those prayers written by nationally known religious leaders such as Archbishop Spellman. Perhaps the most intensive pre-Invasion preparations for a prayer-related event went into readying Independence Hall to broadcast Mayor Samuel's ringing of the Liberty Bell. According to the *New York Journal American*, radio engineers spent weeks preparing the hall for the eventual broadcast.[137]

In the end, the print and broadcast media had collaborated with political and religious leaders, organically and independently of General Eisenhower's own messaging, to sacralize the Invasion by observing it through a national call to prayer. In doing so, they helped to apotheosize the event, to elevate the Invasion's importance and greater significance in the minds of all Americans for decades to come. The veritable icing on the cake would come at day's end, when the commander in chief himself would enjoin all Americans to gather around their radios and pray with him for victory. No one, not even President Roosevelt, was exempt from the "impulse to prayer."

◆ ◆ ◆

Newspapers and radio worked in unison to provide all Americans on D-Day the starkest example of the Invasion's sacred meaning in the form of a prayer written and broadcast by the commander in chief himself, Franklin D. Roosevelt. In a remarkable display of spiritual union with his fellow Americans, FDR demonstrated through the power of his personal example the importance that prayer would play in ultimate victory. In doing so, FDR both acknowledged and channeled the angst all Americans felt by assuring them through the medium of prayer that although the road ahead would be tough and that many young men would die, the inherent goodness of America's cause and of its fighting men would prevail over the forces of evil. Through his demonstrated piety and shared concern for the soldiers' welfare, FDR was stabilizing, or perhaps even elevating, the collective national morale of all Americans in a time of crisis.[138] By closing out the day's Invasion reporting with this prayer, FDR was cementing in America's consciousness the divine nature attending D-Day and its core meaning, a meaning made more powerful through the united message transmitted through Eisenhower's crusading rhetoric, through the thematic framing evident in the newspapers' and radio networks' much-touted national impulse to prayer, and through the tacit endorsement given to each of these two factors by the top American himself, President Roosevelt.

Scores of newspapers throughout America enabled President Roosevelt's national call to prayer to reach a wide and disparate audience by promptly notifying readers of the event and by advertising the broadcast time according to each particular region's war time zone. As soon as news of the scheduled prayer came over the wire, newspapers throughout the country gave FDR's prayer front-page billing while others carved out already precious news space within the paper's main body. In many cases, when and where news of the prayer appeared in a given newspaper depended upon when specific editions hit the presses. The *Boston Traveler*, relying on AP's wire feed, found front-page space to promote the prayer under the heading "FDR To Radio Prayer for Victory: Asks Nation To Join In at 10 Tonight."[139] Thus, Bostonians and all Americans on the East Coast would hear the broadcast at the latest time of day—10 p.m. Eastern war time—just as many people were preparing for bed. At the other end of the spectrum, under Pacific war time, those on the West Coast would hear the prayer broadcast the earliest, at 7 p.m.—just as many listeners were finishing their evening meals and settling in to absorb the day's war news. The *Los Angeles Evening Herald and Express* advertised the prayer in its fifth Invasion extra that day with the heading "FDR in Prayer: To Lead Nation Via Radio Tonight." The news item instructed the people of Los Angeles to tune in at 7 p.m. on one of seven listed radio stations; the *Herald and Express* also specified a rebroadcast time of 11:05 p.m. that evening in case some listeners were unable to hear FDR recite the prayer live.[140] The *San Jose News* even posted an advertisement for Fox West Coast Theatres, promoting FDR's prayer and providing various stage venues where the public could gather and listen together to the broadcast that evening.[141]

Despite regional war time zones, however, almost all Americans tuning in would experience the prayer simultaneously, further enabling a common understanding of how all Americans on 6 June 1944 had served the cause of D-Day by participating in a national, communal prayer with the commander in chief. Even the designation of "war time," established by FDR in 1942 ostensibly to save energy in the spring and summer months, helped remind Americans that they were already tangibly serving their nation by calibrating their daily lives to this war-imposed time regimen. Thus, across the eastern, central, mountain, and Pacific war time zones, a four-hour difference from coast to coast, all Americans would successfully place into practice the notion of an "imagined community" through the common, and simultaneous, ceremony of prayer.[142]

The newspapers did not merely advertise FDR's scheduled prayer broadcast, they also printed the complete text of the prayer so all Americans could familiarize themselves with the words before reciting the epistle in unison with FDR later that night. All three main wire services—AP, UP, and INS—fed their subscribers not simply news of the prayer and its scheduled broadcast time but also the prayer itself. The *Cincinnati Times-Star*, the *Columbus Citizen*, the *Elizabethton Daily Star*, the *Erie Dispatch Herald*, and the *Fresno Bee*, for example, all provided the verbatim text of FDR's 525-word prayer the moment it became available around mid-day on 6 June.[143] CBS and NBC also broadcast the text of FDR's prayer at "dictation speed" to allow listeners to copy each word verbatim.[144] The *Boston Traveler* even featured an AP report from Washington, DC, describing how FDR, upon completing the prayer, dispatched a copy to the House of Representatives by motorcycle messenger. After this dramatic delivery, claimed the report, the House chaplain, Dr. James Shera Montgomery, read the prayer aloud on the floor. Moreover, Dr. Montgomery broke with custom by asking members to join with him in the opening invocation and to stand in silent prayer, further suggesting not only that America's political leaders, like FDR, were heeding the impulse to prayer but also that D-Day was of such significance as to warrant a break with House tradition.[145]

Attending notifications of the prayer's broadcast and its text were sometimes conflicting details about how FDR came to craft his D-Day prayer. Before America learned of the Allied invasion, FDR had addressed all Americans via radio on the night of 5 June 1944 to celebrate Rome's liberation by Allied forces earlier that day while also cautioning that hard fighting still lay ahead. A few hours later, German news reports signaled that the Invasion of Normandy had begun. The wire services, especially the AP, initially reported that immediately after the Rome broadcast, FDR, with foreknowledge of the Invasion, had "closeted himself in his bedroom" with blackout curtains drawn in order to begin writing his D-Day prayer.[146] The UP version, as reported in the *Seattle Star*, described FDR as spending "the tense early invasion hours writing a prayer which he will read to the nation over all radio networks" that evening.[147] FDR's presidential secretary Stephen T. Early began his daily press conference, according to an AP story, by explaining to reporters that FDR, fully informed about D-Day's start date and time, had in fact begun drafting the Invasion prayer days earlier and had only finished it that night. In reality, the president had leaned heavily upon the talents of Robert Sherwood, Pulitzer Prize–winning playwright and presidential speechwriter, to craft a carefully articulated message infused with religious sentiment much like Eisenhower's Order of the Day.[148] Early's statement reassured the public that America's commander in chief, who had begun monitoring Invasion reports that night at 11:30 p.m., had received plenty of sleep and, by implication, did not stay awake all night writing the Invasion prayer from scratch. Instead, FDR had remained "intimately abreast of the operations" and in full command. In effect, Americans could take comfort in knowing that while preparing to engage in spiritual leadership of the nation, FDR was not forsaking his practical, hands-on leadership of the war.[149]

At 10 p.m. EWT the messaging platform for D-Day shifted decisively from newspapers to radio as an estimated 90 million people tuned in to join FDR in prayer. According to *BBA* magazine, FDR's radiocast was "the first time a President of the United States led the nation in prayer over combined networks and independent stations." Everyone prayed simultaneously in a common tongue with the commander in chief. Radio, according to *BBA*, became FDR's "pulpit."[150]

When the hour struck, announcers throughout the nation introduced the president, who immediately began reading from the same prayer script disseminated throughout the day by newspapers from coast to coast. Listeners followed along from these newspapers as FDR read slowly and deliberately in his familiar New York patrician accent. He opened with some handwritten lines added before the broadcast to explain his earlier silence about the Invasion during his Rome broadcast. "My Fellow Americans," he began. "Last night, when I spoke with you about the fall of Rome, I knew at that moment that troops . . . were crossing the Channel." With these introductory words, FDR asserted his common nationhood with all listeners and that, as commander in chief, he was fully informed and in control, setting the tone for a prayer intended to reassure all Americans while acknowledging the difficult road that lay ahead.

Next, the president focused on the prepared text of the prayer, opening with perhaps the most memorable, most dignified words of the entire orison, replete with religious imagery and language that deliberately cast the Invasion as a sacred undertaking. With an unmistakable gravity in his voice, FDR asked his audience to join him in prayer: "Almighty God: Our sons, pride of our nation, this day have set upon a mighty endeavor, a struggle to preserve our Republic, our religion, and our civilization, and to set free a suffering humanity." Like Eisenhower, FDR framed the Invasion in moralistic terms as a high-stakes enterprise undertaken by America's peace-loving sons, who fought to liberate others and "not for the lust of conquest." FDR warned that the enemy was strong, so he instructed all Americans to steel themselves for the trials ahead and the inevitable loss of human life. He even employed descriptive imagery—"The darkness will be rent by noise and flame"—to stimulate listeners' imaginations about the horrors faced by America's fighting men. But he also invoked God's grace for those at home, all of whom must "rededicate [them]selves in renewed faith in Thee in this hour of great sacrifice."

FDR further instructed Americans not to allow the impulse to pray to dissolve after D-Day but to sustain it for the long term, "to devote themselves in a continuance of prayer" each day as they "redoubl[ed] the contributions [they] make in the physical and material support of our armed forces." Most tellingly, FDR linked his own moralistic message to the one expressed by Eisenhower in the supreme commander's Order of the Day by asking the Lord for "faith in our united crusade," establishing for Americans an unmistakable consistency in messaging between the president and his top military commander leading the Invasion. FDR reinforced Eisenhower's characterization of the Invasion as a morally charged Great Crusade spearheaded by divinely motivated American soldiers whose goodness would prevail over "the apostles of greed and racial arrogances"—but likely after much bloodshed and loss. In a segregated America, the clearly hypocritical reference to the enemy's racism likely fell on deaf ears as Americans seized upon FDR's deeper message of America's inherent goodness. The president concluded the six-minute broadcast by beseeching God's blessing in helping America lead the world, along with its sister nations, to establish "a peace invulnerable to the schemings of unworthy men." FDR ended the transmission without deviation from the prepared script, allowing listeners to absorb the words and to ponder the serious tone of his delivery. Although no evidence exists to suggest that FDR and Eisenhower collaborated on the Order of the Day and the presidential prayer, FDR clearly seized upon the Invasion-as-crusade trope from Eisenhower's message and deliberately included it to sacralize the Invasion narrative for all Americans. But more importantly, these complementary messages would signal to America's enemies that they faced a nation united in what amounted to no less than a religious fervor dedicated to their ultimate defeat.[151]

◆ ◆ ◆

Author and scholar James P. Moore Jr. has argued that "during times of domestic and international conflict, Americans of every persuasion have repeatedly turned to prayer to acknowledge the presence of a higher power, to put life and death into perspective, and to take stock of the consequences of human decision and action." Americans on D-Day clearly fell in line with Moore's assertion by reacting to the Invasion with an "impulse to prayer." But in the case of D-Day, the print and broadcast media deliberately enabled this reflexive response by advancing religiously charged messaging through its consistent, and often emphatic, reporting on General Eisenhower's moralistic Great Crusade missive, on where and when all Americans were to fulfill their social expectation to pray, and on when to tune in to hear the commander in chief close out the day's Invasion news on a prayerful note. This combined reporting, facilitated by widely used wire service feeds and made more powerful because the religious themes comported so well with American sensibilities of the time, contributed to a deliberately constructed thematic framing of D-Day as an extraordinary and sacred military undertaking in the greatest war the world had ever seen—a "crusade" that transcended mere political differences with enemy nations and instead took on the flavor of a morally charged struggle for the survival of civilization and freedom. In this characterization, D-Day marked the beginning of the end in a desperate battle between good and evil. The medium of prayer further enabled this sacralization of the D-Day narrative because, as Moore further claimed, it "offered a way for people across religious, racial, ethnic, economic and social lines to come together to share such a seminal event," to see the Invasion through the same religiously shaded prism.[152] Thus, on 6 June 1944 an "imagined community" of American newspaper readers and radio listeners—all social contemporaries—came away with the clear notion that D-Day was, among other things, a sacred event, in turn giving rise to another of the four core themes comprising the emerging D-Day narrative.

CHAPTER 6

Only the Very Best

The Invasion Leaders and Their Fighting Men

The liberation of Europe is not being accomplished by robots. The story of the Second Front is the story of your son, your kid brother. . . . From commanders down to buck privates, the Allied invasion army is a human army.

—Charles Shaw, CBS war correspondent
broadcasting from London, 6 June 1944[1]

Gen. Dwight D. Eisenhower, supreme commander of the Allied Expeditionary Force, stood on the rooftop of the 101st Airborne Division headquarters building in Newbury, England, with members of his staff and, according to a UP report appearing in American newspapers on D-Day, "cheered" on his men as he "watched a mighty airborne armada form in the sky and wing toward France" in the waning daylight hours of 5 June 1944.[2] These American paratroopers would be among the first troops to land in occupied France to fulfill the promise of their supreme commander's Great Crusade by engaging directly in "the elimination of Nazi tyranny over the oppressed peoples of Europe."[3]

Since issuing the order to launch the Invasion eighteen hours earlier, an inwardly anxious Ike decided to visit some of the troops that morning beginning with a stop in Portsmouth, where he met with members of two British divisions—the 3rd and the 50th—as they loaded onto their ships and landing craft. Following an afternoon press briefing with SHAEF's four accredited war correspondents—Robert Barr of the British Broadcasting Corporation (BBC); Stanley Burch of Reuters, the British wire service; Ned Roberts of the UP; and Merrill "Red" Mueller of NBC—in which he told the reporters that the Invasion was on, Ike traveled unannounced to an airfield at Newbury to speak to the men of the 101st Airborne Division as they prepared to board the aircraft that would deliver them to France. The grinning, gregarious supreme commander, undoubtedly weighed down by the great responsibility he shouldered, mingled informally among the paratroopers. He quizzed them on their hometowns as Mueller and Roberts, who had accompanied Ike on the visit, recorded the event for the press pool. The *Seattle Daily Times* became one of the first newspapers to publish the now-famous AP Wirephoto of Ike chatting with the young paratroopers late on D-Day. The supreme commander knew that many of the young "Screaming Eagles" would not be alive when the sun rose the next morning.[4] At that point, Eisenhower was doing all that one could expect of a senior leader in command of such a massive and complex operation—he was spending time with the men and women who would make Operation Overlord a reality and, hopefully, defeat the Nazi aggressors.

◆ ◆ ◆

For the press on D-Day, Dwight D. Eisenhower represented the very best of the leaders—and soldiers—America had to offer to the global war effort. Elevating the status and capacity of a man like Eisenhower fed directly into the final two thematic frames shaping the enduring American D-Day narrative. America's newspaper and broadcast editors wanted the reading public to see D-Day through the prism of these themes, affording the editors and their staffs a strong measure of agency as morale boosters and contributors to the Invasion's success. These thematic frames in turn directly influenced the public's understanding of what the Invasion should mean to them and, ostensibly, stiffened their resolve for the final push against Nazi Germany.

The first of these final two thematic frames, and the third theme overall, cast the Allied Invasion leaders, most notably the American Invasion leaders, as the right men with the right experience and expertise to lead the troops to victory on the European continent. The fourth and final theme emerged through the press' collective characterization of America's young fighting men overseas as morally pure, well-trained, courageous, and selfless citizen-soldiers. These soldiers were the very embodiment of American values and, for many, of American exceptionalism. These young men manning the front lines of liberty with their very lives represented all that was good in America, and the broadcast and print media ensured that their reportage publicly testified to their courage and sacrifice. Such a portrayal elided troubling instances that might complicate the narrative—soldiers whose training left them unprepared, commanders relieved for not measuring up, and newfangled equipment that failed catastrophically at the decisive moment—in favor of an idealized, oversimplified vision of the landing forces. The one key factor that destabilized both of these thematically dominant characterizations was how the mainstream press excluded the glaring fact that the United States as a nation overtly and structurally prevented Black soldiers from sharing in the same combat opportunities as White soldiers. In effect, Black soldiers had no fundamental opportunity to share in the nation's adulation for its fighting troops. How could the press claim that only America's best soldiers were fighting at the tip of the spear when a large male segment of America's 13 million Blacks—10 percent of the U.S. population—were denied the right to fight?[5]

Despite the omission of Black soldiers from the narrative, America's radio networks and newspapers advanced these final two thematic frames in three specific ways. First, they conveyed the third theme, which cast the Allied senior leaders as the best men for the task at hand, by promoting and celebrating the American commander of the operation, Gen. Dwight D. Eisenhower, as the right man for the job. They also highlighted the collective body of senior Allied commanders as having the combined capacity to best Germany's finest, most seasoned leaders, such as Field Marshal Erwin Rommel. Finally, the press developed the fourth and final theme—that America's soldiers were the best and most courageous warriors in the Invasion—by highlighting the soldiers' training, intrepidity, spirit, and links to their hometown roots. Along with the first two themes shaping the D-Day reportage—that the Invasion was the war's greatest enterprise and a sacred undertaking—these final two thematic frames focusing on the Invasion leaders and America's fighting men rounded out the four elements that came to define the enduring, and largely anodyne, D-Day narrative for decades to come.

The emphasis on the very best leaders and soldiers shaping the D-Day reportage contrasted with the newspaper coverage of two earlier invasions in the European theater in very nuanced and, in some cases, very overt ways. When reporting on Operation Torch in North Africa on 8 November 1942 and Operation Husky in Sicily on 10 July 1943, America's newspapers revealed a clear progression in how they covered General Eisenhower, who served as the supreme commander for both operations. While early editions on D-Day splashed photographs of Ike across their front pages accompanied by celebratory language of his martial prowess, newspapers reporting on Torch on 8 November 1942, the first Allied invasion in the west, simply offered stock photos of Eisenhower in his dress uniform under bland captions that read "Heads Invasion" or "In Command."[6] At that point, Ike did not have a track record to celebrate. But after the Allied success in North Africa, Ike's command abilities appeared to be no longer in question. In the reporting on Husky nine months later, his name appeared in bold, almost celebratory pronouncements attesting to his growing reputation as a successful commander. For example, the *Chicago Daily Tribune*'s headlines announcing the Sicily landings exclaimed, "Eisenhower Strikes!" while the *Dunkirk Evening Observer* reported, "Eisenhower Commands Great Amphibious Operation."[7] Thus, Ike's media stature evolved steadily leading up to D-Day thanks to his continued operational successes, with the press's martial apotheosis of the supreme commander reaching a crescendo with the D-Day reportage.

When identifying or describing the Allied senior leaders, the newspapers covering Torch and Husky offered very little—a stark contrast from the broader D-Day reporting. Granted, Allied commanders such as Montgomery, Patton, and others did in fact receive frequent mention in America's newspapers and on the radio, but the intense emphasis and positive reviews these senior flag officers received in America's newspapers on D-Day broke with these earlier reporting paradigms. And even though reporting on the North Africa landings proved very

American-centric, by the time of the Sicily operation, American newspaper headlines and front-page stories spelled out plainly that Husky involved not only American but Canadian and British troops as well.[8] The D-Day reporting built upon this multinational theme, especially when describing the martial prowess of the senior Allied leaders.

Coverage of the American troops throughout the war had always been strong and represented one of many common threads connecting all of America's newspapers, but the reporting on D-Day reflected a change in approach leading up to the Invasion. While most newspapers featured items emphasizing the military service of their "hometown boys," the reporting on Torch and Husky only referred to the troops participating directly in the operation in broad terms—essentially as nameless, faceless GIs making up, in the case of Torch, "powerful American expeditionary forces" hitting the beaches.[9] These generalized descriptions of the American troops' collective "power" did little to humanize them in the ways that war correspondents and feature writers approached their characterizations of the Invasion troops on 6 June 1944. The war correspondents on D-Day found ways to portray American soldiers with greater detail and texture; the reporting was something different—something that transcended all earlier reporting paradigms.

For all the emphasis America's newspapers and radio networks placed on boosting the images and military capabilities of the Allied senior leaders, the news media did not give themselves any room to parry possible counterpoints if their wire sources provided reports contradicting or destabilizing this thematic frame in the overall D-Day narrative. Although America's newspaper editors and radio broadcasters broadly advanced this core theme organically and systematically on 6 June 1944, their war correspondents accompanying the Invasion troops were actively trying to provide reports that had the power to compromise that very boosterism. Specifically, if the war correspondents on Omaha Beach had succeeded in getting their dispatches off the beach and across the wires, the as-yet unresolved situation on Omaha, if reported in the papers and on radio, would almost certainly have destabilized the news media's thematic frame that America's best leaders had managed to secure the beachheads efficiently and with minimal loss of life. With a six- to ten-hour time lag in reporting nationwide, Americans would not have learned by the end of 6 June 1944 if Omaha had or had not fallen to the American landing forces. Such an open question would have raised concerns about American generalship and altered, or at least called into question, the type of D-Day narrative advanced by the collective news media. In many ways, the press and radio were staking their credibility on their overly optimistic narrative of the Invasion. In fact, Lt. Gen. Omar Bradley, whose 1st Infantry Division and 29th Infantry Division were caught up in the bloodbath on Omaha, considered evacuating the beachhead because the reports he was receiving on his flagship suggested the assault had failed. The press would only report much later that certain colonels and generals on the beaches had risen to the challenge and broken the Omaha Beach stalemate before the sun set on D-Day. But such clarity was lacking at the moment, and the lag in reporting and the problems getting reports off the beaches by men like the AP's Don Whitehead allowed the best-leader theme to go unchallenged—at least in the first 24 hours of the Invasion reportage.[10]

◆ ◆ ◆

America's newspapers shaped their Invasion reportage to advance the thematic frame that the Allied Invasion troops, particularly the Americans, benefitted directly from the Allies' best senior leaders by first emphasizing with photographs the American commander who not only led the effort but who also embodied the Allied senior leaders' finest attributes—Gen. Dwight D. Eisenhower. Along with their bold headlines and news summaries attesting to the Invasion's grand scale and significance, most newspapers nationwide leveraged their ability to employ visual representations of the news by interspersing photographs of the supreme commander throughout their pages. These images appeared with headings or captions that indicated something all Americans had come to know leading up to 6 June 1944—that Ike, a leader with a proven track record of success, was at the helm. Such images reminded all Americans that their young citizen-soldiers were in good hands. Moreover, for those Americans who saw the war from an American-centric perspective, the fact that an American officer was in charge of American lives likely offered them added comfort.

The photographs local editors selected to portray the supreme Allied commander generally depicted him as a man in full command of his environment. These images showed Ike—normally wearing his familiar short-waisted, British-style jacket and side cap with four stars—as sporting either his characteristic, confident grin or his more serious, stoic demeanor. Accompanying most of these photographs were headings clearly identifying him as the man in charge. The *Miami Herald* included a previously well-publicized photograph of a stern-faced Ike at his desk taken shortly after he assumed command of Operation Overlord in January 1944. Similarly, the *Detroit News* published an image of Ike under large letters identifying the general as simply "Invasion Chief Gen. Dwight D. Eisenhower." For its part, the *Sheboygan Press* featured a grinning portrait of Ike under the straightforward heading of "Allied Supreme Commander." The *Daily News* of Los Angeles strayed slightly from the norm by publishing a front-page image of Ike above a quotation from the supreme commander. It was essentially an edict designed to inspire confidence among the reading public in the operation and its troops: "Keep your faith." As Ike's Order of the Day testified, faith played a large role in the supreme Allied commander's operational calculus, so his admonition to the American public to stay the course undoubtedly carried great weight. A more dramatic portrayal of Eisenhower as the supreme commander appeared inside the *Knoxville News-Sentinel* with an image of Eisenhower, his four stars clearly visible, checking his watch under the heading "Gen. Eisenhower Gives Command To Invade." Although the picture did not in fact capture the precise moment Eisenhower gave the order to launch Overlord—since members of the press were not present at that early-morning gathering of senior leaders—the editorial framing surrounding the photograph undoubtedly impressed upon the American public that the right man for the job was fully in command.[11]

More dramatic images depicting Ike in the field in England supervising the troops during pre-Invasion training tended to elicit a greater sense of the "man in command" framework that America's editors wanted to convey. An image in the *Rochester Times-Union* portrayed Eisenhower pointing out something to a young American officer as British officers General Montgomery and Air Marshal Tedder watched nearby. The *Times-Union* framed the image to impress upon readers Ike's undisputed leadership: "America's Eisenhower Points the Way." But the *Times-Union* also included a caption to ensure readers understood the close Allied partnership at work in Overlord by explaining, "British and Americans [understood] each other perfectly as General Eisenhower discusse[d] Allied strategy" with the two British flag officers.[12]

Vermont's *Burlington Free Press* perhaps made the most extensive use of photographs to reveal the principal qualities and characteristics that, in their estimation, made General Eisenhower a successful commander throughout the war. By leveraging five photographs from an AP feature beginning with Ike's time in the Mediterranean theater, the *Free Press* labeled the supreme Allied commander as "Ike the Invader" and then, using each photograph, described in a few sentences the qualities that made him the "No. 1 invader of World War II": industry, intelligence, diplomacy, good humor, and thoroughness.[13] The pervasive use of Eisenhower's image on D-Day had the ultimate effect of linking the man directly and permanently to the Invasion. In effect, the name Eisenhower became synonymous with the word "D-Day." But providing an imagistic record of Eisenhower in America's newspapers on D-Day was not the only way the press rendered the supreme commander in a three-dimensional—and very human—manner.

In addition to using imagistic means to promote General Eisenhower as a man fully capable of prosecuting such a massive enterprise as Overlord, Americas' newspapers liberally scattered numerous feature articles throughout their pages designed to reveal the man in greater detail than photographs would permit. Many of these short news items, mostly produced by overseas correspondents at SHAEF headquarters, burst across the wires and into America's newsrooms as soon as news of the Invasion broke. These brief word sketches defined Eisenhower not simply as an effective commander, but as representing a typical American upbringing—a man who hailed from the same small towns and who embodied the same American values as the troops he led. The war correspondents and America's newspaper editors worked in tandem to shape the content and headings of these brief biographical sketches to show American readers that Ike, for all his gifts, was one of them.

The most ubiquitous biographical sketch dotting America's newspapers on 6 June 1944—and the one that likely shaped most of America's impression of Eisenhower on D-Day—was penned by overseas correspondent Paul Kern Lee of the AP's foreign staff. In his brief analysis of the supreme commander, Lee cast Ike as "a quiet, methodical American soldier" who lived by the creed "of taking big risks for big stakes."[14] For Lee, Eisenhower was unassuming and not flashy, a quality that likely agreed with an American public seeking a direct path to victory with no frills attached. Moreover, Ike's track record of military successes up to that point more than justified his rapid rise through the ranks and his place as commander of what Lee described as "history's greatest overseas invasion."[15] But in Lee's assessment, one of Ike's greatest successes had been in "getting American, British, and French forces to work together as an [*sic*] harmonious team," which in turn made Eisenhower the "inevitable" choice for supreme Allied commander.[16]

Lee even unpacked for America's readers the German-language origin of Ike's name—"Eisenhauer," or "iron striker"—as a way to portray further the general's inborn steely resolve and risk-taking nature. But perhaps the one quotation Lee captured from Ike that proved most endearing and resonant to America's audiences was the baseball metaphor the supreme commander used when asked to explain his command philosophy. Ike simply replied, "You can't hit a home run by bunting; you have to step up and take your cut at the ball."[17] The use of this metaphor, based upon the beloved all-American sport, resonated so much with rewrite men and editors nationwide that some of them referred to it directly in the heading to Lee's piece. The *Johnson City Press-Chronicle* in Tennessee, for instance, labeled Lee's article as "General 'Ike' Takes a Full

Cut at Ball."[18] No singular metaphor could more effectively elicit from American readers the sense that Ike was truly one of them—a simple, unobtrusive man who exuded the values of Main Street America and an uncompromising optimism.[19]

Other small features built upon the descriptions and characterizations of General Eisenhower reflected in Lee's article, particularly the notion that some considered Ike to be "A 'Lucky' General." The AP's Wes Gallagher sent a short item over the wires on D-Day (in addition to his front-page news summaries) portraying Ike's successful decisions in previous operations as partly due to luck. Gallagher, who had covered Eisenhower in North Africa, explained how Ike had selected the date for the North African landings sixty days in advance "with the scientific odds nine-to-one against him" that French Morocco's "iron coast" would not support landings except for a brief three-day window. But as Ike's luck would have it, the waters were calm on that day. Ike had similar luck, explained Gallagher, when he selected invasion dates in advance for the Sicily and Salerno landings. In Gallagher's estimation, if luck was a necessary ingredient in the success of large operations such as Overlord, then Ike had it in abundance. But Gallagher was quick to point out that the supreme commander was not superstitious, a point Gallagher blatantly contradicted when he explained that Ike carried with him on "'tough' days" a small purse containing lucky coins, which he had "rubbed" prior to the invasions in North Africa, Sicily, and Salerno. Gallagher ended by speculating "that there was no doubt [Ike] was rubbing them last night."[20]

Some correspondents emphasized Eisenhower's youth and virility and the advantages those factors afforded the supreme Allied commander on D-Day. Paul Kern Lee revealed that Ike would be fifty-four years old on 14 October 1944, a fact that war correspondent James Wellard of the *Chicago Daily Times* accentuated in his own sketch of Eisenhower.[21] Wellard celebrated Eisenhower as "the youngest commander-in-chief of the vast Allied and enemy armies entering the final trial of strength." Wellard was correct: Ike's opposite, Germany's commander in chief West was Field Marshal Gerd von Rundstedt, whose age on D-Day was sixty-nine, making him Ike's senior by sixteen years. Wellard made much of this distinction by claiming that with Eisenhower, "the accent is definitely on youth—on the new and virile ideas of the new military theory." For Wellard, this youthfulness suggested that Eisenhower's mastery of modern operational doctrine put him well ahead of his aged, and implicitly backward, German counterpart. Moreover, explained Wellard, Eisenhower openly admitted that he was not infallible, but this youthful commander in chief "was a soldier's soldier" who willingly carried the burden of command and who "never pass[ed] his responsibilities to subordinates."[22]

While many correspondents placed Eisenhower on an even higher pedestal—exalting him like no other Allied military figure at the time—some reporters sought to accentuate his humanity and common decency by revealing that the supreme Allied commander felt deeply anxious about Overlord even while projecting outward confidence. Red Mueller, who was situated at SHAEF headquarters when news of D-Day broke, broadcast his own assessment of Ike at 8:24 a.m. EWT, a report that later appeared in many newspapers. In the report, Mueller described asking Ike on the drive out to visit the 101st Airborne Division how his nerves were holding up. Ike replied in a Midwest vernacular that undoubtedly resonated with Main Street America: "I'm so goll durn nervous I boil over."[23] If America was nervous about D-Day, so was Ike.

Despite this inner nervousness, explained Mueller, Ike exuded an infectious confidence in his troops through the easy way he interacted with the men on the eve of the Invasion. In his CBS broadcast, Mueller explained that once the D-Day order had gone out, "there [was] nothing more tactically useless than a supreme commander, except as an inspiration." Mueller claimed, "I have never seen *any* commander receive greater acclaim for buoying his men more than does General Eisenhower."[24] He described in detail how Eisenhower interacted with, and inspired, the troops. The supreme Allied commander would roll up to the troops in his staff car amid cheers of "Ike! Ike!" and begin verbally sparring with the men in his easy manner. Mueller quoted several exchanges between the supreme commander and the troops, such as the banter between Ike and a young soldier, who told his commander in chief that "he was an expert rifleman." "'Good,' said the General, 'that's the way we'll win.'"[25]

Another common frame running throughout all the various biographical and personal sketches of General Eisenhower was the supreme commander's ability to maintain a fully functional, multinational coalition—and to be acceptable to all parties involved. As Paul Kern Lee claimed in his portrayal of Ike, getting the British, French, and Americans to work together was his greatest success.[26] Geoffrey Parsons Jr. of the *New York Herald Tribune* reported on D-Day that Eisenhower, ever the diplomatic leader and ally, maintained daily contact with General Charles de Gaulle, whom many Americans nationwide already knew to be a difficult personality from earlier reporting. But Parsons's simple report, for all its sparseness, suggested to American readers that Ike was a leader who built bridges to others.[27] Most importantly, the press collectively cast Ike on D-Day as acceptable to all Allied parties. James Wellard testified in his report: "I have never heard a Briton, official or private citizen, object to Ike's role as supreme commander." He continued, "They are heartily in favor, are actually inspired by the fact."[28]

Perhaps the most effective and powerful attestation to General Eisenhower's complete and confident command of Operation Overlord was the supreme commander's direct message to the people of occupied Europe. A mere fifteen minutes following the release of Communiqué No. 1, the radio networks broadcast Eisenhower's message to the "People of Western Europe" live from London at 3:47 a.m. EWT. Although the American public had often heard Ike's voice over the radio, they had never heard him broadcast a message directly to the people the Allies were liberating at the precise moment of an operation's execution. In North Africa, Ike had read a message from President Franklin D. Roosevelt; it was broadcast at the moment of invasion, but the American public only learned about the message through subsequent newspaper reportage.[29] On D-Day in Normandy, the American broadcast networks allowed the American people to eavesdrop on a key operational message at the very moment the intended recipients—the "People of Western Europe"—were hearing it. This immediacy caught listeners in its grip.[30]

The content of the supreme commander's message to the people of Western Europe clearly exhibited Eisenhower's full command of the operation and a clear sense that the man in charge had complete confidence in his mission and in the Invasion's outcome. In his calm, even, and deliberate Midwestern accent, Ike informed his European audience, "A landing was made this morning on the coast of France . . . in conjunction with our great Russian allies." But Ike's core message reflected that of a commander issuing orders to the very people he sought to liberate. He warned them against premature action, which "may prevent you from being of maximum help to your country in the critical hour." His words sought to inspire and uplift as he acknowledged in his broadcast the "heroic deeds of Frenchmen who have continued their struggle against the Nazis and their Vichy satellites." But, he warned, this landing represented only the "opening phase of the campaign in Western Europe" and that "great battles lie ahead"—but "together we shall achieve victory." This message left no doubt that Overlord was in good hands.[31]

The profundity of reporting on General Eisenhower on D-Day helped to advance the thematic frame that the Allies' senior leaders had the capacity, talent, experience, and leadership skill to prosecute Overlord successfully. Most importantly, those very qualities, and other uniquely American attributes, resided in the man at the top—the man they came to identify most with the Invasion at that moment and for decades to come, Gen. Dwight D. Eisenhower. The reportage on Eisenhower on 6 June 1944 clearly smacked of unrestrained hero worship, but the press felt obliged to instill in this one man all the qualities of a military leader that would undoubtedly put unsettled American hearts and minds at ease. They knew Ike was that man, and they framed their reporting in newsrooms across the country to match that messaging. But perhaps the key trait these collective portraits of Ike advanced to the public was his ability to bring Allied leaders together toward a common cause—he was the supreme *Allied* commander, after all. This trait would prove critical as the press further celebrated the collective excellence of the American and British senior leaders who, all Americans hoped and prayed, would lead the way to victory.

◆ ◆ ◆

Although Gen. Eisenhower became the dominant symbol of the competence, skill, and ability of the Invasion's senior leaders, the newspapers did not hide the fact that the supreme commander, and the Allied forces more broadly, further benefited from a much larger, multinational team of experienced and capable senior officers. These senior flag officers, drawn primarily from the U.S. and British armed forces, received almost universal attention and publicity in America's newspapers to convince an uneasy American public that the lives of the nation's young men and women were in excellent hands. Perhaps most importantly, the newspapers' collective emphasis on this thematic frame was by far the single most inclusively multinational aspect of the broader reportage on D-Day. In other words, the senior Allied leaders designated by the *St. Joseph News-Press* as the "Big Chiefs of the Second Front" received equal attention from America's newspaper editors—be they British or American.[32] This inclusiveness helped to temper the overarching American-centric perspective that dominated both the newspaper and radio coverage of D-Day, which resulted from the prevailing reliance in the American press on dispatches and bulletins emanating from the U.S. wire services and other overseas American news sources. In fact, the American reporting on D-Day caused the British Ambassador in Washington, DC, to express "dismay over those U.S. headlines that suggested the Americans had invaded France by themselves."[33] However, by giving equal billing to the British senior leaders, America's newspapers acknowledged the one trait that made Eisenhower acceptable to all Allied parties—his ability to unify all members of the alliance in the furtherance of victory.

America's newspaper editors, who exercised their legitimate roles as active participants in the Invasion's success, framed their biographical sketches of the Allied senior leaders to demonstrate the wide range of abilities and experience each man offered the Invasion effort, regardless of any previously well-publicized battlefield setbacks suffered by these men prior to the Invasion. The leaders receiving the most direct photographic and biographical emphasis by the press were the eight core members of what Chicago's *Daily News* defined as the "Supreme high command."[34] The first of those eight leaders was General Eisenhower who, despite the individual attention he received on D-Day, obtained added emphasis as one of these eight Allied leaders. Following closely behind Ike appeared the four British senior leaders in the high command: General Sir Bernard Law Montgomery, the ground commander of the Allied assault forces and the 21st Army Group; Air Chief Marshal Sir Arthur Tedder, deputy supreme commander; Air Chief Marshal Trafford L. Leigh-Mallory, Allied Air Force commander; and Admiral Sir Bertram Home Ramsay, Allied naval commander. Rounding out the group of eight were three American senior leaders: Lt. Gen. Omar Bradley, senior American ground forces and First Army commander; Lt. Gen. Carl "Tooey" Spaatz, U.S. Strategic Air Forces commander; and Lt. Gen. James H. "Jimmy" Doolittle, commander of the U.S. Eighth Air Force. A few newspapers added one or two additional senior Allied leaders, but this core group of eight senior leaders were the ones who were directly engaged in Operation Overlord and who received primary attention in America's newspapers.[35] Unsurprisingly, all of these Invasion leaders were White men, since the U.S. Army had in its ranks at the time what the *Detroit Tribune*, a Black weekly, described as the Army's "lone Negro general," Brig. Gen. Benjamin O. Davis Sr., who achieved his rank arguably because of the backing of the Black press. Davis had no direct role in the Invasion. Instead, as a deputy to the inspector general of the Army, Davis made inspection tours of Black troops throughout the Army. With so many White officers among the Invasion's most senior leaders, Black Americans had cause to view D-Day as just another chapter in a White man's war.[36]

First and foremost, America's newspaper editors presented the American public with photographic images of these eight all-White senior leaders upon whom so much depended on 6 June 1944. The individual photographs (or, in some cases, artist renderings) of these eight leaders appeared almost universally throughout America's newspapers on D-Day generally grouped together on a single page.[37] This physical placement of the images not only suggested Allied unity but also that the Invasion effort relied *equally* on both American and British leadership—four American senior leaders and four British senior leaders. The Canadian leadership interests were, naturally, ensconced within the British command hierarchy. The most important aspect of providing these photographs to the American public was that it allowed readers to see—to visualize—who these men were in a physical sense. The images used by the editorial staffs tended to be stock photographs collected prior to the Invasion by combined press sources in London or by the individual papers themselves for this very purpose—to celebrate the capabilities of these men and instill public faith and confidence in the Invasion's command team.

The images appearing in the papers varied slightly, but each newspaper generally crafted portrayals of the senior leaders as confident, serious, and self-assured. The most commonly published photographs of General Eisenhower and General Montgomery often toggled between their serious and smiling facial expressions. Air Marshal Tedder's images always portrayed him with a beaming smile while balancing his pipe between his lips. Air Chief Marshal Leigh-Mallory and Admiral Ramsay each appeared in formal portraits (the latter in his dress uniform with full medals), which evinced a distinguished, confident air. Two lieutenant generals—Bradley and Spaatz—offered American readers a slight smile while nearly all images of Lieutenant General Doolittle used by the press portrayed him grinning widely from ear to ear—a potent reflection of his self-confidence. These images allowed American readers to discern those often-intangible features of a person that speak to different people in different ways. America's newspaper editors hoped that the reading public would see in those faces, some familiar and others not, an expression of the collective wisdom, experience, and skill of the Invasion's command team. All told, these were the leaders whose faces all Americans would forever associate with turning such a complex operational plan into a successful reality.

The newspapers did not simply rely on photographs of these eight senior leaders to convince the American public that these men were the very best America and her Allies had to offer. They also crafted brief biographical sketches to accompany the photographs to provide further information that profiled each man's specific military successes, his hometown (to link him to the folks at home), his personal attributes, and his age, which had the dual role of suggesting youthful vitality and hard-earned experience. For instance, the word picture used to define the supreme Allied commander cast Ike as a fifty-three-year-old "canny Kansan who knit American, British and French forces in north [*sic*] Africa into unified command . . . decisive, but diplomatic." At age fifty-six, General Montgomery had been a "professional soldier [for] 35 years," according to his write-up; he was said to be a "hatchet-faced, hard-fighting, hard-bitten" soldier who had "won fame" in North Africa by "smashing" Rommel's Afrika Korps at El Alamein. Air Marshal Tedder was said to be a "quiet, sardonic scholar who sparked air support which spearheaded African victory" and who, as holder of the Royal Air Force's "oldest pilot's certificate, 1911," saw war as "a beastly thing." Admiral Ramsay at sixty-one was the "shy Scot who planned allied amphibious operations against Sicily and Italy" and who "won fame as the man who got the British army out of Dunkerque." Air Marshal Leigh-Mallory, according to his narrative, already had experience "maintaining air supremacy over hotly-contested beachheads" because "he [had done it] over the blazing beach of Dieppe in August, 1942." Lieutenant General Spaatz (nicknamed "Tooey"), appeared, in the press' eyes, as a "taciturn, tough-jawed Pennsylvania Dutchman" who thought his promotion to general would "cut into his flying" and whose credo for his airmen was simple: "The army air force must operate as a team, with minds, hearts and hands." Missouri-born Lieutenant General Bradley, according to the bio, "display[ed] rock-like imperturbability in [the] face of danger" and was also the "quiet-mannered hero of American victory at Bizerte." The youngest of the group at age forty-seven, Lieutenant General Doolittle, received acclaim in his summary as "the man who bombed Tokyo"; he was the "little Californian with the big grin [who had] been setting flying records for the last 25 years." All told, these summaries cast the "Supreme Invasion Command" as the right men for the mission and upon whom all Americans could rely to get the job done and bring their men and women home safely.[38]

If this portfolio of photographs and brief biographical sketches did not persuade the American public that the Allies had the very best senior leaders on their team, then the numerous individual features published about many of these leaders—British and American alike—drove the point home. Nearly every member of the eight senior leaders profiled in these collective snippets received individual treatment in separate feature articles spread throughout America's newspapers. These essays expanded on each leader's background and provided greater depth and texture to each man's character and capabilities. Not every newspaper included features of this nature on all eight men; the number of articles featuring the individual British leaders appeared in fewer newspapers, suggesting that when pressed for space, editors opted to provide their American readership with the more in-depth personal histories of the American senior leaders. Overall, the approach to publishing these stories nationwide remained remarkably balanced and fair—a clear demonstration by the newspapers to their readers that America needed these British senior leaders as much as they needed America.

This reliance on British generalship was most apparent in the fact that General Montgomery, commanding the Allied ground forces as well as the 21st Army Group, received more individual attention in America's newspapers than any other leader besides General Eisenhower. Two of the U.S. wire services' finest overseas correspondents, the AP's Paul Kern Lee and the UP's James C. McGlincy, each crafted in-depth portrayals of Montgomery that smacked of pure hagiography. In fact, the first sentence of Lee's feature hailed "Monty" as the "possessor of perhaps the most glittering reputation of all the Allied invasion commanders."[39] In his depiction, McGlincy portrayed Monty as a highly confident commander who admitted openly that "The invasion will be a rough show but it will succeed." McGlincy recounted how Monty believed the Invasion would be a reunion between him and German Field Marshal Erwin Rommel, whom McGlincy described as Monty's "defeated antagonist of the African desert campaign." The message: Rommel was no match for the British commander. Lastly, and in keeping with Allied diplomacy, Monty applauded American troops as "fine fighters" and admitted that "he was happy to be commanding American assault forces and working again—as in Tunisia—under an American commander." Montgomery's generous comments likely helped to salve any concerns the American and British people might have had about the Allies' ability to work in harmony.[40]

If the American newspaper-reading public did not have an opportunity to digest either of these two wire service portraits of General Montgomery, then radio gave them an opportunity to hear about the British commander from a different source. At 10:15 p.m. EWT, only a few minutes after President Roosevelt finished reading his D-Day prayer over the networks, CBS's Quentin Reynolds took to the microphone and offered his own adulatory assessment of General Montgomery. He described the general as having "an amazing spiritual quality that you don't often find in a successful general," a characteristic that, along with Monty's dedication to daily Bible readings, appealed to the more religious members of the American public and on a day when nearly everyone in America was praying for the Invasion's success. Reynolds went on to celebrate Montgomery as "a colorful, almost a legendary figure" who, oddly enough, abhors "bloodshed." He also noted that the British commander had a "habit of being right" about most things happening on the battlefield. But Reynolds obviously knew his audience and the angst they felt about D-Day, so he drove home the thematic frame characterizing the day's reportage of the Allied senior leaders by stating, "If your son serves under Montgomery, he serves under the greatest tactical general in the world, and he serves under a man who is vitally concerned with the welfare and the safety of every one of his men."[41]

Although General Montgomery received the lion's share of attention among the features focusing on the British senior leaders, some newspaper editors found (or even made) space to include articles on the other three British officers—Air Marshal Tedder, Air Marshal Leigh-Mallory, and Admiral Ramsay. These inclusions were largely scattershot among America's newspapers and far fewer in number than those items spotlighting the American senior leaders. However, these individual features, emanating from the AP and other news sources, appeared in sufficient quantity on D-Day to add greater depth and texture to the human aspects of these otherwise unknown British officers.

The brief word sketches accompanying the British senior leaders' photographs succeeded only in providing the highlights of each officer's military bona fides. However, the stand-alone features sought to make these men appear more relatable as human beings with, in many cases, average interests, a penchant for humor, and an enduring devotion to duty. For instance, according to one feature writer, in addition to his prowess as an air commander, Air Marshal Tedder now held the "highest place in the high command that has ever fallen to an Air Force man," a singular achievement marking him as a top-shelf senior leader. On a more personal level, Tedder was an amateur artist who carried his watercolors with him everywhere, had "bright and piercing eyes," and a "sharp cutting humor." Perhaps the one fact about him that evoked empathy from American readers was that his eldest son had died fighting the Luftwaffe in the skies over Britain.[42]

According to an AP feature, Tedder's fellow air marshal, Leigh-Mallory, had been a clergyman's son who had set out to become a lawyer when World War I broke out and after the war decided to "[devote] himself to military and aviation problems as an instructor." Leigh-Mallory, known as "L-M" throughout the RAF, was profiled by Tom Wolf, a Newspaper Enterprise Association (NEA) syndicated writer. Wolf noted that the air marshal was described by his former subordinates as "extremely fair" but "utterly ruthless in breaking even personal friends who let the service down." The biographical sketch of Admiral Ramsay lauded him "as the man who got the British army out of Dunkerque," which resulted in a hitherto unknown detail about the admiral—his nickname of "Dynamo," the code name for the evacuation operation. These added details pressed American readers to connect on a more intimate level with these men who, although leaders from another country, shared many traits and interests with other American leaders and, for that matter, many average Americans.[43]

The American Invasion leaders received similar, but more prolifically published, stand-alone tributes. Like those of their British counterparts, these profiles also highlighted personal attributes not captured in the briefer thumbnail sketches accompanying the photographic collages. Lt. Gen. Omar N. Bradley, according to one feature, was "the tall and lanky" general whose II Corps captured 25,000 German troops in North Africa; an AP feature noted that Bradley had been a former West Point tactics instructor who readily "translate[d] his theories into victorious action." Like many average Americans, he liked to hunt, golf, and play bridge. But one feature writer added a fourth pastime to those three hobbies—Bradley liked to fight.[44]

Like the articles on Bradley, the AP feature on Lieutenant General Spaatz divulged to American readers personal qualities that made him the right man to blunt the Luftwaffe's efforts to thwart the Invasion. Spaatz came off to American readers as a true, hard-edged warrior who, "despite Eisenhower's frowns, [had] made a number of combat bombing missions on particularly tough assignments." His achievement in shooting down two German planes during World War I earned him the Distinguished Service Cross and, as one article suggested, made him into a hands-on leader who was not afraid to risk his own life. Spaatz spoke bluntly and played poker badly, but "flying [was] his religion—and all agree he does it marvelously well." Fellow Army Air Forces Lt. Gen. James H. Doolittle's profile highlighted the fact that his Tokyo bombing raid of April 1942 had resulted in his promotion to brigadier general and the award of the Medal of Honor. But perhaps the most surprising detail for American readers was the fact that this diminutive hero also held a doctorate in aeronautics from the Massachusetts Institute of Technology, the first issued in the United States. Doolittle was called "one of the greatest pilots of all time" and "one of the best aeronautical engineers in the world." As these stand-alone profiles suggested, these senior leaders all had the right stuff, professionally and personally, to lead Operation Overlord to a successful conclusion.[45]

From NBC's Washington studio at 10 a.m. EWT on 6 June 1944, reporter Nancy Osgood elicited statements of confidence in the troops and promises of home-front support from Mrs. Carl A. Spaatz and Mrs. James H. Doolittle as well as from the wives of two American admirals—Mrs. Harold R. Stark, whose husband commanded U.S. Naval Forces Europe, and Mrs. Alan G. Kirk, whose husband commanded the Western Naval Task Force. Even General Eisenhower received on-air support from his wife, Mamie, who could not be present in the studio because, as Osgood explained, she was attending the West Point graduation of her son, John. Nevertheless, Osgood read aloud Mrs. Eisenhower's written expression of complete confidence that their men would be victorious and that the task now for everyone on the home front was to remain "as cheerful and as busy as possible."[46]

The press did not neglect to highlight the actions on D-Day of the one American senior officer in Washington, DC, who commanded the nation's greatest respect and to whom General Eisenhower reported—Gen. George C. Marshall, the Army chief of staff. Knowing about Marshall's activities on the evening of 5 June 1944 became a key objective for the Washington bureaus of both wire services, presumably because they knew their reading audience would want to know that the top general officer, the very exemplar of American generalship, was alert and at the helm—even though he was thousands of miles from the actual landings. His actions on the eve of D-Day had the power to demonstrate confidence in the operation or concern that Overlord might (or already had) hit some snags.

Oddly enough, the AP story that appeared in morning editions on 6 June 1944 actually sowed confusion about Marshall's activities on the eve of D-Day. One AP version reported that Marshall had departed his office in the Pentagon at 5 p.m. EWT and did not return until the next morning, suggesting that the Army chief had such faith in the operation's success that his presence was not necessary.[47] But other versions appearing in later editions put Marshall in his office almost continuously on Monday, 5 June, except for a brief interlude in which he attended an evening ceremony at the Soviet Embassy to receive the Order of Suvorov.[48] His remarks at that event, as reported by the UP, dripped with confidence in the Allied forces' ability to defeat the Germans. The news item quoted Marshall as saying that the last push against Germany will be "a battle to the death for the Nazis and a battle to victory for the Allies." He added the rare acknowledgment that the Red Army had carried a heavy burden in the war and that Soviet armies were now in "the actual process of destroying the Nazi military formations on the Eastern Front."[49] Marshall's confidence, and his recognition of Russia's sacrifice, undoubtedly resonated with the practical-minded American public who wanted the war concluded as quickly as possible.[50] And despite earlier confusion in the reporting, most AP pieces appearing in the newspapers on D-Day put Marshall squarely on the job all night long.[51]

As a way of enhancing further the thematic frame that the Allied senior leaders were the best men to lead Overlord, several press reports appearing in America's newspapers on D-Day compared the Allied leaders with their German counterparts—often in unflattering ways for the enemy. In fact, the press's representations of the German senior leaders came the closest on D-Day to the type of anti-German propaganda advanced by George Creel during World War I.[52] For the most part, the press on D-Day did not venture too deeply into propaganda's waters—but in some cases they got their feet wet. Understandably, the German leaders received far less attention in America's newspapers, and the type of attention they received toggled between bland assessments of their wartime accomplishments and uncomplimentary characterizations of their alleged personal attributes. Unsurprisingly, America's news editors generally painted a bleak picture of German generalship.

Like the coverage of the eight principal Allied Invasion leaders, some newspapers published a photo collage of the German flag officers, most notably with two key field marshals—von Rundstedt and Rommel—along with brief biographical narratives of each man. The less-than-flattering images portrayed several of the German generals, particularly von Rundstedt and Colonel-General Johannes Blaskowitz, as aged men in their sixties glaring stiffly into the camera while wearing outdated, prewar German uniforms. Rommel, though, always appeared in pictures taken in the North African desert and was visibly the youngest (and most dangerous) general among a cast of seemingly over-the-hill German leaders. The brief word descriptions further complemented these images in derisive ways, such as Rommel's depiction as "one of the fiercest leaders in the 1940 Battle of France" and von Rundstedt's portrayal as a member of the "Prussian military caste" whose "sole hobby is war." In short, these men bore little resemblance to the Allied senior leaders, who, by comparison, evinced greater humility and, unlike someone of the "Prussian military caste," bore a common connection with the soldiers they led and the hometowns and families they left behind.[53]

Although Field Marshal von Rundstedt represented General Eisenhower's direct German counterpart, and whom CBS's William Shirer lauded over the air as "undoubtedly the best general Hitler has," American newspapers cast Rommel as the Allied leaders' biggest threat and compared the "Desert Fox" directly to Ike and Montgomery.[54] In fact, a widely published AP piece bluntly asserted that Rommel was a kind of physical manifestation of Adolf Hitler's tactical genius, and who, like Der Führer, had "built a legend of invincibility around himself." Essentially, Rommel was Hitler's vessel, a channeler of the dictator's supposed battlefield acumen brought to bear against the Invasion forces in the person of the "Desert Fox." The *Toledo Times* put it most succinctly: "Rommel Means Hitler."[55]

Despite these negative characterizations of Germany's senior leaders, these Wehrmacht officers proved to be highly capable and worthy adversaries for the Allies in Normandy—a reality that would later demonstrate the perils of Creel-style propaganda when the bitter fighting on the beaches and later in the hedgerows of Normandy told a different story.

America's newspapers and radio networks made clear through the use of excessively obsequious language that the Allied senior leaders, particularly American flag officers, represented the very best men to lead the Invasion. American reportage trumpeted this theme over the airwaves and in newsprint to afford anxious American readers on the home front a measure of comfort in knowing that their young men and women in harm's way were in the very best hands. On the evening of D-Day, Major George Fielding Eliot, military analyst for CBS, acknowledged that some Americans had likely rebuffed such glowing characterizations of American generals. Eliot broadcast his own candid assessment that "the present American Army is the most capably commanded army" ever fielded at the outset of a war. But for the more skeptical and discerning listeners, he explained, "I don't mean to say that all our general officers are perfect, but as a whole they represent a far higher average of leadership and all-around military capability than the generals of any of our other wars."[56]

◆ ◆ ◆

The notion that America's—and the Allies'—finest senior leaders were piloting the Invasion went hand in hand with the fourth and final thematic frame emerging from the American press on D-Day: that the American troops these officers led were also the best, most well-trained, and gallant men to spearhead Operation Overlord. America's newspapers and radio networks cast the average soldier, sailor, and airman on D-Day as inherently pure, selfless, and brave, essentially reluctant citizen-soldiers whose goal was to liberate and not to conquer. The central belief that these young men, prepared for combat by America's athletic fields, farms, and Main Streets, were the very best the nation had to offer appeared to be a major factor uniting all Americans in 1944. Moreover, these troops enjoyed the unshakeable confidence of their families and their hometown neighbors. "Mom and Pop" America placed great faith in its young men, whom they liked to see as wholesome and decent, and the press took great pains to reinforce this lofty, and often exaggerated, ideal on D-Day to bolster the home front's continued support for these troops and, evidently, for the greater war effort.

In portraying U.S. troops in this manner, America's radio and newspaper editors also sought to alleviate their readers' angst over the fate of the overall Invasion effort and of their troops' well-being by illustrating in detail precisely how well-trained, well-equipped, and highly motivated America's soldiers, sailors, and airman were on D-Day. The press conveyed an impression of the troops' collective courage, confidence, and morale while also linking these men directly to the communities and jobs they left behind, deepening home-front connections to the actual Invasion. Newspapers also reminded their readers that many of these troops were women, mostly nurses, who trained in the same mud and rain as their male counterparts and whose roles as healers would prove invaluable once the shooting started. Unsurprisingly, the newspapers took even less notice of the contributions of Black soldiers participating in the Invasion effort. Hearkening back to the words of Gen. John J. Pershing—the man who commanded the D-Day troopers' fathers in World War I—Americans were reminded that their young men and women participating in Operation Overlord would live up to the legacy of victory earned on the same European battlegrounds a generation earlier.

In reality, most Americans certainly understood that these portrayals of America's fighting men and women glossed over those cowards, dolts, and dullards who infected the ranks and in past battles had contributed to failures and reversals. But in general, word had reached most Americans through trusted messengers such as correspondent Ernie Pyle that the average soldier, for all his shortcomings, was doing fine. In his widely read 1943 book *Here Is Your War*, Pyle admitted that after the debacle at Kasserine Pass in Tunisia, "folks at home must have been disappointed" in the troops. But they had nothing to fear. Pyle, as an eyewitness to the battle, saw "nothing wrong with the American soldier." In fact, wrote Pyle, "his fighting spirit was good," and his morale was "okay." What the American soldier gained from Kasserine, suggested Pyle, was experience. The more he fought, "the more of a fighting man he became."[57] And that experience, along with excellent training, made GI Joe a mortal threat to the Germans, and the press pushed that very point with vigor.

The newspapers led the way in casting America's fighting men as well-trained, highly skilled warriors by widely publishing an official War Department story on D-Day that was released to the wire services after SHAEF announced the Invasion. The article focused on any angst or misgivings members of the populace might have harbored secretly or openly about the ability of American troops to crack the German coastal defenses. The article, whose title in the *Chicago Daily News* read "Infantry Specially Trained To Knock Out Pillboxes," sought to undermine any German propaganda efforts at making the coastal defenses seem impenetrable by explaining that the U.S. Army's infantrymen had received special training to overcome these very types of defenses. According to the official release, these "assault tactics, perfected in North Africa, Sicily and Italy, were drilled into troops in Great Britain for months before the actual invasion." Those infantry units "designated for the spearhead of the attack," continued the article, received this "special training." The report further explained that although reducing fortifications was an engineer task, experience had shown that preparing the infantry to breach the defenses would be more "effective." For American readers, this information meant their men did indeed have the know-how to defeat the German "concrete emplacements" in what the article described as one of the most "dangerous operations of modern war" but that "American doughboys [had] proved," albeit with little supporting evidence, that they could do it. Most importantly, insisted the article, the "key to success [was] plain, old-fashioned fortitude, spelled with a capital G"—ostensibly meaning "guts." Thus, the official narrative emanating from Washington, DC, maintained that while the troops had the knowledge, skill, weapons, and training to breach Hitler's Fortress Europe, the special ingredient that each man had to bring with him was, quite simply, courage.[58]

The most significant message conveyed by the War Department's assault team article was the fact that America's military leaders had made good use of the lessons learned during previous invasions. The AP's Hal Boyle drove that point home by readily acknowledging something the War Department had already admitted—that "landing on a hostile shore against entrenched opposition is the most difficult of military tasks." According to Boyle, the Allies who were poised to assault Hitler's "Atlantic Wall" were taking "the most titanic gamble of our time"—"but a gamble in which, with proper preparation, the odds [were] in their favor." This "proper preparation" was leveraging that "vital factor"—experience—gained from the landings in Africa and Italy, experience that Boyle implied had shaped the GIs' and their Allied counterparts' training for the Invasion and gave them, along with their courage, that extra edge over the enemy. Paul Kern Lee also chimed in with his own dispatch claiming that "with every battle, with every new campaign, the Allies learned something new and stored it away until the great invasion of western Europe should call upon all their courage and cleverness and skill." With this type of editorial boosterism,

Mom and Pop America could take comfort in knowing their young men had benefitted from the sacrifices made by soldiers who spearheaded past invasions and learned some very hard lessons.[59]

Some war correspondents even participated directly in the realistic, live-fire training developed and executed for the assault troops, in turn allowing them to report on the realism, detail, and complexity of the Invasion rehearsals. For instance, the *San Francisco Chronicle*'s foreign editor, Peter D. Whitney, gained rare access to the Infantry Assault Training Center in England in which he and other reporters "took part in a mimic battle with live ammunition in an exhibition that involved air strafing, artillery bombardment, tanks, Bangalore torpedoes, bazookas and flamethrowers." Although deeply impressed by what he had witnessed, Whitney asked the officer in charge, a veteran of the landings in Sicily and Italy, what would happen if the Germans repulsed the Allied assault. The officer shot back a response that undoubtedly pleased American readers: "They don't fail. These guys are on the beach to stay."[60] In other words, suggested the officer, the troops' high-quality training and preparation had fortified them with the fieldcraft necessary to defeat any German threat. They were the best, most capable soldiers to eliminate the Nazi threat.

In a further effort to help American readers visualize the realistic nature of the pre-Invasion training for D-Day, many newspapers published photographs of the GIs engaged in that dramatic type of training. These photographs, published in accordance with censorship guidelines, allowed the newspapers, as a visual medium, to help the American public imagine with greater clarity just how rigorously the troops had prepared for Overlord. Although many images were clearly staged, most of them portrayed actual training events in England or the United States and, in some cases, depictions of earlier landings in other combat operations. In the absence of being able to publish actual Invasion photographs owing to the procedural breakdown between the correspondents on the beachheads and their London offices, a large percentage of newspapers on D-Day filled their pages with these training images to give their readers some appreciation of their soldiers' commitment to the Invasion's success and, most likely, to provide an impressionistic glimpse of the kind of beachhead combat these young GIs were facing.

In almost every case, the photographs published by America's newspapers depicted GIs in aggressive, confident poses or demonstrating their acquired skill in landing on beaches and clearing obstacles. The *Chicago Daily News* attempted to capture the dedication and demeanor of the average fighting man by publishing an image of a U.S. soldier in camouflage garb looking directly into the camera above a caption that read: "This Yank, outfitted and trained for his job, looks forward with a determined calm. He is set to carry out his mission."[61] Such images were intended to represent all U.S. fighting men who were ready to get the job done. But most of the images showed GIs engaged in collective training as combat units and using an abundance of newfangled, state-of-the-art military equipment. The New York *Daily News* printed nine photos of GIs engaged in a variety of pre-Invasion training activities. One photograph depicted a large air drop of paratroopers over Northern Ireland with a caption explaining how these airborne troopers had "perfected the technique with which they attack Axis strategic airdromes behind the invasion coastal area." Another of the nine images showed GIs "armed for action," climbing down rope ladders from transport ships and into landing craft. A third image showed U.S. infantrymen mounted atop several tanks above a caption describing how such mechanized units would "back the initial landings and sweep spearheads into Fortress Europe."[62] The editors of the *Johnson City Press-Chronicle* made clear that they were publishing training photos of paratroopers exiting their aircraft, infantrymen charging off of landing craft, and mortar crews laying in their guns to give readers a sense of "[How] It May Have Looked."[63] Some captions attending these images employed snappy, idiomatic jargon to further convey the idea that "these boys mean business." The use of such photographs in America's newspapers on D-Day further amplified the superlative nature of the American GI's training and preparation and the added notion that these men were far better warriors than their German counterparts.

One element common to the training and other photographs published by newspapers on D-Day was the deliberate portrayal of the abundance of new, state-of-the-art equipment sported by the American soldier and his Allied counterparts. The AP and UP in particular, relying on official sources, dutifully drove this point home by dispatching over the wires several widely published articles describing the surfeit of cutting-edge combat gear, rations, and vehicles supposedly available to the invaders.[64] One story dispatched by the AP's London office focused on General Eisenhower's chief ordnance officer, Brig. Gen. Henry Benton Sayler, who was responsible for "build[ing] up the vast stocks of guns, tanks, ammunition, trucks and spare parts for the smash across the channel." The article quoted Sayler as proclaiming (hyperbolically, for German consumption) that the men and women whom America was sending to invade Europe comprised "the best equipped army that ever existed."[65] Even the AP's Don Whitehead, a discerning veteran of numerous amphibious landings, managed to get a brief dispatch onto the wires from a docked "Invasion Ship" in which he insisted that the "quality, variety and the amount of equipment [was] almost beyond belief." He added, "Never has the United States sent an army into battle so well equipped."[66]

Filling out these huge stockpiles of equipment were items of new military technology that, whatever they might be, would make America's fighting men indisputable peer competitors when facing their German counterparts on the battlefield. A UP report issued from Detroit on D-Day quoted War Production Board chairman Donald M. Nelson, accosted by reporters while departing Detroit after the Invasion's announcement, as stating that "at this moment there are weapons and equipment in use on the invasion front that the public have never seen or even heard of" and that "match weapon for weapon everything the enemy has been able to devise." Thus, American newspaper readers would perceive their troops on D-Day to be the most capable, best-equipped warriors ever to take to the field of battle—even if Mom and Pop America was not quite sure exactly what those "secret weapons" were (one of them was the aforementioned "rocket launcher, or bazooka").[67] All that mattered, suggested the reportage, was that the troops were benefitting from the very best war implements that American industry and intellect could provide to the nation's community of precious young soldiers.

Perhaps the largest resource stockpiled by America and her Allies on D-Day, according to one UP feature, was the human resource—the sheer number of Allied troops assembled for the Invasion itself and for the follow-on operations. The feature stated that the Invasion operation is "giving the Germans just a sampling of the great hordes that are to follow and complete the job of knocking Hitler off the map of Europe." British experts, the writer explained, estimated "that a successful invasion will require from 60 to 70 divisions—that is, from 900,000 to 1,050,000 men even to open a western front." Although the public's response to such a wide-ranging estimate of human commitment to the war in Europe remains unclear (the actual number of Allied ground troops participating in Overlord was around one-third of that estimate), the scope and scale of the human effort must have given home-front Americans pause and, for propaganda purposes, underscored for the Germans the true nature of the Allied commitment. The most sobering assessment advanced by this article was the fact that "What ever [*sic*] the total, the world knows that the final invading force will be predominantly American."[68] Despite any misgivings American readers may have had about these troop numbers, the core thematic message was clear: these young GIs were the best-trained, best-equipped troops invading the European continent, and they had in abundance, and in direct support, all the rifles, grenades, bazookas, aircraft, tanks, and flamethrowers they needed to be successful. In fact, in one widely disseminated news item on 6 June 1944, the UP's Sandor S. Klein quoted a "headquarters report" that, rather tellingly, described each American fighting man as "a walking arsenal."[69]

Although well trained and well equipped, these American troops evinced a quiet courage the reporters wanted to convey to the folks at home. Already heroes in the eyes of most Americans, these men (and women, in many cases) demonstrated, as suggested by the reportage, a subtle type of courage leading up to H-Hour on D-Day by calmly preparing to thrust themselves into a battle that was nothing less than a frontal attack straight into the teeth of enemy fire. Some news items, such as the War Department's story describing the infantry's special training to overcome German pillboxes, declared bluntly in the AP version that those ground troops preparing to assault the beachheads were "some of the bravest soldiers in the U.S. Army."[70] But for the most part, the dispatches published in America's newspapers avoided such direct attestations of bravery and instead highlighted the troops' silent, subtle courage. For instance, a report issued by the UP described Army engineers and their naval comrades loading landing craft at an English port as carrying out these activities "very quietly and without tension," exhibiting a unique form of quiet courage.[71]

The radio networks also broadcast reports to their listeners throughout D-Day testifying to this same brand of subtle courage evident in most GIs. Most notable was the first-person broadcast described previously and made by NBC's Wright Bryan, who had returned on a C-47 transport after it delivered a group of American paratroopers over Normandy. During the flight, according to Bryan, the airborne troopers remained calm and steadfast. Once the green light began blinking, explained Bryan, the men exited the aircraft into the night sky without hesitation—an indisputable act of bravery. The paratroopers were heavily laden with arms and equipment, and one jumper stumbled as he "shuffled" to—and past—the door; the energy of the troopers behind him in his "stick" knocked him out of the way as they exploded out of the aircraft. By the time the poor fellow could regain his feet it was too late to jump; he had to accompany the plane back to England. He was inconsolable.[72] A Chicago *Daily Times* piece describing Bryan's broadcast explained that the soldier's angst rested in his belief that his buddies might "think he was 'yellow.'"[73] But the correspondents framed the scene to suggest that the opposite was true: this young man's fear of being branded a coward testified more to his courage than if he had made the jump.

Another approach to allowing listeners to recognize and appreciate the underlying courage of the young men hitting the beaches came from CBS's Quentin Reynolds, who celebrated the mettle of "GI Joe" by describing how such men overcame their fears. Reynolds told his audience that he knew GI Joe because "I saw him in action at Sicily and Salerno and I know his reactions . . . his hopes and fears." He imagined for listeners how difficult the Channel crossing must have been for the fighting men. As the armada neared the coastline, Reynolds imagined, "GI Joe tightened up" and "kept telling himself that he wasn't afraid," even as his "nervousness increased." But once he hit the beach's cold water, said Reynolds, "the nervousness left GI Joe." Instead, this once-anxious young man "looked coolly ahead." When "he saw a flash, he automatically lifted his tommy gun" and returned fire. For Reynolds, GI Joe's courage resulted from his excellent training, which assured listeners that bravery would flow from such preparedness as a natural attribute.[74] Reynolds's fictionalized report contributed to the growing aura surrounding the capabilities and courage of the average American soldier. Some details may have been accurate, but others were exaggerated. In fact, such musings deviated from normal journalistic practice and instead ventured into the world of mythmaking.

The one group of American invaders receiving special emphasis on D-Day were the paratroopers, whose airborne exploits and unique battlefield insertion method made them into exemplars of GI derring-do and overall soldier excellence. Many of the stock photographs appearing in the newspapers depicted paratroopers in action as they courageously floated to earth in the absence of cover, ready to fight the instant they hit the ground. As evidenced by a myriad of early radio broadcasts—such as Wright Bryan's eyewitness account—these specially trained men led the way and became the first to touch French soil during the Invasion. When the early newspaper editions hit the stands, scores of them carried a report by the AP's Howard Cowen describing the collective body of paratroopers as "studded with battle-hardened veterans of the Sicilian and Italian campaigns" whose landings alone represented "the first blow of the long-awaited western front [aimed] squarely [at] the enemy's vitals." Cowan described the airborne troopers as the "Allies' toughest, wiriest men of war" who carried "weapons from the most primitive to the most modern" in order "to disrupt and demoralize" the Germans' defensive efforts.[75] A complementary (and syndicated) story from correspondent

B. J. McQuaid of the *Chicago Daily News* foreign service captured the confident attitudes of several paratroopers he interviewed a few days before the Invasion began. "Sure the German is tough," insisted one paratrooper, "but we are a lot tougher." According to this same airborne soldier, "We are the best fighting outfit in the world [and can] handle anything there is." Other troopers echoed this man's sentiments, including the confidence they had in their leaders.[76] Correspondents Cowan and McQuaid each revealed enough to the American public about the paratroopers to make clear the challenges they faced as the Invasion's spearheading force but also how tough and ready these men were to take on the German occupiers. As portrayed by the press, they were America's best soldiers—and they had the very best leaders showing them the way. Thus, Mom and Pop America could find solace in knowing such men filled out the ranks of America's citizen-soldiers, even though they knew deep down that such characterizations were well over the top.

The confidence and high morale exuded by the paratroopers represented a key attribute American war correspondents and broadcasters wanted to project onto all American fighting men for their respective audiences on D-Day. Radio set the stage early by broadcasting a taped interview by CBS's Charles Collingwood with troops on board a landing craft at 9:15 a.m. EWT. Against a backdrop of bustling noise and soldier chatter, Collingwood asked SSgt. Alexander Ham of Chicago if he was worried. The sergeant shot back, "No, it doesn't worry me any." Collingwood received that same display of casual confidence from an interview with a nearby officer, a Captain Wood, who told the reporter that the ship-loading "seem[ed] to have gone without any bit of trouble" and that the men were settled in and ready to go.[77]

The newspapers provided readers with further illustrations of the troops' high morale. The AP's Don Whitehead, who had marveled at the abundance of equipment available to the troops, wrote from a landing craft still in port that the "morale of American troops is running high." Their "spirits are up," claimed Whitehead, because they can now "see the beginning of the end of war," a sentiment that fully agreed with the same mission-focused attitude held by the American public and "Dr.

Win-the-War" himself—President Roosevelt.[78] But Whitehead was careful not to cast the GIs as blindly stumbling into an unknown danger zone. The men were not displaying "a false optimism," he explained, because "they know what lies of ahead of them" and "many will die on the beaches of Normandy." Despite this knowledge they remained "grimly confident" of their success.[79] The hard-charging, confident image the press bestowed upon the troops almost certainly raised the men's stock in the eyes of the American public, but some correspondents also juxtaposed these characterizations against images of young men who, while confident and courageous, were also struggling with fear and doubt.

In an attempt to reveal what she imagined as the emotional state of men entering combat for the first time, Marjorie Van de Water of the *Flint Journal* crafted a fictional letter from a young GI to his mother—the kind of letter that "will never be sent home by any soldier taking part in the invasion." This fictional soldier, imagined Van de Water, told his mother that as he sat "waiting and listening," his "knees [kept] knocking together." Although it was not cold, the fictional trooper admitted, "I am shivering" and "my throat is burning." But Van de Water depicted a transformation in the young man as he overcame his fears upon hitting the beach under enemy fire. He returned fire with his rifle, and the "kick against my shoulder never felt so good." This young man had become a seasoned combat veteran within minutes.[80] This image of the citizen-soldier—the reluctant warrior—fell in line with how home-front America wanted to see their young fighting men. One article appearing in Maine's *Waterville Morning Sentinel* reinforced this positive image of the troops by quoting a colonel who had just returned from the Pacific. The colonel bore witness to the fact that America's "boys" (as he called them) "go into war proud of their weapons and their ability to fight with a deadly coolness[,] which makes them a better soldier." In other words, they were not ideologues bent on hatred or destruction but men who had a dangerous job to do for all the right reasons—and they had the proper mindset, tools, and courage to do it.[81]

Although the news primarily emphasized the fighting men, the newspapers found space in their D-Day editions to highlight the Invasion contributions of Army women, specifically nurses. One AP feature asserted that the "first American women onto the continent after the beachhead is gained will be the U.S. Army nurses." The feature focused on two second lieutenants, Lilyan Emmons of Chicago and Marion L. Hemmesch of New Rockford, North Dakota, and how each officer endured a rigid training regimen "to prepare for battle conditions." Using gender-discriminating language of the time that needlessly emphasized the women's personal appearance, the feature described how Lilyan, "a blue-eyed blonde," trained rigorously as part of an evacuation hospital so that she would be ready to treat casualties once the Invasion began. Likewise, "Marion, an attractive brunette" assigned to an air evacuation squadron, would fly in transport planes shuttling wounded to U.S. Army hospitals in England. The article further revealed that except for firearms, each woman would carry the same heavy equipment as the average fighting man. The writer further explained that all members of the Women's Army Corps (WAC) heading to the continent thereafter would carry "the same 50 pounds of equipment as the Army ground nurses." Thus, as this feature suggested, America's young women shared many of the same physical burdens and dangers as their male counterparts.[82]

The mainstream press' rather cursory mention of women in the D-Day narrative highlighted another significant exclusion in the day's Invasion reportage—the role of America's Black soldiers in the Invasion. This glaring omission, evident throughout the pages of America's newspapers, undermined the theme suggesting that America had sent forth its very best soldiers to defeat Hitler's minions when in fact a significant number of willing American men—Black men—had been denied the right to fight equally alongside White soldiers on the landing beaches. The closest any Black soldier came to participating equally in the beach fighting alongside his White countrymen was as a member of the sole all-Black unit to take part in the landings—the 320th Barrage Balloon Battalion. The 320th's task was to inflate and deploy tethered balloons above the beaches; these aerial obstacles were designed to prevent German aircraft from strafing the landing troops and naval vessels anchored offshore. Elements of this battalion landed at both Omaha and Utah Beaches after the first few waves came ashore and suffered casualties throughout the day. In fact, one of the battalion's medics, Cpl. Waverly B. Woodson Jr., performed multiple acts of valor on Omaha Beach, treating wounded GIs while ignoring his own injuries. His actions eventually led to his White commanders considering him for the Medal of Honor, but the citation was ultimately downgraded to the Bronze Star. At the time, America's White press ignored Woodson, his comrades in the 320th, and the contributions of other Black troops, leaving the weekly Black papers to fill the void in the days following 6 June 1944.[83]

The *Pittsburgh Courier* consistently argued that Black men were as capable of fighting as gallantly as their White counterparts. The *Courier* pointed to the valorous actions of a cook, Ck3c Doris "Dorie" Miller, at Pearl Harbor on 7 December 1941. Miller was a Black galley sailor who manned an antiaircraft (AA) turret despite having never received training on the weapon system; he fired the AA guns until his ammunition ran out. For his gallantry that day, Miller was awarded the Navy Cross, at the time the third highest military decoration in the U.S. Navy. The *Courier*'s larger point in highlighting Miller's bravery was to illustrate in stark terms the capacity of Black men to face the enemy's guns in direct combat and give a good accounting of themselves.[84] In other words, America was failing to tap into the abilities and courage of Black men, who had much to offer America's armed forces. Ultimately, the general absence of Black troops among the Army's combat arms forces destabilized the very D-Day narrative the media was constructing. America could not claim to send its very best young men into battle when the nation excluded so many of those men from the decisive actions on the landing beaches of Normandy. A government survey even highlighted the fact that the "one dominant, swelling and poignant plaint of Negroes everywhere was: 'If you want to win the war so badly, why don't you let us fight?'"[85]

Throughout the war America's Black newspapers had railed against the U.S. government—the War Department and the Navy Department specifically—for excluding Black men from serving in all military capacities, especially the infantry. The "Double V" campaign, initiated in February 1942 by the *Pittsburgh Courier* and generally adopted by the Black press and Black leaders nationwide, held to the belief that "[B]lacks would have to serve as equals in the armed forces in order to gain eventual equality."[86] Essentially, Black editors and leaders knew that if Black men were not allowed to fight *during* the war, they would not be treated like men *after* the war.[87] Despite many gains made by Blacks in the armed forces leading up to D-Day, such as receiving commissions in the Air Forces, the Marine Corps, and the Coast Guard, the numbers of Black infantry troops were decreasing.[88] The Black press pounced on Secretary of War Henry L. Stimson for claiming that this decrease resulted from Black soldiers' lower educational levels and failing to master, according to the *Pittsburgh Courier*, "the technique of modern weapons." America's Black newspaper editors could only express astonishment at Stimson's claim.[89]

Stimson's abhorrent statement did not mean the War Department had excluded Black troops from all combat-arms jobs. Black war correspondent William Randolph Dixon Jr. reported in the 10 June 1944 issue of the *Pittsburgh Courier*, the first edition of this Black weekly published after D-Day, that "all-Negro combat units" in England were undergoing field artillery, tank destroyer, and antiaircraft training for the Invasion. However, according to Dixon, their actual participation in the assault phase of D-Day remained in question. He claimed that the massive scale of the Invasion prevented him from reporting on their participation, a surprisingly feeble attempt on his part to gloss over the glaring reality that the U.S. armed forces had again denied Black troops the opportunity to fight as equals with White soldiers, especially as infantry soldiers.[90] In fact, Dixon offered no evidence that he was even aware that a lone, all-Black unit—the 320th Barrage Balloon Battalion—had set foot on the beaches that morning, albeit as a supporting unit. Dixon's quixotic statement seemingly tabled for the moment the *Courier's* militant, outspoken stance in favor of an overt demonstration of Black support for the war effort.

While the nationally distributed and syndicated newspaper stories did much to celebrate the capacity, courage, and training of America's invading troops (minus the contributions of Black soldiers), local newspapers perhaps did the most to connect those men directly to their hometown communities. Most of America's local newspapers on D-Day published the names and photographs of local men whom family members knew or suspected were participating directly in Operation Overlord. For instance, the *St. Joseph News-Press* published a photograph of Lawrence G. Reno, a "corporal technician," wearing his tan Army shirt and visor cap with a caption indicating that he had "arrived in England, according to word received by his wife." A photograph of Pfc. Ronald Tilbury appeared in the same edition also stating that he had "arrived in England, according to word received by his parents." These "arrivals in England" suggested both men were likely involved in the Invasion. Further solidifying the connection between the fighting men and their local communities was the fact that the newspapers routinely published the specific addresses of these men or their families. The paper revealed that Mrs. Reno, for instance, lived at 2324 South Fourth Street while Private First Class Tilbury's family resided at 617 Shady Avenue.[91] Likewise, the *Rochester Times-Union* published an image of Lt. Col. Frank S. Perego sitting in his aircraft's cockpit above a caption proudly reporting that "Perego, son of Mr. and Mrs. Frank H. Perego, 90 Bristol Street, Canandaigua, was one of the first airmen returning to England after participating in the invasion of France this morning."[92] The *Winston-Salem Journal* posted twelve photographs of local men in uniform while specifying the hometowns of all twelve men, the names of their parents, and where they had received their training.[93]

Some local newspapers did not publish photographs of their hometown men in uniform but only listed their names and other information. The *Cincinnati Times-Star*, for example, published the names of "Cincinnati Airborne Troops," who were "presumably among the first airborne troops to land on the European continent." The men's addresses were also published and, as a unique touch, their previous civilian occupations juxtaposed against their new jobs in the Army. For instance, Pfc. Harry L. Burg of 3712 River Road had been a sheet metal worker but was now a rifleman, while fellow paratrooper Sgt. Charles Easter of 5805 Madison Road, formerly a pressman, was now a squad leader.[94] These explicit connections between the men and their neighborhoods, appearing in papers nationwide, became a source of local pride; they linked America's communities directly to the ongoing Invasion. While proud of their highly trained and courageous local men and their known or unknown contributions to the Invasion effort, local community members knew they could suffer the effects of the Invasion on a personal level if their young men became casualties or, worse, were killed in action.

While most newspapers on D-Day generally avoided any speculation about American casualties in keeping with Office of Censorship guidelines, some newspapers dealt directly with the anguish that mothers, fathers, sons, and daughters were experiencing about the fates of their loved ones overseas.[95] The *Flint Journal* published the following candid reminder: "Lest We Forget: War Casualties To Date: 599." The item broke the numbers down to show that 391 deaths came from Flint and the remaining 208 dead from the Flint area.[96] Such a harsh statistic offered on D-Day attested to the editor's desire to remind the local folks of war's cost; it also represented a not so subtle attempt to energize home-front support of the troops. Clearly, the prospect of high casualties haunted most Americans, and the *Akron Beacon Journal* perhaps did the most to reveal on D-Day the nature of the anxiety felt by average Americans who, in many cases, had family members in harm's way. The *Journal* published an article by Helen Waterhouse, who had taken to the streets of Akron to assess the home-front mindset following the Invasion's announcement. The title of her piece, "How Is My Son Faring? Anxious Relatives Await Invasion News," encapsulated the apprehension felt by the people with whom she spoke. Waterhouse wrote that "white-faced, tense, but with great courage," Akron's families received the news of D-Day. She explained metaphorically that these families "'went under the knife' of anxiety, suspense and uncertainty with a deep conviction that their men have the best in training and equipment." She witnessed fathers, mothers, brothers, sisters, and children rapidly buying up newspapers while others clung to their radios "hungrily grasping for every bulletin that flashed out to interrupt scheduled programs." What Waterhouse truly learned was that "over many homes hung the big, unanswered question: Where is

Bill today? Jack? Harry? Frank?" Her sensing of the population revealed a mixture of pride and confidence in the troops but, justifiably, a standing fear "racing through [their] minds" that a telegraph boy might deliver to the front door a "casualty message."[97]

But undergirding these fears was a hardened stoicism, almost fatalism. One father she interviewed stated forthrightly: "Whatever happens, his home folks must not let him down today." A mother of four sons serving on the European front echoed this father's sentiment by saying "grimly" that "we must be mighty brave people today," for we "have got to try to be worthy of them." Another father said, "I must have faith now that [my son] will live through this" just like he survived "the horrible near-annihilation of the tank corps in Tunisia and at the Kasserine Pass."[98] These expressions most likely represented the same attitudes felt by many Americans on D-Day, but the angst the home-front family members experienced also revealed an underlying desire to live up to the soldiers' example. Although Waterhouse's report suggested that the troops represented the very best of America, the fighters could only succeed if they had a solid home-front foundation in support of their efforts.

But how might the news media's thematic frame that only America's bravest, best-trained, and best-equipped soldiers were cracking the German beach defenses have stood if actual reports of the carnage, chaos, and confusion on Omaha Beach had managed to appear in newspapers and over the airwaves? In many ways, such reports, likely appearing out of context, would have called into question the GIs' abilities as soldiers in much the same way that these reports would have raised questions about Eisenhower's, Montgomery's, or the other Allied senior leaders' competence and skill to fight and win. Once again, by advancing this theme so robustly as one of the centerpieces of the American D-Day narrative, the news media risked its credibility. As journalists, they were obligated to report any and all progress of the Invasion, even the bad news. But how might newspaper editors and broadcasters have shaped such news? Would they have downplayed disappointing, even pessimistic, reports from Omaha Beach or elsewhere in favor of hewing to their more optimistic tone? Would they have invoked censorship guidelines to avoid reporting such information? Would they have fallen prey to George Creel's propagandistic tactics from World War I by mixing truths with half-truths and even deliberate untruths? Ultimately, America's press editors and broadcasters never faced this choice on D-Day.

While the press unswervingly conveyed the notion that the front-line troops fighting on D-Day were worthy of home-front support, the radio networks and newspapers also expressed to their listeners and readers an equally unflinching confidence in the GIs' ability to live up to their fathers' examples during World War I. This confidence came across loudly in an almost universally broadcast and published statement made by the man who led the GIs' fathers to victory in World War I—General of the Armies John J. Pershing. The eighty-three-year-old Pershing's message first went out over the airwaves an hour after Communiqué No. 1. The *Fresno Bee* claimed Pershing "was the first high ranking official in the nation's capital to hail the landing of Allied troops on the French coast."[99] An NBC reporter in Washington read Pershing's statement aloud, in which the former American Expeditionary Force commander linked the legacy of his doughboys who fought for liberty in 1917 and 1918 to the current war of European liberation fought by the sons of those very same men. Pershing declared, "I have every confidence that they, together with their gallant brothers-in-arms, will win through to victory." Thus, America's well-trained, well-equipped, and well-bred citizen soldiers had the backing of the man who had led their fathers to success a generation earlier—a powerful endorsement from perhaps the most well-respected general officer in America. The man whose command abilities embodied success had now bequeathed that same confidence to another generation of young men, the World War II generation, which according to Pershing, "would bring freedom to peoples who have been enslaved."[100]

◆ ◆ ◆

The two final thematic frames shaping the press' narrative of the Invasion on 6 June 1944—that the best Allied leaders were leading the very best American troops in carrying out Operation Overlord—came to define, along with the first two themes, the enduring narrative of the Invasion in the decades that followed. America's radio networks and newspapers clearly showed themselves to be team players who were, after all, rooting for the home team. In many instances, they flirted with producing propaganda; but for the most part, they stuck to their sources. And so, in a remarkable and generally organic nationwide effort predicated on a largely professional response to what the American news media all agreed was the biggest story up to that point in the war, they managed to imbue the D-Day narrative with a tightly packaged set of four thematic frames, vestiges of which would remain fundamentally unaltered in America's collective psyche for the next three-quarters of a century—a narrative that remained most evident in the national-level commemorations of D-Day that marked each passing decade.

CHAPTER 7

Confirming America's Enduring D-Day Narrative

There is no question . . . that members of the media have some autonomy and authority to depict the world according to their own ideas.

—Michael Schudson[1]

Within minutes of finishing his "Boys of Pointe du Hoc" speech on 6 June 1994, President Ronald Reagan had cast himself, like other U.S. presidents before him and those who would follow, as the custodian of America's enduring D-Day narrative. By summing up the four thematic frames of the D-Day narrative as formulated by the radio networks and newspapers on 6 June 1944, Reagan had once again confirmed a fundamental understanding of America's shared perception that the Invasion was in fact a monumental, highly significant, and sacred undertaking. It was led by the best of America's and her Allies' senior leaders and carried out by the best-trained, morally virtuous soldiers, sailors, and airmen that America could offer. Although Reagan had selected the venue and overarching theme for his speech, he was communicating the D-Day narrative through the words of his two most gifted speechwriters, Peggy Noonan and Anthony Dolan. Their research exposed them to the long-standing D-Day narrative that represented America's sentimental, self-affirming storyline of the Invasion.[2] But Reagan was the one who gave life and new purpose to their words and to the overall D-Day narrative by articulating it to a global audience within a Cold-War framework. This framework celebrated democracy and human rights worldwide while signaling to the Soviet Union the lengths to which the United States would go to preserve these ideals if they ever came under threat—even from a former World War II ally. Thus, this thematically framed D-Day narrative, deeply ensconced in the nation's belief system, has persisted through the intervening years; only the lessons that American presidents have drawn from that narrative have changed over time. President Reagan clearly demonstrated that national-level commemorations of D-Day have served as an effective litmus test for the staying power of this narrative and as the best means of perpetuating its thematic frame.

Reagan had chosen to revitalize America's media-constructed D-Day narrative at a fortuitous time in U.S. history. Most of America's World War II veterans were reaching retirement age and with time on their hands were becoming more introspective and vocal about their wartime experiences. Many men joined or rejoined veterans' organizations associated directly with their old outfits to catch up and reminisce with wartime comrades they had not seen in decades. Some of them even looked back upon their war years through the filtering lens of the "good war" trope. This sanitized view of World War II helped the veterans and Americans of all ages push aside the dark shadow cast by the Vietnam War and instead celebrate the moral righteousness of an earlier conflict that ostensibly united all Americans in common cause of liberating oppressed peoples and defeating the evil Axis regimes.[3] Thus, the D-Day narrative created by the press conformed neatly with this desire to engage in the collective understanding of a war that supposedly unified Americans instead of polarizing them—a war in which the American people were the "good guys."

◆ ◆ ◆

The D-Day narrative and its four key themes remained remarkably unchanged and found ready reinforcement in the press in the days and months after D-Day and leading up to Victory in Europe (VE) Day on 8 May 1945. For the newspapers in particular, D-Day (or the "Invasion") became "the Battle for Normandy" as early as 7 June 1944. With the initial landings complete and the beachheads generally secure, front pages rightly focused on the current battlefield situation as the Allies pushed hard against stiff German resistance in the hedgerows of Normandy. For instance, the headlines appearing on the front pages of the *Springfield Evening Union* for the three days following the Invasion focused exclusively, and predictably, on the inland fighting and attempts by the Allies to expand the beachheads seized on D-Day.[4] Each day that passed saw news of D-Day fade.

Despite the shift in focus, features and articles revealing previously unknown details of D-Day continued to appear in America's newspapers in the days and weeks following the Invasion, and these added details further reinforced the thematic frames advanced in the 6 June 1944 reportage. Fresh photographs of actual Invasion scenes, along with more expanded maps that enlarged the fighting area, provided readers with an even broader perspective of the scope, scale, and significance of D-Day.[5] The *Los Angeles Evening Herald Express* of 8 June 1944 even provided an advanced look at one of Robert Capa's soon-to-be-famous photographs of Omaha Beach on its front page, the bulk of which the American public would not see until *Life*'s June 1944 issue. The lone, grainy Capa image captured the intensity of the beachhead fighting by portraying several GIs taking cover behind obstacles in the surf under heavy German fire, a powerful visual testament to the courage of the average American soldier as he confronted the enemy's beach defenses head-on.[6]

Even more first-person eyewitness accounts from reporters who had landed on the Invasion beaches also appeared in the papers, further highlighting the danger faced by the attacking GIs and their battlefield successes. The *Los Angeles Times*' Tom Treanor, in a report published on 8 June 1944, described his landing experience on D-Day; he noted the "heavy casualties," adding that "men, jeeps, bulldozers and other equipment moving" on the beach was a sign that American arms had carried the day.[7] The *Baltimore New-Post*'s Louis Azrael described in a 9 June 1944 report how he had accompanied the GIs as they hit the beaches and how American infantrymen "rooted out the Germans with rifle or grenade" from their "little cliffside holes."[8] In spite of these emerging details of bitter fighting and carnage, the D-Day narrative of 6 June 1944, with all of its optimistic tones and anodyne imagery, still held fast in America's consciousness.

The weekly news magazines, which could not match the daily newspapers' up-to-the-moment reporting on D-Day, soon began filling gaps in the initial Invasion coverage. As the days and weeks passed, more relaxed censorship revealed less sanitized Invasion details, which produced further stories and particulars of the landings—and, remarkably, further thematic underscoring—from America's magazine correspondents. Since these reporters had longer lead times for their stories, they were able to amass more details and craft lengthier reports than their daily newspaper brethren.

The news magazines appearing in the first two weeks after the Invasion contained the most extensive D-Day coverage before shifting their primary focus onto the more current battlefield developments in Normandy. The more prominent weekly news magazines—*Time, Newsweek, Life,* and even the *New York Times* magazine—featured Invasion-themed covers promoting, among other subjects, the senior Allied leadership through artists's renderings or photographs of American generals, including Eisenhower, Spaatz, and Bradley, as well as British General Montgomery.[9] These magazines also included many more photographs of the actual beach landings than the D-Day newspapers—images unavailable to the press on 6 June 1944. Several issues carried photographs of Eisenhower meeting with the 101st Airborne's paratroopers before they left for Normandy, again reinforcing the two themes related to strong senior leaders and intrepid GIs. *Life* magazine perhaps did more than any other weekly to jolt Americans into reality by featuring Capa's arresting images of the Omaha Beach assault. The grainy, blurry images of GIs desperately seeking cover while under withering enemy machine-gun fire gave the images an impressionistic motif, crystallizing for Americans at home the raw courage required of their men to engage in such a deadly frontal assault. This impressionistic veil defied the average American's efforts to peel it back for a more detailed look, forever adding to the mystique that would attend all future attempts to comprehend what happened on "Bloody Omaha."[10] Even more dramatically, one image taken by an Acme photographer on an unspecified beach that appeared in the 19 June 1944 issues of *Time, Newsweek,* and

Life showed the bodies of dead GIs laying in a row on the beach awaiting recovery. *Time*'s caption simply stated the obvious: "For them the Atlantic Wall was real."[11]

The magazines also reinforced all four thematic frames through the more expanded narratives they published, which synthesized much of the same reporting that emerged on D-Day but with added details from war correspondents of all stripes whose pooled stories did not filter into London offices until days after the Invasion. Like the other magazines, *Time* and *Life* used more detailed maps with their D-Day narratives to highlight the scale and significance of the Invasion effort.[12] Additionally, eyewitness accounts by war correspondents that did not cross the wires until days after the Invasion began helped put more meat on the bones of the D-Day narrative. *Time*'s war correspondent William Walton jumped into Normandy with American paratroopers and captured the frenetic and daring nature of the airborne side of the operation, while *Newsweek*'s Kenneth Crawford landed with one of the first waves to assault the beaches and attested to the gallantry of the average American infantryman.[13] The magazines even captured the sacralization theme by reporting that D-Day was in fact a "Day of Prayer" and that President Roosevelt had invested the Invasion with the same moralistic undertones used by General Eisenhower with his Great Crusade.[14] *Newsweek* claimed that the publicly advertised build-up to the Invasion and the fact that "the crusaders faced deadlier weapons and hardier risks than ever before" added to the solemnity of D-Day and the "widespread restraint" it evoked among the populace. Such restraint, the story suggested, added to the sanctified nature of the event in terms of its importance to the war effort and to the lives of thousands of reluctant citizen-soldiers who were risking everything for a higher ideal than the one espoused by Nazism.[15] In the days immediately following 6 June 1944, the D-Day narrative as framed by the four thematic elements we have enumerated had further strengthened its grip on the American press and the American public, in spite of the harsher details of the fighting that were seeping into the reportage. By late June 1944, the D-Day narrative was well enough established to resist modification.

Several monthly magazines hitting the stands in July and August further expanded the media-constructed D-Day narrative and many of its thematic elements. *Look* magazine's 11 July 1944 issue reinforced the theme of gifted and highly capable senior Allied leaders by placing a colorized photograph of General Eisenhower on the front cover with binoculars in hand—a commanding image magnified by the magazine's large-sized format. Inside, an article entitled the "Invasion Heroine: The Flying Nurse" illuminated the gallant efforts of Army nurses charged with caring for wounded GIs. The feature, replete with numerous photographs of the nurses in action, framed the women's efforts to correspond with the narrative theme that America had given to the Invasion only her best, most skilled soldiers. One photograph singled out Lt. Jean Tolen of Minneapolis, who "typifies the American girls, trained nurses in civilian life who have volunteered for one of the war's most dangerous jobs."[16] In short, many of America's young women, also products of Main Street U.S.A., played significant roles in D-Day. Many Black soldiers played noteworthy (albeit supporting) roles in the Invasion, but unlike their White countrymen, they remained largely invisible in the pages of these magazines.

One of the most impactful eyewitness testimonies to the difficulties faced by America's resolute infantrymen on Omaha Beach came from *Collier's* war correspondent and literary legend Ernest Hemingway. In his exposition of the beach landing published in the 22 July 1944 issue, Hemingway described in riveting detail the difficulties faced by the GIs while under heavy German fire. From his position on a landing craft vehicle, personnel (LCVP), Hemingway bore witness to a beachhead strewn with the bodies of men from the initial waves who had fallen to enemy fire, each one "looking like so many heavily laden bundles." This imagery alone evoked the thematic frame that America's finest troops had faced the enemy's guns bravely and that many had died in the process. Although a gifted writer, Hemingway recognized the limits of his own ability to communicate the chaos he witnessed. He admitted that "real war is never like paper war, nor do accounts of it read much the way it looks."[17] Hemingway's description also had the power to suggest a contradictory interpretation that might have destabilized the D-Day narrative by intimating that for all their courage, the GIs might not have been as well trained or as prepared for the beach assaults as the news media claimed.

Additional Invasion details appeared in magazines such as the *Reader's Digest* as late as August 1944. In the issue for that month, stories by three accredited war correspondents reinforced all four thematic frames attending the D-Day narrative. Allan A. Michie's recounting of "The Great Decision"—prefaced by a heading of "The Invasion: Great Event in History"—underscored the theme associated with the Invasion's scope and significance as well as the notion that able senior Allied leaders conducted the Invasion with skill and wisdom. Frederic Sondern Jr., accredited to the U.S. Navy, evoked the scope and scale of the Invasion effort by depicting the massive size of the naval contribution and how skilled Allied admirals guided the enormous fleet across the Channel. Lastly, Ira Wolfert, landing in the afternoon, marveled at the skill of the combat engineers, who had lost one man dead and seventeen wounded clearing German mines from beachhead paths leading off the beaches.[18] All told, America's magazine editors kept the D-Day narrative alive throughout most of the summer months, but less conventional media representations of the Invasion in the weeks that followed also helped to reinforce the press' overarching narrative, embedding it even more firmly into America's collective consciousness.

In addition to the newspapers and radio networks, less conventional media-type devices helped to further establish the thematic frames governing the D-Day narrative in America's shared perspective. Stamp collecting was one such unconventional technique; philatelists memorialized the grand significance of the Invasion by purchasing a wide variety of postal covers commemorating the operation on D-Day. Stationers printed and sold various envelopes complete with simple D-Day messages or more graphically detailed Invasion motifs by early afternoon on 6 June 1944.[19]

Another less conventional format came in the form of trading cards depicting "Signal Corps Photos" of the Invasion, many of which had passed the censors on 6 June 1944 and appeared in the newspapers. The two-by-three-inch cards, each with captions on the back side, depicted senior American leaders such as Eisenhower and Bradley. This fifteen-card set graphically captured the American press' narrative of D-Day.[20]

Another visual means of conveying the scope and significance of the Invasion as well as the challenges faced by American leaders and soldiers came in the form of newsreels shown to theatergoers. These film shorts contained footage that helped to capture those aspects of the Invasion that radio and newspapers could not convey. By D-Day, the time lag for newsreel footage of an event appearing in theaters had dropped to around ten days, so the American viewers were able to develop a better visual understanding of the Invasion's magnitude much sooner than the war coverage in months past. Several newsreel companies existed at the time, such as Fox (with its "Fox Movietone News"), Paramount, Metro-Goldwyn-Mayer ("News of the Day"), Universal, Pathé, and Official Films.[21] However, each company's D-Day newsreel productions generally contained the same footage because of pooling requirements; the only differences were in how the various companies edited and framed the images. The footage brought elements of the Invasion narrative to life and further underscored the press's thematic frames.[22] The "Invasion" newsreel produced by Official Films, for instance, featured the thundering sounds of naval gunfire and artillery accompanied by a narrator reminding audiences of the massive scope and scale of the Invasion effort. Audience members witnessed air bombardments, exploding German aircraft, Allied troops landing on the beaches under fire, wounded GIs huddled under a cliff, and swamped amphibious tanks languishing in the surf. The imagery pulled no punches, and censors even approved the release of one scene in which several GIs appeared rushing across an open beach as two of the men were hit and collapsed in a heap. The troops' obvious gallantry needed no further explication.[23]

Newsreels changed from week to week to follow the war's progress, so most audiences only saw a specific reel during the week in which it played. Thus, a less conventional means of thematic reinforcement came in the form of a silent 16mm version of the same newsreel footage produced by Castle Films and sold to the public, who could watch the footage repeatedly at home as a narrative-reinforcing medium.[24]

In the same way that commercially produced newsreels and hard-copy newspapers allowed Americans to reexperience the Invasion narrative visually and in textual form, some radio networks produced 78 rpm recordings of the actual Invasion broadcasts that offered their listeners the means to reexperience the actual D-Day broadcasts as often as desired, making these record sets into another reinforcing medium for the D-Day narrative. NBC, for example, produced a four-disc set of the network's breaking Invasion coverage.[25] Americans had at their fingertips multiple ways to reexperience and reinforce the media's thematically framed D-Day narrative in the weeks that followed the Invasion. For those radio listeners keeping up with the war's progress in real time, numerous companies produced "Invasion" editions of European maps that listeners could use to track the fighting and the expanding Invasion effort.[26] Once more, Americans had at their disposal inexpensive ways to revisit the Invasion narrative as the press constructed it, further strengthening the news media's thematically constructed story of D-Day.

By early August 1944 the press's emphasis on the D-Day narrative faded temporarily as the news focused on the Allied forces pushing the Wehrmacht out of France and, by mid-spring 1945, into the heart of Germany. Coverage of D-Day trailed off until the Invasion's one-year anniversary followed a month after VE Day. Some press outlets mentioned the Invasion, but few Americans took notice. Many of them—especially the veterans of D-Day—opted to forget what they had experienced on 6 June 1944 in the short term. Instead, the limited American news coverage of D-Day on the Invasion's anniversary took on a somber tone. For instance, the *Stars and Stripes*, a U. S. Army newspaper run exclusively by soldiers for the troops, released an article by G. K. Hodenfield on 3 June 1945; Hodenfield had landed with the Rangers on Pointe du Hoc. The article chronicled Hodenfield's observations on returning to the American landing beaches a year later. He expressed an unusual sense of melancholy in observing the silence and renewal evident on Omaha and Utah Beaches, each one nearly free of battlefield detritus and showing scant evidence that a year earlier these places had been the centerpieces of the Invasion storm. Hodenfield, who had witnessed the grand spectacle of the Invasion landings firsthand, felt "sadness in seeing the desolation of Omaha Beach today; there is irreverence in its quiet." Weeds had overgrown Pointe du Hoc, and young couples strolled arm in arm on the cleared beaches. In many ways, Hodenfield could not reconcile in his mind the sudden retreat from the world stage, as evidenced by the few physical reminders remaining, of the great endeavor called Operation Overlord. The press did not even report the fact that General Eisenhower, still commanding the European theater of operations, had declared that all occupation troops observe 6 June 1945 as a holiday but without fanfare or formal ceremonies. Instead, Eisenhower directed that his troops use the day to reflect on the Allied Expeditionary Force's accomplishment of the "primary purpose and aims which inspired this tremendous amphibious operation."[27] The press barely took notice. For the moment, the press' D-Day narrative and its four attendant themes had fallen dormant in America's collective consciousness following the Allied victory. However, the D-Day narrative would reemerge in the decades that followed—and when America needed it most.[28]

Despite initial postwar resistance by Americans to push D-Day and the war in general into the darkest recesses of the human mind, D-Day continued to remain a powerful national topic. Most significantly, the four themes framing the media-constructed D-Day narrative largely resisted any modification in the seven decades following the Invasion, perhaps because those themes—in the hagiographic and sometimes hyperbolic forms they took as framing devices for the press—offered Americans a largely nostalgic, sanitized view of the event that, as Michael Dolski has argued, "confirm[ed] cherished national self-perceptions . . . of America's selfless sacrifice to restore order in the world."[29] Dolski's particular analysis of D-Day in America's collective memory after VE Day and in the decades that followed found the four thematic elements of the Invasion narrative firmly ensconced in American culture and memory. Local hometown commemorations as well as novels, recordings, books, blockbuster movies, board games, and, most significantly, national commemorations all revealed vestiges of the Invasion's four key themes.[30]

How and why did such a media-constructed, thematically framed narrative of D-Day endure in America's collective consciousness over the decades? First and foremost, the endurance of this narrative attests to the sheer power of the news media to shape how Americans see and understand world events in the moment and over time. But D-Day represented a perfect storm for the media, a unique moment in time when everything lined up to enable the creation of a theme-based narrative. In many ways, D-Day represented a special case as a major event during World War II. Everyone knew the Invasion was coming six months in advance, so the individuals with the primary responsibility for framing the news reportage on D-Day—America's news editors and their overseas sources—had time to prepare written and on-air features, analyses, maps, and photographs that allowed them to shape a national, and largely calculated, narrative of D-Day with great effect for their readers and listeners. But, most tellingly, the news they could not predict or control, such as the dispatches that never made it off the beaches, played a major role in shaping, or rather circumscribing, how Americans perceived D-Day.

If the news media on 6 June 1944 constructed an enduring, thematically shaped narrative of D-Day based largely on the newspaper and radio press reporting, then an effective litmus test for verifying that phenomenon perhaps rests in Barry Schwartz's belief that "historical remembering," even for a media-generated narrative produced decades earlier, occurs through the act of *commemoration*. According to Schwartz, historical remembering relies on "chronicling," which on 6 June 1944 occurred through the act of capturing the Invasion in newspapers and radio recordings in order to make the event "historically real."[31] If the press' thematically framed narrative of D-Day endured, it should be evident in how America has commemorated, and continues to commemorate, the Invasion in the years after the landings.

◆ ◆ ◆

The thematically framed D-Day narrative, born on 6 June 1944 in America's newspapers and over the radio networks, did in fact endure over the decades as America's agreed-upon version of that event, most notably in national commemorations that were often as much about emphasizing the needs of the present as the needs of the past. And these commemorations, enhanced by the trappings of pageantry, represent the truest test for the enduring quality of this media-constructed D-Day narrative. This phenomenon is most evident in the speeches given by U.S. presidents during international D-Day commemorations in Normandy every decade since the fortieth anniversary in 1984, when President Ronald Reagan gave his famous "Boys of Pointe du Hoc" speech. War-weariness and other significant political events and national crises kept U.S. presidents before Reagan from commemorating D-Day on site, but these presidents, such as Dwight D. Eisenhower, still issued statements or sent representatives to convey their messages. In all cases, the D-Day narrative and its four themes—that it was the most significant event of the war in terms of its contribution and scale; that it was a sacred undertaking; that the Allies had the best and brightest senior leaders; and that the American fighting man was a virtuous, gallant, and reluctant warrior—all framed this one standing narrative.

D-Day commemorations immediately following the war tended to be small-scale, localized affairs in which communities such as Bedford County, Virginia, memorialized their war dead by installing plaques or other reminders of the local men's sacrifice. In fact, the Invasion hit the Bedford community hardest. Company A, 116th Infantry Regiment, part of the 29th Infantry Division—a National Guard unit with local roots in Virginia and Maryland—comprised mostly Bedford County men who landed in the first wave on Omaha Beach. That distinction—the first to land on D-Day's bloodiest beach—cost Company A, and Bedford by default, nineteen men killed that day, the most of any single community in the United States.[32] Like the people of Bedford, other communities nationwide "were left to confront the holes wartime losses had torn through their social fabric."[33] In a general sense, the pain of such losses focused most Americans on the immediate future and not the past, even though the media-constructed D-Day narrative remained in the recesses of their shared consciousness. In these early years, D-Day's meaning remained mutable. Granted, most Americans still considered the Invasion to have been a significant operation in the war, but they had yet to recognize its true value as an exemplar of American values and exceptionalism.[34]

Considering the American people's war-weariness and efforts to reconcile their battlefield losses from all theaters of the war, commemorations of D-Day in the first three decades after the Invasion remained remarkably subdued and discreet. On Overlord's tenth anniversary on 6 June 1954, Dwight D. Eisenhower, former supreme allied commander and now the U.S. president, did not appear in Normandy to mark the occasion. Instead, he released a written statement acknowledging the milestone. The overarching tone of Eisenhower's declaration was one of hope for the future while still recognizing past Allied cooperation and suffering. Three of the four thematic frames were evident in the text, but the heavy moralism found in his "Great Crusade" language during the Invasion did not ring loudly, most likely because Ike and the war-weary nation had just concluded another bloody conflict, the Korean War, a year earlier. Eisenhower still acknowledged the Invasion's significance in his message by describing it as an operation that "set in motion a chain of events which affected the history of the entire world." Moreover, he stated that "some of the most cherished memories of that campaign" were of his "friendly cooperation" with distinguished senior leaders such as Montgomery, Bertram Ramsay, and Arthur Tedder as well as a number of French marshals, including Alphonse Juin and Phillippe Leclerc. Their "joint labors," he explained, made D-Day possible. And despite the Cold War, the always diplomatic Ike even praised his cooperation with Soviet marshal Georgy Zhukov. But Eisenhower, in advancing what would become the dominant theme of the D-Day narrative over time, reserved his most laudatory comments for the average soldiers of all nations, whose "skill, determination and self-sacrifice" made D-Day a success.[35]

The next ten-year anniversary of D-Day on 6 June 1964 came in the wake of President John F. Kennedy's assassination and at the moment President Lyndon B. Johnson was struggling to push his civil rights bill through Congress. Consumed by this legislative priority, Johnson remained in Washington, DC, and instead dispatched a twenty-two-person delegation to Normandy led by General of the Army Omar Bradley, one of the Invasion's key leaders. Bradley's appearance alone called to mind a massive Invasion effort led by skilled senior leaders and the overarching significance of the Invasion, the remembrance of which merited the general's physical presence in Normandy. General Bradley read a statement from the president that evoked elements of the thematic D-Day narrative, primarily the acknowledgment that it was, in Johnson's words, "America's sons and those of our gallant allies [who] helped carry freedom back to the continent where it was cradled." Even as Johnson honored American and Allied war dead, his language more readily embraced the moralism behind the Invasion as a sacred undertaking in which "we shall not permit the light of freedom to be extinguished on any continent again" as "the rays of [a new] dawn are piercing through the shadows." According to Johnson, "Freedom is not the cause of America alone . . . nor the hope of Western man alone," language that emulated the crusading rhetoric used by Eisenhower on the eve of D-Day. Central to this rhetoric was Johnson's stated vision, like Ike's "Great Crusade" vision, of a "world without tyranny, without war, without aggression, without oppression." Once more, a presidential statement honoring D-Day captured many of the thematic elements that shaped the media-constructed D-Day narrative, even as those themes became grist for political and foreign policy matters, particularly Johnson's emphasis on further cooperation within the "Atlantic alliance."[36] Thus, President Johnson used an American media narrative from the past—in this case D-Day and its moralistic undercurrents—to "legitimate," in the words of Paul Connerton, "a present social order."[37]

For D-Day's thirtieth anniversary commemoration on 6 June 1974, General Bradley once again led the American delegation on behalf of the president, in this case Richard Nixon, who was only two months away from resigning his office due to the Watergate scandal. Bradley carried no remarks from the president. Only the eighty-one-year-old general's presence, as the last living Allied senior leader, testified to the themes addressing the Invasion's greater significance and the skilled senior leaders who made it happen—all embodied in the person of Bradley himself. Most notably, the anniversary in Normandy that year witnessed the most Allied D-Day veterans of any previous commemoration—about 1,500 were in attendance.[38] The veterans were reaching retirement age and looking back upon their wartime experiences with introspection and even nostalgia. Their collective interest in World War II's past and the developing meaning of D-Day to the American populace opened the door for the first D-Day commemoration to feature the attendance and remarks of an American president in Normandy, a circumstance that would provide powerful evidence of the endurance of America's media-constructed D-Day narrative.

The presence of President Ronald Reagan in Normandy to commemorate the fortieth anniversary of D-Day in 1984 became a watershed moment in validating the narrative that underlay America's broader understanding of the Invasion.[39] The scene that opened this study found President Reagan standing on Pointe du Hoc before the dagger-shaped monument to men of the 2nd Ranger Battalion, who had scaled the hundred-foot cliff behind him using ropes and ladders while under intense German machine-gun fire from above. For the first time, an American president had assumed the mantle of keeper and conveyor of America's D-Day narrative by delivering a powerful and memorable address that captured all four of the major thematic frames that shaped the radio and newspaper reportage of 6 June 1944 and the subsequent narrative that became how the nation continued to view the operation.

Even though Reagan's speech was clearly political and directed toward America's Cold War adversary, the Soviet Union, the president and his speechwriters still managed to synthesize into this single oration four key themes that encompassed the distinctively American narrative developed in the press the moment the Invasion happened. First, he celebrated the grand scale of the Invasion, hyperbolically casting it as "a giant undertaking unparalleled in human history" while also acknowledging the Soviet Union's major contribution to defeating the Wehrmacht. Second, he cast all American soldiers as moralistic liberators, young "boys" who took up arms to "liberate, not to conquer." These young GIs, claimed Reagan, fought for freedom and democracy, driven by a love for liberty and a hatred of "tyranny." Third, the virtuous motives of these young American men sanctified their endeavor, thus giving "Providence [a] great hand in the events that would unfold" on the beaches and cliffs of Normandy. "God," insisted Reagan, "was an ally in this great cause," and the prayers of those fellow Americans at home "filling the churches" that Tuesday morning further buttressed the overarching devotion that underscored the troops' collective valor. Last, highly skilled, divinely inspired senior leaders were the right officers to lead these men in battle. Under their exceptional leadership, the troops would neither "fail" nor "forsake" God and the folks at home. In short, according to Reagan's rendition, D-Day was the seminal, liberating battle of World War II, a divinely sanctioned enterprise fought by intrepid, liberty-loving soldiers led by the best leaders of any army or navy in the world. No newspaper or radio broadcast on 6 June 1944 could have summed up the Invasion narrative any better and illustrate what it should mean to all Americans.[40] Perhaps most importantly, Reagan's speech had a performative aspect to it, delivered in the early afternoon when Americans at home could tune in to watch. This performative aspect, combined with the speech's dramatic locale and its trappings of pageantry, invested D-Day with a powerful, enduring meaning. This combination of factors allowed a very specific narrative of D-Day to persist even more deliberately from that point forward, setting down a marker that transformed the commemoration of D-Day into an American tradition.[41]

The metamorphosis from commemoration to tradition became most evident a decade after Reagan's oration, when President Bill Clinton attended the fiftieth anniversary events in Normandy and gave numerous speeches, all of which evoked the four major themes of the D-Day narrative. In one sense, Clinton's physical presence reinforced the thematic frame that D-Day was a sacred event in American history and that the blood of American soldiers, sailors, and airmen had sanctified the beaches, cliffs, and drop zones of Normandy. Journalist David Jackson summed it up best when he wrote, "D-Day has become a moment of national consecration—and a pilgrimage for modern presidents." According to Jackson, Normandy had become a sacred site that U.S. presidents felt obliged to visit as a way of celebrating American sacrifice, military prowess, and exceptionalism on the world stage. Omaha Beach, Utah Beach, and Pointe du Hoc had become, collectively, an American mecca.[42]

President Clinton spoke a total of four times in Normandy on 6 June 1994, and each one of his orations hewed faithfully to the American D-Day narrative. His first speech, given aboard the USS *George Washington* off the coast of Normandy at 7:21 a.m. local time to honor the U.S. Navy's role in the Invasion, powerfully evoked the first, and principal, theme by describing the operation as "the pivot point of the war, perhaps the pivot point of the 20th Century." He acknowledged the sacralization theme inherent in the D-Day narrative by quoting Eisenhower's Order of the Day, in which the supreme commander wrote: "Let us all beseech the blessing of almighty God upon this great and noble undertaking." Clinton further described how all Americans on D-Day "spoke softly to God" when news of the Invasion broke. He even described how workers in a Brooklyn shipyard knelt together and recited the Lord's Prayer upon hearing the news. Within these same religious overtones, Clinton acknowledged the "raw courage" of "legions of [freedom-loving] young men packed into landing craft" on their way to seize the beaches, led by the "brilliant planning" of senior leaders such as "General Eisenhower and his Allied staff."

President Clinton's second speech, given on Pointe du Hoc at 8:45 a.m. and in the precise spot where Ronald Reagan had delivered his oration a decade earlier, served as an even more powerful rendition of the D-Day narrative. He began by immediately comingling two of the key thematic frames—the scope and significance of the Invasion and its broader sacralization—by declaring to his audience: "We stand on sacred soil," a place where fifty years earlier "a miracle of liberation began." "On that morning," the president continued, "democracy's forces landed to end the enslavement of Europe." He once again acknowledged that on D-Day "the peoples of democracy prayed that they had done their job right." He saluted the abilities of the Allied senior leaders by celebrating the choices of those "lion-hearted leaders to rally their people" as well as the choices "of their soldiers to carry on that fight." He described in detail how Lt. Col. James Rudder of the 2nd Ranger Battalion led his 224 men up the "unforgiving cliffs" where he now spoke, braving German bullets and grenades from above to gain the heights and seize the artillery batteries thought to be on the ground above them. These young men, Clinton explained, "fought for the very survival of democracy" while "under the gaze of a loving God." These themes, as synthesized by the president, captured deftly the D-Day narrative in a way that flattered most Americans' sensibilities and reinforced the power of democracy, particularly since Clinton took time to point out in his speech that five years earlier, another "miracle of liberation" had taken place "when the rotting timbers of communism came tumbling down."

Clinton's third speech of the day at Utah Beach concentrated almost exclusively on the American and Allied losses experienced on the beaches while still managing to incorporate vestiges of the other themes. He combined the first theme, the Invasion's scope and significance, with the fourth theme, the valor and skill of the average soldier, by expressing the troop's sacrifices on D-Day in terms of "thousands and thousands of American, Canadian, and British troops . . . killed or wounded on one brutal day." According to Clinton, these soldiers, as well as French civilians and those who fought with the Resistance, "gave everything they were, or what they might have become, so that freedom might live." American troops in particular, explained Clinton in moralistic terms, embodied a "confident clarity born of relentless training and the guiding light of a just cause." For his homage to excellent American military leadership, Clinton eschewed any mention of the senior Allied leaders and instead captured the theme of America's best leaders in action by quoting a single American commanding officer, Col. Russell "Red" Reeder, who, upon learning that the 4th Infantry Division had landed in the wrong sector on Utah Beach, said, "It doesn't matter. We know where to go." In closing, Clinton confirmed D-Day's sacralization in America's collective consciousness by thanking those survivors who returned "to this hallowed ground" for their sacrifices, which had brought America "50 years of freedom."

President Clinton's fourth and final speech at the U. S. Cemetery in Colleville-sur-Mer, on the heights above Omaha Beach, captured more poignantly than his other addresses that day the media-constructed narrative of D-Day. He invoked the scale and significance of the Invasion and its moral justness by casting D-Day as "part of the biggest gamble of the war, the greatest crusade, yes, the longest day." In effect, Clinton averred, "June 6th, 1944, was the least ordinary day of the 20th Century." He sacralized the cemetery as "this hallowed place that speaks . . . in silence." Instead of focusing on capable, well-seasoned senior Allied leaders, Clinton chose once again to pay homage to American leadership as embodied in a more junior officer, in this case the 1st Infantry Division's Capt. Joe Dawson, who led his men in securing "a foothold for freedom." And the superb soldiers he led, explained Clinton, "saved the world." Their valor on D-Day compelled them to disembark their landing craft and move "away from their youth and toward a savage place many of them would sadly never leave." But, as Clinton proclaimed, moral righteousness remained on their side as they willingly took on "one of the greatest forces of evil the world has ever known." In seeking a broader message to convey to his audience, Clinton reminded the attendees that "just as freedom has a price, it also has a purpose, and its name is progress." In this case, the morality tale of the D-Day narrative allowed the American president to declare to all Americans and the world that "our mission is to expand freedom's reach forward." In effect, Clinton used his speeches not just to validate the D-Day narrative or to legitimate a present social order, but to erect guideposts to steer that social order toward a brighter and better future.[43]

For the sixtieth anniversary commemoration in 2004, President George W. Bush, as part of his own presidential pilgrimage to Normandy, spoke alongside French president Jacques Chirac at the site of President Clinton's final speech ten years earlier—the Normandy American Cemetery and Memorial at Colleville-sur-Mer overlooking Omaha Beach.[44] Following President Chirac's remarks, President Bush took to the podium and essentially recited theme by theme the media-constructed narrative of D-Day created on 6 June 1944. Bush described the magnitude of the operation by describing how "more than 12,000 Allied aircraft and about 5,000 Naval vessels" took to the air and the seas to carry out General Eisenhower's Order of the Day. Newspapers on D-Day used almost the very same numbers of aircraft and ships to communicate the operation's grand scale, further testifying to the press's powerful influence in creating the D-Day narrative. Bush further captured the Invasion's overarching significance by describing how multiple Allied nations had come together and "liberated a conquered Europe" and then stood together "for the freedom of all Europe."

Bush also invoked the sacralization theme by describing how President Roosevelt had taken to the airwaves on D-Day and prayed for God's blessing for "America's sons" and to lead them "straight and true" in their fight against evil. He even drew directly on the D-Day reportage by explaining how New York's *Daily News* had "pulled its lead stories to print the Lord's prayer on its front page." Perhaps the most striking image emanating from Bush's oration arose when he conflated two of the themes—the sacralization of D-Day and the virtue of the typical American GI—by relating how one soldier carried with him "the memory of three paratroopers dead and hanging from telephone poles 'like a horrible crucifixion scene.'" He even described the many Bibles that washed up on the beaches "mixed with the wreckage of war." With these images, Bush had deliberately apotheosized the American soldier on D-Day and sanctified each GI's endeavors and sacrifice. In keeping with the theme of sacrifice and valor, Bush told the story of one GI, Technician 5th Grade John Pinder Jr. Although he was gravely wounded, Pinder delivered his radio equipment onto the beach and then made three more trips through the surf under heavy fire to salvage more equipment. The Germans shot him two more times, and he died on the beach. Bush also acknowledged the leadership contributions of talented senior Allied leaders such as Eisenhower and Bradley, to whom he attributed the success of the Invasion as captured in Ike's own vernacular: "This operation is planned as a victory, and that's the way it is going to be." Bush's supplication, rich in imagery and metaphor, not only embodied all aspects of the D-Day narrative but clearly left a bread-crumb trail of references leading directly back to the newspaper and radio reportage of 6 June 1944.[45]

The "presidential pilgrimage" to Normandy continued with the seventieth anniversary of D-Day in 2014, when President Barack Obama, like Presidents Clinton and Bush before him, addressed a crowd of dignitaries, veterans, and other attendees at the cemetery above Omaha Beach and repeated in his own way the Invasion narrative that had by then taken hold firmly in America's collective consciousness. Obama wasted no time in bringing to bear the significance and scale of the operation and its sacred status in America's mindset. He began by declaring, "If prayer were made of sound, the skies over England that night would have deafened the world." The president shared how "fresh-faced GIs," America's virtuous and valiant soldiers, implored God to give them strength—or in one case, "give me guts." These men were not simply America's finest warriors but also critical agents in a historical undertaking, a collection of "150,000 souls" upon whose efforts that day "hung more than the fate of a war, but rather the course of human history." The sacrifice of each man, suggested Obama, "is written in the blood on these beaches, and it will endure for eternity." And in even more pointed moralistic language that further invoked D-Day's sanctified status, the president deemed Omaha Beach to be "democracy's beachhead" and the men who landed there a "powerful manifestation of America's commitment to human freedom." Obama's rhetoric masterfully wove in each element of the four thematic frames shaping the American D-Day narrative; yet despite his celebration of the fighting men's sacrifice and legacy, he still managed to acknowledge the contributions of the Invasion's senior leaders by mentioning General Bradley and an American general on Omaha Beach who spurred on the stalled troops by barking, "If you're Rangers . . . lead the way!"—an inspirational inducement that yielded the Ranger motto.

In relating these thematically consistent elements of the Invasion storyline by using other examples of individual soldier valor, President Obama fully assumed the mantle of guardian of America's D-Day narrative. His choice of language revealed his belief that the commemoration activities in Normandy represented a larger commitment to the nation's collective understanding of D-Day. In fact, he made clear to his audience that they had all come together that day to ensure that the soldiers' sacrifices remained "seared into the memory of a future world."[46]

Only five years later, President Donald J. Trump stood on the same ground to commemorate the seventy-fifth anniversary of the Invasion and offered his audience another rendition of the American D-Day narrative with all four themes intact. Trump's version fully sacralized the Invasion using high-minded, amply moralistic language that cast the American Cemetery above Omaha Beach as "Freedom's Altar" and the ground upon which he and his audience stood that day as "sacred Earth." He reiterated the thematic significance of the Invasion effort as a battle "for the survival of liberty" led by young men—products of America's farms, cities, and industrial towns—who had "enlisted their lives in a Great Crusade" and the "eternal struggle between good and evil." In Trump's eyes, the Allies represented "a liberation force of awesome and breathtaking scale" carried over the water by "the largest naval armada in the history of the world." Like President Clinton, President Trump eschewed examples of the more senior Allied leaders in action and instead cast his focus on ground-level leaders, such as the 16th Infantry Regiment's commander, Col. George Taylor, and the gallant Capt. Joe Dawson, "the son of a Texas preacher." But Trump's greatest emphasis, like most of his predecessors, remained on the sacrifices made by the individual GI. The president made clear his view of the significance of D-Day in the American psyche by stating that "Americans are drawn to this place as though it were part of our very soul." Trump explained that Americans journeyed to Normandy not only to salute what the GIs had done there decades earlier but "because of who they were." "In defeating evil," proclaimed the president, "they left a legacy that will last not only for a thousand years, but for all time . . . as long as freedom keeps its hold on the human heart."

Trump had effectively molded his speech within the framework of the four media-constructed themes in the D-Day narrative. In doing so, he gave Americans back home a powerful reminder of how they viewed themselves and the United States on the global stage. The clearest message here was that the American D-Day narrative constructed by America's newspapers and radios on 6 June 1944—and its four thematic frames—had truly endured.[47]

CODA

The D-Day Narrative as an American Myth

Next to cultural fantasies[,] historical truths can appear sacrilegious.

—Paul Jankowski[1]

As of this writing, seventy-eight years have passed since the D-Day Invasion took place. Most significantly, the thematically framed narrative of that event as constructed by the American press in a single day of reporting—6 June 1944—has genuinely endured. Today, in the twenty-first century's third decade, the media's ability to agree on a single narrative for a major news event seems next to impossible. Ideological differences, distrust of government, and political advocacy have infected newspapers, radio networks, and above all, cable television news, compelling them to challenge each other's interpretations of world and domestic events. This breakdown was magnified by Walter Cronkite's declaration in February 1968 that "we are mired in stalemate" in Vietnam, poking serious holes in the government's optimistic messaging.[2] Reporters were no longer rooting for the home team as they had a generation earlier, and partisan divides in both government and the press only increased over time. Perhaps the closest the U.S. press has come in the past twenty years to agreeing on a common narrative for a major news event was on 11 September 2001, when nearly all Americans agreed that the terrorist attacks in New York, in the skies over Pennsylvania, and at the Pentagon were what the *Honolulu Advertiser* called America's "second Pearl Harbor."[3] But within a matter of weeks, political finger-pointing and ideology regained their footing among America's news media. Apparently, only a direct attack on the American homeland had the power to bring the American news media together, and even then only for a short time.

When the subject was D-Day, however, the news media in 1944 not only crafted a common narrative about the Invasion, but that narrative remained in America's consciousness long after the last Allied soldier left the beachhead. America's chief executives have remained the primary guardians and promulgators of this single, common narrative. They will likely continue to make their pilgrimages to Normandy on key anniversaries to commemorate this historical manifestation of American exceptionalism. The D-Day narrative, although sanitized, sacralized, and memorialized, has allowed Americans to look back on 6 June 1944 and see themselves as they hope the world sees them today—as liberators on a moralistic crusade to advance the American theology of freedom throughout an oppressed world.

Even as more details of the horrors faced by the GIs on the beaches of Normandy emerged over the years, the American D-Day narrative has remained unaltered—a testament to the capacity of the news media to shape how Americans perceive world events. Even graphic representations of the carnage on Omaha Beach, revealed years after the landings by historians and filmmakers, never diluted the romanticism baked into America's D-Day story by a whole host of agents—newspaper editors, war correspondents, broadcasters, military officials overseas and at home, and the consumers of news themselves: the American people. Historian S. L. A. Marshall, whose 1960 magazine article "First Wave of Omaha Beach" in the *Atlantic* described in stark terms the slaughter on that beach, and filmmaker Steven Spielberg, with his graphic representation of the event in *Saving Private Ryan* (1998), each sought to pierce the veil of nostalgia in order to remind Americans of war's unforgiving violence and to caution future generations against the reflexive use of military power as a primary means to solve global challenges.[4] Even the efforts of historians to place D-Day into proper context when compared to other large-scale World War II operations (such as the massive Red Army offensives on the eastern front) have done little to knock D-Day from its romanticized perch. Instead, these efforts appear to have further sanctified the Invasion and elevate it to a higher level of American mythology. And that myth, born in the press on a single day and committed to America's collective consciousness in the same moment, demonstrates how powerful the news media can be in shaping our view of the world and the events that take place in it—now and into the future.

News reporting in the moment, when assuming the thematic trappings of mythmaking, can become a powerful force in masking reality. Such potent storytelling stymies any subsequent effort by historians to reveal greater truths and more meaningful interpretations, particularly when the myth manifests itself in a physical form. That reification of the media-induced mythology of D-Day exists today in the physical presence of the National D-Day Memorial located in Bedford, Virginia. The statuary and overall structure of the memorial powerfully captures all four themes of the American D-Day narrative. The sheer size of the memorial's physical layout attests to the significance and scale of the operation. The cathedral-like archway overlooks realistic statues of GIs crawling forward on a Normandy beach among fountain bursts simulating German small-arms fire; this dramatic presentation conveys the Invasion's sanctified nature and the sacrifice of America's virtuous and valorous soldiers. Likewise, a pavilion housing a lifelike statue of General Eisenhower and busts of the other Allied senior leaders decorate a garden that celebrates the gifted and inspired leaders who guided Operation Overlord to its successful outcome. The D-Day narrative now has a physical monument to its existence and to its growing status as an American myth.[5] In the words of President John F. Kennedy, "The great enemy of truth is very often not the lie—deliberate, contrived and dishonest—but the myth—persistent, persuasive and unrealistic."[6]

NOTES

Introduction

1. Douglas Brinkley, *The Boys of Pointe du Hoc: Ronald Reagan, D-Day, and the U.S. Army 2nd Ranger Battalion* (New York: William Morrow, 2005), 228.
2. I capitalize "Invasion" to distinguish it from other "invasions" conducted in the Mediterranean and the Pacific. The media invested the term "Invasion" with new meaning when they used it in the context of D-Day.
3. The complete text of President Reagan's Pointe du Hoc speech appears in Brinkley, 225–32; Video of President Reagan's speech is available online at https://www.youtube.com/watch?v=eEIqdcHbc8I.
4. Dwight D. Eisenhower, *Crusade in Europe* (Garden City, NY: Doubleday, 1948), 220.
5. Gordon A. Harrison, *Cross-Channel Attack* (Washington, DC: Office of the Chief of Military History, Department of the Army, 1951), 1.
6. Cornelius Ryan, *The Longest Day: June 6, 1944* (New York: Simon and Schuster, 1959); *The Longest Day,* directed by Ken Annakin, Andrew Marton, Bernhard Wicki, and Darryl F. Zanuck. Darryl F. Zanuck Productions and Twentieth-Century Fox Film Corporation, (1962; Los Angeles, CA: 2002), DVD.
7. "D-Day Plus 20 Years: Eisenhower Returns to Normandy," aired June 6, 1944, on CBS Reports, 81 minutes, 47 seconds. The specific segment from the program I describe here is available online at https://www.youtube.com/watch?v=qNsi4Z8Q12M.
8. Stephen E. Ambrose, *D-Day June 6, 1944: The Climactic Battle of World War II* (New York: Simon and Schuster, 1994), 24.
9. Ambrose, 495–96.
10. Tom Brokaw, *The Greatest Generation* (New York: Random House, 1998).
11. *Saving Private Ryan,* directed by Steven Spielberg. DreamWorks Pictures and Paramount Pictures, (Glendale, CA: 1998). DVD
12. Eric Foner, *Give Me Liberty! An American History,* 5th ed. (New York: W. W. Norton, 2017), 871.
13. *Editor & Publisher* 77, no. 15 (8 April 1944) 7. Cited hereafter as *E&P.*
14. Daniel J. Boorstin, *The Image: A Guide to Pseudo-Events in America* (New York: Vintage Books, 1961), 10.

15. Michael Dolski, *D-Day Remembered: The Normandy Landings in the American Collective Memory* (Knoxville: University of Tennessee Press, 2016), 8–14.
16. See Sarah J. Purcell, *Sealed with Blood: War, Sacrifice, and Memory in Revolutionary America* (Philadelphia: University of Pennsylvania Press, 2002), and Carol Reardon, *Pickett's Charge in History and Memory* (Chapel Hill: University of North Carolina Press, 1997) for further discussions of the importance of Bunker Hill and Gettysburg in American memory.
17. George H. Roeder Jr., *The Censored War: American Visual Experience During World War Two* (New Haven: Yale University Press, 1993), 15.
18. Andrew Whitmarsh, *D-Day in Photographs* (Cheltenham, UK: The History Press, 2009), 87; Paul Adair, *Hitler's Greatest Defeat: The Collapse of Army Group Centre, June 1944* (London: Arms and Armour Press, 1994), 171.
19. For the war's impact on the Soviet Union, see Gerhard L. Weinberg, *A World at Arms: A Global History of World War II* (New York: Cambridge University Press, 2005), 897–900. On how the Soviet Union defeated German land power, see Richard Overy, *Why the Allies Won* (New York: W. W. Norton, 1995), 1–2 and 314–25.
20. Allan M. Winkler, *The Politics of Propaganda: The Office of War Information, 1942–1945* (New Haven: Yale University Press, 1978), 12–13.
21. Capt. Harry C. Butcher, USNR, *My Three Years with Eisenhower* (New York: Simon and Schuster, 1946), 610.
22. For example, *El Paso Times*, 9 August 1942, and *San Bernardino Daily Sun*, 9 August 1942.
23. *Detroit Free Press* vol. 112, no. 188 (8 November 1942).
24. *Chicago Sunday Tribune*, 8 November 1942; *Los Angeles Times*, 8 November 1942. Other representative examples include the *Clarion Ledger* (Jackson, MS), 8 November 1942; *Las Cruces Sun-News*, 8 November 1942; *Philadelphia Inquirer*, 8 November 1942; *Hartford Courant*, 8 November 1942; and *Democrat Chronicle* (Rochester, NY), 8 November 1942.
25. *New Castle* (PA) *News*, 10 July 1943; *Indianapolis Star*, 10 July 1943. Other representative examples include the *St. Louis Star-Times*, 10 July 1943; *Chicago Daily Tribune*, 10 July 1943; *Los Angeles Times*, 10 July 1943; and *St. Louis Post-Dispatch*, 10 July 1943.
26. *Akron Beacon Journal*, 10 July 1943; *Dunkirk* (NY) *Evening Observer*, 10 July 1943.
27. John McDonough, "The Longest Night: Broadcasting's First Invasion," *American Scholar* 63, no. 2 (Spring 1994): 194.
28. *Radio News 1942* vol. 2, N1942.2, 187838, Old Time Radio CD, files 420810 and 421108, https://www.otrcat.com/p/cbs-world-new-today.

29. Patrick S. Washburn, *A Question of Sedition: The Federal Government's Investigation of the Black Press During World War II* (New York: Oxford University Press, 1986), 39.
30. *Sheridan* (WY) *Enterprise,* 12 June 1918; *Evening Public Ledger* (Philadelphia), 3 April 1918.
31. Dolski, 3.

Chapter 1. Anticipating the "Explosion"

1. "D Day Guidance for the Press" (Secret), 31 May 1944, National Archives and Records Administration II (NARA II hereafter), Records Group (RG) 331, Box 3, "Press Policy," NAI 613109, Decimal File 000.7–1, 1.
2. "D Day Guidance for the Press," 1.
3. *United States Summary: Census of 1940,* Table 2B, 8, https://www2.census.gov/prod2/decennial/documents /33973538v1ch02.pdf.
4. David M. Kennedy, *Freedom from Fear: The American People in Depression and War, 1929–1945* (New York: Oxford University Press, 1999), 675.
5. Max Hastings, *Overlord: D-Day and the Battle for Normandy* (New York: Simon and Schuster, 1984), 349.
6. Michael C. C. Adams, *The Best War Ever: America and World War II* (Baltimore and London: Johns Hopkins University Press, 1994), 68.
7. Peter Margaritas, *Bust Eisenhower: The Message That Almost Ruined D-Day,* 3rd ed. (Privately published, 2009, 2014, and 2015), 5.
8. Michael Schudson, *The Power of News* (Cambridge, MA: Harvard University Press, 1995), 15.
9. Benedict Anderson, *Imagined Communities* (London and New York: Verso, 2006), 35–36.
10. Schudson, *The Power of News,* 14.
11. Schudson, *The Power of News,* 19–25; Michael Schudson, *The Sociology of News,* 2nd ed. (New York and London: W. W. Norton, 2011), 22–24, 164; Jürgen Habermas, *The Structural Transformation of the Public Sphere: An Inquiry into a Category of Bourgeois Society* (Cambridge, MA: MIT Press, 2001), 183.
12. Schudson, *The Power of News,* 37.
13. N. W. Ayer and Son's *Directory of Newspapers and Periodicals 1944,* ed. J. Percy H. Johnson (Philadelphia: N. W. Ayer and Son, 1944), 11.
14. Gwenyth L. Jackaway, *Media at War: Radio's Challenge to the Newspapers, 1924–1939* (Westport, CT: Praeger, 1995), 16.
15. David Lloyd Jones, "The U.S. Office of War Information and American Public Opinion During World War II" (PhD diss., State University of New York, 1976), 3–4, 32.

16. Lee Finkle, *Forum for Protest: The Black Press During World War II* (Rutherford, NJ: Fairleigh Dickinson University Press, 1975), 56.
17. Oliver Gramling, *AP: The Story of News: Editions for the Armed Services, Inc.* (New York: Farrar and Rinehart, 1940), 23.
18. Jackaway, 16.
19. Richard R. Lingeman, *Don't You Know There's a War On? The American Home Front from 1941–1945* (New York: G. P. Putnam's Sons, 1970), 311.
20. Original United Press newswire feed for 6 June 1944 (*Sunbury Daily Item*, Sunbury, PA).
21. Sherman H. Dryer, *Radio in Wartime* (New York: Greenburg Publishers, 1942), 152.
22. Bill Mauldin, *Up Front* (New York: Henry Holt, 1945), 20–22.
23. Gramling, 21–23.
24. Gramling, 25.
25. Michael Schudson, *Discovering the News: A Social History of American Newspapers* (New York: Basic Books, 1978), 4–8.
26. Gramling, 287–92.
27. Schudson, *Discovering the News*, 144–48.
28. Gramling, 394–411.
29. Washburn, 39.
30. Washburn, 39.
31. Finkle, 9.
32. Finkle, 10, 192.
33. See the *Arkansas State Press*, 9 June 1944; *The Echo* (MS), 9 June 1944; *Century Voice* (Yazoo City, MS), July 1944; and *Mississippi Enterprise*, 24 June 1944.
34. *Plaindealer* (Kansas City, KS), 16 June 1944.
35. Washburn, 84.
36. Washburn, 54.
37. Finkle, 10.
38. Washburn, 58.
39. Theodore F. Koop, *Weapon of Silence* (Chicago: University of Chicago Press, 1946), 176.
40. Michael Stamm, *Sound Business: Newspapers, Radio, and the Politics of New Media* (Philadelphia: University of Pennsylvania Press, 2011), 4.
41. Anderson, 63; Mary L. Dudziak, *War Time: An Idea, Its History, Its Consequences* (Oxford: Oxford University Press, 2012), 19–20; Stamm, 8–9, 30–31; Kennedy, 228–29.

42. Lingeman, 233–34.
43. Dryer, 45.
44. Hadley Cantril, *Public Opinion 1935–1946* (Princeton, NJ: Princeton University Press, 1951), 523–26; Dryer, 56–58.
45. Dryer, 41.
46. Stamm, 4.
47. Stamm, 3.
48. Stamm, 195.
49. Jackaway, 89; Stamm, 11.
50. Jackaway, 4, 29–33; Stamm, 11–13, 81–85, 93–101.
51. Jackaway, 45–48.
52. Jackaway, 49–70.
53. Michele Hilmes, ed., *NBC: America's Network* (Berkeley: University of California Press, 2007), 3–4.
54. Jackaway, 131.
55. Dryer, 41.
56. Hilmes, 12–17, 85–96; Stamm, 71–74, 110.
57. Stamm, 45–54; Koop, 177; Hilmes, 12.
58. Dryer, 309–10. This specific provision in the Communications Act of 1934 appeared in Section 606 (c), Title VI.
59. Lingeman, 235.
60. Stamm, 30–31.
61. *The Columbia Program Book: Spring 1944* (New York: Columbia Broadcasting System, 1 May 1944), 4, 5, 7.
62. Dryer, 59–60.
63. Lingeman, 233.
64. Edward Davidson and Dale Manning, *Chronology of World War Two* (London: Cassell, 1999), 11, 43; Lingeman, 233–34; Stamm, 101–3.
65. Noam Chomsky, *Media Control: The Spectacular Achievements of Propaganda*, 2nd ed. (New York: Seven Stories Press, 2002), 11–12; Anthony Rhodes, *Propaganda: The Art of Persuasion: World War II* (New York: Chelsea House, 1976), 139.
66. Dryer, 87–88; Alan M. Winkler, *The Politics of Propaganda: The Office of War Information 1942–1945* (New Haven: Yale University Press, 1978), 1.
67. Garth S. Jowett and Victoria O'Donnell, *Propaganda and Persuasion*, 6th ed. (Los Angeles and London: SAGE, 2015), 2–8.
68. Chomsky, 11.
69. Susan A. Brewer, *Why America Fights: Patriotism and War Propaganda from the Philippines to Iraq* (Oxford: Oxford University Press, 2009), 53–55.

70. *Red, White, and Blue Series No. 9: War Labor and Peace: Some Recent Addresses and Writings of President Wilson* (Committee on Public Information, March 1918).
71. Winkler, 2–3.
72. George Creel, *How We Advertised America: The First Telling of the Amazing Story of the Committee on Public Information That Carried the Gospel of Americanism to Every Corner of the Globe* (New York: Harper and Brothers, 1920), xv and 4–7; *Red, White, and Blue Series No. 9*; Koop, 156; Brewer, 63.
73. Brewer, 56.
74. Jowett and O'Donnell, 244–45; Brewer, 76; Jeffrey A. Smith, *War and Press Freedom: The Problem of Prerogative Power* (New York: Oxford University Press, 1999), 139.
75. Koop, 156–59.
76. Sam Lebovic, *Free Speech and Unfree News: The Paradox of Press Freedom in America* (Cambridge, MA: Harvard University Press, 2016), 124–25.
77. Brewer, 71.
78. Brewer, 84.
79. Winkler, 3.
80. Brewer, 85; Edward Bernays, *Propaganda.* (Brooklyn: IG Publishing, 2005), 63–69.
81. John Morton Blum, *V Was for Victory: Politics and American Culture During World War II* (New York and London: Harcourt Brace Jovanovich, 1976), 21.
82. Winkler, 22.
83. Lebovic, 113–15.
84. Blum, 29–30.
85. Winkler, 28–29.
86. Winkler, 20.
87. Executive Order 9132, *The American Presidency Project*, http://www.presidency.ucsb.edu/ws/index.php?pid=16273.
88. Paul M. A. Linebarger, *Psychological Warfare* (Washington, DC: Combat Forces Press, 1954), 93; Winkler, 30–31.
89. Emphasis in original. Executive Order 9132.
90. Winkler, 60–62
91. See George H. Roeder Jr., *The Censored War: American Visual Experience During World War Two* (New Haven: Yale University Press, 1993), 78.
92. Brewer, 89.

93. Winkler, 66–71, 125–31; Lebovic, 116; Blum, 41.
94. Michael S. Sweeney, *Secrets of Victory: The Office of Censorship and the American Press and Radio in World War II* (Chapel Hill: University of North Carolina Press, 2001), 2.
95. Executive Order 8985, Establishing the Office of Censorship, *The American Presidency Project,* https://www.presidency.ucsb.edu/documents/executive-order-8985-establishing-the-office-censorship.
96. Sweeney, 22.
97. Byron Price, *A Report on the Office of Censorship* (Washington, DC: United States Government Printing Office, 1945), 4; Koop, 9.
98. Koop, 19.
99. Executive Order 8985, Establishing the Office of Censorship.
100. Emphasis in original. Price, 8; Koop, viii; Sweeney, 51.
101. Price, 6.
102. Lebovic, 124–25.
103. Sweeney, 92.
104. Price, 38.
105. The War Department, not the Office of Censorship, withheld images of American dead during the first twenty-one months of the war to avoid demoralizing the home front. Military authorities felt that neither the press nor the public wanted that much candor. See Roeder, 8, 13.
106. Price, 35–37.
107. *Code of Wartime Practices for American Broadcasters,* edition of February 1, 1943 (Washington, DC: United States Government Office of Censorship), 6–8.
108. Price, 32.
109. Koop, 27–28.
110. Lebovic, 132.
111. Only one true failure of the press code occurred during the entire war. In June 1942, the *Chicago Tribune* published a story about the Japanese naval forces at Midway suggesting that the United States had broken the Japanese naval code. Providentially, the Japanese navy did not catch on. See Lebovic, 130.
112. Price, 40.
113. Koop, 235–46.
114. *E&P* 77, no. 15 (8 April 1944): 7.
115. *E&P* 77, no. 15 (8 April 1944): 7.
116. Jackaway, 89; Stamm, 11–14.
117. *E&P* 77, no. 5 (29 January 1944): 7.

118. *E&P* 77, no. 7 (12 February 1944): 54; *E&P* 77, no. 11 (11 March 1944): 11; *E&P* 77, no. 14, (1 April 1944): 8; *E&P* 77, no. 18 (29 April 1944): 28; *E&P* 77, no. 20 (13 May 1944): 9; *Broadcast and Broadcast Advertising* (*BBA* hereafter) 26, no. 5 (31 January 1944): 63; *BBA* 26, no. 10 (6 March 1944): 16, 52; *BBA* 26, no. 21 (22 May 1944): 24.
119. *BBA* 26, no. 16 (17 April 1944): 16.
120. *BBA* 26, no. 22 (29 May 1944): 14.
121. If the OWI provided any official guidelines for how the radio networks and the newspaper press should shape their reporting of the Invasion, the trade journals have remained silent on that fact.
122. "D Day Guidance for the Press" (Secret), 31 May 1944, NARA II, Records Group (RG) 331, Box 3, "Press Policy," NAI 613109, Decimal File 000.7–1, 1.
123. "D Day Guidance for the Press" (Secret), 31 May 1944, 1.
124. *Rocky Mountain News*, 4 June 1944, 8; Col. Barney Oldfield, USAF, *Never a Shot in Anger* (New York: Duell, Sloan, and Pearce, 1956), 68–69; Margaritas, 11–18.
125. Oldfield, 68; Margaritas, 9.
126. *Rocky Mountain News*, 4 June 1944, 8.
127. Oldfield, 59, 64–69; Margaritas, 7; Koop, 240.
128. Margaritas, 4; *Rocky Mountain News*, 4 June 1944. I have relied on the AP story explaining the details behind the error that appears in this specific newspaper; many other newspapers throughout the country carried the same AP story with little or no modification; *AP Inter-Office*, "Invasion Issue" (June–July 1944): 7–8, provided additional details and background; *BBA* 26, no. 24 (12 June 1944): 18.
129. *The Battle Creek (MI) Enquirer and News*, 4 June 1944; *Rocky Mountain News*, 4 June 1944.
130. Roeder, 15.
131. *E&P* 75, no. 42 (17 October 1942): 10.
132. *E&P* 77, no. 7 (12 February 1944): 54.
133. *E&P* 77, no. 22 (27 May 1944): 5.
134. *E&P* 77, no. 22 (27 May 1944): 11.
135. *E&P* 77, no. 22 (27 May 1944): 11.
136. *BBA* 26, no. 5 (31 January 1944): 46.
137. Letter to the author by Andrew A. "Andy" Rooney, 20 February 1998.
138. *Time*, 1 May 1944, 17; *E&P* 77, no. 20 (13 May 1944): 9.
139. *Time*, 1 May 1944, 17, 26.
140. *Time*, 1 May 1944, 25; *Time*, 15 May 1944, Pony Edition: Specially Printed for Air Transport, 8.

141. For an excellent study of Operation Fortitude, see Anthony Cave Brown, *Bodyguard of Lies* (New York: Harper and Row, 1975); *Time*, 1 May 1944, 24, 27.

Chapter 2. "Invasion by Airwave"

1. *H Hour-1944* (National Broadcasting Company, 1944), 1, 4.
2. *CBS News on D-Day* (New York: Columbia Broadcasting System, 1945), 3, 9–11; John McDonough, "The Longest Night: Broadcasting's First Invasion," *American Scholar* 63, no. 2 (Spring 1994): 199; *Newsweek*, 19 June 1944, 95.
3. Despite my best efforts, I have been unable to locate printed sources or archival recordings of how the Mutual Broadcasting System and the Blue Network broke the news of D-Day on their respective networks. For that reason, CBS and NBC receive the most coverage in this study as exemplars of how the broadcast networks handled D-Day, simply because both of those networks established a written record of their performance in the form of two self-produced booklets: *CBS News on D-Day* (1945) and *H Hour-1944* (1944). The nonprofit Internet Archive hosts complete sound files for the first twenty-four hours of D-Day broadcasting for CBS at https://archive.org/details/CBD440606CBSDDayCBS, and for NBC at https://archive.org/details/NBC-CompleteBroadcastDDay.
4. *H Hour-1944*, 2.
5. McDonough, 194–95.
6. David M. Kennedy, *Freedom from Fear: The American People in Depression and War, 1929–1945* (New York: Oxford University Press, 1999), 229.
7. Susan A. Brewer, *Why America Fights: Patriotism and War Propaganda from the Philippines to Iraq* (Oxford: Oxford University Press, 2009), 93.
8. Gunnar Horn, "Radio Journalism," *English Journal* 34, no. 5 (May 1945): 257; James Rowland Angell, "Radio and National Morale," *American Journal of Sociology* 47, no. 3 (November 1941): 352–54; Hadley Cantril, *Public Opinion 1935–1946* (Princeton, NJ: Princeton University Press, 1951), 523–26.
9. Sherman H. Dryer, *Radio in Wartime* (New York: Greenberg, 1942), 54; *NBC and You: An Account of the Organization, Operation and Employee-Company Policies of the National Broadcasting Company designed as a Handbook to aid you in your daily work* (National Broadcasting Company, 1944), 15; Benedict Anderson, *Imagined Communities* (London: Verso, 2006), 35–36.
10. *NBC and You*, 8–9; Michael Stamm, *Sound Business: Newspapers, Radio, and the Politics of New Media* (Philadelphia: University of Pennsylvania Press, 2011), 101–3.
11. Dryer, 46.

12. Horn, 258.
13. See Gwenyth L. Jackaway, *Media at War: Radio's Challenge to the Newspapers, 1924–1939* (Westport, CT: Praeger, 1995).
14. McDonough, 194–95.
15. McDonough, 193.
16. *H Hour-1944*, 30–32; *BBA* 26, no. 19 (8 May 1944): 8.
17. *BBA* 26, no. 19 (8 May 1944): 8.
18. *CBS News on D-Day*, 2.
19. *BBA* 26, no. 19 (8 May 1944): 8, 52.
20. *BBA* 26, no. 19 (8 May 1944): 8.
21. *CBS News on D-Day*, 4; *NBC and You*, 42.
22. *NBC and You*, 25; Stamm, 31–32.
23. *BBA* 26, no. 19 (8 May 1944): 52.
24. *CBS News on D-Day*, 9.
25. McDonough, 197.
26. *BBA* 26, no. 19 (8 May 1944): 7.
27. *NBC and You*, 20.
28. *CBS News on D-Day*, 3.
29. *CBS News on D-Day*, 7–8.
30. *BBA* 26, no. 22 (29 May 1944): 14; *BBA* 26, no. 19 (8 May 1944): 52.
31. *BBA* 26, no. 19 (8 May 1944): 8.
32. *BBA* 26, no. 19 (8 May 1944): 52; McDonough, 201.
33. *CBS News on D-Day*, 4–5.
34. *BBA* 26, no. 19 (8 May 1944): 52.
35. McDonough, 196–97; *NBC and You*, 53–54.
36. *BBA* 26, no. 19 (8 May 1944): 7; *BBA* 26, no. 24 (12 June 1944): 40. Colonel Kirby came from a radio background himself before taking a position with the War Department in 1940.
37. *BBA* 26, no. 19 (8 May 1944): 7–8. The BBC had offered to provide eyewitness news accounts of the Invasion for independent, non-network stations in the United States; *BBA* 26, no. 24 (12 June 1944): 68.
38. *BBA* 26, no. 26 (26 June 1944), 16; *BBA* 26, no. 24 (12 June 1944): 70; *AP Inter-Office* 2, no. 8 (June–July 1944): 7.
39. "Public Relations Plan 'Overlord,'" dated 1 May 1944, National Archives and Record Administration II (NARA II hereafter), Records Group (RG) 331, Box 3, "Press Policy," NAI 613109, Decimal File 000.7–1.
40. *BBA* 26, no. 21 (22 May 1944): 16; *CBS News on D-Day*, 6–7; *Newsweek*, 8 May 1944, 79.
41. *BBA* 26, no. 19 (8 May 1944): 8; *BBA* 26, no. 24 (12 June 1944): 61, 70; *BBA* 26, no. 26 (26 June 1944): 16; *Time*, 19 June 1944, 68.

42. McDonough, 195; *BBA* 26, no. 19 (8 May 1944): 8, 52.
43. Letter to "All Unit Commanders, Allied Expeditionary Force, Subject: Accredited War Correspondent," (Restricted), 11 May 1944, NARA II, RG 331, Box 3, "Press Policy," NAI 613109, Decimal File 000.7–1.
44. *CBS News on D-Day*, 18; *BBA* 26, no. 22 (29 May 1944): 14; *BBA* 26, no. 24 (12 June 1944): 70.
45. *BBA* 26, no. 22 (29 May 1944): 14.
46. *BBA* 26, no. 16 (17 April 1944): 16.
47. *Code of Wartime Practices for American Broadcasters*, edition of February 1, 1943 (Washington, DC: U.S. Government Office of Censorship).
48. McDonough, 197.
49. *BBA* 26, no. 22 (29 May 1944): 48.
50. *BBA* 26, no. 19 (8 May 1944): 54.
51. *CBS News on D-Day*, 8.
52. *CBS News on D-Day*, 85.
53. McDonough, 195; David Paul Nord, *Communities of Journalism: A History of American Newspapers and Their Readers* (Urbana: University of Illinois Press, 2001), 254.
54. McDonough, 194–95.
55. *Time*, 19 June 1944, 68.
56. McDonough, 194.
57. *BBA* 26, no. 19 (8 May 1944): 8; *Newsweek*, 19 June 1944, 95; *CBS News on D-Day*, 14; *BBA* 26, no. 24 (12 June 1944): 9, 65; *H Hour-1944*, 1–2.
58. *Newsweek*, 19 June 1944, 95.
59. *BBA* 26, no. 24 (12 June 1944): 10, 59.
60. *BBA* 26, no. 24 (12 June 1944): 61.
61. *CBS News on D-Day*, 14.
62. McDonough, 197; *CBS News on D-Day*, 2.
63. McDonough, 197.
64. Dryer, 175–76.
65. "George Fielding Eliot, 76, Dies; Military Writer of World War II," *New York Times*, 22 April 1971, 44 (*New York Times* online archives: https://www.nytimes.com/1971/04/22/archives/george-fielding-eliot-76-dies-military-writer-of-world-war-11.html); *BBA* 26, no. 24 (12 June 1944): 10; McDonough, 199; *CBS News on D-Day*, 14, 24.
66. *BBA* 26, no. 24 (12 June 1944): 59; *H Hour-1944*, 4.
67. For background on Kaltenborn, see https://coutant.org/kaltenborn.html.
68. *CBS News on D-Day*, 15.
69. McDonough, 199.
70. *CBS News on D-Day*, 4.
71. *BBA* 26, no. 24 (12 June 1944): 66.

72. *Newsweek*, 19 June 1944, 95; *BBA* 26, no. 24 (12 June 1944): 9.
73. *BBA* 26, no. 24 (12 June 1944): 10.
74. *CBS News on D-Day*, 13.
75. *BBA* 26, no. 24 (12 June 1944): 59.
76. *H Hour-1944*, 3.
77. Horn, 257.
78. McDonough, 194.
79. *CBS News on D-Day*, 11–12.
80. *BBA* 26, no. 24 (12 June 1944): 11.
81. McDonough, 200.
82. McDonough, 196.
83. *BBA* 26, no. 24 (12 June 1944): 10; *CSB News on D-Day*, 14; McDonough, 200.
84. I transcribed all direct quotations from the online archive of CBS's D-Day coverage at https://archive.org/details/CBD440606CBSDDayCBS (hereafter cited as CBS Sound Files), File 440606, Part 001.
85. CBS Sound Files, File 440606, Part 001.
86. *CBS News on D-Day*, 11–15.
87. *CBS News on D-Day*, 15; McDonough, 200.
88. *CBS News on D-Day*, 15.
89. CBS Sound Files, File 440606, Part 001.
90. Sound files for NBC's D-Day coverage are at https://archive.org/details/NBCCompleteBroadcastDDay (hereafter cited as NBC Sound Files), CBD-440606, NBC0250 (Music and News) and NBC0300 (Music and News).
91. McDonough, 194, 200–201.
92. *CBS News on D-Day*, 16.
93. McDonough, 201.
94. CBS Sound Files, File 440606, Part 001.
95. *BBA* 26, no. 24 (12 June 1944): 62; The Public Relations Plan for Overlord (1st Draft), dated 13 March 1944, identifies Dupuy as SHAEF's Public Relations Officer. NARA II, RG 331, Entry NM8 56, Box 3, Press Policy, Decimal File 000.7–1; McDonough, 201–2.
96. McDonough, 202; SHAEF finalized the wording for Communiqué Number 1 in a memorandum dated 30 May 1944. NARA II, RG 331, Entry NM8 56, Box 3, Special Announcements and Bulletins, Decimal File 000.7–3. The final wording appeared in "Communiqué No. 1, SHAEF, 6 June 1944," NARA II, RG 331, Entry NM8 56, Box 3, Communiqués thru 27 June 1944, Decimal File 000.71–2.
97. SCAF No. 22, 7 May 1944, NARA II, RG 331, Entry NM8 56, Box 3, Special Announcements and Bulletins, Decimal File 000.7–3.
98. NBC Sound Files, CBD-440606, NBC0330 (News).
99. CBS Sound Files, File 440606, Part 001; McDonough, 202.

100. *CBS News on D-Day,* 19–20; CBS Sound Files, File 440606, Part 001; NBC Sound Files, CBD-440606, NBC0330 (News).
101. *CBS News on D-Day,* 19–20; CBS Sound Files, File 440606, Part 001; NBC Sound Files, CBD-440606, NBC0330 (News); *BBA* 26, no. 24 (12 June 1944): 10; Edward R. Murrow read the text of Eisenhower's Order of the Day over the networks precisely as it was printed on the small leaflets issued to the Invasion troops.
102. *CBS News on D-Day,* 20; *H Hour-1944,* 4; NBC Sound Files, CBD-440606, NBC0330 (News); CBS Sound Files, File 440606, Part 002.
103. *CBS News on D-Day,* 20–21; *H Hour-1944,* 5; McDonough, 203; *BBA* 26, no. 24 (12 June 1944): 10; CBS Sound Files, File 440606, Part 002; NBC Sound Files, CBD-440606, NBC0330 (News).
104. SCAF No. 33, 24 May 1944, NARA II, RG 331, Entry NM8 56, Box 3, Special Announcements and Bulletins, Decimal File 000.7–3; NBC Sound Files, CBD-440606, NBC0330 (News); CBS Sound Files, File 440606, Part 002; *CBS News on D-Day,* 1, 20–21; *H Hour-1944,* 5.
105. *CBS News on D-Day,* 23–24; *H Hour-1944,* 5; McDonough, 203; CBS Sound Files, File 440606, Part 002; NBC Sound Files, CBD-440606, NBC0415 (News); *E&P* 77, no. 25 (17 June 1944): 5, 25.
106. *CBS News on D-Day,* 31, puts sunrise in New York at 4:29 a.m. local mean time.
107. McDonough, 204.
108. *CBS News on D-Day,* 27.
109. *CBS News on D-Day,* 26–27; CBS Sound Files, File 440606, Part 002. I have corrected minor transcription errors in *CBS News on D-Day* by comparing the booklet's broadcast quotations with sound files of the broadcasts.
110. *H Hour-1944,* 6; NBC Sound Files, CBD-440606, NBC0330 (News).
111. *CBS News on D-Day,* 29–30.
112. *H Hour-1944,* 6–7.
113. *CBS News on D-Day,* 32; *H Hour-1944,* 6–7.
114. McDonough, 208.
115. *CBS News on D-Day,* 31.
116. *CBS News on D-Day,* 39.
117. McDonough, 207–8; NBC Sound Files, CBD-440606, NBC0930 (News and NBC Orchestra).
118. *CBS News on D-Day,* 39.
119. *H Hour-1944,* 11.
120. CBS Sound Files, File 440606, Part 008.
121. *CBS News on D-Day,* 40; McDonough, 207; *BBA* 26, no. 24 (12 June 1944): 61; CBS Sound Files, File 440606, Part 007.
122. *CBS News on D-Day,* 41.
123. *H Hour-1944,* 4 and 10; McDonough, 207; *Time,* 19 June 1944, 68.

124. *Time*, 19 June 1944, 68, reported that the CBS-Hooper survey estimated that listening was 82 percent above normal. A D-Day CBS-Hooper survey released after the Invasion refined that number to 78 percent. *BBA* 26, no. 25 (19 June 1944): 16.
125. *CBS News on D-Day*, 40–41, 44, and 47–48.
126. *CBS News on D-Day*, 32–33; McDonough, 205, states that neither broadcasts nor recordings were allowed in the House of Commons.
127. *H Hour-1944*, 7; CBS Sound Files, File 440606, Part 007.
128. *H Hour-1944*, 13–14.
129. *H Hour-1944*, 13; "21 Army Group: Personal Message from the C-in-C," signed B. L. Montgomery, General.
130. *CBS News on D-Day*, 49–50; *H Hour-1944*, 15; CBS Sound Files, File 440606, Part 0013.
131. *BBA* 26, no. 24 (12 June 1944): 38.
132. *CBS News on D-Day*, 31; McDonough, 204.
133. *BBA* 26, no. 24 (12 June 1944): 64.
134. *BBA* 26, no. 24 (12 June 1944): 10.
135. *H Hour-1944*, 7; NBC Sound Files, CBD-440606, NBC0700 (News).
136. *H Hour-1944*, 12; NBC Sound Files, CBD-440606, NBC1230 (News).
137. *H Hour-1944*, 19–20; NBC Sound Files, CBD-440606, NBC1630 (News).
138. *CBS News on D-Day*, 55–58; "Communiqué No. 2, 6 June 1944," NARA II, RG 331, Entry NM8 56, Box 3, Communiqués thru 27 June 1944, Decimal File 000.71–2.
139. *CBS News on D-Day*, 1, 68–69.
140. See https://archive.org/details/1940RadioNews/1940–09–20-CBS-Edward-R-Murrow-During-Blitz.mp3 and https://archive.org/details/1940RadioNews/1940–09–22-CBS-Edward-R-Murrow-London-Rooftop-Blitz.mp3 for the 20 September 1940 and 22 September 1940 broadcasts by Edward R. Murrow of German air raids on London.
141. See John Keegan, *The Face of Battle* (New York: Penguin, 1976).
142. McDonough, 210.
143. *BBA* 26, no. 19 (8 May 1944): 7.
144. McDonough, 210.
145. *Newsweek*, 3 July 1944, 64.
146. *Newsweek*, 3 July 1944, 64.
147. *BBA* 26, no. 24 (12 June 1944): 11.
148. *BBA* 26, no. 24 (12 June 1944): 11.
149. *BBA* 26, no. 24 (12 June 1944): 18; *Time*, 19 June 1944, 68; *E&P* 77, no. 25 (17 June 1944): 5, 25.
150. Lieutenant Colonel Cole later received the Medal of Honor for his actions in Normandy. See Leonard Rapport and Arthur Norwood Jr., *Rendezvous with*

Destiny: History of the 101st Airborne Division (Old Saybrook, CT: Konecky and Konecky, 1948), 813.

151. *CBS News on D-Day*, 23–24; *H Hour-1944*, 5; NBC Sound Files, CBD-440606, NBC0415 (News); CBS Sound Files, File 440606, Part 002.
152. *CBS News on D-Day*, 28–29; McDonough, 204; CBS Sound Files, File 440606, Part 003. In the CBS Sound Files, between Parts 002 and 003, Richard Hottelet's broadcast at 5:07 a.m. EWT is missing. I relied on a recording of Hottelet's broadcast on YouTube at https://www.youtube.com/watch?v=I8xkQ05VT_k.
153. *CBS News on D-Day*, 75–77; CBS Sound Files, File 440606, Part 021; *Time*, 19 June 1944, 68–69; McDonough, 209.
154. In an unsigned letter from among the wartime letters of Mrs. Horace S. Sargent of Auburndale, Massachusetts, the writer described her experience of listening to the D-Day broadcasts as "very thrilling." In particular, she commented on George Hicks's report by explaining that she remained tuned in "till 11.30 p.m. when I listened over the radio at my bedside to a broadcast from a U.S. flag-ship off the coast of France describing the scene of action as things were actually happening."
155. *BBA* 26, no. 24 (12 June 1944): 11.
156. McDonough, 209.
157. *CBS News on D-Day*, 77–79; George Hicks's entire fourteen-minute broadcast of the German air attack is online at https://www.youtube.com/watch?v=AnomrhP6sVs.
158. McDonough, 210.
159. *BBA* 26, no. 25 (19 June 1944): 40.
160. *BBA* 26, no. 25 (19 June 1944): 16.
161. *BBA* 26, no. 22 (29 May 1944): 14; *CBS News on D-Day*, 18.
162. Richard R. Lingeman, *Don't You Know There's a War On? The American Home Front, 1941–1945* (New York: G. P. Putnam's Sons, 1970), 242–43.
163. *H Hour-1944*, 25; NBC Sound Files, CBD-440606, NBC2215 (Bob Hope).

Chapter 3. "Invasion On!"

1. *Akron Beacon Journal*, 6 June 1944.
2. *Newsweek*, 19 June 1944, 73; *Daily News* (New York), 6 June 1944.
3. David Paul Nord, *Communities of Journalism: A History of American Newspapers and Their Readers* (Urbana: University of Illinois Press, 2001), 246–47.
4. Benedict Anderson, *Imagined Communities* (London: Verso, 2006), 35–36.
5. Michael Stamm, *Sound Business: Newspapers, Radio, and the Politics of New Media* (Philadelphia: University of Pennsylvania Press, 2011), 4. For example, the circulation for the *Daily News* of New York, already the largest in the nation, jumped more than 400,000 on 7 June 1944 to 2,424,161. Also see *Newsweek*, 19 June 1944, 73.

6. John McDonough, "The Longest Night: Broadcasting's First Invasion," *American Scholar* 63, no. 2 (Spring 1994): 194–95; Steven Casey, *The War Beat: The American Media at War Against Nazi Germany* (New York: Oxford University Press, 2017), 224.
7. *E&P* 77, no. 19 (6 May 1944): 13; *E&P* 77, no. 20 (13 May 1944): 65.
8. *E&P* 77, no. 23 (3 June 1944): 37.
9. Jürgen Habermas, *The Structural Transformation of the Public Sphere: An Inquiry into a Category of Bourgeois Society* (Cambridge, MA: MIT Press, 2001), 183.
10. For example, see the New York *Daily News*, 6 November 1942, and the 11 July 1943 issue (*Sunday News*).
11. Oliver Gramling, *AP: The Story of News: Editions for the Armed Services, Inc.* (New York: Farrar and Rinehart, 1940), 287–92.
12. *Negro Star* (Wichita, KS), 9 June 1944; *Arkansas State Press*, 9 June 1944; *Echo* (MS), 9 June 1944.
13. *Arkansas State Press*, 9 June 1944; *Plaindealer* (Kansas City, KS), 16 June 1944; *Detroit Tribune*, 10 June 1944.
14. Patrick S. Washburn, *A Question of Sedition: The Federal Government's Investigation of the Black Press During World War II* (New York: Oxford University Press, 1986), 54, 132, 192–93; *Echo* (Meridian, MS), 9 June 1944, 3.
15. *Pittsburgh Courier*, 10 June 1944.
16. *The American Heritage College Dictionary*, 3rd ed. (Boston: Houghton Mifflin, 1993), 714.
17. *The Cincinnati Enquirer*, Vol. CII, no. 213, 8 November 1942; *The Anniston Star*, Vol. 60, no. 276, 8 November 1942; *The San Bernardino Daily Sun*, 49th Year, 8 November 1942.
18. *Gettysburg Times*, 10 July 1943; *Herald and News* (Klamath Falls, OR), 10 July 1943; *Honolulu Advertiser*, 10 July 1943.
19. *E&P* 77, no. 21 (20 May 1944): 6.
20. "D Day Guidance for the Press" (Secret), 31 May 1944, NARA II, Records Group (RG) 331, Box 3, "Press Policy," NAI 613109, Decimal File 000.7–1, 1.
21. From this point forward, I rely on a corpus of sixty original newspapers from 6 June 1944 in my possession. These newspapers are all complete, highly legible, and display the colors (such as red) used to communicate news of D-Day. I also referred to some newspapers in the Library of Congress, the British Newspaper Archive, and Newspapers.com; *N.W. Ayer and Son's Directory of Newspapers and Periodicals 1944* (Philadelphia: N. W. Ayer and Son, 1944) lists 1,859 daily newspapers in print in 1944. The newspapers in my corpus represent all five regions of the United States: Northeast (17), Southwest (2), West (including Hawaii) (19), Southeast (5), and Midwest (17).

22. *Daily News* (New York), 6 June 1944; *State Journal* (Lansing, MI), 6 June 1944; *Los Angeles Evening Herald and Express*, 6 June 1944; *Toledo Times*, 6 June 1944.
23. *Daily Times* (Chicago), 6 June 1944; *Detroit News*, 6 June 1944; *San Francisco Examiner*, 6 June 1944.
24. *San Francisco Chronicle*, 6 June 1944.
25. *Service Men, Civilians Greet Invasion*, 6 June 1944, photograph, AP Wirephoto.
26. *Newsweek*, 19 June 1944, 73.
27. *E&P* 77, no. 24 (10 June 1944): 11.
28. *Pittsburgh Sun-Telegraph*, 6 June 1944; *Wichita Falls* (TX) *Record News*, 6 June 1944; *Erie* (PA) *Dispatch-Herald*, 6 June 1944; *Abilene* (TX) *Reporter-News*, 6 June 1944; *Pasadena* (CA) *Independent*, Invasion Extra, 6 June 1944; *Seattle Daily Times*, 6 June 1944; *Call Bulletin* (San Francisco), 6 June 1944.
29. *Seattle Star*, 6 June 1944; *Montana Standard*, 6 June 1944.
30. Bill Mauldin, *Up Front* (New York: Henry Holt, 1945), 20–22.
31. Representative sources include the *Boston Traveler*, 6 June 1944; *Cincinnati Times-Star*, 6 June 1944; *Journal—Every Evening* (Wilmington, DE), 6 June 1944; *Akron Beacon Journal*, 6 June 1944; and *Evening World-Herald* (Omaha), 6 June 1944.
32. *Chicago Daily News*, 6 June 1944; *Daily News* (Los Angeles), 6 June 1944; *Sun* (New York), 6 June 1944; *Columbus Citizen* (OH), 6 June 1944; *Fresno* (CA) *Bee*, 6 June 1944; *Elizabethton* (TN) *Daily Star*, 6 June 1944; *San Jose News*, 6 June 1944.
33. *Toledo Times*, 6 June 1944; *Wichita Falls* (TX) *Record News*, 6 June 1944.
34. *Plaindealer* (Kansas City, KS), 16 June 1944; *Pittsburgh Courier*, 10 June 1944.
35. Gramling, 287–92.
36. Peter Maslowski, *Armed with Cameras: The American Military Photographers of World War II* (New York: Free Press, 1973), 4–9.
37. George H. Roeder Jr., *The Censored War: American Visual Experience During World War Two* (New Haven: Yale University Press, 1993), 17.
38. Roeder, 62.
39. Gordon A. Harrison, *Cross-Channel Attack* (Washington, DC: Office of the Chief of Military History, Department of the Army, 1951), 254–57.
40. *CBS News on D-Day*, 29–30; *AP Inter-Office* (June–July 1944): 10–11.
41. *Montana Standard*, 6 June 1944, 10; *Daily News* (New York), 6 June 1944, 18–19; *Akron Beacon Journal*, 6 June 1944, 3.
42. Maslowski, 3–8, 68. Additionally, the Army Air Forces had combat camera units, and the Navy had combat photography units.
43. *E&P* 77, no. 24 (10 June 1944) 10; *Newsweek*, 19 June 1944, 74; *Time*, 19 June 1944, 48.

44. *Life*, 19 June 1944, 25–31.
45. Robert Capa, *Slightly Out of Focus* (New York: Modern Library, 2001), 141–52.
46. *AP Inter-Office* (June–July 1944): 39.
47. *Chicago Daily News*, 6 June 1944.
48. *E&P* 77, no. 24 (10 June 1944): 35; *Newsweek*, 19 June 1944, 74; *Time*, 19 June 1944, 48.
49. Representative sources include the *Akron Beacon Journal*, 6 June 1944; *Baltimore News-Post*, 6 June 1944; *Chicago Daily News*, 6 June 1944; *Los Angeles Evening Herald and Express*, 6 June 1944; *Seattle Star*, 6 June 1944; *New York World-Telegram*, 6 June 1944, 3; and *Cincinnati Times-Star*, 6 June 1944, 8.
50. *Binghamton* (New York) *Press*, 6 June 1944, 3; *Columbus Citizen*, 6 June 1944, 2; *New York Journal American*, 6 June 1944, 2.
51. *Binghamton* (New York) *Press*, 6 June 1944, 3; *Call Bulletin* (San Francisco), 6 June 1944, A.
52. *Binghamton* (New York) *Press*, 6 June 1944, 3.
53. *Evening World-Herald* (Omaha), 6 June 1944; *Baltimore News-Post*, 6 June 1944, B; *Los Angeles Evening Herald and Express*, 6 June 1944, A–3; *New York World-Telegram*, 6 June 1944, 2.
54. *Boston Traveler*, 6 June 1944, 23; *Cincinnati Times-Star*, 6 June 1944; *Seattle Daily-Times*, 6 June 1944, 8.
55. *Seattle Daily-Times*, 6 June 1944, 1, 8.
56. John Keegan, *The Face of Battle* (New York: Penguin Books, 1976).
57. Roeder, 1.
58. *AP Inter-Office* 2, no. 8 (June–July 1944): 39.
59. *Pontiac Daily Press* (MI), 6 June 1944; *Cincinnati Times-Star*, 6 June 1944, 3; *Baltimore News-Post*, 6 June 1944, 2; *Daily Record* (Boston), 6 June 1944 (Extra), 24; *Daily Times* (Chicago), 6 June 1944, 36.
60. *Rochester Times-Union*, 6 June 1944.
61. *Flint Journal*, 6 June 1944.
62. *E&P* 77, no. 24 (10 June 1944): 78.
63. *Chicago Daily News*, 6 June 1944.
64. *Erie* (PA) *Dispatch-Herald*, 6 June 1944, 13.

Chapter 4. "Nothing Less Than Full Victory"

1. Paul Colford, "D-Day account surfaces, ripped from the AP wire," *AP: The Definitive Source*, 5 June 2014, https://blog.ap.org/behind-the-news/d-day-account-surfaces-ripped-from-the-ap-wire.

2. *AP Inter-Office* 2, no. 8 (June–July 1944): 4; *E&P* 77, no. 24 (10 June 1944): 17.
3. Klaus Schönbach, Ester de Waal, and Edmund Lauf, "Online and Print Newspapers: Their Impact on the Extent of the Perceived Public Agenda," *European Journal of Communication* 20 (2005): 245.
4. Quoted from the AP story for the *Evening Independent* (Massillon, OH), June 1944.
5. In my corpus of sixty original 6 June 1944 newspapers, thirteen carried Wes Gallagher's byline while seven carried that of Virgil Pinkley.
6. Wes Gallagher, *Back Door to Berlin: The Full Story of the American Coup in North Africa* (Garden City, NY: Doubleday, Doran, 1943), 236–37; Steven Casey, *The War Beat: The American Media at War Against Nazi Germany* (New York: Oxford University Press, 2017), 34.
7. Virgil Pinkley, *Eisenhower Declassified* (Old Tappan, NJ: Fleming H. Revell, 1979), 185.
8. *E&P* 77, no. 20 (13 May 1944): 7.
9. *E&P* 77, no. 19 (6 May 1944): 13; *E&P* 77, no. 20 (13 May 1944): 9; *E&P* 77, no. 24 (10 June 1944): 90.
10. Amendment (dated 1 May 1944) to "Operation 'OVERLORD'—Public Relations Plan, Supreme Headquarters, Allied Expeditionary Force," dated 1 June 1944 (Top Secret), NARA II, RG 331, Box 3, "Press Policy," NAI 613109, Decimal File 000.7–1.
11. *Newsweek*, 19 June 1944, 73.
12. Casey, *The War Beat*, 225. Steven Casey puts the number at 530 while Phillip Knightley, *The First Casualty: The War Correspondent, as Hero and Myth-Maker from the Crimea to Iraq*, 3rd ed. (Baltimore: Johns Hopkins University Press, 2004), 352, put the numbers at "no fewer than 558"; Appendix A, Public Relations Plan OVERLORD, Supreme Headquarters, Allied Expeditionary Force, Public Relations Division, dated 1 May 1944, NARA II, RG 331, Box 3, "Press Policy," NAI 613109, Decimal File 000.7–1, provided a final total of 461. The number likely expanded to more than 500 by 5 June 1944.
13. *AP Inter-Office* 2, no. 5 (March 1944): 6.
14. *AP Inter-Office* 2, no. 8 (June–July 1944): 7; *E&P* 77, no. 21 (20 May 1944): 13.
15. Don Whitehead, *Beachhead Don: Reporting the War from the European Theater, 1942–1945* (New York: Fordham University Press, 2004), xvii; *E&P* 77, no. 24 (10 June 1944): 10.
16. Col. Barney Oldfield, *Never a Shot in Anger* (New York: Duell, Sloan, and Pearce, 1956), 74–75.
17. Ray Moseley, *Reporting War: How Foreign Correspondents Risked Capture, Torture and Death to Cover World War II* (New Haven: Yale University Press, 2017), 3.
18. Oldfield, 50–58.

19. Public Relations Plan OVERLORD, Supreme Headquarters, Allied Expeditionary Force, Public Relations Division, dated 1 May 1944.
20. War Department Field Manual (FM) 30–26, *Basic Field Manual: Regulations for Correspondents Accompanying U.S. Army Forces in the Field* (21 January 1942).
21. Edward Kennedy, *Ed Kennedy's War: V-E Day, Censorship, and the Associated Press* (Baton Rouge: Louisiana State University Press, 2012), x.
22. Casey, 223.
23. *E&P* 77, no. 22 (27 May 1944): 31.
24. "Public Relations Plan OVERLORD, Supreme Headquarters, Allied Expeditionary Force," dated 1 May 1944.
25. *E&P* 77, no. 24 (10 June 1944): 10; Moseley, 1.
26. *Pittsburgh-Courier*, 10 June 1944.
27. Kennedy, x.
28. Casey, 5.
29. Knightley, 361.
30. Knightley, 344.
31. Letter to "All Unit Commanders, Allied Expeditionary Force, Subject: Accredited War Correspondent," (Restricted), 11 May 1944, NARA II, RG 331, Box 3, "Press Policy," NAI 613109, Decimal File 000.7–1.
32. Dwight D. Eisenhower, *Crusade in Europe* (Garden City, NY: Doubleday, 1948), 300; Casey, 7; *Regulations for War Correspondents Accompanying Allied Expeditionary Force in the Field* (SHAEF, 1944), 3–4, NARA II, RG 331, Box 3, "Press Policy," NAI 613109, Decimal File 000.7–1.
33. SCAF No. 42, "D-Day Guidance for the Press" (Secret Priority), 31 May 1944, NARA II, RG 331, Box 3, "Press Policy," NAI 613109, Decimal File 000.7–1.
34. Syndicated newspapers received the same consideration as the wire services because they fulfilled a similar function by making news features, commentaries, entertainment articles, and comics available to smaller newspapers.
35. Oldfield, 39–40.
36. Operation Memorandum Number 24, "Press Policy," Supreme Headquarters, Allied Expeditionary Force, dated 24 April 1944 (Restricted), 2, NARA II, RG 331, Box 3, "Press Policy," NAI 613109, Decimal File 000.7–1; *E&P* 77, no. 22 (27 May 1944): 5; "Public Relations Plan 'OVERLORD,' Supreme Headquarters, Allied Expeditionary Force," dated 1 May 1944.
37. Oldfield, 60; *E&P* 77, no. 25 (17 June 1944): 20.
38. Oldfield, 60–61, 74–75.
39. Gordon A. Harrison, *Cross-Channel Attack* (Washington, DC: Office of the Chief of Military History, Department of the Army, 1951), 300–321.
40. Oldfield, 81–82.
41. Whitehead, xix.
42. Quoted in Casey, 242.

43. *Newsweek*, 19 June 1944, 74; Casey, 238.
44. Casey, 234–35. Some correspondents brought carrier pigeons to get stories back to England. Only one pigeon arrived in London after its release. See Moseley, 235.
45. Casey, 8.
46. *AP Inter-Office* 2, no. 8 (June–July 1944): 3–4; *E&P* 77, no. 24 (10 June 1944): 17, 19.
47. *AP Inter-Office* 2, no. 8 (June–July 1944): 3–4; *E&P* 77, no. 24 (10 June 1944), included an advertisement proclaiming INS as the first to flash Communiqué Number 1. Such claims, regardless of their veracity, demonstrate how fiercely the wire services competed with each other.
48. *Elizabethton* (TN) *Daily Star*, 6 June 1944; *Evening Independent* (Massillon, OH), 6 June 1944.
49. The four newspapers I am using for Wes Gallagher's (AP) main story and byline are the *Elizabethton* (TN) *Daily Star*, 6 June 1944; *Evening Independent* (Massillon, OH), 6 June 1944; *Knoxville News-Sentinel*, 6 June 1944; and *Sheboygan Press*, 6 June 1944. For Virgil Pinkley's (UP) main story, I am using *Boston Traveler*, 6 June 1944; *Columbus Citizen*, 6 June 1944; *San Jose News*, 6 June 1944; and *New York World-Telegram*, 6 June 1944.
50. *Evening Independent* (Massillon, OH), 6 June 1944; *Knoxville News-Sentinel*, 6 June 1944.
51. *Elizabethton* (TN) *Daily Star*, 6 June 1944.
52. John Morton Blum, *V Was for Victory: Politics and American Culture During World War II* (New York: Harcourt, Brace Jovanovich, 1976), 12–13.
53. *San Jose News*, 6 June 1944.
54. *CBS News on D-Day* (New York: Columbia Broadcasting System, 1945), 31.
55. *Elizabethton* (TN) *Daily Star*, 6 June 1944.
56. *Boston Traveler*, 6 June 1944.
57. *Knoxville News-Sentinel*, 6 June 1944, 8; *New York World-Telegram*, 6 June 1944, 13; *Sheboygan Press*, 6 June 1944, 19; *Columbus Citizen*, 6 June 1944, 9.
58. *Sheboygan Press*, 6 June 1944; Colford, "D-Day Account."
59. *Boston Traveler*, 6 June 1944; *Columbus Citizen*, 6 June 1944; and *New York World-Telegram*, 6 June 1944.
60. *Boston Traveler*, 6 June 1944, 18.
61. *New York World-Telegram*, 6 June 1944, 13.
62. *New York World-Telegram*, 6 June 1944, 13.
63. *Elizabethton Daily Star* (TN), 6 June 1944.
64. *Sheboygan Press*, 6 June 1944; *New York World-Telegram*, 6 June 1944.
65. *Elizabethton* (TN) *Daily Star*, 6 June 1944.
66. *Boston Traveler*, 6 June 1944; Harrison, Map XXV.

67. *Sheboygan Press,* 6 June 1944; *Boston Traveler,* 6 June 1944, 18; *Columbus Citizen,* 6 June 1944; *San Jose News,* 6 June 1944, 3; *New York World-Telegram,* 6 June 1944, 3.
68. *Sheboygan Press,* 6 June 1944.
69. *Elizabethton* (TN) *Daily Star,* 6 June 1944.
70. *Columbus Citizen,* 6 June 1944.
71. *Elizabethton* (TN) *Daily Star,* 6 June 1944; *Sheboygan Press,* 6 June 1944; *Columbus Citizen,* 6 June 1944.
72. *Boston Traveler,* 6 June 1944.
73. *Evening Independent* (Massillon, OH), 6 June 1944, 2; *Knoxville News-Sentinel,* 6 June 1944, 8.
74. *Knoxville News-Sentinel,* 6 June 1944, 8.
75. *Columbus Citizen,* 6 June 1944, 9.
76. *Boston Traveler,* 6 June 1944, 18; *Columbus Citizen,* 6 June 1944, 9.
77. *Sheboygan Press,* 6 June 1944.
78. *Boston Traveler,* 6 June 1944, 18; *New York World-Telegram,* 6 June 1944, 13.
79. *Columbus Citizen,* 6 June 1944, 9.
80. *Elizabethton* (TN) *Daily Star,* 6 June 1944, 1, 4.
81. *Evening Independent* (Massillon, OH), 6 June 1944, 2.
82. *Columbus Citizen,* 6 June 1944, 9; *New York World-Telegram,* 6 June 1944, 13.
83. *Evening Independent* (Massillon, OH), 6 June 1944; *Knoxville News-Sentinel,* 6 June 1944, 8; *Sheboygan Press,* 6 June 1944, 19.
84. *Boston Traveler,* 6 June 1944, 18.
85. *Elizabethton* (TN) *Daily Star,* 6 June 1944.
86. *Boston Traveler,* 6 June 1944, 18.
87. *Evening Independent* (Massillon, OH), 6 June 1944.
88. *Boston Traveler,* 6 June 1944, 18.
89. See Britain's *Evening Despatch,* 6 June 1944.
90. *Sheboygan Press,* 6 June 1944, 19.
91. *Elizabethton* (TN) *Daily Star,* 6 June 1944.
92. *Columbus Citizen,* 6 June 1944, 9.
93. *San Jose News,* 6 June 1944, 3; *Boston Traveler,* 6 June 1944, 18.
94. *Sheboygan Press,* 6 June 1944, 18.
95. *Boston Traveler,* 6 June 1944, 18; *Columbus Citizen,* 6 June 1944.
96. *Pocatello Tribune* (ID), 6 June 1944; *Newsweek,* 19 June 1944, 73; *E&P* 77, no. 24 (10 June 1944): 17.
97. *Evening Independent* (Massillon, OH), 6 June 1944.
98. *Pittsburgh-Courier,* 10 June 1944.
99. *Pittsburgh-Courier,* 10 June 1944.

100. Knightley, 352.
101. *Democrat and Chronicle* (Rochester, NY), 8 November 1942; *Indianapolis Star*, 10 July 1943.
102. David Paul Nord, *Communities of Journalism: A History of American Newspapers and Their Readers* (Urbana: University of Illinois Press, 2001), 246.
103. Benedict Anderson, *Imagined Communities* (London: Verso, 2006), 35–36.
104. E. B. White, "Sugar-Coating the War News: February 1942," in *Reporting World War II: Part One: American Journalism, 1938–1944* (New York: Library of America, 1995), 301–2.
105. Nord, 254.
106. Knightley, 352.
107. Casey, 230.
108. *Coventry Evening Telegraph*, 6 June 1944; *Manchester Evening News* (Manchester, England), 6 June 1944; *Essex Newsman-Herald* (Chelmsford, England); *Vancouver* (Canada) *Sun*, 6 June 1944; *Leader-Post* (Regina, Saskatchewan), 6 June 1944.
109. Siân Nicholas, "The British press and D-Day: reporting the launch of the Second Front, 6 June 1944," *Media History* 23, nos. 3–4: 496, 500.
110. *E&P* 77, no. 24 (10 June 1944): 17.

Chapter 5. The "Great Crusade":

1. Gen. Dwight D. Eisenhower, "Order of the Day" (original copy in the author's collection).
2. *CBS News on D-Day* (New York: Columbia Broadcasting System, 1945), 19.
3. *CBS News on D-Day*, 17; NARA II, Records Group (RG) 331, Entry NM8 56, Box 3, Press Policy (000.7–1).
4. *Rocky Mountain News*, 4 June 1944, 1, 8; *CBS News on D-Day*, 8; John McDonough, "The Longest Night: Broadcasting's First Invasion," *American Scholar* 63, no. 2 (Spring 1994): 198.
5. *CBS News on D-Day*, 8.
6. Columbia Broadcasting System, *From D-Day Through Victory in Europe: The Eye-Witness Story as Told by War Correspondents on the Air* (New York: CBS, 1945), 12. Wire services such as the AP and INS monitored the German transmissions and forwarded them to their service subscribers.
7. Mary Louise Roberts, *What Soldiers Do: Sex and the American GI in World War II France* (Chicago: University of Chicago Press, 2013), 15.
8. Benedict Anderson, *Imagined Communities* (London: Verso, 2006), 35–36; David Paul Nord, *A History of American Newspapers and Their Readers* (Urbana: University of Illinois Press, 2001), 3.
9. Eisenhower, Order of the Day.

10. Sarah Purcell, *Sealed with Blood: War, Sacrifice, and Memory in Revolutionary America* (Philadelphia: University of Pennsylvania Press, 2002), 11–12.
11. A transcript of Lincoln's Gettysburg Address appears at https://www.ourdocuments.gov/doc.php?flash=true&doc=36&page=transcript.
12. *CBS News on D-Day,* 1.
13. FDR quoted in Susan A. Brewer, *Why America Fights: Patriotism and War Propaganda from the Philippines to Iraq* (Oxford: Oxford University Press, 2009), 87; Eisenhower, Order of the Day.
14. SHAEF Outgoing Message, SCAF 37, dated 7 May 1944, outlines SHAEF's plans for releasing the first communiqué to U.S., British, and Canadian news organizations, NARA II, RG 331, Entry NM8 56, Box 5, Special Announcements and Bulletins (000.77–1); Allan M. Winkler, *The Politics of Propaganda: The Office of War Information, 1942–1945* (New Haven: Yale University Press, 1978), 31, 125–26; *Daily Times (*Chicago), 6 June 1944, 16.
15. Michael Schudson, *The Sociology of News,* 2nd ed. (New York: W. W. Norton, 2011), 24.
16. George H. Roeder Jr., *The Censored War: American Visual Experience During World War Two* (New Haven: Yale University Press, 1993), 3.
17. Brewer, 283.
18. Message Draft, Ray W. Barker Papers, 1942–46, Box 1, Papers Pertaining to COSSAC and SHAEF, 1942–1945 (1), National Archives Identification Number 12010107, Dwight David Eisenhower Presidential Library and Boyhood Home.
19. NBC radio correspondent John MacVane read both Eisenhower's and Montgomery's messages to the troops over the ship's loudspeaker. See John MacVane, *On the Air in World War II* (New York: William Morrow, 1979), 226.
20. Message to Members of the United States Army Expeditionary Forces signed by President Franklin D. Roosevelt (n.p.: 1944); 21 Army Group, Personal Message From The C-in-C, To be read out to all Troops, signed by General B. L. Montgomery (n.p.: 1944). Both documents are originals in author's collection.
21. Message from the supreme commander to be read to troops upon embarkation, classified Secret (n.p.: 1944). Original in author's collection.
22. Michael Korda, *Ike: An American Hero* (New York: Harper Perennial, 2007), 58; Carlo D'Este, *Eisenhower: A Soldier's Life* (New York: Henry Holt, 2002), 9–10.
23. John Morton Blum, *V Was for Victory: Politics and American Culture During World War II* (New York: Harcourt Brace Jovanovich, 1976), 16.

24. George Creel, *How We Advertised America: The First Telling of the Amazing Story of the Committee on Public Information That Carried the Gospel of Americanism to Every Corner of the Globe* (New York: Harper and Brothers, 1920), xiii.
25. Quoted in Winkler, 3.
26. Brewer, 46; Creel, 8. The film *Pershing's Crusaders* (1918) appears at https://www.youtube.com/watch?v=B_Usu_AfAzw.
27. Winkler, 3; Garth S. Jowett and Victoria O'Donnell, *Propaganda and Persuasion*, 6th ed. (Los Angeles: Sage, 2015), 180–82.
28. David R. Woodward, *The American Army and the First World War* (Cambridge: Cambridge University Press, 2014), 389.
29. Winkler, 13.
30. Winkler, 33.
31. Blum, 304.
32. CBS Sound File CBD 440606, https://archive.org/details/CBD440606CBSDDayCBS; Public Relations Plan 'Overlord,' dated 1 May 1944, NARA II, RG 331, Entry NM8 56, Box 3, Press Policy (000.7–1), 1, 4. Unlike Eisenhower's Order of the Day, FDR's and Montgomery's messages received little to no attention.
33. Hadley Cantril, *Public Opinion 1935–1946* (Princeton, NJ: Princeton University Press, 1946), viii, 523–24.
34. See the *Akron Beacon Journal*, 6 June 1944; *Cleveland Plain Dealer*, 6 June 1944; and the *San Francisco Examiner*, 6 June 1944.
35. *Toledo Times*, 6 June 1944.
36. United Press newswire feed for 6 June 1944 (*Sunbury* [PA] *Daily Item*). Original in author's collection.
37. *Johnson City* (TN) *Press-Chronicle*, 6 June 1944.
38. *Knoxville News-Sentinel*, 6 June 1944 (Extra).
39. *Miami Herald*, 6 June 1944 (Extra).
40. Representative sources are *Evening Independent* (Massillon, OH), 6 June 1944 (Invasion Extra); *Knoxville News-Sentinel*, 6 June 1944 (Extra); *Montana Standard*, 6 June 1944; and the *Winston-Salem Journal*, 6 June 1944 (Extra).
41. *Baltimore News-Post*, 6 June 1944; *Los Angeles Evening Herald and Express*, 6 June 1944 (3rd Invasion Extra / Night Edition); *Sheboygan Press*, 6 June 1944.
42. The *Detroit Times*, 6 June 1944 (Extra); *Honolulu Advertiser*, 6 June 1944.
43. *Evening World-Herald* (Omaha), 6 June 1944.
44. *New York Times*, 6 June 1944 (6 a.m. Extra).
45. *Erie* (PA) *Dispatch-Herald*, 6 June 1944, 2, 5; *Journal—Every Evening* (Wilmington, DE), 6 June 1944 (Final Edition), 8; *Akron Beacon Journal*, 6 June 1944, 6.

46. Emphasis added. *Journal—Every Evening* (Wilmington, DE), 6 June 1944 (Final Edition), 8.
47. *Toledo Times*, 6 June 1944 (Extra), 7.
48. *Boston Traveler*, 6 June 1944, 19.
49. *Daily News* (New York), 6 June 1944 (Final), 14.
50. *Journal—Every Evening* (Wilmington, DE), 6 June 1944 (Final Edition), 8.
51. Sources for the invasion of North Africa (Operation Torch) include the *Clarion Ledger* (Jackson, MS), 8 November 1942; *Las Cruces Sun-News*, 8 November 1942; *Philadelphia Inquirer*, 8 November 1942; *Chicago Sunday Tribune*, 8 November 1942; *Detroit Free Press*, 8 November 1942; *Hartford Courant*, 8 November 1942; *Democrat Chronicle* (Rochester, NY), 8 November 1942; and the *Los Angeles Times*, 8 November 1942. For the invasion of Sicily (Operation Husky), sources include the *New Castle* (PA) *News*, 10 July 1943; *Indianapolis Star*, 10 July 1943; *Akron Beacon Journal*, 10 July 1943; *St. Louis Star-Times*, 10 July 1943; *Chicago Daily Tribune*, 10 July 1943; *Los Angeles Times*, 10 July 1943; *Dunkirk Evening Observer*, 10 July 1943; and the *St. Louis Post-Dispatch*, 10 July 1943.
52. Cantril, 744; The United States Summary of the 1940 Census lists the U.S. population, with all territories and the armed forces, as totaling 150,621,231. If Cantril's survey sampling of 96 percent obtained, then nearly 150 million Americans believed in God (or *a* god) in 1944. The U.S. Census stopped asking about religious affiliation in 1936. The 1940 Census summary is available online at https://www2.census.gov/prod2/decennial/documents/33973538v1ch02.pdf.
53. Francis J. Spellman, *The Road to Victory* (New York: Charles Scribner's Sons, 1942), x–xi.
54. Harry Emerson Fosdick, *A Great Time to Be Alive: Sermons on Christianity in Wartime* (New York and London: Harper and Brothers, 1944), 9.
55. Victor Fleming, director, *A Guy Named Joe* (Metro-Goldwyn Mayer Pictures, 1944), DVD; John Cromwell, director, *Since You Went Away* (David O. Selznick Productions, 1943) DVD.
56. *Chicago Tribune*, 10 November 1957.
57. *Chicago Tribune*, 10 November 1957.
58. Roeder, 43.
59. *St. Joseph* (MO) *News-Press*, 6 June 1944, 7.
60. *Sun* (New York), 6 June 1944 (Night Edition), 11.
61. *Sheboygan Press*, 6 June 1944.
62. *Pasadena Independent*, Invasion Extra, 6 June 1944, 2.
63. *Baltimore News-Post*, 6 June 1944; *Boston Traveler*, 6 June 1944.
64. *Binghamton* (NY) *Press*, 6 June 1944 (4th Invasion Extra), 10.
65. *BBA*, 12 June 1944, 18; *Rocky Mountain News* (Denver), 4 June 1944, 1, 8.

66. *Cincinnati Times-Star,* 6 June 1944 (Final Sports Edition); *Daily News* (Los Angeles), 6 June 1944, 2; *Sheboygan Press,* 6 June 1944, 15.
67. *Baltimore News-Post,* 6 June 1944, B.
68. *Binghamton* (NY) *Press,* 6 June 1944 (4th Invasion Extra), 1; *Rochester Times-Union,* 6 June 1944, 4.
69. *Elizabethton* (TN) *Daily Star,* 6 June 1944, 1; *Journal—Every Evening* (Wilmington, DE), 6 June 1944 (Final Edition), 6.
70. *Journal—Every Evening* (Wilmington, DE), 6 June 1944 (Final Edition).
71. *Baltimore News-Post,* 6 June 1944.
72. *Boston Traveler,* 6 June 1944, 2, 19; *Fresno Bee,* 6 June 1944 (Extra), 7A.
73. *Daily News* (New York), 6 June 1944 (Final), 14; *Rochester Times-Union,* 6 June 1944, 2.
74. *Johnson City* (TN) *Press-Chronicle,* 6 June 1944 (2nd Extra); *Journal—Every Evening* (Wilmington, DE), 6 June 1944 (Final Edition), 6; *New York Journal American,* 6 June 1944 (D-Day Extra), 12.
75. *Columbus Citizen,* 6 June 1944, 4; also see the *Pasadena Independent,* Invasion Extra, 6 June 1944, 2; *Sheboygan Press,* 6 June 1944, 8; and *Baltimore News-Post,* 6 June 1944, 1, B.
76. *Detroit Times,* 6 June 1944 (Extra), C–3; *New York Journal American,* 6 June 1944 (D-Day Extra), 15.
77. *New York Herald Tribune,* 6 June 1944, 18.
78. Representative sources are the *Chicago Daily News,* 6 June 1944, 5; *Columbus Citizen,* 6 June 1944, 4; *Daily News* (Los Angeles), 6 June 1944, 2; and *New York Journal American,* 6 June 1944 (D-Day Extra), 12.
79. *Binghamton Press* (NY), 6 June 1944 (4th Invasion Extra), 10.
80. *Boston Traveler,* 6 June 1944, 2.
81. *Cincinnati Times-Star,* 6 June 1944 (Final Sports Edition).
82. *Johnson City* (TN) Press-*Chronicle,* 6 June 1944 (2nd Extra).
83. *Miami Herald,* 6 June 1944 (Extra), 4.
84. *Rochester Times-Union,* 6 June 1944, 1–A.
85. *St. Joseph* (MO) *News-Press,* 6 June 1944, 3.
86. See the *Journal—Every Evening* (Wilmington, DE), 6 June 1944 (Final Edition), front page, 7; and *Seattle Star,* 6 June 1944, 6.
87. *Boston Traveler,* 6 June 1944.
88. *Evening World-Herald* (Omaha), 6 June 1944, 7.
89. *Sheboygan Press,* 6 June 1944, 15.
90. *Daily News* (Los Angeles), 6 June 1944, 2.
91. *Binghamton* (NY) *Press,* 6 June 1944 (4th Invasion Extra), 10.
92. *Cincinnati Times-Star,* 6 June 1944 (Final Sports Edition), 3.
93. *Los Angeles Evening Herald and Express,* 6 June 1944 (5th Invasion Extra), A–4.

94. *Rochester Times-Union*, 6 June 1944, 4.
95. *Sun* (New York), 6 June 1944 (Night Edition), 11.
96. *Journal—Every Evening* (Wilmington, DE), 6 June 1944 (Final Edition).
97. *Boston Traveler*, 6 June 1944, 2; *Cincinnati Times-Star*, 6 June 1944 (Final Sports Edition), 3.
98. *Baltimore News-Post*, 6 June 1944.
99. *Journal—Every Evening* (Wilmington, DE), 6 June 1944 (Final Edition), 6.
100. *Sun* (New York), 6 June 1944 (Night Edition), 11.
101. *Binghamton* (NY) *Press*, 6 June 1944 (4th Invasion Extra), 10.
102. *Boston Traveler*, 6 June 1944, 2; *New York Journal American*, 6 June 1944 (D-Day Extra), 2, 19.
103. *Daily News* (Los Angeles), 6 June 1944, 2.
104. *San Jose News*, 6 June 1944, 9.
105. *Seattle Star*, 6 June 1944, 6.
106. *Erie* (PA*) Dispatch-Herald*, 6 June 1944.
107. *Baltimore News-Post*, 6 June 1944, 3.
108. *Binghamton* (NY) *Press*, 6 June 1944 (4th Invasion Extra), 10.
109. *Boston Traveler*, 6 June 1944, 2, 14, 16, 18, 19.
110. *New York Journal American*, 6 June 1944 (D-Day Extra).
111. *Sheboygan Press*, 6 June 1944, 8, 15.
112. *Sun* (New York), 6 June 1944 (Night Edition), 11.
113. *Boston Traveler*, 6 June 1944, 2.
114. *Cincinnati Times-Star*, 6 June 1944 (Final Sports Edition), 3.
115. *New York Journal American*, 6 June 1944 (D-Day Extra), 12.
116. *Daily Times* (Chicago), 6 June 1944, 6.
117. *Boston Traveler*, 6 June 1944 (Blue Steak Edition), 3, 16.
118. *Elizabethton* (TN) *Daily Star*, 6 June 1944, 4. The same advertisement also appeared in the *Johnson City* (TN) *Press-Chronicle*, 6 June 1944 (2nd Extra), 8.
119. *Johnson City* (TN) *Press-Chronicle*, 6 June 1944 (2nd Extra), 7.
120. *Boston Traveler*, 6 June 1944 (Blue Steak Edition), 17.
121. *Sun* (New York), 6 June 1944 (Night Edition), 9.
122. *Seattle Star*, 6 June 1944, 10.
123. *Akron Beacon Journal*, 6 June 1944, 9; *Miami Herald*, 6 June 1944 (Extra), 8–B; *St. Joseph* (MO) *News-Press*, 6 June 1944, 11.
124. *BBA* 26, no. 24 (12 June 1944): 59; Michele Hilmes, "NBC and the Network Idea: Defining the 'American System,'" *NBC: America's Network*, ed. Michele Hilmes (Berkeley: University of California Press, 2007), 20–21.

125. *BBA* 26, no. 24 (12 June 1944): 59; NBC Sound File CBD 440606, https://archive.org/details/NBCCompleteBroadcastDDay, accessed on 14 March 2017; *Boston Traveler*, 6 June 1944, 13.
126. *New York Journal American*, 6 June 1944 (D-Day Extra), 12.
127. *Cincinnati Times-Star*, 6 June 1944 (Final Sports Edition).
128. *Sheboygan Press*, 6 June 1944, 8.
129. *BBA* 26, no. 24 (12 June 1944): 59.
130. *H Hour-1944* (National Broadcasting Company, 1944), 26.
131. CBS Sound Files, File 440606, Part 010; *CBS News on D-Day*, 43–44.
132. James P. Moore Jr., "American Prayers, on D-Day and Today," *Washington Post*, 6 June 2004, B03, http://www.washingtonpost.com/wp-dyn/articles/A17410-2004Jun5.html.
133. NBC Sound File CBD 440606, https://archive.org/details/NBCCompleteBroadcastDDay; Edna St. Vincent Millay, "Poem and Prayer for an Invading Army," National Broadcasting Company, 1944.
134. *Rocky Mountain News* (Denver), 4 June 1944, 8.
135. *Baltimore News-Post*, 6 June 1944, B.
136. *Cincinnati Times-Star*, 6 June 1944 (Final Sports Edition); *Johnson City* (TN) *Press-Chronicle*, 6 June 1944 (2nd Extra); *Miami Herald*, 6 June 1944 (Extra), 4.
137. *New York Journal American*, 6 June 1944 (D-Day Extra), 12.
138. James Rowland Angell, "Radio and National Morale," *American Journal of Sociology* 47, no. 3 (November 1941): 352.
139. *Boston Traveler*, 6 June 1944.
140. *Los Angeles Evening Herald and Express*, 6 June 1944 (5th Invasion Extra), A–6.
141. *San Jose News*, 6 June 1944, 5.
142. Mary L. Dudziak, *War Time: An Idea, Its History, Its Consequences* (Oxford: Oxford University Press, 2012), 11–15; Anderson, 35–36.
143. *Cincinnati Times-Star*, 4; *Columbus Citizen*, 6 June 1944, 1, 2; *Elizabethton* (TN) *Daily Star*, 6 June 1944; *Erie* (PA) *Dispatch-Herald*, 6 June 1944; *Fresno Bee*, 6 June 1944 (Extra).
144. *CBS News on D-Day*, 43; *H Hour-1944*, 20.
145. *Boston Traveler*, 6 June 1944, 16; Michael Dolski, *D-Day Remembered: The Normandy Landings in the American Collective Memory* (Knoxville: University of Tennessee Press, 2016), 17. Dolski states that both chambers of Congress read the prayer into the official record.
146. For example, *Baltimore News-Post*, 6 June 1944, 2; *New York Journal American*, 6 June 1944 (D-Day Extra), 7.
147. *Seattle Star*, 6 June 1944.
148. Moore, B03; Dolski, 18.

149. *Boston Traveler*, 6 June 1944, 16.
150. *BBA* 26, no. 24 (Washington, DC, 12 June 1944): 38.
151. FDR Presidential Library and Museum, Papers as President, President's Personal File, 1933–1943, National Archives Identifier 197375, Collection Identifier FDR-PPF; transcription posted on the FDR Presidential Library and Museum website, https://fdrlibrary.org/d-day; NBC Sound File CBD 440606, https://archive.org/details/NBCCompleteBroadcastDDay.
152. Moore, B03.

Chapter 6. Only the Very Best

1. *CBS News on D-Day* (New York: CBS, 1945), 80; CBS Sound Files, File 440606, Part 021.
2. *Binghamton* (NY) *Press*, 6 June 1944; David Eisenhower, *Eisenhower at War, 1943–1945* (New York: Vintage Books, 1986), 251–53.
3. Eisenhower, "Order of the Day."
4. *Seattle Daily Times*, 6 June 1944, 8; David Eisenhower, 251–53.
5. Patrick S. Washburn, *A Question of Sedition: The Federal Government's Investigation of the Black Press During World War II* (New York: Oxford University Press, 1986), 5.
6. *Detroit Free Press*, 8 November 1942; *Hartford Courant*, 8 November 1942; *Los Angeles Times*, 8 November 1942.
7. *Chicago Daily Tribune*, 10 July 1943; *Dunkirk* (NY) *Evening Observer*, 10 July 1943.
8. *Chicago Daily Tribune*, 10 July 1943; *St. Louis Post-Dispatch*, 10 July 1943.
9. *Chicago Sunday Tribune*, 8 November 1942.
10. Omar N. Bradley and Clay Blair, *A General's Life* (New York: Simon and Schuster, 1983), 250–52.
11. *Miami Herald*, 6 June 1944, 3; *Detroit News*, 6 June 1944; *Sheboygan Press*, 6 June 1944; *Daily News* (Los Angeles), 54, 6 June 1944; *Knoxville News-Sentinel*, 6 June 1944, 6.
12. *Rochester Times-Union*, 6 June 1944, 4.
13. *Burlington Free Press*, 6 June 1944, 2.
14. Representative sources include the *Intelligencer Journal* (Lancaster, PA), 6 June 1944, 2; *State Journal* (Lansing, MI), 6 June 1944; *Johnson City* (TN) *Press-Chronicle*, 6 June 1944, 17; and *Pittsburgh Sun-Telegraph*, 6 June 1944, B.
15. *Intelligencer Journal* (Lancaster, PA), 6 June 1944, 2.
16. *State Journal* (Lansing, MI), 6 June 1944.
17. *Intelligencer Journal* (Lancaster, PA), 6 June 1944, 2.
18. *Johnson City* (TN) *Press-Chronicle*, 6 June 1944, 17.

19. *Intelligencer Journal* (Lancaster, PA), 6 June 1944, 2.
20. *Chicago Daily News*, 6 June 1944, 3: *Evening World-Herald* (Omaha), 6 June 1944, 4.
21. *Intelligencer Journal* (Lancaster, PA), 6 June 1944, 2.
22. *Daily Times* (Chicago), 6 June 1944, 8.
23. *New York Journal American*, 6 June 1944, 14; *New York World-Telegram*, 6 June 1944, 3.
24. *CBS News on D-Day*, 33–34; CBS Sound Files, File 440606, Part 006.
25. *Daily Times* (Chicago), 6 June 1944, 8.
26. *Intelligencer Journal* (Lancaster, PA), 6 June 1944, 2.
27. *New York Herald Tribune*, 6 June 1944, 8.
28. *Daily Times* (Chicago), 6 June 1944, 8.
29. *Democrat and Chronicle* (Rochester, NY), 8 November 1942.
30. *CBS News on D-Day*, 20; *H Hour-1944* (National Broadcasting Company, 1944), 5; NBC Sound Files, CBD-440606, NBC0330 (News); CBS Sound Files, File 440606, Part 002.
31. *CBS News on D-Day*, 20; *H Hour-1944*, 5; NBC Sound Files, CBD-440606, NBC0330 (News); CBS Sound Files, File 440606, Part 002.
32. *St. Joseph* (MO) *News-Press*, 6 June 1944, 2.
33. Susan A. Brewer, *Why America Fights: Patriotism and War Propaganda from the Philippines to Iraq* (Oxford: Oxford University Press, 2009), 126.
34. *Daily Times* (Chicago), 6 June 1944, 5.
35. Representative sources are the *Daily Times* (Chicago), 6 June 1944, 5; *Detroit News*, 6 June 1944, 2; *Evening World-Herald* (Omaha), 6 June 1944, 8; *Flint Journal*, 6 June 1944, 3; *Honolulu Advertiser*, 6 June 1944; *Intelligencer Journal* (Lancaster, PA), 6 June 1944, 4; *Johnson City* (TN) *Press-Chronicle*, 6 June 1944, 7; and *Miami Herald*, 6 June 1944, 2.
36. *Detroit Tribune*, 10 June 1944; Washburn, 58.
37. *Evening World-Herald* (Omaha), 6 June 1944, 8; *Seattle Star*, 6 June 1944, 16; and *State Journal* (Lansing, MI), 6 June 1944.
38. I used the descriptions found in the *Evening World-Herald (Omaha)*, 6 June 1944, 8, as a single, but representative, source.
39. *Intelligencer Journal* (Lancaster, PA), 6 June 1944, 2.
40. Representative sources include the *Akron Beacon Journal*, 6 June 1944, 3; *Columbus Citizen*, 6 June 1944, 9: *Evening World-Herald* (Omaha), 6 June 1944, 7; *Fresno* (CA) *Bee* 6 June 1944, 6A; and the *Rochester Times-Union*, 6 June 1944, 4.
41. *CBS News on D-Day*, 71–72; CBS Sound Files, File 440606, Part 020.

42. *Columbus Citizen*, 6 June 1944, 3; *Burlington Free Press*, 6 June 1944, 2.
43. *Evening Independent* (Massillon, OH), 6 June 1944, 2; *Pittsburgh Sun-Telegraph*, 6 June 1944, 4; *Wichita Falls Record News*, 6 June 1944, 12.
44. *Columbus Citizen*, 6 June 1944, 7; *Burlington Free Press*, 6 June 1944, 4.
45. Representative sources include: the *Akron Beacon Journal*, 6 June 1944, 4; *Evening Independent* (Massillon, OH), 6 June 1944, 2; *Intelligencer Journal* (Lancaster, PA), 6 June 1944, 4; *Pittsburgh Sun-Telegraph*, 6 June 1944, p. B; and the *Wichita Falls Record News*, 6 June 1944, 12.
46. *H Hour-1944*, 10; *BBA* 26, no. 24 (12 June 1944): 58; NBC Sound Files, CBD-440606, NBC1000 (Nancy Osgood).
47. *Cincinnati Times-Star*, 6 June 1944, 8; *Seattle Daily Times*, 6 June 1944, p. 3.
48. *Evening World-Herald* (Omaha), 6 June 1944, 4; *Chicago Daily News*, 6 June 1944, 3; *Seattle Daily Times*, 6 June 1944, 3.
49. *Chicago Daily News*, 6 June 1944, 3; *Rochester Times-Union*, 6 June 1944, p. 2; *New York World-Telegram*, 6 June 1944, 15.
50. John Morton Blum, *V Was for Victory: Politics and American Culture During World War II* (New York: Harcourt Brace Jovanovich, 1976), 304, 12–13.
51. *Pittsburgh Sun-Telegraph*, 6 June 1944, B; *Sheboygan Press*, 6 June 1944, p. 7; *Journal-Every Evening* (Wilmington, DE), 6 June 1944, 3.
52. See George Creel, *How We Advertised America: The First Telling of the Amazing Story of the Committee on Public Information That Carried the Gospel of Americanism to Every Corner of the Globe* (New York: Harper and Brothers, 1920).
53. *Johnson City* (TN) *Press-Chronicle*, 6 June 1944, 13; *Knoxville News-Sentinel*, 6 June 1944, 2.
54. *CBS News on D-Day*, 72; CBS Sound Files, File 440606, Part 020.
55. *Toledo Times*, 6 June 1944, 3.
56. *CBS News on D-Day*, 64; CBS Sound Files, File 440606, Part 018.
57. Ernie Pyle, *Here Is Your War* (New York: Henry Holt, 1943), 176–78.
58. *Chicago Daily News*, 6 June 1944, 3; *Daily Times* (Chicago), 6 June 1944, p. 4; *Rochester Times-Union*, 4.
59. *Akron Beacon Journal*, 6 June 1944, 5; *Montana Standard* (Butte), 6 June 1944, 11; *Sheboygan Press*, 6 June 1944, 15.
60. *San Francisco Chronicle*, 6 June 1944, D.
61. *Chicago Daily News*, 6 June 1944, 3.
62. *Daily News* (New York), 6 June 1944, 18–19.
63. *Johnson City* (TN) *Press-Chronicle*, 6 June 1944.
64. *New York World-Telegram*, 6 June 1944.
65. *New York World-Telegram*, 6 June 1944, 13.

66. *Evening World-Herald* (Omaha), 6 June 1944.
67. *St. Joseph News-Press*, 6 June 1944, 3; *Johnson City* (TN) *Press-Chronicle*, 6 June 1944, 16.
68. *Honolulu Advertiser*, 6 June 1944.
69. *Rochester Times-Union*, 6 June 1944, 2; *Sheboygan Press*, 6 June 1944, 3; *Binghamton (NY) Press*, 6 June 1944, 4; *Evening World-Herald* (Omaha), 6 June 1944, 8.
70. *Chicago Daily News*, 6 June 1944, 3; *Akron Beacon Journal*, 6 June 1944, p. 2; *Johnson City* (TN) *Press-Chronicle*, 6 June 1944; *Sheboygan Press*, 6 June 1944, 4; *St. Joseph News-Press*, 6 June 1944, 6.
71. *Knoxville News-Sentinel*, 6 June 1944, 1, 2.
72. *CBS News on D-Day*, 23–24; *H Hour-1944*, 5; NBC Sound Files, CBD-440606, NBC0415 (News); CBS Sound Files, File 440606, Part 002.
73. *Daily Times* (Chicago), 6 June 1944, 8.
74. *CBS News on D-Day*, 63–65; CBS Sound Files, File 440606, Part 018.
75. *Daily Times* (Chicago), 6 June 1944, 4.
76. *Chicago Daily News*, 6 June 1944, 4; *Binghamton* (NY) *Press*, 6 June 1944, p. 7.
77. *CBS News on D-Day*, 35–37; CBS Sound Files, File 440606, Part 007.
78. Blum, 12–13.
79. *Evening World-Herald* (Omaha), 6 June 1944; *Seattle Daily Times*, 6 June 1944, 5.
80. *Flint Journal*, 6 June 1944, 4.
81. *Waterville* (Maine) *Morning Sentinel*, 6 June 1944, 6.
82. *Abilene Reporter-News*, 6 June 1944, 15; *Flint Journal*, 6 June 1944, 4; *Intelligencer Journal* (Lancaster, PA), 6 June 1944, 3.
83. See Linda Hervieux, *Forgotten: The Untold Story of D-Day's Black Heroes, At Home and At War* (New York: Harper, 2015), for a detailed account of the 320th Barrage Balloon Battalion's actions on D-Day.
84. Lee Finkle, *Forum for Protest: The Black Press During World War II* (Rutherford, NJ: Fairleigh Dickinson University Press, 1975), 34; Washburn, 53–54.
85. Washburn, 103–4.
86. Finkle, 109–110.
87. Washburn, 54; Finkle, 109–110.
88. Washburn, 132.
89. Finkle, 183.
90. *Pittsburgh Courier*, 10 June 1944.
91. *St. Joseph News-Press*, 6 June 1944, 9, 14.
92. *Rochester Times-Union*, 6 June 1944, 2A.
93. *Winston-Salem Journal*, 6 June 1944, 5.

94. *Cincinnati Times-Star,* 6 June 1944, 4.
95. *Code of Wartime Practices for American Broadcasters,* February 1, 1943 ed. (Washington, DC: United States Government Office of Censorship), 6.
96. *Flint Journal,* 6 June 1944, 2.
97. *Akron Beacon Journal,* 6 June 1944, 5.
98. *Akron Beacon Journal,* 6 June 1944, 5.
99. *Fresno* (CA) *Bee,* 6 June 1944, 7A.
100. *H Hour-1944,* 6; NBC Sound Files, CBD-440606, NBC0415 (News); Representative sources include the *Cincinnati Times-Star,* 6 June 1944, 4; *Daily Times* (Chicago), 6 June 1944, 7; *Evening Independent* (Massillon, OH), 6 June 1944, 2.

Chapter 7. Confirming America's Enduring D-Day Narrative

1. Michael Schudson, *The Sociology of News* (2nd ed.) (New York: W. W. Norton, 2011), 10.
2. Douglas Brinkley, *The Boys of Pointe Du Hoc: Ronald Reagan, D-Day, and the U.S. Army 2nd Ranger Battalion* (New York: William Morrow, 2005), 128–80.
3. Michael Dolski, *D-Day Remembered: The Normandy Landings in the American Collective Memory* (Knoxville: University of Tennessee Press, 2016), 117–18; Philip D. Beidler, *The Good War's Greatest Hits: World War II and American Remembering* (Athens: University of Georgia Press, 1998); John Bodnar, *The "Good War" in American Memory* (Baltimore: Johns Hopkins University Press, 2011).
4. *Springfield* (MA) *Evening Union,* 7–9 June 1944.
5. For instance, *The Denver Post,* 7 June 1944, and *The Knoxville Journal,* 7 June 1944.
6. *Los Angeles Evening Herald Express,* 8 June 1944; *Life,* 19 June 1944.
7. *Los Angeles Times,* 8 June 1944.
8. *Baltimore News-Post,* 9 June 1944.
9. *Time,* 12 June 1944 (Pony Edition), and 19 June 1944; *Life,* 19 June 1944; *New York Times Magazine,* 11 June 1944, and 18 June 1944.
10. *Life,* 19 June 1944, 25–31; Robert Capa, *Slightly Out of Focus* (New York: Modern Library, 2001), 141–52.
11. *Time,* 19 June 1944, 23; *Newsweek,* 19 June 1944, 27; *Life,* 19 June 1944, 33.
12. *Time,* 12 June 1944, 7; *Life,* 19 June 1944, 35.
13. *Time,* 19 June 1944, 29; *Newsweek,* 19 June 1944, 25–28.
14. *Time,* 12 June 1944, 7; *Newsweek,* 19 June 1944, 36–40; Eisenhower, "Order of the Day."
15. *Newsweek,* 19 June 1944, 36–40.
16. *Look,* 11 July 1944, cover and 30–32.

17. *Collier's*, 22 July 1944, 11–13, 56–57.
18. *Reader's Digest*, August 1944, 112–28.
19. Both envelope examples are in the author's collection.
20. "Invasion: 15 Actual Pictures of France" (Richmond, VA: W. R. Thompson, 1944), author's collection.
21. Peter Maslowski, *Armed with Cameras: The American Military Photographers of World War II* (New York: Free Press, 1973), 264; George H. Roeder Jr., *The Censored War: American Visual Experience During World War Two* (New Haven: Yale University Press, 1993), 18.
22. Maslowski, 265.
23. The newsreel "Invasion," produced by Official Films (8472) and edited by Leslie Wink, is a good example of pooled footage made available to the newsreel companies and strung together to create a coherent narrative. https://www.youtube.com/watch?v=JosdZNjDseo.
24. "Rome Falls to the Allies; Invasion of Fortress Europe," *Castle Films News Parade*, no. 153, https://www.youtube.com/watch?v=suWgDJZoo5E.
25. *D Day*, National Broadcasting Company, June 6, 1944 (four-disc record set), ND4-MC-5901 to 5905, ND4-MC-5954 and 5957 to 5959 (n.d.).
26. For example, "Hagstrom's Invasion Map of Europe" (New York: Hagstrom, 1944).
27. Message to the Allied Expeditionary Force from General of the Army Dwight D. Eisenhower, SUBJECT: Observance of June Sixth as a Holiday, Headquarters Channel Base Section, Communications Zone, European Theater of Operations, AG 006, dated 4 June 1945 (author's collection).
28. *Stars and Stripes* (Weekly Supplement), 3 June 1945, 1, 4, 5, 8.
29. Dolski, 3.
30. Dolski, 1–16.
31. Barry Schwartz, "The Social Context of Commemoration: A Study in Collective Memory," *Social Forces* 61, no. 2 (December 1982): 374–402.
32. See Alex Kershaw, *The Bedford Boys* (Cambridge, MA: Da Capo Press, 2003).
33. Dolski, 37–39.
34. Dolski, 40.
35. *D-Day Through the Decades: 1954 Commemoration*, https://www.dday.org/2014/01/14/d-day-through-the-decades-1954-commemoration/.
36. Lyndon B. Johnson, "Remarks to Members of the Delegation to the D-Day Ceremonies," 3 June 1964, https://www.presidency.ucsb.edu/documents/remarks-members-the-delegation-the-d-day-ceremonies.
37. Paul Connerton, *How societies remember* (Cambridge: Cambridge University Press, 1989), 3.
38. *D-Day Through the Decades: 1974 Commemoration*, https://www.dday.org/2014/03/06/d-day-through-the-decades-1974-commemoration/.
39. President Reagan was not the first U.S. present to visit Normandy. In January

1978, Present Jimmy Carter visited the landing beaches and U.S. Cemetery, but his trip did not coincide with an anniversary celebration. See David Jackson, "D-Day has become a presidential pilgrimage," *USA Today*, 5 June 2014, https://www.usatoday.com/story/news/world/2014/06/05/obama-d-day-roosevelt-carter-reagan-bush-clinton/9967199/.

40. The complete text of President Reagan's speech appears in Brinkley, 225–32; video of President Reagan's speech is available online at https://www.youtube.com/watch?v=eEIqdcHbc8I. Reagan spoke at 7:20 a.m. EST to ensure as many citizens as possible in the United States could watch his speech live.
41. Connerton, 4–5.
42. Jackson, "Presidential pilgrimage."
43. *Weekly Compilation of Presidential Documents*, vol. 30, no. 23, Monday, 13 June 1994, 1209–67, 1236–41; Connerton, 3.
44. George W. Bush also spoke at the dedication of the D-Day Memorial in Bedford, Virginia, but his emphasis was on the common D-Day enlisted soldier; see https://georgewbush-whitehouse.archives.gov/news/releases/2001/06/20010606–2.html.
45. "President Bush, President Chirac Mark 60th Anniversary of D-Day," The White House, President George W. Bush, https://georgewbush-hitehouse.archives.gov/news/releases/2004/06/20040606.html.
46. "Remarks by President Obama at the 70th Anniversary of D-Day—Omaha Beach, Normandy," The White House: President Barack Obama, https://obamawhitehouse.archives.gov/the-press-office/2014/06/06/remarks-president-obama-70th-anniversary-d-day-omaha-beach-normandy.
47. "Remarks by President Trump on the 75th Commemoration of D-Day," The White House: President Donald Trump, https://www.whitehouse.gov/briefings-statements/remarks-president-trump-75th-commemoration-d-day/.

Coda. The D-Day Narrative as an American Myth

1. Paul Jankowski, *Verdun: The Longest Battle of the Great War* (Oxford: Oxford University Press, 2013), 254.
2. Cronkite's broadcast on 27 February 1968 is at https://www.cbsnews.com/video/50-years-ago-walter-cronkite-calls-for-the-u-s-to-get-out-of-vietnam/#x.
3. *Honolulu Advertiser*, 12 September 2001.
4. S. L. A. Marshall, "First Wave at Omaha Beach," *Atlantic*, November 1960, 67–72; *Saving Private Ryan*, directed by Steven Spielberg (DreamWorks Pictures and Paramount Pictures, 1998), 169 minutes.
5. Images of the National D-Day Memorial are at www.dday.org.
6. John F. Kennedy, Yale University Commencement Address, 11 June 1962, American Rhetoric Online Speech Bank, https://www.americanrhetoric.com/speeches/jfkyalecommencement.htm.

BIBLIOGRAPHY

Archives and Libraries

29th Infantry Division Archives, Fifth Regiment Armory, Baltimore, MD.

British Newspaper Archive (https://www.britishnewspaperarchive.co.uk/).

Franklin D. Roosevelt Presidential Library and Museum.

Library of Congress, Washington, DC.

National Archives and Records Administration II, College Park, MD.

Newspapers.com. https://go.newspapers.com/welcome?xid=767&gclid=EAIaIQobChMI-PCxlriD5gIVgZ6zCh34pQzNEAAYASAAEgI5C_D_BwE.

Newspapers, 6 June 1944

Abilene Reporter-News

Akron Beacon Journal

Arkansas State Press

Baltimore News-Post

Binghamton (NY) *Press*

Boston Traveler

Burlington (VT) *Free Press*

Call Bulletin (San Francisco)

Chicago Daily News

Cincinnati Times-Star

Cleveland Plain Dealer

Columbus (OH) *Citizen*

Daily News (New York)

Daily News (Los Angeles)

Daily Record (Boston)

Daily Times: Chicago's Picture Newspaper

Detroit News

Detroit Times

Elizabethtown (KY) *Daily Star*

Erie (PA) Dispatch-Herald

Evening Independent (Massillon, OH)

Evening World-Herald (Omaha)
Flint (MI) *Journal*
Fresno (CA) *Bee*
Honolulu Advertiser
Honolulu Star–Bulletin
Intelligencer Journal (Lancaster, PA)
Journal Every-Evening (Wilmington, DE)
Knoxville News-Sentinel.
Los Angeles Evening Herald and Express
Miami Herald.
Montana Standard (Butte, MT)
New York Herald Tribune
New York Journal American
New York World-Telegram
New York Times
Pasadena (CA) *Independent*
Pittsburgh Sun-Telegraph
Pocatello (ID) *Tribune.*
Pontiac (MI) *Daily Press.*
Rochester (NY) *Times-Union*
Rocky Mountain News (Denver)
San Francisco Chronicle
San Francisco Examiner
San Jose News
Savannah Evening Press
Seattle Daily Times
Seattle Post-Intelligencer
Seattle Star
Sheboygan Press
(Brookings) *South Dakota Collegian*
St. Joseph (MO) *News-Press*
State Journal (Lansing, MI)
Sun (New York)
Syracuse Herald-Journal
Toledo Times
Waterville (ME) *Morning Sentinel*
Wichita Falls Record News
Winston-Salem Journal

Newspapers (Other Dates)

Akron Beacon Journal, 10 July 1943

Anniston (AL) *Star*, 8 November 1942

Arkansas State Press, 9 June 1944

Baltimore News-Post, 9 June 1944

Boston Evening Globe, 10 June 1944

Checkerboard: Official Newspaper of the 99th Infantry Division, 24 May 1944

Chicago Daily Tribune, 10 July 1943

Chicago Sunday Tribune, 8 November 1942

Chicago Tribune, 10 November 1957

Christian Science Monitor, 9 June 1944

Cincinnati Enquirer, 8 November 1942

Clarion-Ledger (Jackson, MS), 8 November 1942

Columbus (OH) *Citizen*, 7 June 1944

Daily Mail (London), 7 June 1944

Daily News (New York), 6 November 1942, 11 July 1943

Democrat Chronicle (Rochester, NY), 8 November 1942

Denver Post, 7 June 1944

Detroit Free Press, 8 November 1942

Dunkirk (NY) *Evening Observer*, 10 July 1943

El Paso Times, 9 August 1942

Evening News (London), 9 June 1944

Evening Public Ledger (Philadelphia), 3 April 1918

Gettysburg (PA) *Times*, 10 July 1943

Hartford (CT) *Courant*, 8 November 1942

Herald and News (Klamath Falls, OR), 10 July 1943

Honolulu Advertiser, 10 July 1943, 12 September 2001

Indianapolis Star, 10 July 1943

Knoxville Journal, 7 June 1944, 11 June 1944, and 13 June 1944

Las Cruces (NM) *Sun-News*, 8 November 1942

Los Angeles Evening Herald Express, 8 June 1944

Los Angeles Times, 10 July 1943, 8 June 1944

Negro Star (Wichita, KS), 9 June 1944

New Castle (PA) *News*, 10 July 1943

Oregonian (Portland), 7 June 1944

Philadelphia Inquirer, 8 November 1942

Pictorial Review Supplement: *Europe Invasion!* Issued by King Features Syndicate (New York), 11 June 1944

Pictorial Review Supplement, *Baltimore American*, 9 July 1944

Pictorial Review Supplement, *Times Union* (NY), 7 June 1944

*Plaindealer (*Kansas City, KS), 16 June 1944
PM Daily (New York), 8 June 1944
PM's Sunday Picture News (New York), 11 June 1944
Post-Standard (Syracuse, NY), 7 June 1944
Rocky Mountain News (Denver), 4 June 1944
San Bernardino (CA) *Daily Sun*, 9 August 1942, 8 November 1942
Sheridan (WY) *Enterprise*, 12 June 1918
Springfield (IL) *Evening Union*, 7–9 June 1944
Stars and Stripes, 8–10; 12 June 1944
Stars and Stripes Magazine (insert), 3 June 1945
Stars and Stripes, "History of the Invasion" supplement, 6 June 1949

Trade Journals

AP Inter-Office, March 1944, June–July 1944
Broadcasting and Broadcast Advertising, April, May, and June 1944
Editor & Publisher, May 1944 and June 1944

Primary Periodicals and Specials

Air Trails Pictorial, July 1944
American Rifleman, July 1944
Atlantic, August 1944
Blue Book: Stories of Adventure for Men, by Men, July and September 1944
Bureau of Naval Personnel Information Bulletin, July 1944
Click: The National Picture Monthly, June 1944, July 1944
Collier's, 22 July 1944, 12 August 1944
Coronet, July 1944
Etude, July 1944
GI: Deming Army Air Field, 9 June 1944
Ladies' Home Journal, June 1944
Liberty, 26 August 1944, 16 September 1944
Life, 2 March 1942, 31 January 1944, 19 June 1944, and 3 July 1944
Look, 11 July 1944, 14 August 1944
National Geographic, July 1944, August 1944
News Story and Booktab, August 1944
Newsweek, 8 May 1944, 12 June 1944, 19 June 1944, and 3 July 1944
New York Times Magazine, 2 January 1944, 11 June 1944, 18 June 1944, and 25 June 1944
Pathfinder: Every Week for the Nation's Capital, 24 April 1944, 22 May 1944
Popular Science, July 1944

Reader's Digest, July 1944, August 1944
Saturday Evening Post, 12 August 1944
Saturday Review of Literature, 3 June 1944
Spatters, June 1944
Time, 1 May 1944, 15 May 1944, 12 June 1944, and 19 June 1944
United States News, 9 June 1944
Yank: The Army Weekly, 11 June 1944, 16 June 1944, and 30 June 1944
Yank: The Army Weekly (British edition), 25 June 1944

Pamphlets, Reports, Government Publications, and Nonstandard Media Publications

Book I: 29th Division in France during World War II: Articles prepared by the family of Lieut. Charles M. Sinclair. Baltimore, MD: Fifth Regiment Armory Archives.

CBS News on D-Day. New York: Columbia Broadcasting System, 1945.

Code of Wartime Practices for American Broadcasters, edition of 1 February 1943. Washington, DC: United States Government Office of Censorship.

Columbia Program Book: Spring 1944. New York: Columbia Broadcasting System, 1 May 1944.

Communiqués 1–9, Supreme Headquarters Allied Expeditionary Force, 6–10 June 1944.

Ernie Pyle: Fighting Hearts. New York: Graphic Enterprises, 1944.

General Dwight D. Eisenhower. American War Leader Series, No. 2. Philadelphia: Independence Square, 1944.

H Hour—1944. National Broadcasting Company, 1944.

Millay, Edna St. Vincent. "Poem and Prayer for an Invading Army." National Broadcasting Company, 1944.

NBC and You, National Broadcasting Company, 1944.

Population of the United States: Census of 1940. Comparative figures from 1930 and 1940.

"President's D-Day Prayer." Broadcast nationally June 6, 1944. Franklin D. Roosevelt Presidential Library and Museum. Papers as President, President's Personal File, 1933–1943, NAI: 197375, Collection Identifier: FDR-PPF.

Price, Byron. *A Report on the Office of Censorship*. Washington, DC: United States Government Printing Office, 1945.

Records of Allied and Occupational Headquarters, World War II, National Archives and Records Administration, Records Group 331, Decimal Files, 1944–1945, NAI 613030, Boxes 1, 3, 4, and 5.

Records of the Office of War Information, World War II. National Archives and Records Administration, Records Group 208, Entry 6H, Box 3; Entry 6N, Box 3, Entry 81, Box 4000.

Red, White, and Blue Series No. 9: War Labor and Peace: Some Recent Addresses and Writings of President Wilson. Washington, DC: Committee on Public Information, March 1918.

Regulations for War Correspondents Accompanying Allied Expeditionary Force in the Field. Supreme Headquarters Allied Expeditionary Force, 1944.

War Department Field Manual (FM) 30-26. *Basic Field Manual: Regulations for Correspondents Accompanying U.S. Army Forces in the Field,* 21 January 1942.

War Department Technical Manual (TM) 20-205. *Dictionary of United States Army Terms,* 18 January 1944.

Weekly Compilation of Presidential Documents. Vol. 30, no. 23, Monday, 13 June 1994, 1209–67.

United States Summary: Census of 1940. https://www2.census.gov/prod2/decennial/documents /33973538v1ch02.pdf.

What the Soldier Thinks: A Monthly Digest of War Department Studies on the Attitudes of American Troops. Morale Services Division, Army Service Forces, War Department. Vol. 1, no. 1, December 1943 (Restricted).

Radio Broadcasts

Columbia Broadcasting System (CBS) D-Day Sound Files. https://archive.org/details/CBD440606CBSDDayCBS.

National Broadcasting company (NBC) D-Day Sound Files. https://archive.org/details/NBCCompleteBroadcastDDay.

Radio News 1942. Volumes 1 and 2, Old Time Radio, N1942.1, and N1942.2. OTRCAT.com, MP3 CD.

Commercial and Government Sound Recordings

D Day. National Broadcasting Company, June 6, 1944 (ND4-MC-5901). Private recording, not for public performance, n.d.

D-Day Plus 20, 1944–1964: A Commemorative Documentary Recording and Photographic Album of the Allied Invasion of Normandy, June 6th, 1944. New York: Columbia Records, 1964.

"Those Historic Years": A Recorded History of World War II. Washington, DC: Panacoustic, U.S. Recording Company, n.d.

Published Primary Sources

Bernays, Edward. *Propaganda.* With an introduction by Mark Crispin Miller. Brooklyn: IG Publishing, 2005.

Bradley, Holbrook. *War Correspondent: From D-Day to the Elbe.* New York: Universe, 2007.

Bradley, Omar N. and Clay Blair, *A General's Life.* New York: Simon and Schuster, 1983.

Butcher, Capt. Harry C., USNR. *My Three Years with Eisenhower: The Personal Diary of Captain Harry C. Butcher, USNR, Naval Aide to General Eisenhower, 1942 to 1945.* New York: Simon and Schuster, 1946.

Cantril, Hadley. *Public Opinion 1935–1946.* Princeton, NJ: Princeton University Press, 1951.

Columbia Broadcasting System. *From D-Day Through Victory in Europe: The Eye-Witness Story as Told by War Correspondents on the Air.* New York: Columbia Broadcasting System, 1945.

Creel, George. *How We Advertised America: The First Telling of the Amazing Story of the Committee on Public Information That Carried the Gospel of Americanism to Every Corner of the Globe.* New York: Harper and Brothers, 1920.

Dryer, Sherman H. *Radio in Wartime.* New York: Greenburg Publishers, 1942.

Editors of *YANK* (selected by). *The Best from YANK the Army Weekly.* New York: World Publishing, 1945.

Eisenhower, Dwight D. *Crusade in Europe.* Garden City, NY: Doubleday, 1948.

Fosdick, Harry Emerson. *A Great Time to Be Alive: Sermons on Christianity in Wartime.* New York: Harper and Brothers, 1944.

Gallagher, Wes. *Back Door to Berlin: The Full Story of the American Coup in North Africa.* Garden City, NY: Doubleday, Doran, 1943.

Gramling, Oliver. *AP: The Story of News: Editions for the Armed Services, Inc.* New York: Pub. by arrangement with Farrar and Rinehart, 1940.

Hutton, Bud, and Andy Rooney. *The Story of The Stars and Stripes.* New York: Farrar and Rinehart, 1946.

Johnson, J. Percy, ed. *H. N. W. Ayer and Son's Directory of Newspapers and Periodicals 1944.* Philadelphia, PA: N. W. Ayer and Son, 1944.

Johnson, Lyndon B. "Remarks to Members of the Delegation to the D-Day Ceremonies." 3 June 1964. https://www.presidency.ucsb.edu/documents/remarks-members-the-delegation-the-d-day-ceremonies.

Kennedy, Edward. *Ed Kennedy's War: V-E Day, Censorship, and the Associated Press.* Baton Rouge: Louisiana State University Press, 2012.

Kennedy, John F. *Yale University Commencement Address.* 11 June 1962. *American Rhetoric Online Speech Bank.* https://www.americanrhetoric.com/speeches/jfkyalecommencement.htm.

Koop, Theodore F. *Weapon of Silence.* Chicago: University of Chicago Press, 1946.

Lippman, Walter. *Public Opinion.* Lexington, KY: Renaissance Classics reprint, 2012. First published New York: Harcourt Brace, New York, 1922.

Lopez, Adrian B. *Blitzkrieg Over America: When Will Hitler Invade U.S.A.* New York: War Books, 1940.

MacVane, John. *On the Air in World War II.* New York: William Morrow, 1979.

Mauldin, Sgt. Bill. *This Damn Tree Leaks: A Collection of War Cartoons.* Reprinted from *The Stars and Stripes.* Mediterranean, Italy, 1945.

Mauldin, Bill. *Up Front.* New York: Henry Holt, 1945.

McGurn, Barrett. *YANK, The Army Weekly: Reporting the Greatest Generation.* Golden, CO: Fulcrum, 2004.

Murrow, Edward R. *This Is London.* New York: Schocken Books, 1989.

Oldfield, Col. Barney. *Never a Shot in Anger.* New York: Duell, Sloan, and Pearce, 1956.

Pinkley, Virgil. *Eisenhower Declassified.* Old Tappan, NJ: Fleming H. Revell, 1979.

Pyle, Ernie. *Brave Men.* New York: Henry Holt, 1944.

———. *Here Is Your War.* New York: Henry Holt, 1943.

Reporting World War II: Part One: American Journalism, 1938–1944. New York: Library of America, 1995.

Reporting World War II: Part Two: American Journalism, 1944–1946. New York: Library of America, 1995.

Rooney, Andy. *My War.* New York: Times Books, 1995.

Spellman, Francis J., Archbishop of New York, Military Vicar of the Armed Forces of the United States. *The Road to Victory.* New York: Charles Scribner's Sons, 1942.

Whitehead, Don. *Beachhead Don: Reporting the War from the European Theater, 1942–1945.* New York: Fordham University Press, 2004.

Secondary Sources

Adair, Paul. *Hitler's Greatest Defeat: The Collapse of Army Group Centre, June 1944.* London: Arms and Armour Press, 1994.

Adams, Michael C. C. *The Best War Ever: America and World War II.* Baltimore: Johns Hopkins University Press, 1994.

Ambrose, Stephen E. *D-Day June 6, 1944: The Climactic Battle of World War II.* New York: Simon and Schuster, 1994.

American Heritage Dictionary. 3rd ed. Boston: Houghton Mifflin, 1993.

Anderson, Benedict. *Imagined Communities: Reflections on the Origin and Spread of Nationalism.* London: Verso, 1983.

Angell, James Rowland. "Radio and National Morale." *American Journal of Sociology* 47, no. 3 (November 1941): 352–59.

Balkoski, Joseph. *Beyond the Beachhead: The 29th Infantry Division in Normandy.* Harrisburg, PA: Stackpole Books, 1989.

———. *Omaha Beach: D-Day, June 6, 1944.* Mechanicsburg, PA: Stackpole Books, 2004.

Beidler, Philip D. *The Good War's Greatest Hits: World War II and American Remembering.* Athens: University of Georgia Press, 1998.

Blum, John Morton. *V Was For Victory: Politics and American Culture During World War II.* New York: Harcourt Brace Jovanovich, 1976.

Bodnar, John. *The "Good War" in American Memory.* Baltimore: Johns Hopkins University Press, 2011.

———. *Public Memory, Commemoration, and Patriotism in the Twentieth Century.* Princeton, NJ: Princeton University Press, 1992.

Boorstin, Daniel J. *The Image: A Guide to Pseudo-Events in America.* New York: Vintage Books, 1987.

Brandt, Nat. *Harlem at War: The Black Experience in WWII.* Syracuse, NY: Syracuse University Press, 1996.

Brewer, Susan A. *Why America Fights: Patriotism and War Propaganda from the Philippines to Iraq.* Oxford: Oxford University Press, 2009.

Brinkley, Douglas. *The Boys of Pointe Du Hoc: Ronald Reagan, D-Day, and the U.S. Army 2nd Ranger Battalion.* New York: William Morrow, 2005.

Brokaw, Tom. *The Greatest Generation.* New York: Random House, 1998.

Brown, Anthony Cave. *Bodyguard of Lies.* New York: Harper and Row, 1975.

Buchanan, A. Russell. *Black Americans in World War II.* Santa Barbara: Clio Books, 1977.

Caddick-Adams, Peter. *Sand and Steel: The D-Day Invasion and the Liberation of France.* New York: Oxford University Press, 2019.

Casey, Steven. *Cautious Crusade: Franklin D. Roosevelt, American Public Opinion, and the War Against Nazi Germany.* New York: Oxford University Press, 2001.

——— *The War Beat, Europe: The American Media at War Against Nazi Germany.* New York: Oxford University Press, 2017.

Censer, Jack R. (with William Miller). *On the Trail of the D.C. Sniper: Fear and the Media.* Charlottesville: University of Virginia Press, 2010.

Chandler, David G., and James Lawton Collins Jr., eds. *The D-Day Encyclopedia.* New York: Simon and Schuster, 1994.

Chomsky, Noam. *Media Control: The Spectacular Achievements of Propaganda.* 2nd ed. New York: Seven Stories Press, 1991, 1997, and 2002.

Colford, Paul. "D-Day account surfaces, ripped from the AP wire." *AP: The Definitive Source* website, 5 June 2014. https://blog.ap.org/behind-the-news/d-day-account-surfaces-ripped-from-the-ap-wire.

Colman, Penny. *Where the Action Was: Women War Correspondents in World War II.* New York: Crown Publishers, 2002.

Connerton, Paul. *How Societies Remember.* Cambridge: Cambridge University Press, 1989.

Davidson, Edward, and Dale Manning. *Chronology of World War Two.* London: Cassell, 1999.

D'Este, Carlo. *Eisenhower: A Soldier's Life.* New York: Henry Holt, 2002.

Dolski, Michael, Sam Edwards, and John Buckley, eds. *D-Day in History and Memory: The Normandy Landings in International Remembrance and Commemoration.* Denton, TX: University of North Texas, 2014.

Dolski, Michael. *D-Day Remembered: The Normandy Landings in the American Collective Memory.* Knoxville: University of Tennessee Press, 2016.

Dower, John W. *War Without Mercy: Race and Power in the Pacific War.* New York: Pantheon Books, 1986.

Dudziak, Mary L. *War Time: An Idea, Its History, Its Consequences.* Oxford: Oxford University Press, 2012.

Eisenhower, David. *Eisenhower at War, 1943–1945.* New York: Vintage Books, 1986.

Finkle, Lee. *Forum for Protest: The Black Press During World War II.* Rutherford: Fairleigh Dickinson University Press, 1975.

Foner, Eric. *Give Me Liberty! An American History.* 5th ed. New York: W. W. Norton, 2017.

Fussell, Paul. *Wartime: Understanding and Behavior in the Second World War.* New York: Oxford University Press, 1990.

Gallup, George. *A Guide to Public Opinion Polls.* Princeton: Princeton University Press, 1944.

Gay, Timothy M. *Assignment to Hell: The War Against Nazi Germany with Correspondents Walter Cronkite, Andy Rooney, A. J. Liebling, Homer Bigart, and Hal Boyle.* New York: NAL Caliber, 2012.

Habermas, Jürgen. *The Structural Transformation of the Public Sphere: An Inquiry into a Category of Bourgeois Society.* Translated by Thomas Burger and Frederick Lawrence. Cambridge, MA: MIT Press, 2001.

Halbwachs, Maurice. *The Collective Memory.* Translated from the French by Francis J. Ditter Jr. and Vida Yazdi Ditter. 1950; reprint. New York: Harper Colophon Books, 1958.

Harrison, Gordon A. *Cross-Channel Attack.* Washington, DC: Office of the Chief of Military History, Department of the Army, 1951.

Hastings, Max. *Overlord: D-Day and the Battle for Normandy.* New York: Simon and Schuster, 1984.

Hatch, Alden. *General Ike: A Biography of Dwight D. Eisenhower.* Chicago: Consolidated Book Publishers, 1944.

Herman, Edward S., and Noam Chomsky. *Manufacturing Consent: The Political Economy of the Mass Media.* New York: Pantheon Books, 2002.

Hervieux, Linda. *Forgotten: The Untold Story of D-Day's Black Heroes, At Home and At War.* New York: Harper, 2015.

Hilmes, Michele, ed. *NBC: America's Network.* Berkeley, Los Angeles: University of California Press, 2007.

Hollister, Paul, and Robert Strunsky. *From D-Day through Victory in Europe*. New York: Columbia Broadcasting System, 1945.

Horn, Gunnar. "Radio Journalism." *The English Journal* 34, no. 5 (May 1945): 257–60.

Jackaway, Gwenyth L. *Media at War: Radio's Challenge to the Newspapers, 1924–1939*. Westport, CT: Praeger Publishers, 1995.

Jackson, David. "D-Day has become a presidential pilgrimage." *USA Today*, 5 June 2014. https://www.usatoday.com/story/news/world/2014/06/05/obama-d-day-roosevelt-carter-reagan-bush-clinton/9967199/.

Jamieson, John. "Censorship and the Soldier." *Public Opinion Quarterly* 11, no. 3 (Autumn 1947): 367–84.

Jankowski, Paul. *Verdun: The Longest Battle of the Great War*. Oxford: Oxford University Press, 2013.

Jones, David Lloyd. "The U.S. Office of War Information and American Public Opinion During World War II." PhD diss., State University of New York, 1976.

Jowett, Garth S., and Victoria O'Donnell. *Propaganda and Persuasion*. 6th ed. Los Angeles: SAGE, 2015.

Kammen, Michael. *Mystic Chords of Memory: The Transformation of Tradition in American Culture*. New York: Vintage Books, 1991.

Keegan, John. *The Face of Battle*. New York: Penguin Books, 1976.

Kennedy, David M. *Freedom from Fear: The American People in Depression and War, 1929–1945*. New York: Oxford University Press, 1999.

Kershaw, Alex. *The Bedford Boys*. Cambridge, MA: Da Capo Press, 2003.

Knightley, Phillip. *The First Casualty: The War Correspondent as Hero and Myth-Maker from the Crimea to Iraq*. Baltimore: Johns Hopkins University Press, 2004.

Korda, Michael. *Ike: An American Hero*. New York: Harper Perennial, 2007.

Landsberg, Alison. *Prosthetic Memory: The Transformation of American Remembrance in the Age of Mass Culture*. New York: Columbia University Press, 2004.

Lebovic, Sam. *Free Speech and Unfree News: The Paradox of Press Freedom in America*. Cambridge: Harvard University Press, 2016.

Le Goff, Jacques. *History and Memory*. 1977; reprint. New York: Columbia University Press, 1992.

Linebarger, Paul M. A. *Psychological Warfare*. Washington: Combat Forces Press, 1954.

Lingeman, Richard R. *Don't You Know There's a War On? The American Home Front from 1941–1945*. New York: G. P. Putnam's Sons, 1970.

Margaritas, Peter. *Bust Eisenhower: The Message That Almost Ruined D-Day*. 3rd ed. n.p.: privately published, 2015.

Marshall, S. L. A. "First Wave at Omaha Beach." *Atlantic*, November 1960, 67–72.

Martin, Ralph G. *The GI War 1941–1945*. Boston: Little, Brown, 1967.

Maslowski, Peter. *Armed with Cameras: The American Military Photographers of World War II*. New York: Free Press, 1993.

McDonough, John. "The Longest Night: Broadcasting's First Invasion." *American Scholar* 63, no. 2 (Spring 1994): 193–211.

McLuhan, Marshall. *The Medium and the Message: Understanding the Information World*. n.p.: Clearfield Group, 2016.

Moore, James P., Jr. "American Prayers, on D-Day and Today." *Washington Post*, 6 June 2004, B03. http://www.washingtonpost.com/wp-dyn/articles/A17410-2004Jun5.html.

———. *One Nation Under God: The History of Prayer in America*. New York: Doubleday, 2005.

Moseley, Ray. *Reporting War: How Foreign Correspondents Risked Capture, Torture and Death to Cover World War II*. New Haven: Yale University Press, 2017.

Nicholas, Siân. "The British press and D-Day: reporting the launch of the Second Front, 6 June 1944." *Media History* 23, no. 3–4 (September 2017): 489–507.

Nora, Pierre. *Realms of Memory: Rethinking the French Past*. Volume I: *Conflicts and Division*. New York: Columbia University Press, 1996.

Nord, David Paul. *Communities of Journalism: A History of American Newspapers and Their Readers*. Urbana: University of Illinois Press, 2001.

Overy, Richard. *Why the Allies Won*. New York: W. W. Norton and Company, 1995.

Purcell, Sarah J. *Sealed with Blood: War, Sacrifice, and Memory in Revolutionary America*. Philadelphia: University of Pennsylvania Press, 2002.

Rapport, Leonard, and Arthur Norwood Jr. *Rendezvous with Destiny: History of the 101st Airborne Division*. Old Saybrook, CT: Konecky and Konecky, 1948.

Reardon, Carol. *Pickett's Charge in History and Memory*. Chapel Hill: University of North Carolina Press, 1997.

Rhodes, Anthony. *Propaganda: The Art of Persuasion: World War II*. New York: Chelsea House, 1976.

Ricks, Thomas E. *The Generals: American Military Command from World War II to Today*. New York: Penguin Press, 2012.

Roberts, Mary Louise. *What Soldiers Do: Sex and the American GI in World War II France*. Chicago: University of Chicago Press, 2013.

Roeder, George H., Jr. *The Censored War: American Visual Experience During World War Two*. New Haven: Yale University Press, 1993.

Roediger, Henry L., III, and K. Andrew DeSoto. "The Power of Collective Memory: What do large groups of people remember—and forget?" *Scientific American*, 28 June 2016. https://scientificamerican.com/article/the-power-of-collective-memory/.

Rose, Kenneth D. *Myth and the Greatest Generation: A Social History of Americans in World War II*. New York: Routledge, 2008.

Rosenberg, Emily S. *A Date Which Will Live: Pearl Harbor in American Memory.* Durham: Duke University Press, 2003.

Ryan, Cornelius. *The Longest Day: June 6, 1944.* New York: Simon and Schuster, 1959.

Schönbach, Klaus, Ester de Waal, and Edmund Lauf. "Online and Print Newspapers: Their Impact on the Extent of the Perceived Public Agenda." *European Journal of Communication* 20 (2005): 245–58.

Schudson, Michael. *Discovering the News: A Social History of American Newspapers.* New York: Basic Books, 1978.

———. "News, Public, Nation." *The American Historical Review* 107, no. 2 (April 2002): 481–95.

———. *The Power of News.* Cambridge, MA: Harvard University Press, 1995.

———. *The Sociology of News.* 2nd ed. New York: W. W. Norton, 2011.

Schwartz, Barry. "The Social Context of Commemoration: A Study in Collective Memory." *Social Forces* 61, no. 2 (Dec. 1982): 374–402.

Smith, Jeffery A. *War and Press Freedom: The Problem of Prerogative Power.* New York: Oxford University Press, 1999.

Stamm, Michael. *Sound Business: Newspapers, Radio, and the Politics of New Media.* Philadelphia: University of Pennsylvania Press, 2011.

Stenbuck, Jack, ed. *Typewriter Battalion: Dramatic Frontline Dispatches from World War II.* New York: William Morrow, 1995.

Stoler, Mark A. *George C. Marshall: Soldier-Statesman of the American Century.* Boston: Twayne, 1989.

Sweeney, Michael S. *Secrets of Victory: The Office of Censorship and the American Press and Radio in World War II.* Chapel Hill: University of North Carolina Press, 2001.

Terkel, Studs. *The Good War.* New York: Pantheon Books, 1984.

Washburn, Patrick S. *A Question of Sedition: The Federal Government's Investigation of the Black Press During World War II.* New York: Oxford University Press, 1986.

Weinberg, Gerhard L. *A World at Arms: A Global History of World War II.* New ed. New York: Cambridge University Press, 1994, 2nd ed. 2005.

White, Egbert. "A Free Press in a Citizen's Army." *Journal of Educational Sociology* 19, no. 4 (Dec. 1945): 236–48.

Whitton, John B. "Radio after the War." *Foreign Affairs* 22, no. 2 (January 1944): 309–17.

———. "War by Radio." *Foreign Affairs* 19, no. 3 (April 1941): 584–96.

Winkler, Allan M. *Home Front U.S.A.: America during World War II.* Wheeling, IL: Harlan Davidson, 2000.

———. *The Politics of Propaganda: The Office of War Information, 1942–1945.* New Haven: Yale University Press, 1978.

Wood, Edward W., Jr. *Worshipping the Myths of World War II: Reflections on America's Dedication to War.* Washington, DC: Potomac Books, 2006.

Woodward, David R. *The American Army and the First World War.* Cambridge, MA: Cambridge University Press, 2014.

Young, Nancy Beck. *Why We Fight: Congress and the Politics of World War II.* Lawrence: University of Kansas Press, 2013.

Websites (also see Archives and Libraries)

D-Day Through the Decades: 1954 Commemoration. https://www.dday.org/2014/01/14/d-day-through-the-decades-1954-commemoration/.

D-Day Through the Decades: 1974 Commemoration. https://www.dday.org/2014/03/06/d-day-through-the-decades-1974-commemoration/.

National D-Day Memorial, Bedford, VA. www.dday.org.

"President Bush, President Chirac Mark 60th Anniversary of D-Day." The White House, President George W. Bush. https://georgewbush-whitehouse. archives.gov/news/releases/2004/06/20040606.html.

"Remarks by President Obama at the 70th Anniversary of D-Day—Omaha Beach, Normandy." The White House: President Barack Obama. https://obamawhitehouse.archives.gov/the-press-office/2014/06/06/remarks-president-obama-70th-anniversary-d-day-omaha-beach-normandy.

"Remarks by President Trump on the 75th Commemoration of D-Day." The White House: Present Donald Trump. https://www.whitehouse.gov/briefings-statements/remarks-president-trump-75th-commemoration-d-day/.

Television and Film

Annakin, Ken, Andrew Marton, Bernhard Wicki, and Darryl F. Zanuck, directors. *The Longest Day.* Darryl F. Zanuck Productions and Twentieth-Century Fox Film Corporation, 1962. 178 minutes. DVD.

Castle Films News Parade. No. 153, "Rome Falls to the Allies; Invasion of Fortress Europe." Castle Films, n.d.

CBS Reports. "D-Day Plus 20 Years: Eisenhower Returns to Normandy." Aired 1964 on Columbia Broadcasting Systems.

Cromwell, John. *Since You Went Away.* David O. Selznick Productions, 1943. 177 minutes. DVD.

Fleming, Victor, director. *A Guy Named Joe.* Metro-Goldwyn-Mayer Pictures, 1943. 121 minutes. DVD.

Spielberg, Steven, director. *Saving Private Ryan.* DreamWorks Pictures and Paramount Pictures, 1998. 169 minutes. DVD.

Press Feeds

United Press newswire feed for 6 June 1944. Subscription teletype for *Sunbury Daily Item,* Sunbury, PA.

INDEX

ABOUT THE AUTHOR

After twenty-five years as a U.S. Army infantry officer, **Stephen M. Rusiecki** retired and became Dean of Academics of the U.S. Army Inspector General School in 2005. He holds master's degrees in English and history as well as a PhD in history from George Mason University. Dr. Rusiecki's previous books are *The Key to the Bulge: The Battle for Losheimergraben* (1996) and *In Final Defense of the Reich: The Destruction of the 6th SS Mountain Division "Nord"* (Naval Institute Press, 2010). He is a recipient of the Phi Kappa Phi Award for Academic Achievement and has been inducted into the Phi Alpha Theta National History Honor Society and the Golden Key International Honor Society. Dr. Rusiecki's military decorations include the Legion of Merit and the Combat Infantryman's Badge. He is a native of Springfield, Massachusetts, and resides in Dumfries, Virginia, with his wife, Angela, and son, Jonathan.

The Naval Institute Press is the book-publishing arm of the U.S. Naval Institute, a private, nonprofit, membership society for sea service professionals and others who share an interest in naval and maritime affairs. Established in 1873 at the U.S. Naval Academy in Annapolis, Maryland, where its offices remain today, the Naval Institute has members worldwide.

Members of the Naval Institute support the education programs of the society and receive the influential monthly magazine *Proceedings* or the colorful bimonthly magazine *Naval History* and discounts on fine nautical prints and on ship and aircraft photos. They also have access to the transcripts of the Institute's Oral History Program and get discounted admission to any of the Institute-sponsored seminars offered around the country.

The Naval Institute's book-publishing program, begun in 1898 with basic guides to naval practices, has broadened its scope to include books of more general interest. Now the Naval Institute Press publishes about seventy titles each year, ranging from how-to books on boating and navigation to battle histories, biographies, ship and aircraft guides, and novels. Institute members receive significant discounts on the Press' more than eight hundred books in print.

Full-time students are eligible for special half-price membership rates. Life memberships are also available.

For more information about Naval Institute Press books that are currently available, visit www.usni.org/press/books. To learn about joining the U.S. Naval Institute, please write to:

Member Services
U.S. Naval Institute
291 Wood Road
Annapolis, MD 21402-5034
Telephone: (800) 233-8764
Fax: (410) 571-1703
Web address: www.usni.org